AF803924

INTERPRETED LANGUAGES AND COMPOSITIONALITY

STUDIES IN LINGUISTICS AND PHILOSOPHY

VOLUME 89

Managing Editors

LISA MATTHEWSON, *University of British Columbia, Vancouver, Canada*
YAEL SHARVIT, *University of Connecticut, Storrs, USA*
THOMAS EDE ZIMMERMAN, *Johann Wolfgang Goethe-Universität, Frankfurt am Main, Germany*

Editorial Board

JOHAN VAN BENTHEM, *University of Amsterdam, The Netherlands*
GREGORY N. CARLSON, *University of Rochester, U.S.A.*
DAVID DOWTY, *Ohio State University, Columbus, U.S.A.*
GERALD GAZDAR, *University of Sussex, Brighton, U.K.*
IRENE HEIM, *M.I.T., Cambridge, U.S.A.*
EWAN KLEIN, *University of Edinburgh, Scotland, U.K.*
BILL LADUSAW, *University of California, Santa Cruz, U.S.A.*
TERRENCE PARSONS, *University of California, Irvine, U.S.A.*

For further volumes in this series:
http://www.springer.com/series/6556

INTERPRETED LANGUAGES AND COMPOSITIONALITY

by

MARCUS KRACHT

Bielefeld University, Germany

Springer

Marcus Kracht
Bielefeld University
Postfach 100131
33501 Bielefeld
Germany
marcus.kracht@uni-bielefeld.de

ISSN 0924-4662
ISBN 978-94-007-2107-4 e-ISBN 978-94-007-2108-1
DOI 10.1007/978-94-007-2108-1
Springer Dordrecht Heidelberg London New York

Library of Congress Control Number: 2011933831

© Springer Science+Business Media B.V. 2011
No part of this work may be reproduced, stored in a retrieval system, or transmitted in any form or by any means, electronic, mechanical, photocopying, microfilming, recording or otherwise, without written permission from the Publisher, with the exception of any material supplied specifically for the purpose of being entered and executed on a computer system, for exclusive use by the purchaser of the work.

Printed on acid-free paper

Springer is part of Springer Science+Business Media (www.springer.com)

Preface

This manuscript presents an outline of something that I like to call *metatheory of linguistics*. It is not an attempt to replace any existing framework by a new one; it is rather an attempt to provide some results that show us the interconnection between certain requirements on theories. The word "metatheory" emphasizes that I am not trying to establish a new framework or discover concrete properties of languages but that I want to find methods of establishing properties that a given language has. The aim is to find out in what way our initial assumptions about the structure of language or linguistic theory can actually yield an insight into languages and what this insight consists in. I shall isolate a few principles and investigate their empirical potential in this way. One such principle is the *Principle of Compositionality*. It will emerge, for example, that the Principle of Compositionality has no empirical impact whatsoever unless we fix languages to be sets of signs consisting in form and meaning; additionally, when defining form and meaning for natural languages we must make sure that there are restrictions on syntactic and semantic representations and functions. If this is guaranteed, however, we shall show that there can be concrete results about the structure of natural languages.

This book owes much to Keenan and Stabler (2001). However, here the emphasis is quite different. Rather than assuming a particular grammar for a language at the outset, it is our aim to establish to what extent a language determines the grammar that generates it. In contrast to a lot of work in linguistics I do not take syntax as the exclusive source of evidence for structure. Rather, I look at syntax and semantics *together*. Certainly, structural properties determine in which way expressions can be formed but it has often been assumed in linguistic literature that this is effectively all there is to be said about structure. This prejudice is the rather unfortunate heritage of a view promoted mainly—but not exclusively—within Generative Grammar. That linguistics is neither just about form (syntax) nor just about content (semantics) has been emphasized also by Manaster-Ramer and Michalove (2001) in the context of historical linguistics. A reconstruction solely based on either sound or meaning is useless. It must obviously involve both.

Although the style of the book is ostensively neutral, the motivation for this research is the belief that ultimately the Principle of Compositionality is correct. However, the methodology is not to try and verify this (this is impossible) but to see what its consequences are. It turns out to be possible to show that there are noncompositional languages. This means that it is an empirical question whether natural languages are compositional. It should be clear though that no definitive answer can be given for any natural language. The reason for this is a—in my view unavoidable—peculiarity of the whole theory; namely that for a finite language no grammar is needed. A simple enumeration of all items is enough. Hence, we can only fruitfully apply the theory to infinite languages. Thus, when we apply the present theory to a particular language we have to make assumptions about its global nature; and these assumptions are always tentative.

One of the biggest problem areas that I have identified in the course of studying compositionality is the nature of semantics. While the prevailing attitude used to be that meanings are hopelessly unclear, many semanticists nowadays feel that there is not much to discuss either: meanings are objects of the typed universe. Both groups will feel that the present book got it wrong; the first because I include semantics as primitive data, the second because I reject most semantic approaches to compositionality on the grounds that their semantics encodes semantically contingent syntactic structure. My response to the first group is this: if it is possible that humans understand each other and if we do agree that there is such a thing as meaning, which can be preserved—among other—in translation, we must conclude that something of substance can be said about meanings, both concrete and abstract. The response to the second group is more complex. On the one hand, Montague Grammar has enjoyed success and it popularized the notion of compositionality. Nevertheless, I feel that there is a sort of complacency in most research conducted within type logical grammar as a whole. Most questions of actual meaning are not really solved, they are only relegated (for example to lexicology). Instead, many theories of formal semantics are just offering technology without much proof that this is what we really wanted. It is like saying that technological advances have made it possible for man to fly. That is only half true because originally the dream was to fly like a bird. It will take large parts of this book (especially Chapter 4) to work out exactly what is at fault with type theoretical semantics for natural language.

The Principle of Compositionality can be seen as an abstract requirement on the grammar of a language (and therefore, albeit indirectly, on the language itself). The rationale for adopting it, however, comes from an assumption on the architecture of language that is not universally shared. A particularly blatant case of this sort is Generative Grammar, where interpretation is done *after* the structure building has taken place. It will be seen, though, that even if we grant this assumption, there is still so much to take care of that it becomes unclear just why a level such as LF is at all needed and how it can help us. In addition, it turns out that many more frameworks or theories fail to be compositional. This may be surprising since linguists commonly judge theories on the basis of whether they are compositional or not. Thus, if we value compositionality so highly we ought to know what exactly makes a theory compositional. This is what this book is about. Part of my claims may be contentious. For example, I claim below that indices are not part of a syntactic representation. This militates against a number of well-established theories, among them Generative Grammar and Montague Grammar (!). It may therefore be thought that this diminishes the usefulness of the present approach. On the other hand, it is not my task to agree with a theory simply because it is popular. What is at stake is rather the very foundation on which the current theories are built. And in this respect it seems to me that linguistic theory on the whole suffers from a lack of understanding of how solid the ground is on which it rests. The actual syntactic structure, for example, has become highly theory internal in Generative Grammar. The independent evidence of Kayne's Antisymmetry Thesis, for example, was originally quite thin. And it is simply not true that it has been proved to be correct thereafter. Rather, the factual approach has been to adopt it and explore its consequences (just as I adopt here the Principle of Compositionality and explore its consequences). One of the consequences is that one needs a lot more categories, for the theory predicts plenty of movement steps and appropriate landing sites must be furnished. However, a careful review of the syntactic structure of German (within the generative framework) undertaken in Sternefeld (2006) has yielded a far less articulated structure than standardly assumed. Thus, the question as to what categories we need and what structure we should assume seems to be completely open. So, if syntax cannot help out, maybe semantics can lead the way.

This book has basically two parts. The first consists in Chapters 2 and 3, the second in Chapters 4 and 5. The first part develops a mathematical theory of interpreted languages; Chapter 2 provides the background of string languages, using grammars that generate languages from the lexicon, known from Montague Grammar. Chapter 3 then turns to interpreted languages. In the second part, starting with Chapter 4 we zoom in on natural languages. We ask what the meanings of natural language constituents are and how they can be manipulated. Then, in Chapter 5 we apply the theory. We shall show that the notion of a concept defined in Chapter 4 changes the outlook on predicate logic: finite variable fragments are compositional, while with infinite variables the languages have no compositional context free grammar. Then we show how we can argue for structure from a purely semantic point of view.

The current text is a development of ideas found in Kracht (2003). Since then I have spent considerable energy in getting a clearer idea on the central notion of this book, namely compositionality. In the meantime, new articles and books have appeared (for example (Barker and Jacobson, 2007) and the handbook (Werning, Hinzen, and Machery, 2012)) showing that the topic is still a lively issue. I have had the benefit of extended discussions with Damir Ćavar, Lawrence Cheung, Herbert Enderton, Kit Fine, Hans-Martin Gärtner, Ben George, Fritz Hamm, László Kálmán, Ed Keenan, Ben Keil, István Kenesei, Udo Klein, Greg Kobele, András Kornai, Uwe Mönnich, Yannis Moschovakis, Chris Piñón, Nathaniel Porter, Richard Schröder and Ed Stabler. Special thanks also to István Kenesei for his support and to Damir for organising the summer school in Zadar, which got me started on this manuscript. All of them have influenced my views on the subject in numerous ways. Finally, thanks to Richard Schröder and Udo Klein for careful reading. The responsibility for any occurring errors in this text remains entirely with me.

A Note on Notation. This text contains lots of examples and occasional "intermissions". The end of an example or an intermission is marked by ⚽.

Contents

Chapter 1
Synopsis

BEFORE I start with the technical discussion it is perhaps worthwhile to discuss the relevance of the concepts. I shall begin with some notes on the historical context and the current developments before I turn to the questions that I have tried to answer in this book.

Modern linguistics begins with de Saussure, yet he wrote surprisingly little on the subject matter. The famous *Cours de linguistique générale* exists in several editions none of which were published by de Saussure himself. Some years ago, however, a bundle of autographs was found in his home in Geneva, which are, I think, of supreme importance (see the English edition (Saussure, 2006)). We see de Saussure agonize over some quite basic and seemingly innocent problems: one is the distinction between what he calls "parole", a continuous object of changing and elusive nature and "langue", a system of oppositions, in other words a structured object. De Saussure constantly reminds us that all the objects we like to talk about in linguistics are abstractions: meanings, letters, phonemes and so on. The second problem that he deals with, and one that will be central to this book, is that language is a *relation* between form and meaning and not just a system of well-formed expressions.

One might think that one hundred years later we have settled these issues and found satisfactory answers to them. I think otherwise. Both of the problems are to this day unsolved. To understand why this is so it is perhaps useful to look at Chomskyan linguistics. The basic ingredients of Generative Grammar are a firm commitment to discrete objects and the primacy of form over meaning. There is no room for gradience (though occasional attempts have been made even by Chomsky himself to change this). Grammars are rule systems. Moreover, linguistics is for the most part the study of form, be it phonology, morphology or syntax. The rise of Montague Grammar has changed that to some degree but not entirely. One reason for this is that Montague Grammar itself, like Generative Grammar, is rooted in metamathematics, which puts the calculus, the mindless symbolic game, into the centre of investigation.

The present book took its beginning in the realization that what linguists (and logicians alike) call meaning is but a corrupted version thereof. A second, related insight is that linguists rarely if ever think of language as a *relation*. The ambition of the present monograph is to change that. What I shall outline here is a theory of formal languages that are not merely collections of syntactic objects but relations between syntactic objects and their meanings.

M. Kracht, *Interpreted Languages and Compositionality*, Studies in Linguistics and Philosophy 89, DOI 10.1007/978-94-007-2108-1_1,

© Springer Science+Business Media B.V. 2011

> Throughout this book, *language* means a set of signs. Signs are pairs consisting in syntactic objects and meanings. Languages are sets of signs and hence relations between syntactic objects and meanings.

This calls for a complete revision of the terminology and the formal framework. Consider by way of example the syntactic rule

$$\mathtt{S} \to \mathtt{NP}\ \mathtt{VP} \tag{1.1}$$

This rule can be used to replace the string /S/ by the string /NP VP/. (I use slashes to enclose strings so as to show explicitly where they begin and end in running text.) Yet, if language consists in syntactic objects together with their meanings we must ask what the meaning of /S/ is, or, for that matter, /NP VP/. If anything, the meaning of /S/ is the disjunction of all possible meanings of sentences of the language, or some such object. However, notice that /S/ is not an object of the language. The whole point of auxiliary symbols in the grammar is that they are not *meant* to be part of the language for which they are used. And if they are not in the language then they have no meaning, for a language by definition endows only its own constituents with meaning.

Notice that the problem existed already at the inception of grammar as production rules. Grammars never generated only the language they were designed to generate but a host of strings that do not belong to the language. Again this was precisely because they contained auxiliary symbols. While it was unproblematic if only string generation was concerned, the problem becomes more urgent if meanings are considered as well. For now we need to replace the rule by something that replaces not only strings but signs, like this:

$$\langle \mathtt{S}, x\rangle \to \langle \mathtt{NP}, y\rangle\ \langle \mathtt{VP}, z\rangle \tag{1.2}$$

This means something like this: an /S/ that means x can be decomposed into an /NP/ that means y and a /VP/ that means z. This formulation however is unsatisfactory. First, we have lost the idea that /S/ is replaced by the *sequence* of /NP/ followed by /VP/, for we needed to annotate, as it were, the parts by meaning. Second, there is no unique way to derive y and z from x; rather, x is unique once y and z are given. In Montague Semantics, following Frege, z is a function and $x = z(y)$, the result of applying z to y. Thus, it is actually more natural to read the rule from right to left. In this formulation it now reads as follows: given an object α of category NP and meaning y and an object β of category VP and meaning z, the concatenation $\alpha^\frown\beta$ is an object of category S and meaning $z(y)$. The objects can be anything; however, I prefer to use strings. Notice now that we have variables for strings and that we have (de facto) eliminated the syntactic categories. The rule looks more like this now:

$$\langle \alpha, y\rangle, \langle \beta, z\rangle \to \langle \alpha^\frown\beta, z(y)\rangle \tag{1.3}$$

There is a proviso: α must be of category NP, β of category VP. To implement this we say that there is a function f that takes two signs and returns a sign as follows.

$$f(\langle \alpha, y\rangle, \langle \beta, z\rangle) := \begin{cases} \langle \alpha^\frown\beta, z(y)\rangle & \text{if } \alpha \text{ is of category NP} \\ & \quad \text{and } \beta \text{ of category VP,} \\ \text{undefined} & \text{otherwise.} \end{cases} \tag{1.4}$$

This is the formulation that we find in Categorial Grammar and variants thereof. It is, as I see it, the only plausible way to read the rules of grammar. In this formulation the category is not explicit, as we are generating objects of the language intrinsically. The fact that the generated string $\alpha^\frown\beta$ is an S is therefore something that we must be able to recover from the sign itself. Notice that this problem exists also with the input: how do we know whether α is a string of category NP? Where does this knowledge reside if not in the grammar? I shall answer some of these questions below. They show surprising complexity and contrary to popular opinion it is not necessary to openly classify strings into categories.

From this moment on we are faced with plenty of choices. The binary function f takes as its input two signs, each of which consists in two parts. Thus it has in total four inputs. The question is whether the function is decomposable into simpler functions. Some people would argue that this is not so and some theories encode that dictum in one or another form. Yet, from a theoretical point of view it is not good to drop a stronger hypothesis unless one really has to. The plausible hypothesis is this:

Independence. The functions of the grammar that create signs create the components of the signs independently of each other.

This thesis has two parts. One is the so called *Autonomy of Syntax Thesis* and the other the *Compositionality Thesis*. For convenience I spell them out for our example. The autonomy thesis says that whatever $f(\langle \alpha, x\rangle, \langle \beta, y\rangle)$ may be in a given language, the form (or morphology) of the sign is a function of α and β alone, disregarding x and y. The compositionality thesis says that whatever $f(\langle \alpha, x\rangle, \langle \beta, y\rangle)$ may be in a language, its semantics depends only on x and y and nothing else. Thus we have functions f^γ and f^μ such that

$$f(\langle \alpha, x\rangle, \langle \beta, y\rangle) = \langle f^\gamma(\alpha, \beta), f^\mu(x, y)\rangle \tag{1.5}$$

Informally, this says that whatever form the expression takes, it does not depend on the meaning of the component expressions; and whatever meaning the expression has, it does not depend on the form of the component expressions.

What does this Principle of Independence actually say? It is at this point where many linguists start to be very creative. Anything goes in order to prove languages to be compositional. But the problem is that there is little room for interpretation. A language is a relation R between expressions and meanings. What we postulate in the case of f is that there is a pair of binary functions $f^\gamma : E \times E \to E$ and $f^\mu : M \times M \to M$ such that (1.5) holds. What is important is that the input signs are taken from the language R and the output sign must be in R too. Thus, independence means that we have a set of functions that generate R from the lexicon.

All functions are allowed to be partial. Partiality is essential in the generation of the signs. For example, suppose we want to account for the fact that it is grammatical to say "Jack drove the car." but not "Jack drove the bicycle.". Clearly, we must say that "drive" requires a certain kind of vehicle. The nature of the restriction may now be either morphological or semantic. If it is morphological then it may be formulated as a restriction on the function f^{γ} on the expressions. If however it is semantic, what should we do? There are various options. The best is probably to say that the type of vehicle is already implied by the expression and so we cannot use a different one on pain of contradiction. If one dislikes this solution, here is another one. Create two modes, f_1 and f_2 and declare that $f_1^{\mu}(x, y)$ is defined only if y is a motorized (earth bound) vehicle, while $f_2^{\mu}(x, y)$ is defined in cases where y is a different kind of vehicle. What we cannot do, however, is add some material in the syntactic structure that replicates the semantic properties, such as $\mathtt{car}_{\text{motorized}}$ and $\mathtt{bicycle}_{\neg\text{motorized}}$. This is effectively what has been proposed with θ-roles. More often than not they have been used to encode semantic properties in syntax. The converse has also often been done: encode a syntactic restriction in semantics.

There is a lot of terminological ground to be covered here. If the formation of signs is a partial operation the question is whether we can at all distinguish syntactic from semantic deviance. Chomsky argued that we can, and I wish to basically agree with his observation even though it does seem to me that it often requires some education to disentangle ungrammaticality and semantic deviance. If it is therefore possible to distinguish ungrammaticality from semantic deviance, what could be the source of that distinction? It could be this: a sentence is syntactically well-formed if it could be generated looking only at the syntactic composition functions and semantically well-formed if its meaning could be generated looking only at the semantic composition functions. Thus, the fact that we can distinguish between these two notions of (un)acceptability requires that we have independent knowledge of both the syntactic functions and the semantic functions. However, notice that the definition I gave is somewhat strange: how can we know the meaning of an ungrammatical sentence? What is the meaning that it has despite the fact that it is ungrammatical? Unfortunately, I do not have an answer to this question, but it is these kinds of questions that come to the fore once we make a distinction between different kinds of well-formedness. Another problem is why it is that an ungrammatical sentence at all has a meaning. Why is it that sometimes the semantic functions are more general than the syntactic functions and sometimes the syntactic functions more general than the semantic functions? This is not only a theoretical problem. It is important also in language learning: if a child hears only correct input, it will hear sentences that are both grammatical and meaningful, so it can never (at least in principle) learn to distinguish these concepts. Again I have not much to say, I simply notice the problems. In part it is because I am not concerned with learning. Partly, however, it is that—surprisingly—setting up something as simple as a formal theory of interpreted languages as opposed to a formal theory of string languages requires much more care in the definitions, and this task has to come first. Despite the fact that the language is given in a relational form it is not clear how we can or should define from that a grammar that manipulates syntax and semantics independently.

Parts of Chapter 3 are consumed by disentangling various notions of autonomy and compositionality.

Now, as much as one would like to agree with my insistence that the language R is given a priori and cannot be adapted later, there is still a problem. Namely, no one knows for sure exactly how R looks like. This is not only due to the somewhat insufficient knowledge of what is a grammatical constituent. It has to do more with the problem of knowing exactly what the meaning of a given expression actually is. For example, what is the meaning of "drive"? Is it a function, an event, an algorithm? Is it extensional, intensional, time dependent? My own stance here is that basically expressions have propositional content and the meaning of a proposition is its truth conditions. This implies that it is not a function in the sense of Frege (from individuals to truth values) and that the dependencies it displays result from the conditions that it places on the model. Yet, what exactly the formal nature of truth conditions is, is far from clear. Logicians have unfortunately also been quite complacent in thinking that the calculi they have formulated are compositional. They mostly are not. For this reason I have to take a fresh start and develop something of a calculus of truth conditions. The problem is that certain vital constructs in logic must be discarded when dealing with natural language semantics. One of them are variables, another is type theory. To see why this is so we must simply ask ourselves what the semantics of a variable, say, "x" is and how it differs from the semantics of a different variable, say "y". Moreover, these meanings should be given *independently of the form of the expression*. The result is that there is nothing that can distinguish the meaning of "x" from that of "y" because all there is to the difference is the difference in name. Consequently, if names are irrelevant, the meaning of the expression "R(x,y)" is the same as "R(y,x)", that is, we cannot even distinguish a relation and its converse!

This observation has far reaching consequences. For if we accept that we cannot explicate same or different references in terms of variables then the composition of meanings is severely restricted. Indeed, I shall show that it amounts to the restriction of predicate logic to some finite variable fragment. On the other hand, I will argue that nevertheless this is precisely what we want. Consider an ergative language like Dyirbal. Dixon (1994) translates the verbs of Dyirbal by their passives in English. So, the verb meaning "hit" is translated by "is hit by". This makes a lot of sense for Dyirbal, as it also turns out that the transitive object in Dyirbal is the syntactic pivot in coordination. Yet, we may wonder how come that "hit" can at all *mean the same thing as* "is hit by", for "John hits Rover." does not mean the same as "John is hit by Rover.". The answer lies here in a distinction between meaning and meaning composition. The way the verb "hit" composes with a subject expression is certainly different from that of "is hit by". And yet, both have as their truth conditions that someone hit someone.

Similarly, the issue of types is a difficult one. Take once again the meaning of the transitive verb "hit". Montague gave it the type $e \to (e \to t)$ (it is enough to look at the extensional type). This means that it is a function that, when given an object, returns an intransitive verb, which in turn is a function that returns a truth value when given an object. So the first object supplied is the direct object. We could think however that it is just the other way around (compare Dyirbal for that matter):

the first to be supplied is the subject and the direct object comes next. Alternatively we may give it the type $e \bullet e \to t$, which returns a truth value when given a subject paired with an object. Which of the three is correct? The problem is that they are all equivalent: choose one, get the others for free. From a technical viewpoint this is optimal, yet from our viewpoint this says that there is no a priori way to choose the types. Moreover, from a philosophical point of view this gives rise to what has been termed Benaceraff's Dilemma after Benaceraff (1973): if we cannot choose between these formalizations how can we know that any of them is correct? That is, if there are such objects as meanings but they are abstract then how can we obtain knowledge of them? If we are serious about meanings then either we must assume that they are real (not abstract) or else that they do not exist. In particular, the idea that types are abstract properties of objects is just an illusion, a myth. Types are introduced to smoothen the relationship between syntax and semantics. They are useful but not motivated from semantics. In this connection it is important to realize that by semantics I do *not* mean model theoretic semantics. If I did, then any type assignment could be motivated from a needed fit with a particular formal model. Instead, I think of semantics primarily as truth conditions in the world.

In order to understand how this affects thinking semantically, take the sentence "John is hitting Rover.". How can we judge whether this sentence is true? Obviously, it is of no help to say that we have to look whether or not the pair consisting in John and Rover is in the hit-relation. For it is the latter that we have to construct. That we somehow possess a list of pairs where we can look the facts up is no serious suggestion. Obviously, such a list if it ever existed has to be compiled from the facts out there. But how? Imagine we are witnessing some incident between John and Rover or watching a film—where is that relation and how are we to find it? Clearly, there must be other criteria to tell us who is the subject (or first argument) and who is the object (or second argument). So, for a given situation we can effectively decide which object can fill the first slot and which one the second slot so that they come out as a pair in the hit-relation. Once we have established these criteria, however, there is no need to appeal to pairs anymore. For whatever it is that allows us to judge who will be subject, it is this procedure that we make use of when inserting the subject into the construction but not earlier. The pair has become redundant.

A type theorist will object and say: so you are in effect changing the nature of meanings. Now they are functions from scenes (or films) to objects or whatever but still you uphold type distinctions and so you are not eliminating types. I actually agree with this criticism. It is not types as such that I wish to eliminate. There are occasions when types are necessary or essentially equivalent to whatever else we might put in their place. What I contest is the view that the types tell us anything of essence about the syntax of the expressions. We can of course imagine languages where the fit is perfect (some computer languages are of that sort) but the truth is that natural languages are definitely *not* of that kind.

I have said above that language is a relation, that is, a set of pairs. This relation is many-to-many. A given meaning can be expressed in many ways, a given expression may have many meanings. However, one may attempt to reduce the complexity by a suitable reformulation. For example, we may think that an expression denotes not several meanings but rather a single one, say, the set of all its meanings. Call this kind of meaning *set-meaning* and the other the *ground meaning*. Thus, /`crane`/ denotes a set of ground meanings, one covering the bird meaning and the other the machine meaning. This technical move eliminates polysemy and makes language a function from expressions to (set-)meanings. There are however many problems with this approach. The first is that the combination of two set-meanings is much more complex than the combination of ground meanings, for it must now proceed through a number of cases. Consider namely how complex signs are being made. Given a two place function f, a complex sign is made from two simple signs, each being an expression paired with a ground meaning. It is thus particular expressions with particular ground meanings that are composed via f and not expressions with all their meanings or meanings with the totality of their expressions. If an expression is polysemous the claim is therefore that it must enter with any one of its meanings in place of the collection of all its meanings. The expression /`big crane`/ can therefore be formed with two particular meanings for /`crane`/, each of them however taken on its own. The expression is thus again polysemous insofar as the combination of "big" with any of the two ground meanings makes sense. Similarly, /`all cranes`/ can never be a quantification over objects of the expression /`cranes`/ in both senses simultaneously. It can only be either of them: a quantification over some birds, or a quantification over some machines. Lumping the two meanings into a set therefore creates options that languages do not seem to have. Or, more precisely, the fact that a given expression has two ground meanings (= is polysemous) is technically different from it having a set-meaning.

As the reader will no doubt notice the present monograph is quite technical. This is because I felt it necessary to explore certain technical options that the setup allows for. Since the details are essentially technical there is no point in pretending that they can be dealt with in an informal way. Moreover, if we want to know what the options are we better know as exactly as possible what they consist in. It so turns out that we can obtain certain results on the limitations of compositionality. Moreover, I show that certain technical manoeuvers (such as introducing categories or eliminating polysemy) each have nontrivial side effects that need to be addressed. By doing this I hope to provide the theoretical linguist with a tool for choosing among a bewildering array of options.

Chapter 2
String Languages

THIS chapter introduces the notion of a grammar as an algebra. We shall describe how context free grammars and adjunction grammars fit the format described here. Then we shall study syntactic categories as they arise implicitly in the formulation of a grammar and then turn to the relationship between languages, grammars and surface tests to establish structure. We shall meet our first principle: the *Principle of Preservation*.

2.1 Languages and Grammars

Languages in the way they appear to us seem to consist in strings. The text in front of you is an example. It is basically a long chain of symbols, put one after the other. Yet, linguists stress over and over that there is *structure* in this chain and that this structure comes from a *grammar* that generates this language. I shall assume that the reader is familiar with this standard view on language. In this chapter I shall rehearse some of the definitions, though taking a slightly different view. While standard syntactic textbooks write rules in the form of replacement rules (S $\rightarrow$ NP VP) to be thought of as replacing what is to the left by what is to the right, here we take a bottom up view: we define grammars as devices that *combine* expressions. The reasons for this shift have already been discussed; in the next chapter, it will become apparent why there is no alternative to this view. This is also the way in which Montague defined his formation rules.

Although I shall have very little to say about phonology I should make it clear that when I use the terms "alphabet" and "letter" you may replace them by "phoneme inventory" and "phoneme". Likewise, we may decide to include tone and other characteristics into the representation. All this can be done. The only reason that I do not do it is, apart from the fact that I am not a phonologist, that it would distract attention from the central issues. The reader is however asked to keep in mind that the discussion is largely independent of the actual nature and manifestation of the alphabet.

I said that languages are sets of strings. Clearly, there is more to languages, as they also give meanings to the strings. Yet, if we disregard this latter aspect—and maybe some more—we retain as the simplest of all manifestations of a language: that of a *set of strings*. The topic of string languages is very rich since it has been

M. Kracht, *Interpreted Languages and Compositionality*, Studies in Linguistics and Philosophy 89, DOI 10.1007/978-94-007-2108-1_2,

© Springer Science+Business Media B.V. 2011

thoroughly studied in formal language theory. We start therefore by discussing string languages.

Recall that a **string** over some alphabet A is a sequence of letters from A; for example, /abcbab/ is a string over $\{a, b, c\}$. It is also a string over the alphabet $\{a, b, c, d\}$ but not over $\{a, b\}$. Alternatively, a string over A is a function $\vec{x} : n \to A$ for some natural number n (see Appendix A); n is the **length** of $\vec{x}$. If $n = 0$ we get the **empty string**; it is denoted by ε. We write $\vec{x}, \vec{y}$ (with an arrow) for arbitrary strings. Concatenation is either denoted by $\vec{x}^\frown\vec{y}$ or by juxtaposition. In running text, to enhance explicitness, I enclose material strings (or exponents in general) in slashes, like this: /dog/. This carries no theoretical commitment of any sort.

Definition 2.1 Let A be a finite set, the so-called **alphabet**. A^* denotes the set of strings over A, A^+ the set of nonempty strings. A **language over** A is a subset of A^*.

Following Unix convention, we shall enclose names for sets of symbols by colons (for example, :digit:). This way they cannot be confused with sets of strings, for which we use ordinary notation.

Definition 2.2 The union of two sets is alternatively denoted by $S \cup T$ and $S \mid T$. Given two sets S and T we write

$$S \cdot T := \{\vec{x}^\frown\vec{y} : \vec{x} \in S, \vec{y} \in T\}. \tag{2.1}$$

Furthermore, S^n is defined inductively by

$$S^0 := \{\varepsilon\}, \quad S^{n+1} := S^n \cdot S. \tag{2.2}$$

Finally we put

$$S^* := \bigcup_{n \in \mathbb{N}} S^n \tag{2.3}$$

as well as

$$S^+ := S \cdot S^*. \tag{2.4}$$

Typically, we write ST in place of $S \cdot T$. * binds stronger than $\cdot$ and $\cdot$ binds stronger than $\cup$. We shall write $\{x\}$ and x indiscriminately in case x is a single letter.

It is important to note that a language as defined here is a *set*, so it is unstructured. A grammar on the other hand is a *description* or specification of a language. There are two types of grammars: descriptive and generative. Descriptive grammars describe the strings of the language, while generative grammars describe a process that generates them. We shall delay a definition of descriptive grammars. Thus, for now a grammar is a system of rules (or rather functions). It is the grammar that imposes structure on a language. This point seems contentious; in fact, many linguists think differently. They think that the language itself possesses a structure that needs to be described using the grammar. Some are convinced that some descriptions (maybe even a single one) are better than all the others (see Tomalin (2006) on the origin of this view). I consider this belief unfounded. That we know the right grammar when we see it is wishful thinking. It is clear that regularities need accounting for. However, that accounting for them in a particular way will make the rule apparatus more transparent needs to be demonstrated. The most blatant defect of such claims is that no one knows how to define simplicity in an unambiguous way. One exception is perhaps Kolmogorov complexity, which is, however, difficult to use in practice (see Kornai (2007) on that subject). In absence of a unique notion of simplicity we are left with the intuition that a language "calls" for a particular description in the form of a certain grammar. But it may well be that there are different descriptions of the same facts, none of which need to be essentially better than the other. Indeed, if one looks around and studies various frameworks and the way they like to deal with various phenomena, one finds that there is little fundamental consensus; nor is there a criterion by which to judge who is right. Thus, a language may possess various quite different grammars. These grammars in turn impose different structures on the language and it may be impossible to say which one is "correct". Thus a distinction must be made between the set of acceptable strings and the structure that we see in them.

Example 2.1 (See also Example 2.6 below.) The language of *unbracketed* additive arithmetical terms (or *ua-terms* for short) is defined as follows. Consider the set

$$\text{:digit:} := \{\texttt{0}, \texttt{1}, \cdots, \texttt{9}\}. \tag{2.5}$$

An **ua-term** is a string over this alphabet plus the additional symbol /+/ such that it neither ends nor begins with /+/. So it is a member of the following set.

$$\text{UA} := \text{:digit:}^{+}(\texttt{+}\text{:digit:}^{+})^{*} \tag{2.6}$$

Examples are the following.

$$\texttt{0}, \texttt{10}, \texttt{010+7}, \texttt{00+01+31}, \texttt{1001+000+9} \tag{2.7}$$

In practice we think of such a string as consisting in blocks of digits separated by /+/. This is so far just a matter of convenience. We shall see below however what may justify this view.

In contrast to the unbracketed arithmetical terms, the bracketed arithmetical terms (**a-terms**) always have brackets. They are technically strings over a different alphabet, namely :digit:$\cup\{\texttt{+}, \texttt{(}, \texttt{)}\}$. Thus, it is not that we do not write ua-terms with brackets; they do not contain any brackets in the first place. An a-term, by contrast, has them everywhere. (A precise definition of a-terms will be given in Example 2.6.) There are many ways to "analyse" a given ua-term as arising from some a-term. For example, we can think of the ua-term

$$\vec{x}_0\texttt{+}\vec{x}_1\texttt{+}\vec{x}_2\texttt{+}\cdots\texttt{+}\vec{x}_n \tag{2.8}$$

as being derived, among others, in a left bracketed (2.9) or a right bracketed (2.10) way:

$$(\vec{x}_0+(\vec{x}_1+(\vec{x}_2+\cdots(\vec{x}_{n-1}+\vec{x}_n)\cdots))) \tag{2.9}$$

$$((\cdots((\vec{x}_0+\vec{x}_1)+\vec{x}_2)+\cdots\vec{x}_{n-1})+\vec{x}_n) \tag{2.10}$$

Similarly, the ua-term

$$\mathtt{3+1+7+5} \tag{2.11}$$

can be derived from the following a-terms by deleting brackets:

$$\mathtt{(((3+1)+7)+5), ((3+(1+7))+5), (3+((1+7)+5)), (3+(1+(7+5))).} \tag{2.12}$$

There is no way to decide which analysis is correct. ⚽

Example 2.2 The formation of the third singular present of the English verb is identical to the plural of nouns. It consists—irregular forms and idiosyncrasies of spelling aside—in the addition of /`s`/, /`es`/ or /`ses`/, depending on the end of the word. Is there a formal identity between the two or do they just accidentally happen to be the same? ⚽

This last example will be important also when discussing identity of modes in Section 3.1. Let me briefly go into some details. Ordinary languages contain—apart from the obvious alphabetic characters—also punctuation marks; in addition to punctuation marks we find the digits and the blank, written here /␣/ throughout when quoting material language strings and, finally, some less obvious characters such as "newline" or "new paragraph". These should be counted into the alphabet A for the purposes of writing serious grammars for languages. There is, for example, a difference in English between /`black␣bird`/ and /`blackbird`/. In written English the only difference is the presence or absence of the blank; in spoken English this comes out as a different stress assignment. The same goes obviously for punctuation (the difference between restrictive and nonrestrictive relative clauses is signalled by the presence of a comma). Spoken language has intonation, which is absent from written language; punctuation is a partial substitute for intonation. In what is to follow, we will concentrate on written language to avoid having to deal with issues that are irrelevant for the purpose of this book. Writing systems however introduce their own problems. For matters concerning the intricacies of alphabets I refer the reader to Korpela (2006).

Intermission 1 Some interesting facts about punctuation. In general, there is something of a syntax of punctuation marks. Writing no blank is different from writing one blank, while one blank is the same as two (consecutive) blanks. Two periods are likewise the same as one, two commas the same as one and so on. In general, punctuation marks act as separators, not as brackets. This means that they avoid being put in sequence (with minor exceptions such as a period and a comma when the period signals an abbreviation). Separators come in different strengths. For example, a period is a stronger separator than a comma. This means that if a period and a comma will be in competition, the (sentence) period will win. ⚽

Anyone who is nowadays dealing with characters will know that there is a lot of structure in an alphabet, just as the set of phonemes of a language is highly structured. There is first and foremost a division into alphabetic characters, digits, and punctuation marks. However, there is an additional division into such characters that serve as separators and those that do not. Separators are there to define the units ("identifiers" or "words"). For ua-terms, /+/ is a separator. Separators could also be strings, of course. If we want to understand where the words are in a text we break a string at all those positions where we find a separator. Thus, the blank and also punctuation marks are typical separators. But this is not always the case. A hyphen, for example, is a punctuation mark but does not serve as a separator—or at least not always. In programming languages, brackets are separators; this means that the name of a variable may not contain brackets, since they would simply not be recognised as parts of the name. Anyone interested in these questions may consult, for example, books or manuals on regular expressions and search patterns.

While we often think of languages as being sets of strings over a given alphabet, there are occasions when we prefer to think of languages as somehow independent of the alphabet. These viewpoints are not easy to reconcile. We can introduce some abstractness as follows. Let A and B be alphabets and $m : A \to B^*$ a map. m induces a **homomorphism** $\overline{m} : A^* \to B^*$ in the following way.

$$\overline{m}(x_0 x_1 \cdots x_{n-1}) := m(x_0)^\frown m(x_1)^\frown \cdots ^\frown m(x_{n-1}) \tag{2.13}$$

Then $\overline{m}[L]$ is the **realphabetization** of L.

Example 2.3 In German, the **umlaut** refers to the change of /a/, /o/ and /u/ to /ä/, /ö/ and /ü/, respectively. Standard German allows to replace the vowels with dots by a combination of the vowel with /e/ (historically, this is where the dots came from; they are the remnants of an /e/ written above the vowel). So, we have a map m : ä $\mapsto$ ae, ö $\mapsto$ oe, ü $\mapsto$ ue. For all other (small) letters, $m(x) = x$. Hence,

$$\overline{m}(\texttt{Rädelsführer}) = \texttt{Raedelsfuehrer} \tag{2.14}$$

⚽

We now say that we look at a language only up to realphabetization. In linguistics this is done by considering spoken language as primary and all written languages as realphabetizations thereof. Usually we will want to require that $\overline{m}$ is injective on L, but spelling reforms are not always like that. In Switzerland, the letter /ß/ is written /ss/, and this obliterates the contrast between /Maße/ "measures" and /Masse/ "mass". For this reason we shall not deal with realphabetisation except for theoretical purposes, where we do require that $\overline{m}$ be injective. Realphabetizations are not structurally innocent. What is segmentable in one alphabet may not be in another. Imagine an alphabet where /`downtown`/ is rendered by a single letter, say, /⌂/. The map sending /⌂/ to /`downtown`/ makes an indecomposable unit decomposable (/`down`/ + /`town`/). The dependency of the analysis on the alphabet is mostly left implicit throughout this work.

The division into units, which is so important in practical applications (witness the now popular art of tokenisation), is from a theoretical standpoint secondary. That is to say, it is the responsibility of a grammar to tell us what the units are and how to find them. Whether or not a symbol is a separator will be a consequence of the way the grammar works, not primarily of the language itself. This is why we may maintain, at least in the beginning, that the alphabet is an unstructured set in addition to the language. The structure that we see in a language and its alphabet is—as I emphasized above—imposed on it by a system of rules and descriptions, in other words *by a grammar*. This applies of course to phonemes and features in the same way.

In my view, a grammar is basically an interpretation of an abstract language. In computer science one often talks about **abstract** and **concrete syntax**. The abstract syntax talks about the ideal constitution of the syntactic items, while the concrete syntax specifies how the items are communicated. The terminology used here is that of "signature" (abstract) versus "grammar" (concrete).

Definition 2.3 Let F be a set, the set of **function symbols**. A **signature** is a function Ω from F to the set $\mathbb{N}$ of natural numbers. Given f, $\Omega(f)$ is called the **arity** of f. f is a **constant** if $\Omega(f) = 0$.

If f has arity 2, for example, this means that f takes two arguments and yields a value. If f is a function on the set S, then $f : S \times S \to S$. We also write $f : S^2 \to S$. The result of applying f to the arguments x and y in this order is denoted by $f(x, y)$. If f is partial then $f(x, y)$ need not exist. In this case we write $f : S^2 \hookrightarrow S$. We mention a special case, namely $\Omega(f) = 0$. By convention, $f : S^0 \hookrightarrow S$, but there is little gain in allowing a zeroary function to be partial. Now, $S^0 = \{\varnothing\}$, and so f yields a single value if applied to $\varnothing$. However, $\varnothing$ is simply the empty tuple in this connection, and we would have to write $f()$ for the value of f. However, we shall normally write f in place of $f()$, treating f as if it was its own value. The 0-ary functions play a special role in this connection, since they shall form the *lexicon*.

Definition 2.4 A **grammar over** A is a pair $\langle \Omega, \mathcal{I} \rangle$, where Ω is a signature and for every $f \in F$, $\mathcal{I}(f) : (A^*)^{\Omega(f)} \hookrightarrow A^*$. F is the set of **modes** of the grammar. $\mathcal{I}$ is called the **interpretation**. If $\Omega(f) = 0$, f is called **lexical**, otherwise **nonlexical**. The set $\{\mathcal{I}(f) : \Omega(f) = 0\}$ is called the **lexicon** of G, and the set $\{\mathcal{I}(f) : \Omega(f) > 0\}$ the set of **rules**. The **language** generated by G, in symbols $L(G)$, is defined to be the least set S satisfying the following condition for every $f \in F$ and all $\vec{x}_i \in A^*$, $i < \Omega(f)$.

$$\begin{aligned} &\text{If for all } i < \Omega(f) \vec{x}_i \in S \text{ and } \mathcal{I}(f)(\vec{x}_0, \cdots, \vec{x}_{\Omega(f)-1}) \\ &\qquad\qquad \text{exists then } \mathcal{I}(f)(\vec{x}_0, \cdots, \vec{x}_{\Omega(f)-1}) \in S. \end{aligned} \tag{2.15}$$

Example 2.4 Let $F := \{j, t, f\}$, and $\Omega(j) = \Omega(t) = 0$, $\Omega(f) = 2$. $\mathcal{I}$ is defined as follows. $\mathcal{I}(j)$ is a zeroary function and so $\mathcal{I}(j)()$ is a string, the string /`John`/. Likewise, $\mathcal{I}(t)() =$ `talks`. Finally, we look at $\mathcal{I}(f)$. Suppose first that $\mathcal{I}(f)$ is interpreted like this.

$$\mathcal{I}(f)(\vec{x}, \vec{y}) := \vec{x}^\frown\texttt{␣}^\frown\vec{y}^\frown\texttt{.} \tag{2.16}$$

Then the language contains strings like this one:

$$\texttt{John␣talks.␣talks.} \tag{2.17}$$

The function $\mathcal{I}(f)$ needs to be constrained. One obvious way is to restrict the first input to /`John`/ and the second to /`talks`/. An indirect way to achieve the same is this definition.

$$\mathcal{I}(f)(\vec{x}, \vec{y}) := \begin{cases} \vec{x}^\frown\texttt{␣}^\frown\vec{y}^\frown\texttt{.} & \text{if } \vec{x} \text{ ends with /n/} \\ & \quad \text{and } \vec{y} \text{ begins with /t/,} \\ \text{undefined} & \text{otherwise.} \end{cases} \tag{2.18}$$

This grammar generates the following language.

$$\{\texttt{John}, \texttt{talks}, \texttt{John␣talks.}\} \tag{2.19}$$

⚽

Example 2.5 Here is now a pathological example. A set S is called **countable** if it is infinite and there is an onto function $f : \mathbb{N} \to S$. If S is countable we can assume that f is actually bijective. Let $L \subseteq A^*$. L is countable, since A is finite. Let $f : \mathbb{N} \to L$ be bijective. Let now $F := \{b, s\}$, $\Omega(b) := 0$ and $\Omega(s) := 1$. This means that we get the following terms: b, $s(b)$, $s(s(b))$, $s(s(s(b)))$, ... The general element has the form $s^n(b)$, $n \in \mathbb{N}$. This is a familiar way to generate the natural numbers: start with zero and keep forming successors. Further, we put

$$\begin{aligned} \mathcal{I}(b)() &:= f(0) \\ \mathcal{I}(s)(\vec{x}) &:= f(f^{-1}(\vec{x}) + 1) \end{aligned} \tag{2.20}$$

So, we start with the first element in the enumeration f. The number of $\vec{x}$ in the enumeration is $f^{-1}(\vec{x})$. If we add 1 to this number and translate this via f we get the next element in the list. In other words, we have $\mathcal{I}(s)(f(n)) = f(n + 1)$.

This grammar generates L. It follows that every countable language has a grammar that generates it. ⚽

Evidently, any $f \in F$ (that is, every mode) is either lexical or nonlexical. Notice that there are no requirements on the functions, not even that they be computable. (Recently, Lasersohn (2009) has argued that computability may not even be an appropriate requirement for meanings. Without endorsing the argument that he presents I have dropped the requirement here.) We shall introduce restrictions on the functions as we go along. The lexicon is not always considered part of the grammar. I make no principled decision here; it is just easier not to have to worry about the rules and the lexicon separately.

Example 2.6 This is one of our main examples: it will be called *the language of equations*.

$$:\!\mathrm{eq}\!: := :\!\mathrm{digit}\!: \cup \{\texttt{+}, \texttt{-}, \texttt{(}, \texttt{)}, \texttt{=}\} \tag{2.21}$$

$F = \{f_0, f_1, f_2, f_3, f_4, f_5, f_6\}$. $\Omega(f_0) = \Omega(f_1) = 0$, $\Omega(f_2) = \Omega(f_3) = 1$, $\Omega(f_4) = \Omega(f_5) = \Omega(f_6) = 2$. $\vec{x}$ is **binary** if it only contains /0/ and /1/; $\vec{x}$ is an a-term if it does not contain /=/. The modes are shown in Table 2.1. The strings that this grammar generates are of the following form. They are either strings consisting in the letters /0/ and /1/, for example /010/, /11101/, or they are a-terms, like /(1+(01-101))/; or they are equations between two a-terms, like /(1+10)=11/. (A single numeral expression is also an a-term.) ⚽

Given a signature Ω, we define the notion of an *Ω-term*.

Definition 2.5 Let V be a set of variables disjoint from F. Let Ω be a signature over F. An **Ω-term over** V is a string t over $F \cup V$ satisfying one of the following.

❶ $t \in V$,
❷ $t = f$, where $\Omega(f) = 0$,
❸ $t = f^\frown t_0^\frown \cdots {}^\frown t_{n-1}$, where $n = \Omega(f)$ and t_i is an Ω-term for every $i < n$.

Table 2.1 The modes of Example 2.6

$$\mathcal{I}(f_0)() := \texttt{0}$$

$$\mathcal{I}(f_1)() := \texttt{1}$$

$$\mathcal{I}(f_2)(\vec{x}) := \begin{cases} \vec{x}^\frown\texttt{0} & \text{if } \vec{x} \text{ is binary,} \\ \text{undefined} & \text{else.} \end{cases}$$

$$\mathcal{I}(f_3)(\vec{x}) := \begin{cases} \vec{x}^\frown\texttt{1} & \text{if } \vec{x} \text{ is binary,} \\ \text{undefined} & \text{else.} \end{cases}$$

$$\mathcal{I}(f_4)(\vec{x}, \vec{y}) := \begin{cases} \texttt{(}^\frown\vec{x}^\frown\texttt{+}^\frown\vec{y}^\frown\texttt{)} & \text{if } \vec{x}, \vec{y} \text{ are a-terms,} \\ \text{undefined} & \text{else.} \end{cases}$$

$$\mathcal{I}(f_5)(\vec{x}, \vec{y}) := \begin{cases} \texttt{(}^\frown\vec{x}^\frown\texttt{-}^\frown\vec{y}^\frown\texttt{)} & \text{if } \vec{x}, \vec{y} \text{ are a-terms,} \\ \text{undefined} & \text{else.} \end{cases}$$

$$\mathcal{I}(f_6)(\vec{x}, \vec{y}) := \begin{cases} \vec{x}^\frown\texttt{=}^\frown\vec{y} & \text{if } \vec{x}, \vec{y} \text{ are a-terms,} \\ \text{undefined} & \text{else.} \end{cases}$$

The symbol $\mathrm{Tm}_\Omega(V)$ denotes the set of all Ω-terms over V. The set $\mathrm{Tm}_\Omega(\varnothing)$ is of special importance. It is the set of **constant Ω-terms**. A term t is **constant** if $t \in F^+$, that is, if it contains no variables. Given a grammar $G = \langle \Omega, \mathcal{I} \rangle$, we also call an Ω-term a **G-term**.

See Fig. 2.2 on page 36 for an example of term. Notice that the second case is a subcase of the third (where $n = 0$). It is listed separately for better understanding. Some remarks are in order. Standardly, terms are considered abstract, but I thought it easier to let terms also be concrete objects, namely strings. The syntax chosen for these objects is Polish Notation. It has the advantage of using the alphabet itself and having the property of transparency (see page 46 for a definition). Exercises 2.6 and 2.7 show that the language enjoys unique readability. Delaying the justification for the terminology, let us make the following definition.

Definition 2.6 Let t be an Ω-term. s is a **subterm** of t if and only if s is an Ω-term and a substring of t.

Based on the exercises at the end of this section one can show that the language of terms is quite well behaved. A substring that looks like a term actually is a subterm under every analysis. (Consequently there can be only one analysis.)

Proposition 2.1 *Let s and t be Ω-terms and s a substring of t. Then either $s = t$ or $t = f^\frown t_0^\frown \cdots ^\frown t_{n-1}$ for some f and $n = \Omega(f)$ and there is an $i < n$ such that s is a subterm of t_i.*

Given a grammar G we can define the interpretation $\iota_G(t)$ of a constant term t.

❶ $\iota_G(f) := \mathcal{I}(f)$ if $\Omega(f) = 0$,
❷ $\iota_G(f t_0 \cdots t_{n-1}) := \mathcal{I}(f)(\iota_G(t_0), \cdots, \iota_G(t_{n-1}))$, where $n = \Omega(f)$.

We call ι_G the **unfolding function** and say that t **unfolds in G to $\vec{x}$** if $\iota_G(t) = \vec{x}$. If the grammar is clear from the context, we shall write $\iota(t)$ in place of $\iota_G(t)$. Continuing our example, we have

$$
\begin{aligned}
\iota(f_4 f_3 f_0 f_2 f_1) &= \texttt{(}\iota(f_3 f_0)\texttt{+}\iota(f_2 f_1)\texttt{)} \\
&= \texttt{(}\iota(f_0)\texttt{1+}\iota(f_2 f_1)\texttt{)} \\
&= \texttt{(}\iota(f_0)\texttt{1+}\iota(f_1)\texttt{0)} \\
&= \texttt{(01+}\iota(f_1)\texttt{0)} \\
&= \texttt{(01+10)}
\end{aligned}
\tag{2.22}
$$

This establishes the interpretation of constant terms. Since the string functions may be partial not every constant term has a value. Thus, $\iota(t)$ may be undefined. We call

$$\mathrm{dom}(\iota) := \{t \in \mathrm{Tm}_\Omega(\varnothing) : \iota(t) \text{ is defined}\} \tag{2.23}$$

the set of **orthographically definite terms**. The term $f_4 f_3 f_0 f_2 f_1$ is orthographically definite, while the term $f_6 f_6 f_0 f_1 f_1$ is not. This is because once f_6 has been used, it introduces the symbol /=/, and none of the modes can apply further. If t is orthographically definite, so is any subterm of t. Notice that for a grammar G, the language can simply be defined as

$$L(G) := \{\iota(t) : t \in \mathrm{Tm}_{\Omega}(\varnothing)\}. \tag{2.24}$$

Notice that this is different from the standard concept. This difference will be of great importance later on. Standardly, grammars may contain symbols other than the terminal symbols. The nonterminal alphabet contains characters foreign to the language itself. While in formal languages the presence of such characters can be motivated from considerations of usefulness, in our context these symbols make no sense. This is because we shall later consider interpreted languages; and there is, as far as I know, no indication that the nonterminal symbols have any meaning. In fact, in the terminology of this book, by the definition of "language" and "nonterminal symbol" the latter have no meaning. All of this will follow from the principles defined in Section 2.6. The present requirement is weaker since it does not constrain the power of the rules. What it says, though, is that the generation of strings must proceed strictly by using strings of the language itself. Later we shall also require that the strings must be used with the meaning that the language assigns to them.

If we eliminate nonterminal symbols, however, a lot of things change as well. $L(G)$ not only contains the strings at the end of a derivation but every string that is built on the way. If, for example, we write our grammar using context free rules, $L(G)$ not only contains the sentences but the individual words and all constituents that any sentence of $L(G)$ has. Therefore, unlike in traditional linguistic theory, L is not simply assumed to contain sentences but *all constituents*. To distinguish these two notions we shall talk of a **language in the narrow sense** if we mean language as a set of *sentences*; and we speak of a **language in the wide sense**—or simply of a **language**—if we mean language as a set of *constituents*. Notice that the difference lies merely in the way in which the language defines its grammar. As objects both are sets. But a language in the narrow sense leaves larger room to define grammars as languages in the wide sense also fix the set from which constituents may be drawn. Our stance in the matter is that one should start with language in the wide sense. The reasons for this will I hope become clear in Chapter 3. At this moment I would like to point out that for all intents and purposes starting with language in the narrow sense makes the grammar radically underdetermined.

For the working linguist, the choice of L is a highly empirical matter and hence full of problems: in defining L we need to make decisions as to what the constituents of the language are. This means we need more input in the first place. On the other hand, we get a more direct insight into structure. A grammar can only analyse a string into parts that are already members of L. Of course there is still a question of whether a given string really occurs as a constituent (we shall discuss that point later). But it can only do so if it is in L. A side effect of this is that we can sometimes know which occurrences of symbols are syncategorematic. Basically, an occurrence of a symbol is syncategorematic in a string under a derivation if it is not part of any primitive string that the derivation uses. This is admittedly vague; a proper definition must be deferred to Section 2.6.

Example 2.7 I give two alternative formulations of Boolean logic. The alphabet is as follows.

$$:\text{bool}: := \{\mathtt{0}, \mathtt{1}, \mathtt{p}, \neg, \wedge, \vee, \mathtt{(}, \mathtt{)}\} \tag{2.25}$$

The first language is the smallest set S satisfying the equation (here, as in the sequel, $\cdot$ binds stronger than $|$ or $\cup$):

$$S = (\mathtt{p} \cdot (\mathtt{0} \mid \mathtt{1})^*) \cup (\mathtt{(} \cdot \neg \cdot S \cdot \mathtt{)}) \cup (\mathtt{(} \cdot S \cdot (\vee \mid \wedge) \cdot S \cdot \mathtt{)}) \tag{2.26}$$

The other language is the union $D \cup S$, where D and S are the minimal solution of the following set of equations:

$$\begin{aligned} D &= D \cup (\mathtt{0} \mid \mathtt{1}) \cdot D \\ S &= \mathtt{p} \cdot D \cup (\mathtt{(} \cdot \neg \cdot S \cdot \mathtt{)}) \cup (\mathtt{(} \cdot S \cdot (\vee \mid \wedge) \cdot S \cdot \mathtt{)}) \end{aligned} \tag{2.27}$$

It turns out that in both cases S is the same set; however, in the first example the language defined is just S, in the second it is $S \cup D$. S contains `p01`, `(¬p0)`, `(p1∧(¬p1))`. D (but not S) also contains `0`, `111`. ⚽

Given a grammar G and a string $\vec{x}$, we call a term t an **analysis term** or simply an **analysis** of $\vec{x}$ if $\iota(t) = \vec{x}$. A string may have several analysis terms. In this case we say that it is **ambiguous**. If it has none it is called **ungrammatical**. A *grammar* is called **ambiguous** if it generates at least one ambiguous string and **unambiguous** otherwise.

Exercise 2.1 Consider a context free grammar (for a definition, see Section 2.3). Then the language of that grammar generated in the narrow sense is context free, by definition. Show that also the language generated in the wide sense is context free.

Exercise 2.2 Give examples of pairs (L, L') such that L' is a language in the wide sense, and L its narrow restriction, such that (i) L is context free but L' is not, (ii) L' is context free but L is not.

Exercise 2.3 Describe the set of orthographically definite terms for the language of equations.

Exercise 2.4 Write grammars for the unbracketed additive terms, the left and the right bracketed additive terms of Example 2.1, respectively.

Exercise 2.5 Terms are strings, by definition, and can therefore be looked at as members of a language. The methodology of this book can therefore also be applied to them. Consider, by way of example, the strings for terms in Example 2.6. Write a grammar for the set of all constant Ω-terms; then write a grammar for the set of all orthographically definite terms.

Exercise 2.6 The formal notation of terms must be accompanied by a proof that it is uniquely readable. We shall use this and the next exercise to deliver such a proof. Recall that terms are sequences of function symbols, no extra symbol is added. However, not every such sequence is a term. Let Ω be a signature. For $f \in F \cup V$ let $\gamma(f) := \Omega(f) - 1$ and for a string $\vec{x} = x_0 x_1 \cdots x_{n-1} \in F^*$ let $\gamma(\vec{x}) = \sum_{i<n} \gamma(x_i)$. Show the following: if $\vec{x} \in F^*$ is a term, then (i) $\gamma(\vec{x}) = -1$ and (ii) for every proper prefix $\vec{y} = x_0 x_1 \cdots x_{m-1}$, $m < n$, $\gamma(\vec{y}) \geq 0$. (It follows from this that no proper prefix of a term is a term.) *Hint.* Do an induction on the length.

Exercise 2.7 (Continuing the previous exercise). Let $\vec{x} = x_0 x_1 \cdots x_{n-1} \in F^*$ be a string. Then if $\vec{x}$ satisfies (i) and (ii) from the previous exercise, $\vec{x}$ is a term. *Hint.* Induction on n. The cases $n = 0, 1$ are straightforward. Now suppose that $n > 1$. Then $x = x_0 x_1 \cdots x_{n-1}$ and $\gamma(x_0) = p \geq 0$, by (ii). Show that there is a number $i > 1$ such that $\gamma(x_1 \cdots x_{i-1}) = -1$; choose i minimal with that property. Then $\vec{y}_0 = x_1 \cdots x_{i-1}$ is a term, by inductive assumption. If $p > 1$ we have $i < n$, and there is $i' > i$ such that $\vec{y}_0 = x_i x_{i+1} \cdots x_{i'}$ is a term. Choose i' minimal with that property. And so on, getting a decomposition $x_0 \vec{y}_0 \cdots \vec{y}_p$.

Exercise 2.8 Show Proposition 2.1. *Hint.* Assume that $s \neq t$. Then there is a decomposition $t = f^\frown t_0^\frown \cdots ^\frown t_{n-1}$. Now fix a substring occurrence of s in t. Assume that it starts in t_i. Then show that it must also end in t_i.

2.2 Parts and Substitution

We defined a language (in the wide sense) to be the set of all of its constituent expressions. Since we do not discriminate sentences from nonsentences the language contains not only sentences but also parts thereof. We would like to be able to say of some expressions whether one is a part of the other. In particular, we would like to say that /`The cat is on the mat.`/ contains /`on the mat`/ as its part but not, for example, /`cat is on`/ or /`dog`/. In the cases just given this is straightforward: /`cat is on`/ is not in our language (in the wide sense), for it has no meaning; /`dog`/ on the other hand is not a string part of the expression. In other cases, however, matters are not so easy. Is /`Mary ran`/ a part of /`John and Mary ran.`/ or is it not? It is a string part of the sentence and it is meaningful. As it turns out, there is no unique answer in this case. (Curiously enough even semantic criteria fail to give a unanimous answer.) More problems arise, making the notion of *part* quite elusive. One problem is that there are no conditions on the string functions; another is that a given string may have been composed in many different ways. Let us discuss these issues below. We begin however with a definition of *part*.

Definition 2.7 Let G be a grammar. $\vec{x}$ is a **part of** $\vec{y}$ if there are constant terms s and u such that s is a subterm of u and $\iota_G(s) = \vec{x}$ as well as $\iota_G(u) = \vec{y}$.

This definition of *part of* pays no attention to the strings. Instead it looks at the way the strings are obtained through the string functions of the grammar. Thus, any useful restriction will come from restricting the power of string functions.

The definition also pays no attention to the way in which the parts occur in the larger string. Occurrences will be defined in Definition 2.9 and then we shall review Definition 2.7. The examples of this section will show how broad the spectrum of grammars is and how it affects parthood.

Example 2.8 Consider a unary function f which forms the past tense, for example $\mathcal{I}(f)(\texttt{go}) = \texttt{went}$, $\mathcal{I}(f)(\texttt{sing}) = \texttt{sang}$, $\mathcal{I}(f)(\texttt{ask}) = \texttt{asked}$. In this grammar, /go/ is a part of /went/, /sing/ a part of /sang/, /ask/ a part of /asked/. ⚽

Generally, it is actually not assumed that /went/ is literally made from /go/; rather, it is assumed that the verb /go/ possesses different allomorphs and that the context decides which of them is going to be used. This is also my own intuition. Therefore, I shall propose that syntactic functions may not delete material. This will effectively exclude the grammar of Example 2.8. Let us now look at a second example.

Example 2.9 We present two ways of generating the nonempty strings over the alphabet :blet: := $\{\texttt{a}, \texttt{b}\}$ of "binary letters". C_1 consists in the zeroary functions $f_\texttt{a}$, $f_\texttt{b}$ plus the unary functions f_0 and f_1. We have

$$\begin{aligned} \mathcal{I}_1(f_\texttt{a})() &:= \texttt{a} \\ \mathcal{I}_1(f_\texttt{b})() &:= \texttt{b} \\ \mathcal{I}_1(f_0)(\vec{x}) &:= \vec{x}^\frown\texttt{a} \\ \mathcal{I}_1(f_1)(\vec{x}) &:= \vec{x}^\frown\texttt{b} \end{aligned} \tag{2.28}$$

So, $\iota_{C_1}(f_1 f_0 f_0 f_\texttt{a}) = \texttt{aaab}$. This grammar is the "typewriter model" of strings. Strings are generated by appending letters one by one to the initial letter.

The grammar C_2 has the zeroary function symbols $f_\texttt{a}$ and $f_\texttt{b}$ and a binary symbol γ. We have

$$\begin{aligned} \mathcal{I}_2(f_\texttt{a})() &:= \texttt{a} \\ \mathcal{I}_2(f_\texttt{b})() &:= \texttt{b} \\ \mathcal{I}_2(\gamma)(\vec{x}, \vec{y}) &:= \vec{x}^\frown\vec{y} \end{aligned} \tag{2.29}$$

For example, $\iota_{C_2}(\gamma\gamma f_\texttt{a} f_\texttt{a} \gamma f_\texttt{a} f_\texttt{b}) = \texttt{aaab}$.

In C_1, $\vec{x}$ is part of $\vec{y}$ if and only if it is a nonempty prefix of $\vec{y}$. In C_2, $\vec{x}$ is a part of $\vec{y}$ if and only if it is a nonempty subword. ⚽

It is to be noted that both grammars generate the set A^+, so they are extensionally identical. Yet structurally they are different. According to C_2 strings can have many more parts than according to C_1. For example, in C_2 /aaab/ possesses (apart from itself) the parts /a/, /aa/, /aaa/, /b/, /ab/, /aab/. In addition, the string /aa/ has two occurrences in /aaab/, which we may denote as follows: /$\underline{\texttt{aa}}$ab/ and /a$\underline{\texttt{aa}}$b/. (More on occurrences in Definition 2.9 and Section 2.5.) Both occurrences are actually parts of the string. It turns out, though, that not all parts can be parts in one and the same derivation. A more useful notion is in fact defined for a particular analysis term. The relation "is part of" is then the union of the relations "is a t-part of" for all terms t.

Definition 2.8 Let G be a grammar, t a constant term and $\vec{x}$ and $\vec{y}$ strings. We say that $\vec{x}$ is a t-**part of** $\vec{y}$ if $\iota_G(t) = \vec{y}$ and there is a subterm s of t such that $\iota_G(s) = \vec{x}$. In this case there is $t'(x)$ such that $t = t'(s)$.

With certain adaptations we can say that the relation "is a t-part of" is transitive. (If $\vec{y}$ is a t-part of $\vec{z}$ and is the unfolding of s, s a subterm of t, then parts of $\vec{y}$ must be s-parts of $\vec{y}$ in order to be t-parts of $\vec{z}$.) Here is a somewhat surprising result given that the union of transitive relations need not be transitive.

Proposition 2.2 *The relation* **is part of** *is transitive.*

Proof Let $\vec{x}$ be a part of $\vec{y}$ and $\vec{y}$ a part of $\vec{z}$. Then there are terms r and s such that r unfolds to $\vec{x}$ and s unfolds to $\vec{y}$ and r is a subterm of s. Furthermore there are t and u that unfold to $\vec{y}$ and $\vec{z}$, respectively, and t is a subterm of u. Since they unfold to the same string, we may replace t in u by s, giving us a new term u', of which s is a subterm. Since r is a subterm of s, it is also a subterm of u. □

Given a single C_2-term t for /aaab/, the substring occurrences that correspond to the subterms actually form a tree. This is essentially because the grammar encodes a context free analysis. However, C_2 is ambiguous: /aaab/ has several analysis terms and they provide different constituent analyses. The analysis terms are as follows: $\gamma\gamma\gamma f_{\mathtt{a}} f_{\mathtt{a}} f_{\mathtt{a}} f_{\mathtt{b}}$, $\gamma\gamma f_{\mathtt{a}}\gamma f_{\mathtt{a}} f_{\mathtt{a}} f_{\mathtt{b}}$, $\gamma\gamma f_{\mathtt{a}} f_{\mathtt{a}}\gamma f_{\mathtt{a}} f_{\mathtt{b}}$, $\gamma f_{\mathtt{a}}\gamma\gamma f_{\mathtt{a}} f_{\mathtt{a}} f_{\mathtt{b}}$ and $\gamma f_{\mathtt{a}}\gamma f_{\mathtt{a}}\gamma f_{\mathtt{a}} f_{\mathtt{b}}$. On the other hand, C_1 is unambiguous.

Standard tests for constituency in textbooks include the *substitution test*. Before we look in detail at the test let us first say a few words about string substitution.

Definition 2.9 A **(1-)context** is a pair $C = \langle \vec{x}, \vec{z} \rangle$ of strings. Inserting $\vec{y}$ into C results in the string $C(\vec{y}) := \vec{x}\,\vec{y}\,\vec{z}$. We say that $\vec{y}$ **occurs in** $\vec{u}$ if there is a context C such that $\vec{u} = C(\vec{y})$. We also say then that C is **an occurrence of** $\vec{y}$ **in** $\vec{u}$. The result of substituting $\vec{w}$ for $\vec{y}$ in its occurrence C is $C(\vec{w}) = \vec{x}\,\vec{w}\,\vec{z}$.

For example, $C := \langle \mathtt{s}, \mathtt{ish} \rangle$ is a 1-context. $C(\mathtt{elf}) = \mathtt{s}^\frown\mathtt{elf}^\frown\mathtt{ish} = \mathtt{selfish}$. Notice that for any 1-context $C = \langle \vec{x}, \vec{y} \rangle$, $C(\varepsilon) = \vec{x}^\frown\vec{y}$. The substitution test runs as follows.

$$\texttt{John likes cricket.} \tag{2.30}$$

Given a sentence, say, (2.30), we look for the string occurrences that can be substituted for /cricket/ such that the result is once again a sentence. These include /chess/, /vegetables/, /his new home/ and so on. Similarly, we try to substitute for other sequences such as /likes/, /John likes/ and /likes cricket/. The underlying idea is that nonconstituents cannot be substituted for (for example /John likes/) while constituents can. In practice, this test is not without problems, as it often turns out that nonconstituents can be substituted for (as is the case with /John `likes`/, for which we can substitute /`Peter dislikes`/). In fact, it sometimes turns out that the alleged nonconstituent passes all tests and we must be prepared to either strengthen our tests or admit that these really *are* constituents (as some claim is the case with /`John likes`/, see Steedman (1990)). In this section we shall look in some detail at the formal underpinnings of the substitution test.

First of all, we have to ask what we actually mean by substitution and second how it can possibly show us something about the grammars for our language. The answer to the first question is in fact not trivial. In the absence of a grammar the substitution we should be performing is simply *string substitution*. The underlying claim of the constituency test is that it shows us when string substitution is actually *constituent substitution*. This is the case if it can be performed without affecting grammaticality. Here I have *defined* constituent substitution to be substitution on the level of the analysis terms: it is the substitution of one subterm by another. The syntactic tests assume that constituent substitution if defined is always string substitution. This is problematic for two reasons. One is that the two need not be identical because the string functions of the grammar may be different from string polynomials (see the end of this section for a definition). The second is that the substitution can give misleading evidence. We start with some examples to show the point.

Definition 2.10 Let L be a language. Write $\vec{x} \sim_L \vec{y}$ if for all 1-contexts C: $C(\vec{x}) \in L \Leftrightarrow C(\vec{y}) \in L$. The set $\mathrm{Cat}_L(\vec{x}) := \{C : C(\vec{x}) \in L\}$ is called the **string category of $\vec{x}$ in L**.

Obviously, $\vec{x} \sim_L \vec{y}$ if and only if $\mathrm{Cat}_L(\vec{x}) = \mathrm{Cat}_L(\vec{y})$. If string substitution is constituent substitution then the definition above defines exactly the syntactically relevant classes of English. However, mostly this is not a realistic assumption. Let us review how the notion of part can depart from that of a constituent.

Example 2.10 We look at three grammars to form the plural of English. Let F_0 be a list of functions $f_{\vec{x}}$, where in all grammars below $f_{\vec{x}}$ will be evaluated to the string $\vec{x}$. To keep it simple, let $F_0 = F_R \cup F_I$, where $F_R = \{f_{\mathrm{cat}}, f_{\mathrm{dog}}\}$, $F_I = \{f_{\mathrm{sheep}}, f_{\mathrm{mouse}}, f_{\mathrm{ox}}\}$. F_R contains the regular nouns, F_I the irregular nouns. Thus, with $\mathcal{I}_i$ the interpretation function of the grammar P_i we have $\mathcal{I}_i(f_{\mathrm{cat}})() = \mathtt{cat}$, $\mathcal{I}_i(f_{\mathrm{mouse}})() = \mathtt{mouse}$ and so on. Now, put $\Omega_0(f_{\vec{x}}) := 0$. We denote by R_s the set $\{\vec{x} : f_{\vec{x}} \in F_R\}$, R_p the corresponding plural forms, likewise $I_s := \{\vec{x} : f_{\vec{x}} \in F_I\}$, I_p the corresponding plural forms.

The first grammar, $P_1 = \langle \Omega_1, \mathcal{I}_1 \rangle$, is as follows. $F_1 := F_0 \cup \{p\}$, $\Omega_1(p) = 1$, $\Omega_1 \restriction F_0 = \Omega_0$. $\mathcal{I}_1(p)$ is defined on $R_s \cup I_s$, which is all strings that are singular nouns (/`cat`/, /`mouse`/, /`ox`/, but not /`oxen`/) and its output is the corresponding plural. So we have

$$\mathcal{I}_1(p) = \{\langle \mathtt{cat}, \mathtt{cats} \rangle, \langle \mathtt{dog}, \mathtt{dogs} \rangle, \langle \mathtt{sheep}, \mathtt{sheep} \rangle, \langle \mathtt{mouse}, \mathtt{mice} \rangle, \langle \mathtt{ox}, \mathtt{oxen} \rangle\}. \tag{2.31}$$

The second grammar, $P_2 = \langle \Omega_2, \mathcal{I}_2 \rangle$, has instead $F_2 := F_0 \cup \{g, f_{\mathrm{mice}}, f_\varepsilon, f_{\mathrm{s}}, f_{\mathrm{es}}, f_{\mathrm{en}}\}$, where g is a binary function symbol. We put

$$\mathcal{I}_2(g)(\vec{x}, \vec{y}) := \begin{cases} \vec{x}^\frown\vec{y} & \text{if } \vec{x} \in R_s \text{ and } \vec{y} = \texttt{s} \\ & \quad \text{or } \vec{x} = \texttt{sheep} \text{ and } \vec{y} = \varepsilon \\ & \quad \text{or } \vec{x} = \texttt{ox} \text{ and } \vec{y} = \texttt{en}, \\ \text{undefined} & \text{else.} \end{cases} \tag{2.32}$$

In short, $\mathcal{I}_2(g)(\vec{x}, \vec{y})$ is defined only if $\vec{x}$ is a noun root and $\vec{y}$ a proper plural suffix for $\vec{x}$. Since the plural of /mouse/ is not obtained by affixation, it has been added to the lexicon. A variation of this grammar would be to set $\mathcal{I}_2(g)(\texttt{mouse}, \varepsilon) := \texttt{mice}$. Thus, the plural is formed by a zero affix to a different stem.

The third grammar, $P_3 = \langle \Omega_3, \mathcal{I}_3 \rangle$ is a mixture between the two. $F_3 := F_0 \cup \{p, g, f_s, f_{es}\}$. For regular nouns it uses g, for irregular nouns it uses f.

$$\mathcal{I}_3(g)(\vec{x}, \vec{y}) = \begin{cases} \mathcal{I}_2(g)(\vec{x}, \vec{y}) & \text{if } \vec{x} \in R_s, \\ \text{undefined} & \text{otherwise.} \end{cases} \tag{2.33}$$

$$\mathcal{I}_3(p)(\vec{x}) = \begin{cases} \mathcal{I}_1(p)(\vec{x}) & \text{if } \vec{x} \in I_s, \\ \text{undefined} & \text{otherwise.} \end{cases} \tag{2.34}$$

First of all notice that we can distinguish between these grammars in terms of the generated language. It turns out that P_1 generates all and only the singular and plural noun forms. P_2 in addition contains the plural morphs (like /s/, /es/, /en/ and ε). P_3 contains only the regular plural morphs and not ε, for example (though that depends on the exact distribution of the work between f and g). P_1 realizes a model called *item and process*, while P_2 realises a model called *item and arrangement* (see Matthews (1978) for a discussion of these models).

Next we need to look at how constituent substitution works in these examples. Here is an example: in P_2, the string /cats/ is the value of the term $gf_{\mathrm{cat}}f_{\mathrm{s}}$. Replace f_{cat} by f_{dog} and you get the term $gf_{\mathrm{dog}}f_{\mathrm{s}}$, which unfolds to /dogs/. Replace it by f_{mouse} and you get $gf_{\mathrm{mouse}}f_{\mathrm{s}}$, which is undefined. Similarly, replace f_{s} by f_{en} and you get $gf_{\mathrm{cat}}f_{\mathrm{en}}$, which is also undefined.

In P_2, the plural morph is a constituent, so it should be substitutable. Likewise, the root noun is a constituent, so we should be able to substitute for it. Sometimes we can successfully perform such a substitution, as certain nouns accept two plural endings: we have /formulas/ next to /formulae/. Most of the time the substitution will fail though. In P_1 on the other hand the substitution of the plural morph is illicit for a different reason: it is not a constituent. The form /cats/ is the value of pf_{cat}, so the only constituent substitution we can perform is to replace f_{cat} by f_{mouse} and in this case the result is /mice/.

In P_3 string substitution of the plural morph by something else is sometimes licit sometimes not. Let us look now at the substitution of the root noun by another root noun. In P_2 we may exchange /dog/ for /cat/ but not /mouse/. This is because $\mathcal{I}_2(g)(\texttt{dog}, \texttt{s}) = \texttt{dogs}$, which is the result of substituting the substring /cat/ of /cats/ by /dog/, but $\mathcal{I}_2(g)(\texttt{mouse}, \texttt{s})$ is undefined, while applying the string substitution gives /mouses/. Trying the same in P_1 we find that the string substitution facts are similar; however, $\mathcal{I}_2(f)(\texttt{mouse})$ is defined and it gives /`mice`/. Thus, the difference between P_1 and P_2 is that the substitution of the subconstituent /`mouse`/ for /`cat`/ in the derivation is licit in P_1 but illicit in P_2. In P_1, the result of this substitution is different from string substitution, though. ⚽

The grammar P_2 actually uses straight concatenation and the string categories of English actually do tell us about the necessary distinctions we need to make in the paradigms. (Note though that the grammars here do not explicitly mention paradigms. There is no need to do so. The classes are just defined indirectly via the partiality.)

Example 2.11 The next example is a variation of the previous theme. The first grammar, Q_1, has constants for the names /`John`/, /`Alex`/ and /`Pete`/ and for the verb forms, /`sings`/ and /`sing`/, /`runs`/ and /`run`/. It has two binary functions, c and g. Call a sequence $\vec{x}$ an *NP* if it has the form $/x_1\texttt{␣and␣}x_2\texttt{␣and␣}x_3\cdots/$. It is *singular* if it does not contain /`and`/ and plural otherwise.

$$\mathcal{I}(c)(\vec{x},\vec{y}) := \begin{cases} \vec{x}^\frown\texttt{␣and␣}^\frown\vec{y} & \text{if } \vec{x} \text{ and } \vec{y} \text{ are NPs,} \\ \text{undefined} & \text{else.} \end{cases} \tag{2.35}$$

g combines NPs with verb forms. The chosen verb form must agree in number with the sequence. This is done as follows.

$$\mathcal{I}(g)(\vec{x},\vec{y}) := \begin{cases} \vec{x}^\frown\texttt{␣}^\frown\vec{y} & \text{if either } \vec{x} \text{ is a singular NP} \\ & \quad \text{and } \vec{y} \text{ is a singular verb form} \\ & \text{or } \vec{x} \text{ is a plural NP} \\ & \quad \text{and } \vec{y} \text{ is a plural verb form,} \\ \text{undefined} & \text{else.} \end{cases} \tag{2.36}$$

This grammar generates /`John sings`/ (it is the value of $gf_{\text{John}}f_{\text{sings}}$) and /`John and Mary and Alex sing`/ (the value of $gccf_{\text{John}}f_{\text{Mary}}f_{\text{Alex}}f_{\text{sing}}$) but not /`Mary and Alex sings`/. For the second grammar, Q_2, we assume we have only verb roots (form identical with the singulars of the previous grammar) and change the interpretation of g as follows:

$$\mathcal{K}(g)(\vec{x},\vec{y}) := \begin{cases} \vec{x}^\frown\texttt{␣}^\frown\vec{y} & \text{if } \vec{x} \text{ is a plural NP and } \vec{y} \text{ is a verb root,} \\ \vec{x}^\frown\texttt{␣}^\frown\vec{y}^\frown\texttt{s} & \text{if } \vec{x} \text{ is a singular NP and } \vec{y} \text{ is a verb root,} \\ \text{undefined} & \text{else.} \end{cases} \tag{2.37}$$

In Q_1, we can string substitute /`John and Mary`/ for /`John`/ only if the verb form is already plural but not, for example, in /`John sings`/, for we would get /`John and Mary sings`/, which the grammar does not generate. For the same reason it is also not possible to constituent substitute. In Q_2, the constituent substitution gives us different results. Namely, constituent substitution of /`John and Mary`/ for /`John`/

in /`John sings`/ yields /`John and Mary sing`/! This is because the sentence is the value (under $\mathcal{K}$) of $g f_{\text{John}} f_{\text{sing}}$, and we replace f_{John} by $c f_{\text{John}} f_{\text{Mary}}$. This yields the term $g c f_{\text{John}} f_{\text{Mary}} f_{\text{sing}}$, which unfolds to /`John and Mary sing`/. ⚽

The previous examples established two things: first, it may be the case that certain affixes are introduced by the derivation. In this case the string substitution has nothing to do with constituent substitution, since there is no constituent to begin with. Second, there is a difference between string substitution and constituent substitution. It is the latter notion that is dependent on the grammar. It is defined as follows.

We have seen in the previous section how to evaluate constant terms. Now we shall introduce variables over constituents. Thus, we shall allow to write fx and gxy but also $gfxx$, where f is unary and g binary and x and y are variables over terms. For terms containing such variables the interpretation must be a function from values of these variables to strings. Here is a way to implement this idea. The interpretation of a term is a partial function from $(A^*)^{\mathbb{N}}$ to A^*. Here, an infinite sequence $\overline{s} := \langle s_0, s_1, \cdots \rangle$ codes the assignment of strings to the variables that maps x_i to the string s_i. Now put

❶ $\iota_G(x_i)(\overline{s}) := s_i$,
❷ $\iota_G(f)(\overline{s}) := \mathcal{I}(f)$ if $\Omega(f) = 0$,
❸ $\iota_G(f t_0 \cdots t_{n-1})(\overline{s}) := \mathcal{I}(f)(\iota_G(t_0)(\overline{s}), \cdots, \iota_G(t_{n-1})(\overline{s}))$, where $n = \Omega(f)$.

Again, if G is clear from the context, ι_G will be simplified to ι. Notice that if the string functions are partial some of the $\iota_G(t)$ may also be partial functions. In the sequel I shall not use x_0 and x_1 but the usual x, y instead. (ι has been defined in Section 2.1 for constant terms slightly differently. On constant terms the valuation is irrelevant.)

Example 2.12 We continue Example 2.9. Apart from the constant, C_1 has only unary functions, so the terms we can create have at most one variable. Examples are $f_1 x_0$, $f_0 f_1 x_1$, and so on. These describe functions from assignments to strings. The first defines a function from $\overline{s}$ to A^*: $\overline{s} \mapsto s_0{}^\frown\mathtt{a}$. The second is $\overline{s} \mapsto s_1{}^\frown\mathtt{b}$. I shall simplify this by eliminating reference to the entire valuation and replacing s_0 and s_1 by metavariables. This way we get the somewhat simpler expression $\vec{x} \mapsto \vec{x}{}^\frown\mathtt{a}$, $\vec{x} \mapsto \vec{x}{}^\frown\mathtt{b}$. It is possible to describe the totality of definable functions. They all have the form $\vec{x} \mapsto \vec{x}{}^\frown\vec{y}$ for some $\vec{y} \in A^*$ (which may be empty, since we generally also have the term x, which denotes the identity function on A^*).

C_2 has many more functions. In fact, the terms that we can define in C_2 are all the definable string polynomials using constants from A. ⚽

It is the simplifications of the preceding example that I shall adopt throughout. If we have a term $t(x, y, z)$ then the result of filling in the values $\vec{x}$, $\vec{y}$ and $\vec{z}$ for x, y and z, respectively, is denoted as usual by $t(\vec{x}, \vec{y}, \vec{z})$, or—if we want to be very explicit which value is assigned to which variable—by $t(x, y, z)[\vec{x}/x, \vec{y}/y, \vec{z}/z]$. The latter notation is more practical when we suppress the variables in the term itself by writing $t[\vec{x}/x, \vec{y}/y, \vec{z}/z]$. Now let $f : (A^*)^n \to A^*$. Say that it is a **term function** of G if there is a term $t(x_0, x_1, \cdots, x_{n-1})$ such that

$$f(\vec{x}_0, \cdots, \vec{x}_{n-1}) = \iota_G(t[\vec{x}_0/x_0, \cdots, \vec{x}_{n-1}/x_{n-1}]). \tag{2.38}$$

A **polynomial** (over A) is a term in the signature expanded by f_a (with value a) for every $a \in A$. f is a **polynomial function** of G if there is a polynomial $p(x_0, x_1, \cdots, x_{n-1})$ such that

$$f(\vec{x}_0, \cdots, \vec{x}_{n-1}) = \iota_G(p[\vec{x}_0/x_0, \cdots, \vec{x}_{n-1}/x_{n-1}]). \tag{2.39}$$

A particular sort of polynomial is the **string polynomial**. Let A be an alphabet. Then the string polynomials over A are the polynomials defined over the signature $\Omega : \cdot \mapsto 2, \varepsilon \mapsto 0$ in the algebra $\langle A^*, \varepsilon, ^\frown \rangle$. The interpretation is fixed: $\cdot$ is interpreted by concatenation, ε by the empty string and a by a constant yielding the letter a itself. (Bracketing is therefore eliminable since string concatenation is associative.) For example, $p(x_0, x_1) := x_1 \cdot \mathsf{a} \cdot x_1 \cdot x_0 \cdot \mathsf{b}$ is a polynomial. It is interpreted by the following function over A^*.

$$p^{A^*}(\vec{x}, \vec{y}) := \iota_G(t[\vec{x}/x_0, \vec{y}/x_1]) := \vec{y}^\frown \mathsf{a}^\frown \vec{y}^\frown \vec{x}^\frown \mathsf{b} \tag{2.40}$$

Typically, we do not even write the dot, so that $x_0 \cdot x_1$ reduces to $x_0 x_1$.

I close this section with an observation concerning the method of substitution, using Definition 2.10. This test is supposed to reveal something about the structure of the language provided that the grammar for it is some constituent grammar: parts are assumed to be substrings. (If the grammar is not of that form, another form of test is needed.) There are two ways to understand this test, ultimately deriving from two different definitions of language; one is to start with a language as the set of sentences and try to define the constituents smaller than sentences via substitution classes. Another, less ambitious method, starts with a language in the wide sense and tries to find out the constituent *occurrences* in a given string. We shall look here at the first of these interpretations; the other interpretation shall be looked at in more detail later.

Let $L \subseteq A^*$ be a language in the narrow sense and $\vec{x}$ a string. Evidently, there are two cases. Either $\vec{x}$ is not a substring of any string in L, and so $\mathrm{Cat}_L(\vec{x}) = \varnothing$, or it is and then $\mathrm{Cat}_L(\vec{x}) \neq \varnothing$. Apart from this there is nothing of substance one can say about the distribution of categories. There is no theoretical instrument to tell us from the substitution possibilities which are the constituents. This is reflected also in some grammars. In the Lambek Calculus all substrings of a string of the language are given a category.

There is a little bit that we can say about the relationship between the number of categories and L itself. It turns out that if the set of string categories is finite the language is regular. The following proof is based on the Myhill-Nerode Theorem (see Harrison (1978) for a proof).

Theorem 2.1 *A language has finitely many string categories if and only if it is regular.*

Proof Suppose that L has finitely many categories. Intersect the categories with the set $\{\langle \varepsilon, \vec{x} \rangle : \vec{x} \in A^*\}$. This yields a finite set of occurrences of prefixes. By the Myhill-Nerode Theorem, the language is regular. Now assume that the language is regular, and accepted by a finite automaton $\mathfrak{A}$. Let I_i be the language of all strings that lead from the initial state to state i; and let A_j be the language of all strings that lead from j to some accepting state. Then the categories coincide with the sets of pairs $I_i \times A_j$ for all states i and j such that j can be reached from i. □

Exercise 2.9 Describe all unary term functions of C_2, that is, all actions of C_2-terms in one variable.

Exercise 2.10 Verify that the language of ua-terms is defined by the following grammar:

$$\begin{aligned}
\mathcal{I}(n_0)() &:= \mathtt{0} \\
&\ldots\ldots \\
\mathcal{I}(n_9)() &:= \mathtt{9} \\
\mathcal{I}(c_0)(\vec{x}) &:= \vec{x}^\frown\mathtt{0} \\
&\ldots\ldots \\
\mathcal{I}(c_9)(\vec{x}) &:= \vec{x}^\frown\mathtt{9} \\
\mathcal{I}(a_0)(\vec{x}) &:= \vec{x}^\frown\mathtt{+}^\frown\mathtt{0} \\
&\ldots\ldots \\
\mathcal{I}(a_9)(\vec{x}) &:= \vec{x}^\frown\mathtt{+}^\frown\mathtt{9}
\end{aligned} \tag{2.41}$$

Exercise 2.11 (Continuing the previous exercise.) In the grammar of the previous exercise /10+1/ is a part of /10+12/. Simply choose the analysis $n_1 c_0 a_1 c_2$. However, /12/ is not a part of /10+12/ although intuitively it should be. Begin by specifying when a given string is a substring of another. Then write a grammar where only those substring occurrences are parts that should be.

Exercise 2.12 The language of ua-terms is regular. Nevertheless, show that there is no regular grammar that generates exactly this language in the wide sense; this means that L is taken to be the union of all expressions that belong to some nonterminal of the grammar. *Hint.* Regular grammars allow to add only one symbol at a time.

2.3 Grammars and String Categories

In the previous section we looked at string categories defined by replacing substrings by other substrings. In this section we look at a similar but different definition where replacement is done only of constituent occurrences. This definition presupposes a grammar.

Definition 2.11 Let G be a grammar and $\vec{x}, \vec{y} \in L(G)$. We write $\vec{x} \sim_G \vec{y}$ if for every term $t(x_0)$, $\iota_G(t(\vec{x}))$ is defined if and only if $\iota_G(t(\vec{y}))$ is defined. We write $[\vec{x}]_G := \{\vec{y} : \vec{x} \sim_G \vec{y}\}$. These sets are called the **syntactic categories** of G.

We have restricted the definition to strings in $L(G)$. Thus, categories are defined only on the strings of the language. Strings outside the language have no category. An alternative formulation is this: $\vec{x}$ and $\vec{y}$ have the same category if for every pair of terms s_0 and s_1 that unfold to $\vec{x}$ and $\vec{y}$ respectively, $t(s_0)$ is orthographically definite if and only if $t(s_1)$ is. (It is easy to see that if this holds for one pair of terms s_0 and s_1 then it holds for all. See also Definition 2.23.)

Notice that the set of strings on which *no* function is defined is also a syntactic category. For example, in Example 2.1 this category is empty, in Example 2.6 it contains all equations.

There need not be finitely many equivalence classes as the following example shows.

Example 2.13 Let $A := \{\mathsf{a}\}$. $G = \langle \Omega, \mathcal{I} \rangle$ is defined by $\Omega(e) = 0$, $\Omega(f) = \Omega(g) = 1$ and

$$\begin{aligned}
\mathcal{I}(e)() &:= \varepsilon \\
\mathcal{I}(f)(\mathsf{a}^n) &:= \begin{cases} \mathsf{a}^{n-1} & \text{if } n > 0, \\ \text{undefined} & \text{else.} \end{cases} \\
\mathcal{I}(g)(\mathsf{a}^n) &:= \mathsf{a}^{2n}
\end{aligned} \tag{2.42}$$

G generates a^* in a somewhat unconventional way. Namely if $m > n$, then $\mathcal{I}(f)^n(\mathsf{a}^m) = \mathsf{a}^{m-n}$ and $\mathcal{I}(f)^m(\mathsf{a}^m) = \varepsilon$. However, for $n > m$, $\mathcal{I}(f)^n(\mathsf{a}^m)$ is undefined. Thus, $\mathsf{a}^m \sim_G \mathsf{a}^n$ if and only if $m = n$, and so there are infinitely many equivalence classes.

Now, the grammar $H = \langle \Omega', \mathcal{J} \rangle$ with $F' := \{e, h\}$ where $\mathcal{J}(e)() := \varepsilon$ and $\mathcal{J}(h)(\vec{x}) := \vec{x}^\frown\mathsf{a}$ has exactly one class of strings. It is checked that $\mathsf{a}^m \sim_H \mathsf{a}^n$ for all $m, n \in \mathbb{N}$. ⚽

It is linguistic practice not to leave the categories implicit (in the form of domain restrictions) but to make them part of the representation. If we so wish this can be implemented as follows. Let C be a set. A **c-string** is a pair $s = \langle \vec{x}, c \rangle$ where $\vec{x} \in A^*$ and $c \in C$. Given s, we put

$$\varepsilon(s) := \vec{x}, \quad \kappa(s) := c. \tag{2.43}$$

For a set S of c-strings write $\varepsilon[S] := \{\varepsilon(s) : s \in S\}$, $\kappa[S] := \{\kappa(s) : s \in S\}$. A **c-string language** is a subset of $A^* \times C$. A **c-string grammar** is a pair $\langle \Omega, \mathcal{C} \rangle$ where Ω is a signature (with domain F) and $\mathcal{C}$ an interpretation function such that for all $f \in F$ $\mathcal{C}(f) : (A^* \times C)^{\Omega(f)} \hookrightarrow (A^* \times C)$. We define $\iota_G(t)$ for an Ω-term t by

$$\iota_G(f s_0 \cdots s_{\Omega(f)-1}) := \mathcal{C}(f)(\iota_G(s_0), \cdots, \iota_G(s_{\Omega(f)-1})). \tag{2.44}$$

We write t^ε in place of $\varepsilon(\iota_G(t))$ and t^κ in place of $\kappa(\iota_G(t))$. Thus we have

$$\iota_G(t) = \langle t^\varepsilon, t^\kappa \rangle. \tag{2.45}$$

We also use the notation f^ε for the function $\varepsilon \circ \mathcal{C}(f)$ and f^κ for $\kappa \circ \mathcal{C}(f)$. A more detailed discussion can be found in Chapter 3. The categories will be most useful when the string operations of the grammar are independent. We shall deal with grammars acting on several components in Chapter 3.

Example 2.14 The shift to categories is not as innocent as it first appears, for we lose certain properties. Here is an example. The relation "is part of" is no longer transitive. Let $F := \{f_0, f_1, g\}$, $\Omega(f_0) := \Omega(f_1) := 0$ and $\Omega(g) := 1$. $C := \{\alpha, \beta\}$ and $A := \{\mathsf{a}\}$.

$$\begin{aligned}
\mathcal{I}(f_0)() &:= \langle \mathsf{a}, \alpha \rangle \\
\mathcal{I}(f_1)() &:= \langle \mathsf{aa}, \alpha \rangle \\
\mathcal{I}(g)(\langle \vec{x}, c \rangle) &:= \begin{cases} \langle \vec{x}^\frown \mathsf{a}, \beta \rangle & \text{if } c = \alpha, \\ \text{undefined} & \text{else.} \end{cases}
\end{aligned} \tag{2.46}$$

This grammar generates the language $\{\langle \mathsf{a}, \alpha\rangle, \langle \mathsf{aa}, \beta\rangle, \langle \mathsf{aa}, \alpha\rangle, \langle \mathsf{aaa}, \beta\rangle\}$. It turns out that /a/ is a part of /aa/, and /aa/ a part of /aaa/, but /a/ is not a part of /aaa/. ⚽

As the example shows we can no longer simply say that a string occurs as a substring; it occurs in a c-string as a c-string and so the category that it has in that occurrence may also be fixed. For example, /`I see John fly.`/ contains /`fly`/ as a verb and not as a noun.

An important class of (c-string) grammars are the *bottom up context free (c-) grammars*. These are not the same as ordinary CFGs. We shall recall the definition of standard CFGs first and then turn to the bottom up version. Recall that a context free grammar is standardly taken to be a quadruple $G = \langle A, N, S, R \rangle$, where A and N are disjoint sets, $S \in N$ and R a set of replacement rules. They have the form $X \to \vec{y}$, where $X \in N$ and $\vec{y} \in (A \cup N)^*$ is a sequence over $A \cup N$. The rules define a replacement relation in the following way.

Definition 2.12 Let $\rho = \vec{x} \to \vec{y}$ be a rule. We say that $\vec{u}\,\vec{y}\,\vec{w}$ is **1-step derivable** via ρ from $\vec{u}\,\vec{x}\,\vec{v}$, in symbols $\vec{u}\,\vec{x}\,\vec{v} \Rightarrow_\rho \vec{u}\,\vec{y}\,\vec{v}$. For a set R of rules we write $\vec{u}\,\vec{x}\,\vec{v} \Rightarrow_\rho \vec{u}\,\vec{y}\,\vec{v}$ and say that $\vec{u}\,\vec{y}\,\vec{v}$ is **1-step derivable** from $\vec{u}\,\vec{x}\,\vec{v}$ if there is a rule $\rho \in R$ such that $\vec{u}\,\vec{x}\,\vec{v} \Rightarrow_\rho \vec{u}\,\vec{y}\,\vec{v}$. Furthermore, we say that $\vec{w}$ is n-**step derivable** in R from $\vec{v}$ and write $\vec{v} \Rightarrow^n_R \vec{w}$ if either $n = 0$ and $\vec{w} = \vec{v}$ or $n > 0$ and there is a $\vec{u}$ such that $\vec{u}$ is $n - 1$-step derivable from $\vec{v}$ and $\vec{w}$ is 1-step derivable from $\vec{u}$.

Notice that $\vec{v} \Rightarrow^1_R \vec{w}$ and $\vec{v} \Rightarrow_R \vec{w}$ are synonymous, and that $\vec{v} \Rightarrow_{\{\rho\}} \vec{w}$ and $\vec{v} \Rightarrow_\rho \vec{w}$ are also synonymous; R or ρ will be dropped when the context makes clear which rules are being used. Notice furthermore that it may happen that a rule can be applied to a given string in several ways. The rule $\mathsf{A} \to \mathsf{aa}$ can be applied to the string /AcAb/ to yield either /aacAb/ or /Acaab/. Therefore, if we want to know what the result will be after applying the rule we need to identify the occurrence of the left-hand side that is being replaced. When can do this by underlining as follows: $\mathtt{\underline{A}cAb} \Rightarrow \mathtt{aacAb}$ and $\mathtt{Ac\underline{A}b} \Rightarrow \mathtt{Acaab}$. If the occurrence is underlined then the rule *must* be applied to that occurrence. Hence we do not have $\mathtt{\underline{A}cAb} \Rightarrow \mathtt{Acaab}$. Now, suppose we have such a marked string; then the result is still not unique unless we know which rule is being applied. This follows from the fact that several rules may replace a given string. For example, if we also have the rule $\mathtt{A} \rightarrow \mathtt{cd}$ then from /$\mathtt{\underline{A}cAb}$/ we may proceed to /cdcAb/ in addition to /aacAb/. However, if also the resulting string is given, the rule that has been applied can be inferred. Thus, in order to show that a given string $\vec{w}$ is n-step derivable from a string $\vec{v}$ we need to produce a sequence $\langle \vec{v}_i : i < n\rangle$ of length n of marked strings such that $\vec{v}_i \Rightarrow \vec{v}_{i+1}$ for $i < n-1$ and $\vec{v}_{n-1} \Rightarrow \vec{w}$. Such a sequence is called a **derivation**. Notice that the sequence contains marked strings not just strings, though we shall often not show the marks. The derived string is by definition not marked, though it is often added at the end of the derivation sequence so that one can infer the choice of rules in each step.

Given a nonterminal A and a string $\vec{x}$ we write $A \vdash_G \vec{x}$ and say that G **derives** $\vec{x}$ from A if there is an n such that $A \Rightarrow_R^n \vec{x}$.

Definition 2.13 Let $G = \langle S, N, A, R\rangle$ be a CFG. The language of G in the narrow sense is defined by

$$L(G) := \{\vec{x} \in A^* : S \vdash_G \vec{x}\}. \tag{2.47}$$

The language in the wide sense is defined by

$$L^w(G) := \{\vec{x} \in A^* : \text{for some } X \in N : X \vdash_G \vec{x}\}. \tag{2.48}$$

A language L in the narrow (wide) sense is **context free** if there is a context free grammar G such that $L = L(G)$ $(L = L^w(G))$.

Also, write $[A]_G := \{\vec{x} : A \vdash_G \vec{x}\}$. Then $L(G) = [S]_G$. This notion of grammar is top down and nondeterministic. It generates the strings from a single string (consisting in the single letter S).

Example 2.15 Let G be defined as follows.

$$G := \langle\{\mathtt{a}, \cdots, \mathtt{z}, \texttt{\textvisiblespace}\}, \{\texttt{<S>}, \texttt{<NP>}, \texttt{<VP>}, \texttt{<N>}, \texttt{<D>}, \texttt{<VI>}, \texttt{<VT>}\}, \texttt{<S>}, R\rangle \tag{2.49}$$

The alphabet consists in all lower case letters plus the space.

$$\begin{aligned} R = \{ & \texttt{<S>} \rightarrow \texttt{<NP><VP>} \\ & \texttt{<NP>} \rightarrow \texttt{<D><N>} \\ & \texttt{<D>} \rightarrow \texttt{the\textvisiblespace} \mid \texttt{a\textvisiblespace} \\ & \texttt{<N>} \rightarrow \texttt{cat\textvisiblespace} \mid \texttt{dog\textvisiblespace} \mid \texttt{mouse\textvisiblespace} \\ & \texttt{<VP>} \rightarrow \texttt{<VI>} \mid \texttt{<VT><NP>} \\ & \texttt{<VI>} \rightarrow \texttt{runs\textvisiblespace} \mid \texttt{sleeps\textvisiblespace} \\ & \texttt{<VT>} \rightarrow \texttt{sees\textvisiblespace} \mid \texttt{chases\textvisiblespace}\} \end{aligned} \tag{2.50}$$

This grammar generates among others the following strings:

$$
\begin{array}{l}
\texttt{<S>} \\
\texttt{<NP><VP>} \\
\texttt{<D>dog␣<VI>} \\
\texttt{a␣dog␣chases␣the␣cat␣}
\end{array}
\tag{2.51}
$$

Only the last of the four strings is meaningful. A derivation of the third string is as follows.

$$
\langle \underline{\texttt{<S>}}, \underline{\texttt{<NP>}}\texttt{<VP>}, \texttt{<D><N>}\underline{\texttt{<VP>}}, \texttt{<D>}\underline{\texttt{<N>}}\texttt{<VI><D>dog␣<VI>} \rangle \tag{2.52}
$$

Let us now look at a bottom up version of CFGs. Obviously, to get such a grammar we simply turn the rules around. Rather than assuming a rule, say, $\rho = A \to BC$, we define a string function f_ρ of arity 2 such that f_ρ is interpreted as concatenation, which is to say $\mathcal{I}(f_\rho)(\vec{x}, \vec{y}) = \vec{x}^\frown\vec{y}$. However, this function is only defined if $\vec{x}$ is a B-string, that is, if we can derive $\vec{x}$ from B in the grammar and if $\vec{y}$ is a C-string. In this way we guarantee that $\vec{x}^\frown\vec{y}$ is an A-string. In general, for each rule ρ we assume a function symbol f_ρ and an interpretation $\mathcal{I}(f_\rho)$. A rule is of the form $A \to \vec{x}$ for some $\vec{x} \in (A \cup N)^*$.

This means that there is n and $\vec{x}_i \in A^*$, $i < n+1$, and $B_i \in N$, $i < n$, such that

$$
\rho = A \to \vec{x}_0 B_0 \vec{x}_1 B_1 \cdots B_{n-1}\vec{x}_n \tag{2.53}
$$

Then $\Omega(f_\rho) := n$ and its interpretation is

$$
\mathcal{I}(f_\rho)(\vec{y}_0, \cdots, \vec{y}_{n-1}) := \begin{cases} \vec{x}_0\vec{y}_0\vec{x}_1\vec{y}_1 \cdots \vec{y}_{n-1}\vec{x}_n & \text{if for all } i < n\text{:} \\ & \quad \vec{y}_i \text{ is a } B_i\text{-string}, \\ \text{undefined} & \text{else.} \end{cases} \tag{2.54}
$$

We do this for all ρ that do not have the form $A \to B$. It is an easy matter to transform G into a grammar that has no such rules. But this transformation is actually unnecessary. This defines the grammar $G^\blacklozenge$.

Example 2.16 I transform the grammar from Example 2.15. Let us note that the constituents generate only finitely many strings, so we can list them all.

$$
\begin{aligned}
[\texttt{<D>}]_G &= \{/\texttt{a␣}/, /\texttt{the␣}/\} \\
[\texttt{<N>}]_G &= \{/\texttt{cat␣}/, /\texttt{dog␣}/, /\texttt{mouse␣}/\} \\
[\texttt{<VI>}]_G &= \{/\texttt{runs␣}/, /\texttt{sleeps␣}/\} \\
[\texttt{<VT>}]_G &= \{/\texttt{sees␣}/, /\texttt{chases␣}/\} \\
[\texttt{<VP>}]_G &= (\texttt{runs␣} \mid \texttt{sleeps␣}) \mid (\texttt{sees␣} \mid \texttt{chases␣})(\texttt{the␣} \mid \texttt{a␣}) \\
&\quad\ (\texttt{cat␣} \mid \texttt{dog␣} \mid \texttt{mouse␣})
\end{aligned}
\tag{2.55}
$$

Before the transformation we need to consider the rule <VP> → <VI>. This is a unary rule. We eliminate it and add instead the rule

$$\texttt{<S>} \to \texttt{<NP><VI>} \tag{2.56}$$

Now we begin the transformation. The grammar $G^\blacklozenge$ is based on the set $\{f_1, f_2, \cdots, f_{11}\}$ with $\Omega(f_i) = 0$ for $i < 9$ and $\Omega(f_i) = 2$ otherwise. We have

$$\begin{array}{ll}
\mathcal{I}(f_0)() & := \texttt{a␣} \\
\mathcal{I}(f_1)() & := \texttt{the␣} \\
\mathcal{I}(f_2)() & := \texttt{cat␣} \\
\mathcal{I}(f_3)() & := \texttt{dog␣} \\
\mathcal{I}(f_4)() & := \texttt{mouse␣} \\
\mathcal{I}(f_5)() & := \texttt{runs␣} \\
\mathcal{I}(f_6)() & := \texttt{sleeps␣} \\
\mathcal{I}(f_7)() & := \texttt{sees␣} \\
\mathcal{I}(f_8)() & := \texttt{chases␣} \\
\mathcal{I}(f_9)(\vec{x}, \vec{y}) & := \begin{cases} \vec{x}^\frown\vec{y} & \text{if } \vec{x} \in [\texttt{<D>}]_G \text{ and } \vec{y} \in [\texttt{<N>}]_G, \\ \text{undefined} & \text{otherwise.} \end{cases} \\
\mathcal{I}(f_{10})(\vec{x}, \vec{y}) & := \begin{cases} \vec{x}^\frown\vec{y} & \text{if } \vec{x} \in [\texttt{<VT>}]_G \text{ and } \vec{y} \in [\texttt{<NP>}]_G, \\ \text{undefined} & \text{otherwise.} \end{cases} \\
\mathcal{I}(f_{11})(\vec{x}, \vec{y}) & := \begin{cases} \vec{x}^\frown\vec{y} & \text{if } \vec{x} \in [\texttt{<NP>}]_G \text{ and } \vec{y} \in [\texttt{<VI>}]_G, \\ \text{undefined} & \text{otherwise.} \end{cases}
\end{array} \tag{2.57}$$

The reader is asked to check that these modes correspond exactly to the rules of the grammar (in its slight modification). The string /a␣cat␣sees␣the␣dog␣/ is derived by the term $f_{11} f_9 f_0 f_2 f_{10} f_7 f_9 f_1 f_3$, as can be checked. ⚽

$G^\blacklozenge$ is a grammar in the sense of Section 2.1. The grammar $G^\blacklozenge$ generates the language of G in the wide sense, as the following theorem documents.

Proposition 2.3 *Let G be a context free grammar. Then $\vec{x} \in L(G^\blacklozenge)$ if and only if there is a nonterminal X such that $X \vdash_G \vec{x}$. In other words, $L(G^\blacklozenge) = L^w(G)$.*

The proof is a relatively easy induction on the length of derivations. I shall relegate this to the exercises.

Example 2.17 The elimination of unary rules is not as innocent as it first appears. In natural languages there are plenty of examples of zero-derivation. One example is the conversion of adjectives to nouns in Hungarian. Typically, adjectives do not inflect. However, in the absence of a noun they can inflect just as nouns and hence should be regarded as such. Thus, the form /fehéret/ (accusative of /fehér/) must be translated as "a white one". Critically, also the nominative form /fehér/ can be so regarded and hence can be translated as either "white" or "a white one". Given a bottom up grammar these two are now confused. However, as long as we do not treat meaning in addition there is no harm in this. This theme will be picked up in Section 3.4. ⚽

Notice that there is no way to generate *only* the language $L(G)$, which is, all and only the S-strings for the start symbol S. When we do a top down generation we can simply choose to start with the start symbol and all the strings we generate are sentences. However, in the bottom up process we cannot restrict ourselves to generating just the sentences. We must generate all intermediate strings. On the other hand there is no need to generate strings with extraneous symbols. In the c-string grammar we can make up for this defect as follows. For a CFG in the standard sense let

$$L^c(G) := \{\langle\vec{x}, X\rangle : X \in N, X \vdash_G \vec{x}\}. \tag{2.58}$$

So, $L^c(G)$ contains strings together with their categorial information; it does not however single out a particular category. We can derive $L(G)$ from $L^c(G)$ by picking all $\vec{x}$ for which $\langle\vec{x}, S\rangle \in L^c(G)$. This is a different notion of language than the generated language in the wide sense. In the latter we do not know what the categories of the strings are; we just know that they have *some* category. On the other hand, for a language in the wide sense there is no need to construct the categories from the input data (as languages mostly do not always mark their expressions for category). The arity of f_ρ equals the number of nonterminals on the right-hand side of the rule.

The string based version presented above is not an exact equivalent of the grammar G. In the exercises we shall show that these grammars may have quite different derivations. To get a more exact correspondence we turn to c-strings. In the case at hand we choose $C := N$. Thus c-strings are pairs $\langle\vec{x}, X\rangle$ where $\vec{x} \in A^*$ and $X \in N$. The interpretation of the function symbol f_ρ is now the partial function

$$\begin{aligned} \mathcal{C}(f_\rho)(\langle\vec{y}_0, c_0\rangle, \langle\vec{y}_1, c_1\rangle, \cdots, \langle\vec{y}_{n-1}, c_{n-1}\rangle) \\ := \langle\vec{x}_0\vec{y}_0\vec{x}_1\vec{y}_1\cdots\vec{y}_{n-1}\vec{x}_n, f_\rho^\kappa(c_0, c_1, \cdots, c_{n-1})\rangle \end{aligned} \tag{2.59}$$

where

$$f_\rho^\kappa(c_0, \cdots, c_{n-1}) := \begin{cases} A & \text{if for all } i < n\text{: } c_i = B_i, \\ \text{undefined} & \text{else.} \end{cases} \tag{2.60}$$

Then $L(G)$ is a set of pairs $\langle\vec{x}, c\rangle$. We say that $\vec{x}$ **has category** c **in** G if some G-term unfolds to $\langle\vec{x}, c\rangle$. A given string can have several categories.

Example 2.18 We continue the language of equations (Example 2.6 on page 16). The grammar G_Q consists in the alphabet of terminals

$$:\text{bt}: := \{\mathtt{0}, \mathtt{1}, \mathtt{+}, \mathtt{-}, \mathtt{(}, \mathtt{)}, \mathtt{=}\}. \tag{2.61}$$

The alphabet of nonterminals is $N := \{\mathtt{E}, \mathtt{B}, \mathtt{T}\}$, the start symbol /E/ and the set of rules is as follows.

$$\begin{aligned}
&\mathtt{E} \to \mathtt{T=T} \\
&\mathtt{T} \to \mathtt{(T+T)} \mid \mathtt{(T-T)} \mid \mathtt{B} \\
&\mathtt{B} \to \mathtt{B0} \mid \mathtt{B1} \mid \mathtt{0} \mid \mathtt{1}
\end{aligned} \tag{2.62}$$

By default, a derivation starts with the letter /E/. Thus

$$C = \langle\text{:bt:}, N, \mathrm{E}, R\rangle. \tag{2.63}$$

Recall that "|" is an abbreviation. It allows to group together rules with the same left-hand side. Figure 2.1 shows an example of a derivation in G_Q. In each step we replace a single occurrence of a nonterminal by a corresponding right-hand side of (2.62). ⚽

An X-**derivation** is a sequence of strings starting with the nonterminal X, where each nonfirst member is obtained from the previous by replacing a nonterminal symbol in the appropriate way. A **derivation** is an X-derivation with X the top symbol. For our purposes, however, the best objects to deal with are not the derivations but the analysis terms. The analysis term of a derivation is obtained as follows. Assign to each rule ρ with $n(\rho)$ nonterminals on the right a function symbol f_ρ of arity $n(\rho)$. This defines the signature. Start with the variable x_0. A step in the derivation consists in the replacement of an occurrence of a variable x_i by a term of the form $f_\rho(x_{i_0}, x_{i_1}, \cdots, x_{i_{n(\rho)-1}})$ where the x_{i_j} so that in the end no variable occurs twice. This procedure is best explained with the derivation above.

Example 2.19 Continuing Example 2.18. We give the following names to the rules.

$$\begin{array}{ll}
a & \mathtt{E} \to \mathtt{T=T} \\
b & \mathtt{T} \to \mathtt{(T+T)} \\
c & \mathtt{T} \to \mathtt{(T-T)} \\
d & \mathtt{T} \to \mathtt{B} \\
e & \mathtt{B} \to \mathtt{B0} \\
f & \mathtt{B} \to \mathtt{B1} \\
g & \mathtt{B} \to \mathtt{0} \\
h & \mathtt{B} \to \mathtt{1}
\end{array} \tag{2.64}$$

$\mathtt{\underline{E}}$
$\mathtt{\underline{T}=T}$
$\mathtt{\underline{B}=T}$
$\mathtt{0=\underline{T}}$
$\mathtt{0=(T-\underline{T})}$
$\mathtt{0=(T-\underline{B})}$
$\mathtt{0=(\underline{T}-0)}$
$\mathtt{0=(\underline{B}-0)}$
$\mathtt{0=(\underline{B}0-0)}$
$\mathtt{0=(10-0)}$

Fig. 2.1 A derivation in G_Q

$\underline{\texttt{E}}$	$\boxed{x_0}$
$\underline{\texttt{T}}\texttt{=T}$	$f_a \boxed{x_0} x_1$
$\underline{\texttt{B}}\texttt{=T}$	$f_a f_d \boxed{x_0} x_1$
$\texttt{0=}\underline{\texttt{T}}$	$f_a f_d f_g \boxed{x_1}$
$\texttt{0=(T-}\underline{\texttt{T}}\texttt{)}$	$f_a f_d f_g f_c x_0 \boxed{x_1}$
$\texttt{0=(T-}\underline{\texttt{B}}\texttt{)}$	$f_a f_d f_g f_c x_0 f_d \boxed{x_1}$
$\texttt{0=(}\underline{\texttt{T}}\texttt{-0)}$	$f_a f_d f_g f_c \boxed{x_0} f_d f_g$
$\texttt{0=(}\underline{\texttt{B}}\texttt{-0)}$	$f_a f_d f_g f_c f_d \boxed{x_0} f_d f_g$
$\texttt{0=(}\underline{\texttt{B}}\texttt{1-0)}$	$f_a f_d f_g f_c f_d f_e \boxed{x_0} f_d f_g$
$\texttt{0=(10-0)}$	$f_a f_d f_g f_c f_d f_e f_h f_d f_g$

Fig. 2.2 Deriving the term

Thus the symbols are called f_a, f_b, f_c (binary), f_d, f_e, f_f (unary), f_g and f_h (zeroary). The derivation is translated to a term as shown in Fig. 2.2. The variable that is being replaced is surrounded by a box. The exact recipe is this: if the derivation replaces the nth nonterminal counting from the left, then it is the nth variable from the left that is being replaced irrespective of its index. ⚽

Now we shall supply the term symbols with interpretations that match the effect of the rules. Call $\vec{x}$ an X-**string** if $X \vdash_G \vec{x}$. Write $L_X(G)$ for the set of X-strings of G. In our example $L_{\texttt{E}}(G_Q)$ is the set of equations; these are strings of the form /$\vec{x}$=$\vec{y}$/, where both $\vec{x}$ and $\vec{y}$ are T-strings. T-strings are terms; these are strings of the form (a) $\vec{x}$, where $\vec{x}$ consists in 0 and 1 only (a number expression, or a B-string), (b) /($\vec{x}$+$\vec{y}$)/ where $\vec{x}$ and $\vec{y}$ are T-strings, or (c) /($\vec{x}$-$\vec{y}$)/ where $\vec{x}$ and $\vec{y}$ are T-strings. Finally, the B-strings are exactly the strings from $\{\texttt{0}, \texttt{1}\}^+$.

For example, $\rho = \texttt{B} \to \texttt{B1}$ is a rule of G_Q, and so we have a symbol f_ρ with $\Omega(f_\rho) = 1$. The function takes a B-string $\vec{x}$ and appends /1/. Hence:

$$\iota(f_\rho)(\vec{x}) := \begin{cases} \vec{x}^\frown \texttt{1} & \text{if } \vec{x} \text{ is a B-string,} \\ \text{undefined} & \text{else.} \end{cases} \tag{2.65}$$

Similarly, if $\rho' = \texttt{T} \to \texttt{(T+T)}$ we postulate a symbol $f_{\rho'}$ with $\Omega(f_{\rho'}) = 2$ and which acts as follows:

$$\iota(f_{\rho'})(\vec{x}, \vec{y}) := \begin{cases} \texttt{(}^\frown\vec{x}^\frown\texttt{+}^\frown\vec{y}^\frown\texttt{)} & \text{if } \vec{x} \text{ and } \vec{y} \text{ are T-strings,} \\ \text{undefined} & \text{else.} \end{cases} \tag{2.66}$$

As we have briefly noted above, the properties "B-string", "T-string" and so on can actually be defined without making reference to the grammar.

We can use Example 2.19 to show that the transformation $(-)^\blacklozenge$ of CFGs preserves the strings but not the set of terms if applied also to unary rules. The rule d has the form $\texttt{T} \to \texttt{B}$. It is converted into the string function $\mathcal{I}(f_d)(\vec{x}) = \vec{x}$, in other words the identity function. This function is iterable, while the rule is not. Thus the term $f_d f_d f_g$ would evaluate in $G_Q^\blacklozenge$ to /0/.

$$\iota(f_d f_d f_g) = \mathcal{I}(f_d)(\mathcal{I}(f_d)(\mathcal{I}(f_g)())) = \mathcal{I}(f_d)(\mathcal{I}(f_d)(\mathtt{0})) = \mathcal{I}(f_d)(\mathtt{0}) = \mathtt{0} \quad (2.67)$$

However, there is no derivation with term $f_d f_d f_g$. Try to start with the symbol T, for example:

$$\begin{array}{ll} \mathrm{T} & x_0 \\ \mathrm{B} & f_d x_0 \\ ? & f_d f_d x_0 \end{array} \quad (2.68)$$

Similarly if we start with /B/. (If you want a derivation beginning with the start symbol, take the term $f_a f_d f_d f_g f_d f_h$.) It might be deemed that all we have to do is to exclude unary rules. That this is not so is shown in Exercise 2.18.

We can characterize in more exact terms the connection between the two kinds of grammars. Here is a characterization of context free languages in terms of the generating functions. It shows that if the functions are partial functions of a certain kind and such that ranges of functions are subsets of domains (or disjoint) then the generated language is context free (and conversely).

Definition 2.14 Let $G = \langle \Omega, \mathcal{I} \rangle$ be a grammar. G is called a **concatenation grammar** if for all modes f, $\mathcal{I}(f)$ is the restriction of a polynomial function of the string algebra to some arbitrary set of sequences of strings.

This definition says the following. In a concatenation grammar a mode f interpreted as a partial function $\mathcal{I}(f) : (A^*)^{\Omega(f)} \hookrightarrow A^*$. While the domain is some arbitrary set $D \subseteq (A^*)^{\Omega(f)}$, there must exist a polynomial function p such that $\mathcal{I}(f) = p \restriction D$. Notice namely that the string polynomials are total. These polynomials may be arbitrarily restricted. However, as we shall see, in context free grammars there are tight restrictions on these domains. Say a polynomial $p(\vec{x})$ is a **linear string polynomial** if it is composed from the variables x_i and constants such that each x_i occurs exactly once. If p is a polynomial, we denote the induced function by p^{A^*}. $f : (A^*)^n \to A^*$ is a **rectangularly restricted linear string polynomial** if there is a linear string polynomial $p(x_0, \cdots, x_{n-1})$ such that $f \subseteq p^{A^*}(\vec{x})$ and there are subsets $P_i \subseteq A^*$, $i < n$, such that $\mathrm{dom}(f) = \times_{i<n} P_i$. Now recall that the grammar $G^{\blacklozenge}$ uses precisely such functions. Thus we have

Proposition 2.4 *If a language $L \subseteq A^*$ is context free then it has a grammar G in which all function symbols are interpreted by rectangularly restricted linear string polynomials.*

For the converse, a little more is needed. Namely, let H be a grammar such that all $\mathcal{I}(f)$ are rectangularly restricted linear polynomials. So for each f there are sets Q_i^f, $i < \Omega(f)$, such that the domain of $\mathcal{I}(f)$ is $\times_{i<\Omega(f)} Q_i^f$. Assume moreover that for every g and $i < \Omega(g)$: either $\mathrm{rng}(\mathcal{I}(f)) \subseteq Q_i^g$ or $\mathrm{rng}(\mathcal{I}(f)) \cap Q_i^g = \varnothing$. We call this the **connectivity property** for H. For each domain Q we choose a nonterminal N_Q (notice that $N_Q = N_P$ if $P = Q$ as sets). Further, for a function symbol f such that $\mathrm{dom}(\mathcal{I}(f)) = \times_{i<\Omega(f)} Q_i^f$ and $\mathrm{rng}(\mathcal{I}(f)) \subseteq Q_i^g$ we create a rule

$$\rho_f : N_{Q_i^g} \to \vec{x}_0 N_{Q_0^f} \vec{x}_1 N_{Q_1^f} \vec{x}_2 \cdots \vec{x}_{\Omega(f)-1} N_{Q^f_{\Omega(f)-1}} \vec{x}_{\Omega(f)} \tag{2.69}$$

where the $\vec{x}_i$ are chosen such that $\mathcal{I}(f)$ is the restriction of the polynomial

$$p^{A^*}(y_0, \cdots, y_{\Omega(f)-1}) := \vec{x}_0 y_0 \vec{x}_1 y_1 \vec{x}_2 \cdots \vec{x}_{\Omega(f)-1} y_{\Omega(f)-1} \vec{x}_{\Omega(f)}. \tag{2.70}$$

This grammar is such that $\vec{z}$ is an N_Q-string for some Q if and only if $\vec{z} \in L(H)$.

Proposition 2.5 *If H is a grammar such that all $\mathcal{I}(f)$ are rectangularly restricted linear string polynomials and $\mathcal{I}$ has the connectivity property then $L(H)$ is context free.*

Example 2.20 I give some examples to show that none of the conditions can be dropped. First, the functions must be linear string polynomials. Take $f(\vec{x}) := \vec{x}\,\vec{x}$ on the alphabet $\{\mathsf{a}\}$. This function is induced by the polynomial $p(x_0) := x_0 x_0$. It is not linear as the variable x_0 occurs twice on the right. As it happens the function generates the language $\{\mathsf{a}^{2^n} : n \in \mathbb{N}, n > 0\}$ from a. (Assuming we have a single constant c in the signature with interpretation a.) One may be tempted to eliminate the nonlinearity by using the following function instead.

$$f(\vec{x}, \vec{y}) := \begin{cases} \vec{x}\,\vec{y} & \text{if } |\vec{x}| = |\vec{y}|, \\ \text{undefined} & \text{otherwise.} \end{cases} \tag{2.71}$$

This (binary) function is the restriction of the polynomial $p(x_0, x_1) := x_0 x_1$ to the set of all pairs of strings of equal length. Unfortunately, this function is not rectangularly restricted. There are no sets H, K such that the domain of f is $H \times K$ and the set of strings generable from a with this function is again the set $\{\mathsf{a}^{2^n} : n \in \mathbb{N}, n > 0\}$. Finally, consider the following two functions. The first is a modification of f:

$$f(\vec{x}, \vec{y}) := \begin{cases} \vec{x}\,\vec{y} & \text{if } \vec{x}, \vec{y} \in \mathsf{a}^*, \\ \text{undefined} & \text{otherwise.} \end{cases} \tag{2.72}$$

The second is a unary function g defined by

$$g(\vec{x}) := \begin{cases} \vec{x}\,\mathsf{b} & \text{if } |\vec{x}| = 2^n \text{ for some } n, \\ \text{undefined} & \text{otherwise.} \end{cases} \tag{2.73}$$

Both functions are restrictions of linear polynomial functions to some rectangles. Only the connectivity property is lacking. For $Q^g = \{\vec{x} : |\vec{x}| = 2^n \text{ for some } n \in \mathbb{N}\}$, and we have both $\mathrm{rng}(\mathcal{I}(g)) \nsubseteq Q^g$ and $\mathrm{rng}(\mathcal{I}(g)) \cap Q^g \neq \varnothing$. The generated language is

$$\mathsf{a}^+ \cup \{\mathsf{a}^{2^n}\mathsf{b} : n \in \mathbb{N}, n > 0\}. \tag{2.74}$$

This is not context free. Hence all the conditions are really necessary and independent of each other. ⚽

This gives rise to the following definition.

Definition 2.15 A string grammar is called **(bottom up) context free** if it is a concatenation grammar with rectangularly restricted linear string polynomials with the connectivity property.

Notice that "context free" is applied not only to rule based grammars but also to c-string grammars and string grammars alike. Whenever there is risk of confusion, the context free grammars in the sense of this book are called "bottom up context free".

I close this section with some remarks concerning the use of categories as discriminatory devices. Suppose two strings are such that in a language they have the same category. Then we will want to say that they should also be of the same category in the analysing grammar. Recall that in a context free language, the formal concept of identity of category was substitutability in all 1-contexts, written $\vec{x} \sim_L \vec{y}$.

Principle 1 (Identity of Indiscernibles) *Let G be a context free c-grammar. If $\vec{x} \sim_L \vec{y}$ and $\langle \vec{x}, c\rangle \in L(G)$ then also $\langle \vec{y}, c\rangle \in L(G)$.*

We shall not spell out the generalisation to other kinds of grammars, though it is straightforward to do.

Exercise 2.13 In Example 2.14 is was shown that the relation *is a part of* is not transitive. Find an example to show that it is also not antisymmetric. (A relation R is **antisymmetric** if from $x \; R \; y$ and $y \; R \; x$ follows $x = y$.)

Exercise 2.14 A grammar is left regular if the functions are zeroary or unary and the unary functions all have the form $f(\vec{x}) := \vec{x}^\frown a$ for some a. Let L be a language. Define $\vec{x}/L := \{\vec{y} : \vec{x}^\frown\vec{y} \in L\}$. Show that for a regular grammar G generating L: $\vec{x} \sim_G \vec{y}$ if and only if $\vec{x}/L = \vec{y}/L$.

Exercise 2.15 Why does the bottom up grammar $G^\blacklozenge$ not contain any f_ρ for rules of the form $\rho = A \to B$?

Exercise 2.16 Let G be a context free grammar and A a nonterminal. Let $H_A := \{\vec{x} : A \vdash_G \vec{x}\}$. Show that for every $\vec{x} \in H_A$ $H_A \subseteq [\vec{x}]_G$. Give an example to show that equality need not hold!

Exercise 2.17 Prove Proposition 2.3.

Exercise 2.18 Context free grammars allow to tune derivations more finely than grammars in the sense of Definition 2.4. Here is an example, due to Ben George. Let G consist in the rules

$$
\begin{aligned}
\mathtt{S} &\to \mathtt{L} \mid \mathtt{R} \\
\mathtt{L} &\to \mathtt{La} \mid \mathtt{a} \\
\mathtt{R} &\to \mathtt{aR} \mid \mathtt{a}
\end{aligned}
\tag{2.75}
$$

Construct the corresponding grammar and show that it allows for more analysis terms for the string /aaaa/ than does G.

2.4 Indeterminacy and Adjunction

In the previous section we have constructed a "bottom up" version $G^\spadesuit$ of a context free grammar G. (I should stress here, though, that only $G^\spadesuit$, not G, is a grammar in the sense of this book.) In addition to the differences between the types of grammars that I mentioned earlier there is a major difference between G and $G^\spadesuit$. It is that by definition $L(G^\spadesuit)$ is the set of all strings that are constituents for *some* nonterminals as opposed to just the strings corresponding to the start symbol. Thus the standard definition of $L(G)$ for a CFG is contained in $L(G^\spadesuit)$ but the two need not be identical (cf. Proposition 2.3). The difference is exactly between language in the wide sense and language in the narrow sense. Since I insist that the language of a grammar must be taken in the wide sense we must ask if there is a kind of grammar that generates the sentences all by themselves so that the two notions actually coincide for this type of grammar. Such grammars do exist. The adjunction grammars are of this kind. Unfortunately, these grammars turn out to be somewhat different from the grammars previously defined in that the defining operations generally are *relations*. Grammars of this form shall be called *indeterminate grammars* (the label *relational grammar* has already been taken). I shall return to indeterminate grammars again in Section 3.7 in connection with interpreted languages.

Definition 2.16 An **indeterminate grammar over** A is a pair $\langle \Omega, \mathcal{I} \rangle$, where Ω is a signature and for every $f \in F$, $\mathcal{I}(f) \subseteq (A^*)^{\Omega(f)+1}$. F is the set of **modes** of the grammar. The set $\{f : \Omega(f) = 0\}$ is called the **lexicon** of G and the set $\{f : \Omega(f) > 0\}$ the set of **rules**. The **language** generated by G, in symbols $L(G)$, is defined to be the least set S satisfying for every $f \in F$ and all $\vec{x}_i \in A^*, i < \Omega(f)$:

$$\text{If for all } i < \Omega(f) : \vec{x}_i \in S \text{ and if } \langle \vec{x}_0, \cdots, \vec{x}_{\Omega(f)-1}, \vec{y} \rangle \in \mathcal{I}(f) \text{ then } \vec{y} \in S. \tag{2.76}$$

Thus, the output of a rule is not assumed to be unique. In a grammar of the usual sort the output need not exist but if it exists, it is unique. In an indeterminate grammar it need not even be unique. Adjunction grammars are such grammars. They are popular since they generate more than context free languages and enjoy nevertheless quite a simple description. I point out that as soon as we move to interpreted languages it will turn out that the indeterminacy will have to be eliminated; see also the discussion in Section 3.7.

Definition 2.17 A **2-context** is a triple $\gamma = \langle \vec{u}, \vec{v}, \vec{w} \rangle$. The result of inserting a pair $\langle \vec{x}, \vec{y} \rangle$ into γ is defined as follows.

$$\gamma(\langle \vec{x}, \vec{y} \rangle) := \vec{u}\,\vec{x}\,\vec{v}\,\vec{y}\,\vec{w} \tag{2.77}$$

A **2-locale** is a set of 2-contexts. A **string adjunction rule** is a pair $\rho = \langle\langle\vec{x}, \vec{y}\rangle, \Lambda\rangle$, where Λ is a 2-locale.

According to the previous definition, the string relation associated with ρ is

$$\mathrm{Adj}(\rho) := \{\langle\vec{u}\,\vec{v}\,\vec{w}, \vec{u}\,\vec{x}\,\vec{v}\,\vec{y}\,\vec{w}\rangle : \langle\vec{u}, \vec{v}, \vec{w}\rangle \in \Lambda\}. \tag{2.78}$$

Definition 2.18 A **string adjunction grammar** is a pair $A = \langle S, R\rangle$, where S is a finite set of strings and R a finite set of string adjunction rules.

For a string adjunction grammar we define the following signature: let $f_{\vec{x}}$ be a symbol of arity 0 for every $\vec{x} \in S$; and let g_ρ be a symbol of arity 1 for every $\rho \in R$. This defines the signature. The interpretation is given by

$$\mathcal{I}(f_{\vec{x}}) := \vec{x}, \qquad \mathcal{I}(g_\rho) := \mathrm{Adj}(\rho). \tag{2.79}$$

With this definition, the formal apparatus of the previous sections can be used with minor adaptations.

We say that G **generates** $\vec{y}$ in n-steps if the following holds: $n = 0$ and $\vec{y} \in S$ or $n > 0$ and there is a $\vec{z}$ such that A generates $\vec{z}$ in $n - 1$ steps and there is a rule $\langle\langle\vec{x}_0, \vec{x}_1\rangle, \Lambda\rangle$ and $\gamma = \langle\vec{u}, \vec{v}, \vec{w}\rangle \in A^*$ such that $\vec{z}$ possesses the decomposition $\vec{z} = \gamma(\langle\varepsilon, \varepsilon\rangle) = \vec{u}\,\vec{v}\,\vec{w}$ and

$$\vec{y} = \gamma(\langle\vec{x}_0, \vec{x}_1\rangle) = \vec{u}\vec{x}_0\vec{v}\vec{x}_1\vec{w} \tag{2.80}$$

$L(G)$ denotes the set of strings that can be generated in a finite number of steps. An alternative way to define this notion is to define the value of terms to be sets. Namely, $\iota_G(f s_0 \cdots s_{\Omega(f)-1})$ would be the projection to the last component of the following set:

$$\left(\prod_{i<\Omega(f)} \iota_G(s_i)\right) \times A^* \cap \mathcal{I}(f) \tag{2.81}$$

For a zeroary mode $f_{\vec{x}}$ we have

$$\iota_G(f_{\vec{x}}) = (1 \times A^*) \cap \{\vec{x}\} = \{\vec{x}\}. \tag{2.82}$$

The other cases are similar.

Example 2.21 We shall now give a presentation of the E-strings of the grammar from Example 2.18 using a string adjunction grammar. We put

$$S := \{\mathtt{0=0}, \mathtt{0=1}, \mathtt{1=0}, \mathtt{1=1}\} \tag{2.83}$$

The rules are as follows. Let Λ_1 be the set of triples $\langle \vec{u}x, \vec{v}, \vec{w} \rangle$ such that x is either /0/ or /1/ and $\vec{v}\,\vec{w}$ does not begin with /0/ or /1/. (This is equivalent with the following: (1) $\vec{v} \neq \varepsilon$ and $\vec{v}$ does not begin with /0/ or /1/, or (2) $\vec{v} = \varepsilon$ and $\vec{w}$ (!) does not begin with /0/ or /1/.) Let Λ_2 be the set of triples of the form $\langle \vec{u}, \vec{v}, \vec{w} \rangle$, where both $\vec{u}$ does not end with /0/ or /1/, $\vec{w}$ does not begin with /0/ or /1/, while $\vec{v} \in \{\mathtt{0}, \mathtt{1}\}^*$.

$$
\begin{aligned}
\rho_0 &:= \langle \langle \mathtt{0}, \varepsilon \rangle, \Lambda_1 \rangle \\
\rho_1 &:= \langle \langle \mathtt{1}, \varepsilon \rangle, \Lambda_1 \rangle \\
\rho_2 &:= \langle \langle \varepsilon, \mathtt{0} \rangle, \Lambda_1 \rangle \\
\rho_3 &:= \langle \langle \varepsilon, \mathtt{1} \rangle, \Lambda_1 \rangle \\
\rho_4 &:= \langle \langle \mathtt{(}, \mathtt{+0)} \rangle, \Lambda_2 \rangle \\
\rho_5 &:= \langle \langle \mathtt{(}, \mathtt{+1)} \rangle, \Lambda_2 \rangle \\
R &:= \{\rho_0, \cdots, \rho_5\}
\end{aligned}
\tag{2.84}
$$

The signature is $F := \{f_0, \cdots, f_3, g_0, \cdots, g_5\}$, where the f_i are zeroary and the g_i are unary. Further,

$$
\begin{aligned}
\mathcal{I}(f_0) &:= \{\mathtt{0=0}\} \\
\mathcal{I}(f_1) &:= \{\mathtt{0=1}\} \\
\mathcal{I}(f_2) &:= \{\mathtt{1=0}\} \\
\mathcal{I}(f_3) &:= \{\mathtt{1=1}\} \\
\mathcal{I}(g_i) &:= \mathrm{Adj}(\rho_i)
\end{aligned}
\tag{2.85}
$$

Here is an example of a derivation:

$$
\begin{array}{ll}
f_1 & \mathtt{0=1} \\
g_5 f_1 & \mathtt{(0+1)=1} \\
g_2 g_5 f_1 & \mathtt{(0+10)=1} \\
g_5 g_2 g_5 f_1 & \mathtt{(0+(10+1))=1}
\end{array}
\tag{2.86}
$$

The first line is in S. To get from the first line to the second we choose a decomposition of /0=1/ as /$\varepsilon^\frown$0$^\frown$=1/. Thus, choose $\gamma = \langle \varepsilon, \mathtt{0}, \mathtt{=1} \rangle$. This is in Λ_2 since ε does not end in /0/ or /1/, the middle string is a binary string and /=1/ does not begin with /0/ or /1/. Thus we can apply the rule $\langle \langle \mathtt{(}, \mathtt{+1)} \rangle, \Lambda_2 \rangle$.

$$
\gamma(\langle \mathtt{(}, \mathtt{1)} \rangle) = \varepsilon^\frown/\mathtt{(}/^\frown/\mathtt{0}/^\frown/\mathtt{+1)}/^\frown/\mathtt{=1}/ = /\mathtt{(0+1)=1}/
\tag{2.87}
$$

It may be checked that

$$\begin{aligned}
&\iota_G(g_5 g_2 g_5 f_1)\\
&= \{\texttt{((00+1)+1)=1}, \texttt{(00+1)=(1+1)}, \texttt{((0+1)+10)=1}, \texttt{(0+1)=(10+1)},\\
&\quad \texttt{((0+1)+1)=10}, \texttt{(0+1)=(1+10)}, \texttt{(00+(1+1))=1}, \texttt{00=((1+1)+1)},\\
&\quad \texttt{(0+(10+1))=1}, \texttt{0=((10+1)+1)}, \texttt{(0+(1+1))=10}, \texttt{0=((0+1)+10)},\\
&\quad \texttt{(00+1)=(1+1)}, \texttt{00=(1+(1+1))}, \texttt{(0+10)=(1+1)}, \texttt{0=(10+(1+1))},\\
&\quad \texttt{(0+1)=(10+1)}, \texttt{0=(1+(10+1))}\}.
\end{aligned} \tag{2.88}$$

⚽

Example 2.22 (Cf. Example 2.7.) We give another example: Boolean logic in Polish Notation. The alphabet is :bool: $= \{\wedge, \vee, \neg, \mathtt{p}, \mathtt{0}, \mathtt{1}\}$. A term in Polish Notation is either /p/ followed by an index (a sequence of /0/ and /1/) or it is a function symbol f ($\neg$, $\wedge$ or $\vee$) followed by $\Omega(f)$ many terms. The formation rules using adjunction grammars are as follows. The set of start strings is $S := \{\mathtt{p}\}$. The rules are

$$\begin{aligned}
R := \{&\langle\langle \mathtt{0}, \varepsilon\rangle, \langle A^* \cdot \mathtt{p}, \varepsilon, A^*\rangle\rangle,\\
&\langle\langle \mathtt{1}, \varepsilon\rangle, \langle A^* \cdot \mathtt{p}, \varepsilon, A^*\rangle\rangle,\\
&\langle\langle \neg, \varepsilon\rangle, \langle A^*, (\mathtt{p}|\wedge|\vee|\neg) \cdot A^*, \varepsilon\rangle\rangle,\\
&\langle\langle \wedge\mathtt{p}, \varepsilon\rangle, \langle A^*, (\mathtt{p}|\wedge|\vee|\neg) \cdot A^*, \varepsilon\rangle\rangle,\\
&\langle\langle \vee\mathtt{p}, \varepsilon\rangle, \langle A^*, (\mathtt{p}|\wedge|\vee|\neg) \cdot A^*, \varepsilon\rangle\rangle\}.
\end{aligned} \tag{2.89}$$

Using Exercises 2.6 and 2.7 we can see that this preserves termhood: the sum of the elements added in the string is 0, and the sum of the prefixes is positive. The original Polish Notation had no room for indices but they pose no problem here. It is easy to verify that any string in Polish Notation is derivable in this grammar. ⚽

It is easy to generalize the previous example to Polish Notation in general (see the Exercises). Furthermore, I describe in the exercises how one can derive an adjunction grammar for bracketed notation as well.

In the remainder of this section I shall describe two variants of adjunction grammars that have been discussed in the literature.

Definition 2.19 A 2-locale Λ is **factored** if there are sets $S \subseteq A^* \times A^*$ and $C \subseteq A^*$ such that $\Lambda = \{\langle \vec{u}, \vec{v}, \vec{w}\rangle : \langle \vec{u}, \vec{w}\rangle \in S, \vec{v} \in C\}$. A rule is factored if its 2-locale is. A **contextual grammar** is a string adjunction grammar in which every rule is factored.

See Martín-Vide and Păun (1998) for an overview.

The most popular variant of adjunction grammars are however the tree adjunction grammars (TAGs). These grammars can be explained by a method of coding trees into strings. We shall define certain strings that we call trees. Let N be a set, the set of **nonterminal labels**. Then N-**trees** over the alphabet A are strings from $A \cup N \cup \{\mathtt{(}, \mathtt{)}, \lightning\}$. (a) $x \in A^*$ is an N-tree; (b) if $\vec{u}_i$, $i < n$, are N-trees and $X \in N$, then $/(X\vec{u}_0\vec{u}_1 \cdots \vec{u}_{n-1}X)/$ and $/\lightning(X\lightning\vec{u}_0\vec{u}_1 \cdots \vec{u}_{n-1}\lightning X)\lightning/$ is an N-tree. The adjunction rules have the following form. Let $\langle \vec{x}_0, \vec{x}_1 \rangle$ be a pair of strings such that $\vec{x}_0 = /\lightning(X\lightning \cdots /$, $\vec{x}_1 = / \cdots \lightning X)\lightning/$ and $\vec{x}_0\vec{x}_1$ is an N-tree. Such a pair shall be called an N-**adjunction tree**. Given this tree, let

$$\Lambda := \{\langle \vec{u}, \vec{v}, \vec{w} \rangle : \vec{u}\,\vec{v}\,\vec{w} \text{ is an } N\text{-tree}, \vec{v} = (X \cdots X)\}. \tag{2.90}$$

The pair $\langle \langle \vec{x}_0, \vec{x}_1 \rangle, \Lambda \rangle$ is called a **tree adjunction rule**. Notice that the category X of the adjunction string must match the X in the locale. Also, the presence of $\lightning$ blocks adjunction at a node. (The symbol $\lightning$ is not needed to code the tree structure; its sole purpose was to restrict adjunction.) There are many variants of TAGs. We have picked the most common form for comparison. The language generated by a TAG G is however not the string language; rather it is the language of yields. This is defined as follows.

$$\begin{aligned} h^{\lightning}(x) &:= \begin{cases} \varepsilon & \text{if } x \in N \cup \{(,), \lightning\}, \\ x & \text{else.} \end{cases} \\ h^{\lightning}(x_0x_1 \cdots x_{n-1}) &:= h^{\lightning}(x_0)h^{\lightning}(x_1) \cdots h^{\lightning}(x_{n-1}) \end{aligned} \tag{2.91}$$

Then $L_Y(G) := h^{\lightning}[L(G)]$ is the language of the yields, which is by definition the language generated by G.

Exercise 2.19 Verify that the grammars from Examples 2.21 and 2.22 are contextual grammars.

Exercise 2.20 Let Ω be an arbitrary signature. Write an adjunction grammar for all terms in Polish Notation in this signature.

Exercise 2.21 Let Ω be an arbitrary signature. Terms in this signature are now written as follows. If f is binary and s and t are terms, then $/(^\frown s^\frown f^\frown t^\frown)/$ is a term. If f is unary then $/f^\frown(^\frown s^\frown)/$ is a term. If f is ternary and higher order, then $/f^\frown(^\frown s_0^\frown,^\frown,^\frown \cdots^\frown,^\frown s_{\Omega(f)-1})/$ is a term. Use the previous exercise to derive an adjunction grammar for this language.

2.5 Syntactic Structure

Contemporary linguistics insists that what matters is not the string that we see but rather its *structure*. Structure usually means tree structure. It has been stressed by Chomsky that rules operate on constituents and not on strings. Moreover, Transformational Grammar uses representations that contain the structure in them. Formally, however, it is not clear whether the structure needs to be represented. In this section I shall discuss a popular way of encoding structure into the string. Moreover, we shall investigate to what extent a context free language determines the grammar from which it is generated.

Let us take a look at CFGs and tree structures. Given a string $\vec{x}$ and a grammar G that generates it, G assigns a structure to $\vec{x}$ through a term in the following way. Assume a term t for the string $\vec{x}$. Then $t = f_\rho(s_0, \cdots, s_{n-1})$, where $n = \Omega(f_\rho)$.

$$\rho = A \to \vec{x}_0 B_0 \vec{x}_1 B_1 \cdots B_{n-1} \vec{x}_n \tag{2.92}$$

If $n = 0$ then $\rho = A \to \vec{x}_0$ and we just let the tree consist in two nodes, one with label $\vec{x}_0$, and a preterminal with label A. In general, we create a daughter for each B_i and attach the tree for s_i there and a daughter for every nonempty $\vec{x}_i$ whose label will be $\vec{x}_i$ (we avoid positing empty words).

We can code the derivation with a string. This is done by switching to a grammar that distributes brackets, called G^b. This grammar is defined as follows. We introduce for each nonterminal symbol X a pair of brackets $(_X$ and $)_X$. Let $\rho = X \to \vec{Y}$ be a rule. Then

$$\rho^b := X \to (_X \vec{Y})_X \tag{2.93}$$

G^b contains in place of the rules R the set

$$R^b := \{\rho^b : \rho \in R\}. \tag{2.94}$$

Let $\vec{x}$ be a string. Each term t of $\vec{x}$ can be mapped to a term t^b, which is defined by replacing every occurrence of f_ρ by an occurrence of f_{ρ^b}, for every ρ. Thus mapping t into a term t^b of the bracketed grammar we find the string $\vec{x}_t$, which contains a record of t. $\vec{x}$ is obtained from $\vec{x}_t$ by deleting the brackets and the category symbols. More exactly, define a map d as follows.

$$\begin{aligned} d(a) &:= \begin{cases} \varepsilon & \text{if for some } X\text{: } a = (_X \text{ or } a =)_X, \\ a & \text{else.} \end{cases} \\ d(x_0 x_1 \cdots x_{n-1}) &:= d(x_0) d(x_1) \cdots d(x_{n-1}) \end{aligned} \tag{2.95}$$

Notice that the mapping d is many to one, since a given string can have many derivations. Notice also that there may be derivations that lead to the same bracketed string. Thus the structure is intermediate between the string and the derivation, adding detail to the string but not enough to recover the entire derivation.

Example 2.23 Let $G = \langle$:blet:, $\{\mathtt{E}, \mathtt{A}, \mathtt{B}\}, \mathtt{E}, R\rangle$ where R contains the following rules:

$$\begin{aligned} &\mathtt{E} \to \mathtt{AB} \mid \mathtt{BA} \mid \mathtt{EE} \\ &\mathtt{A} \to \mathtt{AE} \mid \mathtt{EA} \mid \mathtt{a} \\ &\mathtt{B} \to \mathtt{BE} \mid \mathtt{EB} \mid \mathtt{b} \end{aligned} \tag{2.96}$$

Now $G^b = \langle$:blet: $\cup \{(_\mathtt{E},)_\mathtt{E}, (_\mathtt{A},)_\mathtt{A}, (_\mathtt{B},)_\mathtt{B}\}, \{\mathtt{E}, \mathtt{A}, \mathtt{B}\}, \mathtt{E}, R^b\rangle$, with R^b consisting in

$$\begin{aligned} \mathtt{E} &\to (_\mathtt{E}\mathtt{AB})_\mathtt{E} \mid (_\mathtt{E}\mathtt{BA})_\mathtt{E} \mid (_\mathtt{E}\mathtt{EE})_\mathtt{E} \\ \mathtt{A} &\to (_\mathtt{A}\mathtt{AE})_\mathtt{A} \mid (_\mathtt{A}\mathtt{EA})_\mathtt{A} \mid (_\mathtt{A}\mathtt{a})_\mathtt{A} \\ \mathtt{B} &\to (_\mathtt{B}\mathtt{BE})_\mathtt{B} \mid (_\mathtt{B}\mathtt{EB})_\mathtt{B} \mid (_\mathtt{B}\mathtt{b})_\mathtt{B} \end{aligned} \tag{2.97}$$

The string /abab/ can be derived in G in several ways. One is given by the sequence /E/, /EE/, /ABE/, /ABAB/ and so on; another is given by the sequence /E/, /AB/, /AEB/, /ABAB/ and so on. These derivations give rise to the following bracketed strings:

$$\begin{aligned} &(_\mathtt{E}(_\mathtt{E}(_\mathtt{A}\mathtt{a})_\mathtt{A}(_\mathtt{B}\mathtt{b})_\mathtt{B})_\mathtt{E}(_\mathtt{E}(_\mathtt{A}\mathtt{a})_\mathtt{A}(_\mathtt{B}\mathtt{b})_\mathtt{B})_\mathtt{E})_\mathtt{E} \\ &(_\mathtt{E}(_\mathtt{A}\mathtt{a})_\mathtt{A}(_\mathtt{B}(_\mathtt{E}(_\mathtt{B}\mathtt{b})_\mathtt{B}(_\mathtt{A}\mathtt{a})_\mathtt{A})_\mathtt{E}(_\mathtt{B}\mathtt{b})_\mathtt{B})_\mathtt{B})_\mathtt{E} \end{aligned} \tag{2.98}$$

Erasing the brackets returns the original string. The derivation /E/, /EE/, /EAB/, /ABAB/ on the other hand yields the first string again. ⚽

Proposition 2.6 G^b *is unambiguous.*

The proof is straightforward. It rests on the usual bracket count of embeddings.

Notice however that the structure of $\vec{x}$ is a derived notion and the bracketed string just a theoretical construct. The structure is actually an *epiphenomenon*. It may be used in theoretical discourse but is in principle eliminable. This will have to be reassessed when we turn to interpreted grammars. We discuss the definitions and results first in the context of CFGs. We shall now discuss the notion of constituent occurrence without adding brackets. Recall the definition of an occurrence from Definition 2.9. Given a grammar G and a term t we can assign constituent occurrences of substrings in a straightforward way. Choose a subterm occurrence s and decompose t into $t = t'(s)$. This means that $t'(x_0)$ is a term with one free variable and it defines a function $\iota_G(t'(x_0)) : \vec{x} \mapsto \vec{u}\,\vec{x}\,\vec{v}$. This means that $\langle \vec{u}, \vec{v}\rangle$ is a 1-context and the substring that occurs in t is $\iota_G(s)$. For a constant term t, $\mathrm{occ}(\vec{y}, t)$ is the set of occurrences of $\vec{y}$ in $\iota_G(t)$.

This definition basically repeats what is intuitively known. Moreover, from the derivation we can uniquely assign a category to the string occurrence. The following formalizes the known substitution principle.

Definition 2.20 Let G be a CFG, t an A-analysis of the string $\vec{x}$ and C an occurrence of $\vec{y}$ in $\vec{x}$. If $C \in \mathrm{occ}(\vec{y}, t)$ then C is said to be a **constituent occurrence of $\vec{y}$ in $\vec{x}$ under the analysis** t. If $C \notin \mathrm{occ}(\vec{y}, t)$, the occurrence is said to be an **accidental B-occurrence under** t if $\vec{y} \in L_B(G)$. G is **transparent** if no constituent has an accidental occurrence in a string of $L(G)$. A language is **transparent** if it has a transparent grammar.

Notice that we look at occurrences under a given analysis term t. A given string $\vec{x}$ can in principle have several analyses. Suppose that a context free language L is transparent. Then given a string $\vec{x} \in L$ we know that every substring occurrence of $\vec{x}$ that is in L also is a constituent occurrence under every analysis. Thus any context free grammar will assign the same constituent tree to $\vec{x}$. This is very useful for languages of analysis terms, because we need to know that they are structurally unique. This is the case for $\mathrm{Tm}_\Omega(V)$, as the next theorem asserts.

Proposition 2.7 *The language* $\mathrm{Tm}_\Omega(V)$ *is transparent.*

Proof (For notation and facts see Exercises 2.6 and 2.7.) Let s and t be terms and $C = \langle \vec{u}, \vec{v} \rangle$ an occurrence of s in t. We shall show that s is actually a subterm occurrence of t by induction on t. For either (a) $\vec{u} = \varepsilon$ or (b) $\vec{u} \neq \varepsilon$. If (a) is the case then $\vec{v} = \varepsilon$, that is, $s = t$, or else s is a proper prefix. This cannot be, since this would imply $\gamma(s) \geq 0$. Now in case (b) there is an i such that the named occurrence begins in t_i. (Case 1) The occurrence is contained in t_i, that is, $t_i = \vec{x} s \vec{y}$ for some $\vec{x}$ and $\vec{y}$. Then we are done by inductive hypothesis. (Case 2) s overlaps with t_i. Then we have $\vec{x}$, $\vec{y}$ and $\vec{z}$ all nonzero such that $t_i = \vec{x}\,\vec{y}$ and $s = \vec{y}\,\vec{z}$. Now note that since $-1 = \gamma(t_i) = \gamma(\vec{x}) + \gamma(\vec{y})$ and $\gamma(\vec{x}) \geq 0$ (since t_i is a term) we must have $\gamma(\vec{y}) < 0$. But then s is not a term since $\gamma(\vec{y}) \geq 0$ if $\vec{y}$ is a proper prefix. So this case does not arise and we are done. □

Every constituent occurrence in $\vec{x}$ under t corresponds to a subterm occurrence in t. We use this for the following definition. A term is simple if it has no nontrivial subterms.

Definition 2.21 Let G be a CFG, t an A-analysis of the string $\vec{x}$ and C an occurrence of a letter b in $\vec{x}$. C is **syncategorematic** if the term to which b belongs is not simple. A substring occurrence is syncategorematic if every letter is syncategorematic and belongs to the same subterm. G is in **standard form** if no string has syncategorematic occurrences.

This definition can easily be generalized. For a CFG, being in standard form means that the right-hand side of a rule cannot contain both a nonterminal and a terminal letter. For example, the standard formulation of regular grammars is that they have rules of the form $A \to xB$ or $A \to x$. Such grammars are not standard. It is easy to convert a CFG into standard form. However, notice that this changes the language of the grammar, since for us the language contains all constituents.

Example 2.24 We continue Example 2.23 above. The first derivation given by the sequence /E/, /EE/, /ABE/, /ABAB/, /aBAB/, /abAB/, /abaB/, /abab/. In the string we have the constituent occurrences $\langle \varepsilon, \varepsilon \rangle$, $\langle \varepsilon, \text{ab} \rangle$, $\langle \text{ab}, \varepsilon \rangle$ of category E; the occurrences $\langle \varepsilon, \text{bab} \rangle$ and $\langle \text{ab}, \text{b} \rangle$ of category A; and the occurrences $\langle \text{a}, \text{ab} \rangle$ and $\langle \text{aba}, \varepsilon \rangle$ of category B. The string /ab/ has an accidental occurrence $\langle \text{a}, \text{b} \rangle$. The string /aa/ has no accidental occurrence although it is a substring of /aabb/. ⚽

Proposition 2.8 *Let* G *be a CFG,* $\vec{x} \in L(G)$ *and* t *an analysis term. Fix a constituent occurrence of* $\vec{y}$ *in* $\vec{x}$ *under* t*. If* $\vec{y}$ *occurs as* A *in the context* C*, and* $\vec{z}$ *is any string of category* A *of* G*, then* $C(\vec{z}) \in L(G)$.

Suppose now that we wish to give a syntactic analysis of a string language L. We assume that the analysis is given in terms of a CFG. If this is so, we know that the set of strings of L fall into finitely many classes, say, S_i for $i < n$ and that if $\vec{x}, \vec{y} \in S_i$ then each constituent occurrence of $\vec{x}$ can be substituted by $\vec{y}$ and each constituent occurrence of $\vec{y}$ can be substituted by $\vec{x}$. This superficially looks like a way to discover the grammar behind a given language.

The problem with this idea is that we do not know whether a given occurrence is a constituent occurrence. However there is one exception: a single letter wherever it occurs can only occur as a constituent on condition that the grammar contains no syncategorematic occurrences of symbols. It is easy to massage any CFG into such a form without losing anything.

Example 2.25 The language of equations. In the form presented in Example 2.18 on page 34. This grammar introduces /=/, the operation symbols and the brackets in a syncategorematic way. It can be reformulated as follows. The original rule set is

$$\begin{aligned} &\mathtt{E} \rightarrow \mathtt{T=T} \\ &\mathtt{T} \rightarrow \mathtt{(T+T)} \mid \mathtt{(T-T)} \mid \mathtt{B} \\ &\mathtt{B} \rightarrow \mathtt{B0} \mid \mathtt{B1} \mid \mathtt{0} \mid \mathtt{1} \end{aligned} \tag{2.99}$$

Now introduce a nonterminal for each symbol. For example, introduce /O/, /C/, /Q/ together with the unary rules

$$\begin{aligned} &\mathtt{O} \rightarrow \mathtt{(} \\ &\mathtt{C} \rightarrow \mathtt{)} \\ &\mathtt{P} \rightarrow \mathtt{+} \\ &\mathtt{M} \rightarrow \mathtt{-} \\ &\mathtt{Q} \rightarrow \mathtt{=} \end{aligned} \tag{2.100}$$

Next replace the occurrence of the syncategorematic symbols above by the corresponding nonterminal:

$$\begin{aligned} &\mathtt{E} \rightarrow \mathtt{TQT} \\ &\mathtt{T} \rightarrow \mathtt{OTPTC} \mid \mathtt{OTMTC} \mid \mathtt{B} \\ &\mathtt{B} \rightarrow \mathtt{B0} \mid \mathtt{B1} \mid \mathtt{0} \mid \mathtt{1} \end{aligned} \tag{2.101}$$

It is possible to simplify this grammar; we group /P/ and /M/ into just one symbol, say, /H/. Then we have the following rule set:

$$\begin{aligned} &\mathtt{O} \rightarrow \mathtt{(} \\ &\mathtt{C} \rightarrow \mathtt{)} \\ &\mathtt{H} \rightarrow \mathtt{+} \mid \mathtt{-} \\ &\mathtt{Q} \rightarrow \mathtt{=} \\ &\mathtt{E} \rightarrow \mathtt{TQT} \\ &\mathtt{T} \rightarrow \mathtt{OTHTC} \mid \mathtt{B} \\ &\mathtt{B} \rightarrow \mathtt{B0} \mid \mathtt{B1} \mid \mathtt{0} \mid \mathtt{1} \end{aligned} \tag{2.102}$$

⚽

Notice that the grammars (2.100) and (2.102) are not only different grammars; they in fact generate different languages. For example, the string /(/ is in the language of (2.102) but not in (2.100). This is a consequence of the fact that we defined $L(G)$ to contain *all* constituents of G, not just the sentences.

Let us now turn to the idea of recovering the grammar from the set of strings. We start with the assumption that our language is generated by a context free grammar. This means that constituents are strings, and that a string is a part of another string only if it is a subword. The standard substitution method starts with the language L and establishes for every $\vec{x} \in L$ the set of contexts:

$$\mathrm{cnt}_L(\vec{x}) := \{\langle \vec{u}, \vec{v} \rangle : \vec{u}\,\vec{x}\,\vec{v} \in L\}. \tag{2.103}$$

The syntactic classes are the context sets so obtained. We present an example first.

Example 2.26 (Continuing Example 2.11.) The language M is generated by u, defined by

$$\begin{aligned} t &:= \texttt{Alex}_\sqcup \mid \texttt{Pete}_\sqcup \mid \texttt{Mary}_\sqcup \\ u &:= t(\texttt{and}_\sqcup t)^*(\texttt{sing}_\sqcup \mid \texttt{run}_\sqcup \mid \texttt{sings}_\sqcup \mid \texttt{runs}_\sqcup) \end{aligned} \tag{2.104}$$

We consider words as units together with a following blank. (This makes the calculations easier.) The context sets are as follows. Here is a more succinct definition of the language:

$$\begin{aligned} a &:= \texttt{and}_\sqcup \\ v &:= \texttt{sings}_\sqcup \mid \texttt{runs}_\sqcup \\ w &:= \texttt{sing}_\sqcup \mid \texttt{run}_\sqcup \\ u &= tv \mid t(at)^+w \end{aligned} \tag{2.105}$$

It turns out that the syntactic classes are the following: $\mathrm{cnt}_M(v)$, $\mathrm{cnt}_M(tv)$, $\mathrm{cnt}_M(w)$, $\mathrm{cnt}_M(a)$, $\mathrm{cnt}_M(t)$, $\mathrm{cnt}_M(ta)$, $\mathrm{cnt}_M(at)$, $\mathrm{cnt}_M(tat)$, $\mathrm{cnt}_M(atat)$, $\mathrm{cnt}_M(atw)$, $\mathrm{cnt}_M(tatw)$. These are more classes and more constituents than were present in the original grammar even if we massaged the syncategorematic occurrences away. ⚽

The exercises give one more example. The problem with the substitution method is that there is no way of telling whether an occurrence is accidental or not. Consequently, the method will return context sets that are the sets of nonconstituent occurrences. In fact, we may end up with infinitely many context sets (see the exercises). And this is not because of the finiteness of the data: even if we had all data in our hands, the grammar is still underdetermined. Thus, there is some art involved in establishing the subset of constituent occurrences. This set can be different from the one for the original grammar. However, in the absence of decisive evidence this is the best one can do.

Under certain circumstances we can know in advance that the set of nonterminals is going to be finite. A particular case is provided by *primitive languages*.

Definition 2.22 A language is called **primitive** if every substitution class contains a string of length 1, that is, consisting in a single letter.

Evidently, since the alphabet is finite, there are finitely many substitution classes. This does not guarantee the uniqueness of the solution (see the Exercises) but it narrows the choice considerably.

The language defined in Example 2.25 is not primitive. This is because the set of E-strings (which form a substitution class!) consists in strings of length of at least 3: an equation sign, and two terms on either side. Terms may not be empty, they have a length of at least 1.

Primitive languages can easily be turned into CFGs. Just observe that for each letter a there is a substitution class $[a]_L$. Let N_a be the nonterminal representing this class (if $[a]_G = [b]_G$ then also $N_a = N_b$). The rules are of the form

$$\begin{array}{ll} N_a \to a & a \in A \\ N_a \to N_{c_0} N_{c_1} \cdots N_{c_n} & c_0 c_1 \cdots c_n \in [a]_L \end{array} \tag{2.106}$$

This set is typically infinite but a finite subset is enough to generate L, by assumption on L.

We shall finally turn to the abstract case.

Definition 2.23 Let u and v be constant Ω-terms and G a grammar. We say that u and v are **categorially equivalent**, in symbols $u \sim_G v$, if for all terms $s(x)$: $s(u)$ is orthographically definite if and only if $s(v)$ is. They are **intersubstitutable**, in symbols $u \approx_G v$, if and only if they are categorially equivalent and $\iota(s(u)) \in L(G)$ if and only if $\iota(s(v)) \in L(G)$.

This definition does not talk about strings; it talks about terms. This is because the term may be very complex while the string is very simple. Moreover, in absence of any condition on the form of the rules it is not possible to assign any sensible structure to the string.

Example 2.27 Here is a context sensitive grammar, consisting in the following rules.

$$\begin{aligned} \mathtt{S} &\to \mathtt{ATB} \\ \mathtt{T} &\to \mathtt{x} \mid \mathtt{xT} \\ \mathtt{Ax} &\to \mathtt{xA} \\ \mathtt{AB} &\to \mathtt{y} \end{aligned} \tag{2.107}$$

In a derivation, first /A/ is generated to the left of the string. However, when the last rule applies, /A/ has to be to the right. The system of constituents formed by this grammar is quite confusing. It puts the occurrence of /y/ into a constituent with all occurrences of /x/ (for each occurrence of /x/ there is a separate constituent, though). ⚽

Notice also that adjunction grammars in the general form may fail to allow for an unequivocal assignment of structure. This is why tree adjunction grammars work differently from string adjunction grammars. In TAGs the constituent structure is by definition preserved while in string adjunction grammars it need not be.

Exercise 2.22 Show that the substitution classes of a context free grammar (construed as a grammar in the sense of this book in the straightforward way) are of the following form. Let N be the set of nonterminals, and $P \subseteq N$. Then a string $\vec{x}$ is said to be of *class* P if for all $Y \in N$: $Y \Rightarrow^* \vec{x}$ if and only if $Y \in P$.

Exercise 2.23 Apply the method of context sets to grammar C_1 of Example 2.9. Show that the grammar that this gives is C_2 (also from Example 2.9)! Show that the language generated by either grammar is primitive.

Exercise 2.24 Let G consist in the rules $\mathsf{S} \to \mathsf{ab} \mid \mathsf{aSb}$. Establish the context sets of all substrings and show that there are infinitely many of them. Show that infinitely many context free grammars can be postulated on the basis of these sets.

Exercise 2.25 Let G be a context free grammar. Try to establish an inductive definition of $\mathrm{occ}(\vec{y}, t)$. *Hint.* This definition will have to be inductive in the length of $\vec{y}$ and t.

2.6 The Principle of Preservation

We have seen that the effect of substitution is unpredictable unless restrictions are placed on the nature of the string functions. We propose here two principles that simplify the situation. In the most ideal case, functions are only able to change a string by appending material to its left or right. If we required this we get something slightly more general than context free grammars. To get some more freedom we propose that grammars do not operate on the set A^* but on some slightly more general set of exponents, which we equate with $(A^*)^m$ for some m, or perhaps $\bigcup_{m \in \mathbb{N}} (A^*)^m$, as proposed in Kracht (2003).

Principle 2 (Structure) ***Exponents*** *are sequences of strings.*

This is a heavy restriction but it still allows substantial freedom, more than is immediately apparent. First of all, we have not said anything at all about the alphabet from which the strings are formed. In conjunction with the Principle of Structure Preservation this will simply be equivalent to saying that letters are alphabetic letters; but I think matters are not that easy. The problems of this viewpoint will be discussed below. Let us for the moment remain with the idea that the alphabet is simply the standard typographical alphabet. Then exponents are strings of that alphabet—or, as I proposed above, sequences thereof. This latter qualification is important. Consider the following principle.

Principle 3 (Structure Preservation) *A rule may not break any string of the exponent or delete any parts of it.*

This can be formalized as follows. The interpretation of a function symbol f is a function from $\Omega(f)$ many m-tuples to a single m-tuple of strings. So, $\mathcal{I}(f) = \langle t_0, t_1, \cdots, t_{\Omega(f)-1}\rangle$, where the t_i are terms in $m < \Omega(f)$ variables that are polynomial functions in the string algebra

$$\langle A^*, \varepsilon, ^\frown \rangle \tag{2.108}$$

over the signature $\Omega_\frown := \{\langle \varepsilon, 0\rangle, \langle ^\frown, 2\rangle\}$. This means further that t_i may use variables, constants for letters of A and for the empty string and concatenation.

What these principles rule out is deletion of any kind; they also rule out breaking a constituent. However, what they *do* allow is discontinuity. A constituent may consist in a bounded number of parts. Typically, we find that constituents consist in just 1 or 2 strings. Examples of the latter kind are the verbs of German (after verb-second has applied), the crossed dependencies in Dutch infinitives and split-DPs. Occasionally we find languages that seem to have arbitrarily fragmented DPs, like Warlpiri or Jiwarli. However, even in the case of these languages it is not entirely clear that the approach does not work; for these languages do not break embedded clauses either. This needs further work.

We have so far only spoken about breaking or deleting strings. The next principle talks about rules in the sense of nonconstant functions (see Definition 2.3).

Principle 4 (Syncategorematicity Prohibition) *A rule may not add any occurrence of a given symbol.*

Again, this can be formalized by saying that the interpretation of functions uses only definable term functions in $\Omega_\frown$, not polynomials. This allows for complete reduplication (as in Malay) and it also allows for partial reduplication (modulo a regular relation), as long as the parts can be represented as strings. The way it does so is by stipulating that a given string may be repeated. This in fact does *not* mean that a fixed symbol is introduced since the nature of the string to be reduplicated is unknown. An alternative to reduplication is the following. We allow to concatenate two strings $\vec{x}$ and $\vec{y}$ *on the condition that they are identical.* Thus, the formation of the plural in Malay can be expressed in two ways: by a reduplication rule, using a function

$$r(x) = x^\frown x \tag{2.109}$$

or by partial concatenation, using the function

$$c(x, y) = \begin{cases} x^\frown y & \text{if } x = y, \\ \text{undefined} & \text{else.} \end{cases} \tag{2.110}$$

The advantage of the latter is that every occurrence of a letter can be uniquely traced back to a leaf. The disadvantage is that it creates too many substitution classes.[1] Apart from this it is hard to distinguish this approach from the one based on duplication, the more so since the rule is completely general and the categories will anyway turn out to be eliminable from the formulation of a grammar.

Another hard case to treat is the so-called **tmesis**. This is the coordination of parts that are not words by themselves. For example, in German we have the words /Urfeind/ and /Erzfeind/, both formed from /Feind/ "enemy" and a prefix /Ur/ "since very long ago" and /Erz/ "arch-". What is striking is that while neither prefix can be on its own, it is possible to say

Ur- und Erzfeind (2.111)

Similarly, verbal prefixes can be separated

auf- und abladen "load and unload" (2.112)

Tmesis can be applied at the juncture of compounds and with certain prefixes. It is in particular not free to apply to any morphological part of the word. A proper formulation of tmesis under the conditions just sketched is not impossible but requires great care.

What the principle does *not* allow is the addition of any concretely specified symbol. For example, it may not say: "add an /s/ at the end". This must be represented alternatively as a binary rule concatenating the string to $\vec{x}$. Again, requiring this we do not so much restrict *what* can be done but rather *how* it can be done. Yet, there is a problem with this requirement and it runs as follows. We practically assume that bound forms are also part of the language; that is, the plural /s/ of English, even though it cannot occur on its own, is part of the English language. However, this might just be an artefact of the requirement that only words are free forms; and we may say that the language consists in more that just the free forms. The semantics of the plural on the other hand is unproblematic or at least not more problematic than that of any other item.

Now we turn to the question of the alphabet and the nature of the underlying strings. Here, as so often, no unique solution can be given. Two extremes exist: on the one hand we have alphabetic systems that are more or less sound based (with complications of their own). On the other we have ideographic systems like Chinese, which make a single letter correspond (again more or less) to a morpheme. Chinese presents a good example of the predicament we are facing: if we base our analysis on the *sounds* then there are about 100 letters (vowels in four tones plus

[1] If we look at this rule in combination with semantics (anticipating the next chapter) we find that the reduplication approach will form the plural in the semantics by performing the step from properties of individuals to properties of sets of individuals. The partial concatenation approach however makes the plurals appear more like *dvandva*-compounds. The idea is that in the Malay plural noun /anak-anak/ "children", we get the plural meaning from extrapolating a dvandva from "child" and "child" rather than (the more natural) dvandva formed from different parts.

consonants), or maybe somewhat more, given that pauses and intonation contours must be taken on board as well. If, however, we base our analysis on the alphabet of *characters* then we have an alphabet of up to 50,000 "letters". (The Chinese Standard Interchange Code, the most comprehensive of the lists, has close to 50,000 characters.) The question that naturally arises is this: which of the two should we choose? In principle, it seems, we should be able to do both but writing systems can be so artificial that it seems we ought to exclude some of them from the analysis.[2] But even if we do, the sound based approach presents difficulties of its own. One is that the notion of part is somewhat obscure. For example, we say that a string $\vec{x}$ is *part* of a string $\vec{y}$ if it is a subword. Thus, we may for example say that /`eel`/ is part of /`reel`/, or /`ice`/ is part of /`rice`/. If we apply our substitution tests, however, we get quite a bizarre picture of the language. Thus, we would like to apply substitution only to constituents, or, as we have said above, study those strings (or sequences) that can be substituted for a single letter. If *letter* can be equated with *morph*, or *morpheme*, we would get a far more interesting grammar from our substitution tests than if we insisted on sounds (or alphabetic characters). The disadvantage of the method is that it presupposes what it ought to reveal: the primitive parts. However, as we shall see in the next chapter, the notion of a morph(eme) makes perfect sense, because once we add the meaning the alphabetic characters are in fact *not* the most basic elements but the morph(eme)s.

In stratificational linguistics we actually pursue *both* analyses at once. There are various strata at which we have structure. Such frameworks have been pursued among others by Lamb (1966) and Mel'čuk (1993–2000). In our view the various levels are mostly epiphenomenal and can be reconstructed on the basis of the language (as a set) itself. I shall briefly discuss the reconstruction of levels in Section 3.7.

Even if all this is granted, we still face a number of problems. Suppose, for example, that our language is based on morphemes, which are the letters of our alphabet. Then, by our principles above, these letters must surface in our strings (or sequences of sounds). It follows that morphemes are sequences of characters of the alphabet. If that is so, we must address exceptions to strict concatenation. I mention here as representatives: final devoicing (as found in Russian and German, for example), vowel harmony (as found, say, in Finnish, Hungarian and Turkish), consonant lenition in Welsh, or consonant gradation in Sami (Svenonius, 2007). Let us discuss the first case. Final devoicing is a process that turns any consonant in the coda of a syllable into a voiceless consonant. For example, there are two nouns in German, /`Rad`/ [ʁa:t] "bicycle" and /`Rat`/ [ʁa:t] "council". They sound exactly the same. On the other hand, their respective genitives, /`Rades`/ [ʁa:dəs] and /`Rates`/ [ʁa:təs], do not. The reason is that the rules of segmentation put the stop into the onset of the next syllable, where it does not undergo devoicing. If we base ourselves

---

[2] There was once a way to write in Japan that used only Chinese characters and even Chinese word order. The characters were augmented with numbers so that one knew in which way to read the characters. Now, not only do the characters come out differently (the character for mountain is read "yama" in Japanese and "shān" in Chinese), but they are also arranged according to Chinese syntax.

on the written forms, no problem. The sounds however do pose a problem. What can be the solution?

One solution ultimately rests on the distinction between complete and incomplete forms. Suppose that the base form comes without word end markers. So they would be [ʁa:d] and [ʁa:t], respectively. Now, when we attempt to pronounce such a word, we must speak it in isolation, so we add a word boundary marker to its left and right: [#ʁa:d#] and [#ʁa:t#]. After that, there is a process that will produce the required form. This solution does explain the different outcomes but it falls short of complying with the Principle of Preservation. This applies to all other phenomena listed above, which is why we have mentioned them. We shall therefore relax this principle a little bit. We shall assume that it is not the actual surface forms that must be preserved but a more abstract form.

If we left matters at that we would basically remove all restrictions. We need to restrict the abstraction. This is done as follows. We operate now with two levels: SP (the surface phonological level) and DP (the deep phonological level). Each of the levels uses the same alphabet (tentatively). The principles apply only to DP. The actual strings of SP are obtained by applying a finite state transducer. In other terms, the relation between DP and SP is a *regular relation* (see Kracht (2003) for definitions and discussion). To account for German devoicing, we assume that at DP no devoicing applies. The relation to SP, however, is such that every consonant that happens to be syllable final is devoiced. This can be achieved using a finite state transducer.

Let us briefly touch on the question of c-languages. If one wishes to include categories into the language then the Principle of Preservation loses some of its bite. It would namely be possible to introduce material into the category part where it is invisible to the principles formulated above. I assume therefore that when categories are added they cannot introduce a finer distinction than already present in the functions.

Principle 5 (Categorial Granularity) *For a c-grammar* G *and the associated string grammar* H, *if* $\langle \vec{x}, c\rangle \in L(G)$ *and* $\vec{y} \sim_H \vec{x}$ *then also* $\langle \vec{y}, c\rangle \in L(G)$.

Thus, the set of categories cannot differentiate the exponents in a finer way than the string functions. The way this is phrased makes the principle somewhat circular. But you need to recall that the string categories are derived from the string functions and ultimately from the language itself. Thus, bringing in an extra set C of categories really is to serve the purpose of explicitly coding the categorial facts rather than bringing back a lost dimension. However, I should note that adding categories even with the Granularity Principle brings in extra power.

Exercise 2.26 German nouns are written with an initial upper case letter. However, in compounds only the first letter is in upper case. For example, /`Auto`/ "car" and /`Bahn`/ "way" result in the compound /`Autobahn`/ "highway". (Observe similarly /`Erzfeind`/ in the example above.) Propose a solution to this. *Hint.* There are (at least) two solutions. One uses the regular relations, the other proposes several forms for the same word.

Chapter 3
Compositionality

THE principle of compositionality is introduced in this chapter: it concerns the relationship of strings with their meanings. To be able to formulate it properly, we shall have to introduce interpreted languages and grammars for them.

3.1 Compositionality

Let us begin with some exegetical remarks concerning the notion of compositionality. Here is what I regard as a standard definition.

> The meaning of a complex expression is a function of the meanings of its parts and the mode of composition by which it has been obtained from these parts.

Almost every word of this definition is in need of explanation. We begin with the subject of the sentence: *the meaning of a complex expression*. To use this expression here means to acknowledge that there first of all *are* expressions and meanings; and that expressions have meanings. Immediately we start to ask ourselves what expressions *are* and what meanings *are*. Since meanings are attributed to expressions, I take this to say that whatever expressions are, they must be part of the language to begin with. Thus, strictly speaking, expressions must be strings. However, we have settled the question somewhat differently in Section 2.6; there we concluded that expressions are *sequences* of strings. Moreover, they must be sequences of strings of which we know what their meaning is. This is implicit in the use of the definite determiner in "the meaning of an expression". The use of the definite determiner is somewhat troublesome: it may mean that an expression has one and only one meaning; it may also mean that its meaning is not arbitrary. If taken in the first sense expressions are unambiguous. I take this to be incorrect and not the way in which "the" is to be understood here (see also the discussion in Section 3.5). Rather, I wish to plead that we interpret this as follows: given that we are under way to investigate *some given* meaning of an expression, which is one of the many that it may have but we have fixed that one as opposed to others, we have a recipe to get *this* meaning from whatever the components mean. Thus, the definite determiner points to an implicitly made choice. I defer a definition of what meanings are. So far we know this much: there are expressions (sequences of strings) and meanings;

M. Kracht, *Interpreted Languages and Compositionality*, Studies in Linguistics and Philosophy 89, DOI 10.1007/978-94-007-2108-1_3,
© Springer Science+Business Media B.V. 2011

a language consists in a relation between the two. This is the original idea laid out in Saussure (2011).

One word still remains to be discussed: *complex*. To say whether an expression is simple or complex cannot be determined intrinsically; in fact, "complex" here means the following. We are given a grammar G of the expressions. An expression is G-**simple** if it is the value in G of a simple term; and an expression is G-**complex** if it is the value in G of a complex term. Often, we omit mentioning the grammar. It turns out that one and the same expression can both be simple and complex; this is the case with idioms, for example. But it is also the case with false idioms such as /`caterpillar`/. This expression is both simple and complex, at least if we assume a grammar of English where compounding is performed by concatenation. Notice that so far the grammar is just a context free grammar for tuples of strings and knows nothing about the meaning. To make sense of the above definition, however, we must assume that the grammar also handles meanings together with expressions. We wish to say, for example, that idioms are simple. For although as expressions they are complex, their meaning is not derived from the meanings that any proper parts have.

We are thus led to assume that the definition of compositionality talks about *languages as relations between expressions and meanings and grammars that generate such relations from a given finite set*. It is this type of language and grammar that we shall look at in detail in this chapter. We call them *interpreted languages* and *interpreted grammars*. To finish explicating the definition, let us assume that we have such a grammar that generates not just expressions but pairs of expressions and meanings. Such pairs we call from now on *signs*. A sign is thus a pair $\sigma = \langle e, m\rangle$, where e is the *exponent* of σ and m the *meaning*. While it cannot be said that in a given language a given expression has just one meaning and a given meaning has just one expression, it is true by definition that a given sign has exactly one exponent and one meaning. It is thus more appropriate to exchange "expression" in the above definition by "sign". It therefore reads as follows.

> The meaning of a complex sign is a function of the meanings of its parts and the syntactic rule by which it has been composed from these signs.

Let us try to understand this definition further. A grammar generates signs; it starts with a lexicon, which we may take to be a finite list of signs. In addition it has some functions to generate signs from signs, in the same way as a string grammar generates strings from strings.

A sign σ is simple if and only if it is the value of a simple term; it is complex if and only if it is the value of a composite term. A given sign can be both simple and complex. The previous problems have now disappeared. An idiom for example is a sign that is simple but not complex, because its meaning is not obtainable in the grammar in a regular way. (To be more exact, idioms are signs whose exponent has another meaning together with which it forms a complex sign. The definition of *idiom* is a truly delicate affair.) So, the definition begins by assuming that we have a grammar G and a sign σ. Furthermore, we assume that there is a term function $p(\vec{x})$ and signs $\sigma, \sigma_0, \cdots, \sigma_{n-1}$ such that

$$\sigma = t(\sigma_0, \cdots, \sigma_{n-1}). \tag{3.1}$$

In that case assume that $\sigma_i = \langle e_i, m_i \rangle$ and $\sigma = \langle e, m \rangle$. Then

$$m = F(t, m_0, \cdots, m_{n-1}) \tag{3.2}$$

for some F that depends only on G. We can without further ado write t^μ for the function $F(t, \_, \cdots, \_)$. Then the previous means that

$$m = t^\mu(m_0, \cdots, m_{n-1}). \tag{3.3}$$

It follows by a simple argument (induction on the length of t) that it is enough to require (3.3) for t a basic function of G.

At last we need to clarify the notion of a *mode of composition*. First of all, we use the same terminology as in the preceding chapter. We assume that we have a finite set F of function symbols forming a signature $\langle F, \Omega \rangle$ together with Ω. As we saw above, for each $f \in F$ there is an f^μ satisfying (3.3). This is the meaning function; there also is a function f^ε such that

$$e = f^\varepsilon(\sigma_0, \cdots, \sigma_{\Omega(f)-1}). \tag{3.4}$$

We shall see later that one will also have to impose some restrictions on f^ε. Crucially, we may understand *mode* as referring just to f, or as referring in fact to f^ε. Suppose for example that we have the following language L.

$$L = \{\langle \mathsf{a}, 0 \rangle, \langle \mathsf{b}, 1 \rangle, \langle \mathsf{ab}, 2 \rangle, \langle \mathsf{ab}, 3 \rangle\} \tag{3.5}$$

Assume that /ab/ is to be considered complex. If we understand a mode to be a syntactic function then this language cannot be compositional, for there is only one function to compose /a/ and /b/.[1] To make this even more precise: we shall assume that what counts in the specific case is not the function as a whole but rather what it does to the specific elements at hand. That is to say that we can also define the following function:

$$f(x, y) := \begin{cases} x^\frown y & \text{if } x = \mathsf{a} \text{ and } y = \mathsf{b}, \\ y^\frown y & \text{if } x = \mathsf{aa} \text{ and } y = \mathsf{b}, \\ \text{undefined} & \text{else.} \end{cases} \tag{3.6}$$

This is a different function but on the strings of the language it shows no difference to plain concatenation. We say therefore that f and g *count as the same mode* exactly when $f^\varepsilon(\vec{\sigma}) = g^\varepsilon(\vec{\sigma})$. (Recall in this connection Example 2.2. The plural of

[1] Well, there are two: $f(x, y) := x^\frown y$ and $g(x, y) := y^\frown x$. But this can be handled by constructing a more complex example.

regular nouns and the third singular of regular verbs are for these purposes formed by the same mode, assuming their arity to be the same.) There are languages that satisfy compositionality even with this strict identity of modes; many computer languages are of that form. There is simply only one way to combine two constituents semantically; the surface syntax may be flexible (allowing the use of brackets, for example) but this is just a means of identifying the constituents. However, semantically, there is just one way to combine two meanings. Natural languages are quite different in this respect. Many expressions are constructionally ambiguous and that accounts for many meaning differences.

Let us now settle down on the final definition of compositionality (see the extended discussion in Section 3.3):

> A language L is *compositional* if there is a grammar G based on a signature $\langle F, \Omega\rangle$ such that (i) $L = L(G)$ and (ii) for each $f \in F$ there is a function f^{μ} such that if $\sigma = \langle e, m\rangle$ and $\sigma_i = \langle e_i, m_i\rangle$, $i < \Omega(f)$, are signs such that
>
> $$\sigma = f(\sigma_0, \cdots, \sigma_{\Omega(f)-1}) \tag{3.7}$$
>
> and g counts as the same mode as f then
>
> $$m = g^{\mu}(m_0, \cdots, m_{\Omega(f)-1}). \tag{3.8}$$

Notice that from (3.7) we deduce that

$$m = f^{\mu}(m_0, \cdots, m_{\Omega(f)-1}), \tag{3.9}$$

since f is the same as f. However, there could be more modes that are the same as f. Three notions of sameness come to mind: (a) $f = g$ (symbolic identity), (b) $f^{\varepsilon} = g^{\varepsilon}$ (extensional identity) and (c) $f^{\varepsilon}(\vec{\sigma}) = g^{\varepsilon}(\vec{\sigma})$ (casewise identity). Option (c) is the least strict on the functions (and therefore induces the strictest condition on compositionality); in this case, any two functions which are defined at all on the input (and return the output string) are the same for the purpose of the definition.

A last point to mention is that strings may have *categories*. In this case we may further refine the notion of identity, allowing functions to depend on the categories of the arguments. I shall discuss the ramifications of this option below.

I shall now review some alternative definitions of compositionality. First, there is a tradition to use a more elaborate structure than the string, namely a tree structure defined over the string. In fact there are several such structures, and it is one of them that is actually interpreted, namely LF. The meaning of a particular LF is actually independent of the way in which it was obtained; however, as it has internal structure, its meaning can be obtained with reference to that structure. I shall return to the question of the viability of this proposal in Section 5.4. Here I just notice that to safeguard themselves from a different interpretation of compositionality some people have named the concept used here **rule-to-rule compositionality**, or **direct compositionality** (see the volume Barker and Jacobson (2007)). I shall not follow this usage, partly because I think that the alternative notions are too weak to yield interesting results.

More interesting therefore are definitions that are more restrictive than the one given here. Szabó (2000) gives the following definition.

> The meaning of a complex expression is determined by the meaning of its constituents and by its structure.

In his discussion, Szabó focuses mainly on the word "determines". The idea is that "determines" refers to some causal connection. Thus a language that uses just any function is not good enough. Some essential link must exist between the structure and the meaning. Thus, Szabó claims, we are led to assume that in order for the meaning to be determined by the structure, meanings must be structured and there must be a kind of structural parallel between syntax and semantics. The arguments by Pagin (2003) go in the same direction, though his reasons are slightly different. Pagin argues that speakers and hearers must be able to effectively find meanings associated with expressions and conversely and it is hard to imagine how that can be done without some kind of structural similarity. The structure in meaning is language independent, so this would among others imply a certain similarity between all human languages. I have chosen not to go that way. One reason for my choice is that the structure of meanings is something that we believe is too poorly understood to give insightful results at this point; thus, I am not arguing that meanings are not structured, I am only saying that the actual structure they have—whatever it may be—is very hard to determine. The recent discussion in King (2007) I do not find very revealing in this connection and too much language bound. Should it turn out that meanings *are* structured our approach is nevertheless not invalid; there will then be more conditions on syntactic structure. I think that one need not believe in structured meanings in order to establish a difference between just any kind of meaning composition function and one that is "good", that is, "compositional". I shall return to the question of natural meaning functions in the next chapter.

Another notion of compositionality is that of Hodges (2001). In essence, the definitions are the same as the ones given here; there are however some technical differences that need to be pointed out. The main difference is that Hodges assumes that meanings are given to an expression through a function; thus an expression always has a unique meaning. This simplifies the technical apparatus and works well for artificial languages, but for natural language this is actually a problematic assumption. Notice that it eliminates ambiguity. Words such as /bank/ or /crane/ will not be considered ambiguous by the grammar. Moreover, the semantic functions f^{μ} will operate on the total meaning. This means the following: an adjective such as /big/ does not simply operate on the different meanings of /crane/ independently; rather, it operates on the combined meaning of the two. Let us make that concrete. /crane/ either means a type of birds—call this meaning crane'_b—or a type of machines—call the meaning crane'_m. The meaning function now associates with it the concept $\mathsf{crane}'_b \vee \mathsf{crane}'_m$, which is true of x if and only if x is either a bird crane or a machine crane. The meaning big' of /big/ on its part takes the whole concept and forms the concept of being-a-big-crane. Evidently, big bird cranes are far smaller than big machine cranes, so we expect the idea of a big bird-or-machine-crane to be different from both.

We may try to save the theory by proposing that the meaning of an ambiguous item is the set of different meanings it has otherwise. Thus, we assign to /`crane`/ the meaning $\{\mathsf{crane}'_b, \mathsf{crane}'_m\}$. This opens problems of its own. For example, an adjective will now apply to a set of what we otherwise would call meanings. How does it apply to such a set? We will have to say that it applies to each member individually. Thus we are already imposing a structure onto semantics (that meanings are sets) that languages cannot override. Everything stands and falls with the question whether a language contains genuinely ambiguous expressions. A defender of the functional view will have to claim that expressions are not ambiguous in this sense; they simply mean what they mean in all their totality. This is difficult to maintain since it would deprive us of the possibility of differentiating between idiomatic and nonidiomatic meanings of expressions. The expression "He kicked the bucket" will have to have both the literal and the idiomatic reading as its meaning simpliciter without there being a way to say what it is that makes the idiomatic reading idiomatic.

Another problem with the functional account is that it assumes that all ambiguity is spurious. Suppose namely that there is a string $\vec{x}$ that can be derived in several different ways. As the meaning of $\vec{x}$ is assumed to be unique, we want each of the derivations to give us the unique reading. This is problematic for reasons of structural ambiguity.

```
__ is square free or it is a product of two        (3.10)
prime numbers and greater than 100.
```

This description can be read in two ways. It says that the number is greater than 100, and it is either square free of the product of two primes. Alternatively, the number is either square free or it is not and in the latter case the product of two primes and greater than 100. In the second reading 71 satisfies the description, in the first reading it does not. The values for each of the readings can be obtained using a compositional grammar. However, the sum of all values cannot be so given, since it would require the grammar to know in each case about alternative readings. This cannot work. Of course, such a claim needs rigorous proof. We shall return to this matter in Section 3.5.

I also add another feature that is frequently encountered in artificial languages but not in human languages. I have given above an example of a language that figures in Zadrozny (1994) to show that there are languages that we intuitively consider not compositional. A critical analysis of this example reveals that the intuition is based on the assumption that what is graphically complex (here the string /ab/) also is syntactically complex. Since alphabets are small, "graphically complex" cannot always mean "consists in more than one letter". Rather, it is taken to mean: consists in more than one identifier, where identifiers are sequences of letters not interrupted by special symbols. More complex criteria can be imagined; what is important is that syntactic complexity is decidable regardless of the underlying grammar. That this is so is a *design property* of formal languages; it is built into the parser. It allows tokenisation to precede syntactic analysis. We cannot likewise assume human languages to be built this way. The said property, that complexity is decidable on the basis of the string alone, is called **morphological transparency**. Human languages are therefore in general morphologically intransparent. Idioms are a case in point.

3.2 Interpreted Languages and Grammars

We assume the setup of the previous chapter. As we have said, objects of a language are sequences of strings over some alphabet (modulo a regular transduction). To avoid having to talk about the exact nature of syntactic objects, we assume that they come from a set E. E can for example be A^*, but different choices are possible (and often necessary).

To differentiate languages as sets of strings from the interpreted languages defined below we shall call sets of strings **string languages** (though in fact we have allowed the exponents to be *sequences* of strings).

Definition 3.1 Let E and M be sets (of exponents and meanings, respectively). The members of $E \times M$ are called **signs**. For a sign $\sigma = \langle e, m\rangle$ define

$$\varepsilon(\sigma) := e, \qquad \mu(\sigma) := m. \tag{3.11}$$

e is the **exponent** of σ and m its **meaning**. A set $L \subseteq E \times M$ is called an **interpreted language over** E. The projection

$$\varepsilon[L] := \{e : \text{there is } m \in M : \langle e, m\rangle \in L\} \tag{3.12}$$

is called the **string language of** L and the set

$$\mu[L] := \{m : \text{there is } e \in E : \langle e, m\rangle \in L\} \tag{3.13}$$

the **expressive power of** L.

The meaning of σ is not to be confused with its **denotation**, a term that I wish to avoid since it is often used in a purely extensional sense, while meaning is intensional.

Definition 3.2 Let L be an interpreted language. L is **unambiguous** if for every $\langle e, m\rangle, \langle e, m'\rangle \in L$ we have $m = m'$. L is **monophone** if for every $\langle e, m\rangle, \langle e', m\rangle \in L$ we have $e = e'$.

Thus a language is generally defined to be a set of signs; that a sign is seen here just as a pair and not a triple (see Section 3.2) is mainly due to the fact that form and meaning are the most obvious components of it. The exponent can be seen, heard or touched (think of Braille letters) and the meaning—although somewhat hard to establish in exact detail—is what makes language a symbolic system. With this definition we also return to the roots. The definition of a sign pairing form and meaning is due to Saussure (2011). (Chomsky also endorsed that view in Chomsky (1993), though the exponents in Generative Grammar are far more complex.) De Saussure uses the words **signifier (signifiant)** and **signified (signifié)**, rather than *exponent* and *meaning*. The straightforward generalization of the definition of grammar would be the following.

Definition 3.3 Let E be a set of exponents and M a set. An **interpreted grammar** is a pair $G = \langle \Omega, \mathcal{I} \rangle$ where Ω is a finite signature and $\mathcal{I}$ a function that assigns to a symbol $f \in F$ a partial $\Omega(f)$-ary function on $E \times M$:

$$\mathcal{I}(f) : (E \times M)^{\Omega(f)} \hookrightarrow (E \times M). \tag{3.14}$$

Furthermore,

$$L(G) := \{\iota(t) : t \in \mathrm{Tm}_{\Omega}(\varnothing)\} \tag{3.15}$$

is the **language generated by** G.

To put it somewhat more simply, given E and M, the set $S := E \times M$ is the **space of signs**. If f is a function symbol, $\mathcal{I}(f)$ is a partial n-ary function on S. Indeed, the definitions of the previous chapter can be imported without much adaptation. The only difference is that where we generated strings (or sequences thereof) now we generate signs.

I remark here that we can always choose E and M in a such a way that $E = \varepsilon[L(G)]$ and $M = \mu[L(G)]$, though of course $L(G)$ need not be identical with $E \times M$.

Example 3.1 (See also Example 2.5) If G is a grammar, $L(G)$ is either finite or countable. This is because we can effectively enumerate the terms and there are only countably many terms. Let now L be countable. Then there is a bijection $f : \mathbb{N} \to L$. Define the grammar G in the same way as in Example 2.5. It is easy to see that the terms are of the form $s^n b$ for some $n \in \mathbb{N}$. For this term we have $\mathcal{I}(s^n b) = f(n)$. Thus this grammar generates L. We conclude that a language has a grammar if and only if it is finite or countable. ⚽

We refer the reader to Appendix A for the relationship between a partial function $f : A \hookrightarrow B \times C$ and the projections $\pi_B \circ f : A \hookrightarrow B$ and $\pi_C \circ f : A \hookrightarrow C$. We apply this to the case at hand. The symbol f is interpreted by a function $\mathcal{I}(f) : (E \times M)^{\Omega(f)} \hookrightarrow (E \times M)$ and so we can factor $\mathcal{I}(f)$ into a *pair* of partial functions

$$f^{\varepsilon} := \pi_E \circ \mathcal{I}(f), \qquad f^{\mu} := \pi_M \circ \mathcal{I}(f). \tag{3.16}$$

This means in more detail that for all signs σ_i, $i < \Omega(f)$, we put

$$\begin{aligned} f^{\varepsilon}(\sigma_0, \cdots, \sigma_{\Omega(f)-1}) &:= \varepsilon(\mathcal{I}(f)(\sigma_0, \cdots, \sigma_{\Omega(f)-1})), \\ f^{\mu}(\sigma_0, \cdots, \sigma_{\Omega(f)-1}) &:= \mu(\mathcal{I}(f)(\sigma_0, \cdots, \sigma_{\Omega(f)-1})). \end{aligned} \tag{3.17}$$

It follows that we have

$$\mathcal{I}(f)(\sigma_0, \cdots, \sigma_{\Omega(f)-1}) = \langle f^\varepsilon(\sigma_0, \cdots, \sigma_{\Omega(f)-1}), f^\mu(\sigma_0, \cdots, \sigma_{\Omega(f)-1})\rangle. \tag{3.18}$$

This is written in a more concise form as

$$\mathcal{I}(f) = f^\varepsilon \times f^\mu. \tag{3.19}$$

Here, $f \times g$, where $f : A^n \to C$ and $g : A^n \to D$ are functions, is a function from A^n to $C \times D$ defined by

$$(f \times g)(x_0, \cdots, x_{n-1}) := \langle f(x_0, \cdots, x_{n-1}), g(x_0, \cdots, x_{n-1})\rangle. \tag{3.20}$$

(Notice that we write $f(x_0, \cdots, x_{n-1})$ in place of $f(\langle x_0, \cdots, x_{n-1}\rangle)$.) Now, in place of a single interpretation function $\mathcal{I}$ we may also consider having *two* such functions, namely $\mathcal{I}^\varepsilon$ and $\mathcal{I}^\mu$, which we get as follows.

$$\mathcal{I}^\varepsilon(f) := \pi_E \circ \mathcal{I}(f), \qquad \mathcal{I}^\mu(f) := \pi_M \circ \mathcal{I}(f). \tag{3.21}$$

As we shall see, having two independent interpretations changes things dramatically. So we shall give the new construct a name and call it a *bigrammar.*

Definition 3.4 Let E be a set of exponents and M a set of meanings. A **bigrammar** over E and M is a triple $G = \langle \Omega, \mathcal{I}^\varepsilon, \mathcal{I}^\mu\rangle$ where Ω is a finite signature and $\mathcal{I}^\varepsilon$ and $\mathcal{I}^\mu$ functions that assign to a mode f two partial functions, namely $\mathcal{I}^\varepsilon(f) : (E \times M)^{\Omega(f)} \hookrightarrow E$ and $\mathcal{I}^\mu(f) : (E \times M)^{\Omega(f)} \hookrightarrow M$.

The concept of a bigrammar is a different concept, as we shall show. If $G = \langle \Omega, \mathcal{I}^\varepsilon, \mathcal{I}^\mu\rangle$ is a bigrammar then put $\mathcal{I}(f) := \mathcal{I}^\varepsilon(f) \times \mathcal{I}^\mu(f)$. Then $G_\times := \langle \Omega, \mathcal{I}\rangle$ is an interpreted grammar. Conversely, given an interpreted grammar $G = \langle \Omega, \mathcal{I}\rangle$, put $G^\times := \langle \Omega, \mathcal{I}^\varepsilon, \mathcal{I}^\mu\rangle$ as in (3.21); this is a bigrammar.

It is easy to see that for every interpreted grammar G, $G = (G^\times)_\times$. However, it is not generally the case that $H = (H_\times)^\times$ for every bigrammar H. This is because several distinct bigrammars may define the same interpreted grammar. Notice namely that

$$\mathrm{dom}(\mathcal{I}^\varepsilon(f) \times \mathcal{I}^\mu(f)) = \mathrm{dom}(\mathcal{I}^\varepsilon(f)) \cap \mathrm{dom}(\mathcal{I}^\mu(f)). \tag{3.22}$$

However, the grammar $G_\times$ has the property that

$$\mathrm{dom}(f^\varepsilon) = \mathrm{dom}(f^\mu). \tag{3.23}$$

Hence, a bigrammar of the form $G^\times$ satisfies

$$\mathrm{dom}(\mathcal{I}^\varepsilon(f)) = \mathrm{dom}(\mathcal{I}^\mu(f)). \tag{3.24}$$

We call a bigrammar satisfying (3.24) **balanced**. The following is easy to see.

Proposition 3.1 *Let H be a bigrammar. Then H is balanced if and only if $H = (H_\times)^\times$.*

Proof Clearly, if $H = (H_\times)^\times$ then H is of the form $G^\times$ and so is balanced. Conversely, if H is balanced then $\mathrm{dom}(\mathcal{I}(f)) = \mathrm{dom}(f^\varepsilon) = \mathrm{dom}(f^\mu)$ and so we have $\mathrm{dom}(\mathcal{I}^\varepsilon(f) \times \mathcal{I}^\mu(f)) = \mathrm{dom}(\mathcal{I}(f))$. It follows that $f = \mathcal{I}^\varepsilon(f) \times \mathcal{I}^\mu(f)$ and so $H = (H_\times)^\times$. □

The terminology of Section 2.1 for grammars is taken over unchanged. For example, the definition of analysis term is the same (it involves only the underlying signature) and the interpretation is defined inductively in the same manner. The reason is that the same signature can be applied to generate string languages and to generate interpreted string languages (and even more complex languages, which we shall consider below in Section 3.3). It just depends on the function $\mathcal{I}$ what types of objects are generated. This is one of the reasons for our abstract definition of grammars using signatures. For example, given an interpreted grammar $G = \langle \Omega, \mathcal{I} \rangle$, we define the interpretation of a constant term t by induction as follows:

$$\iota_G(f s_0 s_1 \cdots s_{\Omega(f)-1}) := \mathcal{I}(f)(\iota_G(s_0), \iota_G(s_1), \cdots, \iota_G(s_{\Omega(f)-1})). \tag{3.25}$$

We use also the following notation. For terms t we let t^ε be the exponent of $\iota(t)$ and t^μ its meaning. A term t is **semantically definite** if t^μ exists; and it is **orthographically definite** if t^ε exists. We say that t is **definite** if it is both orthographically and semantically definite and **indefinite** otherwise. In a balanced bigrammar a term is definite iff it is semantically definite iff it is orthographically definite. In general however they are different but only slightly. For a term of the form $t = f(u_0, \cdots, u_{\Omega(f)-1})$ we either have that one of the u_i is indefinite, in which case t is indefinite. Or all of the u_i are definite and then t can be orthographically but not semantically definite, or semantically but not orthographically definite (or neither orthographically nor semantically definite).

Terms that contain variables are interpreted as partial functions from $S^{\mathbb{N}} \hookrightarrow S$, where S is the space of signs, here $E \times M$. Given a sequence $\langle \sigma_0, \sigma_1, \cdots \rangle$ of signs $\iota(t)$ computes the value of t where for every $i \in \mathbb{N}$, x_i is interpreted as σ_i.

Example 3.2 Let $E := A^*$ where $A := \{$0, 1, +, -, (,), =$\}$. Let $M := \mathbb{Z} \cup \{\top, \bot\}$. $F := \{f_0, f_1, f_2, f_3, f_4, f_5, f_6\}$. $\Omega(f_0) := \Omega(f_1) := 0$, $\Omega(f_2) := \Omega(f_3) := 1$, $\Omega(f_4) := \Omega(f_5) := \Omega(f_6) := 2$. $\vec{x}$ is **binary** if it only contains /0/ and /1/; $\vec{x}$ is a **term** if it does not contain /=/. The grammar is shown in Fig. 3.1. The signs that this grammar generates are of the following form. They are either strings of 0s and 1s, paired with the number that they represent as binary numbers. Or they are terms, interpreted in the usual way; or they are equations between two such terms. A single numeral expression is also a term. An equation is either true (in which case it is interpreted by $\top$) or false (in which case it is interpreted by $\bot$). ⚽

$$
\begin{aligned}
\mathcal{J}(f_0)() &:= \langle \mathtt{0}, 0\rangle \\
\mathcal{J}(f_1)() &:= \langle \mathtt{1}, 1\rangle \\
\mathcal{J}(f_2)(\langle \vec{x}, m\rangle) &:= \begin{cases} \langle \vec{x}\mathtt{0}, 2m\rangle & \text{if } \vec{x} \text{ is binary,} \\ \text{undefined} & \text{else.} \end{cases} \\
\mathcal{J}(f_3)(\langle \vec{x}, m\rangle) &:= \begin{cases} \langle \vec{x}\mathtt{1}, 2m+1\rangle & \text{if } \vec{x} \text{ is binary,} \\ \text{undefined} & \text{else.} \end{cases} \\
\mathcal{J}(f_4)(\langle \vec{x}, m\rangle, \langle \vec{y}, n\rangle) &:= \begin{cases} \langle \mathtt{(}\vec{x}\mathtt{+}\vec{y}\mathtt{)}, m+n\rangle & \text{if } \vec{x}, \vec{y} \text{ are terms,} \\ \text{undefined} & \text{else.} \end{cases} \\
\mathcal{J}(f_5)(\langle \vec{x}, m\rangle, \langle \vec{y}, n\rangle) &:= \begin{cases} \langle \mathtt{(}\vec{x}\mathtt{-}\vec{y}\mathtt{)}, m-n\rangle & \text{if } \vec{x}, \vec{y} \text{ are terms,} \\ \text{undefined} & \text{else.} \end{cases} \\
\mathcal{J}(f_6)(\langle \vec{x}, m\rangle, \langle \vec{y}, n\rangle) &:= \begin{cases} \langle \vec{x}\mathtt{=}\vec{y}, \top\rangle & \text{if } \vec{x}, \vec{y} \text{ are terms and } m = n, \\ \langle \vec{x}\mathtt{=}\vec{y}, \bot\rangle & \text{if } \vec{x}, \vec{y} \text{ are terms and } m \neq n, \\ \text{undefined} & \text{else.} \end{cases}
\end{aligned}
\tag{3.26}
$$

Fig. 3.1 A grammar for binary strings

Example 3.3 We shall now define an unbalanced bigrammar that defines the same interpreted language as the grammar in the previous example. The semantic functions are shown in Figs. 3.2 and 3.3. For the bigrammar $G = \langle \Omega, \mathcal{K}^\varepsilon, \mathcal{K}^\mu\rangle$ we find that $G^\times = \langle \Omega, \mathcal{J}\rangle$. However, it does not satisfy the equations (3.24). For example, we find that $\mathcal{K}^\varepsilon(f_2)(\langle \mathtt{(1+1)}, 2\rangle)$ is undefined while $\mathcal{K}^\mu(f_2)(\langle \mathtt{(1+1)}, 2\rangle) = 4$, since $\mathcal{K}^\mu$ does not look at the exponent. Notice that the semantic functions are not total but could easily be made to be. Notice also that they do not depend on the exponent, so they can be further simplified. This will be discussed in detail in Section 3.3. ⚽

$$
\begin{aligned}
\mathcal{K}^\varepsilon(f_0)() &:= \mathtt{0} \\
\mathcal{K}^\varepsilon(f_1)() &:= \mathtt{1} \\
\mathcal{K}^\varepsilon(f_2)(\langle \vec{x}, m\rangle) &:= \begin{cases} \vec{x}\mathtt{0} & \text{if } \vec{x} \text{ is binary,} \\ \text{undefined} & \text{else.} \end{cases} \\
\mathcal{K}^\varepsilon(f_3)(\langle \vec{x}, m\rangle) &:= \begin{cases} \vec{x}\mathtt{1} & \text{if } \vec{x} \text{ is binary,} \\ \text{undefined} & \text{else.} \end{cases} \\
\mathcal{K}^\varepsilon(f_4)(\langle \vec{x}, m\rangle, \langle \vec{y}, n\rangle) &:= \begin{cases} \mathtt{(}\vec{x}\mathtt{+}\vec{y}\mathtt{)} & \text{if } \vec{x}, \vec{y} \text{ are terms,} \\ \text{undefined} & \text{else.} \end{cases} \\
\mathcal{K}^\varepsilon(f_5)(\langle \vec{x}, m\rangle, \langle \vec{y}, n\rangle) &:= \begin{cases} \mathtt{(}\vec{x}\mathtt{-}\vec{y}\mathtt{)} & \text{if } \vec{x}, \vec{y} \text{ are terms,} \\ \text{undefined} & \text{else.} \end{cases} \\
\mathcal{K}^\varepsilon(f_6)(\langle \vec{x}, m\rangle, \langle \vec{y}, n\rangle) &:= \begin{cases} \vec{x}\mathtt{=}\vec{y} & \text{if } \vec{x}, \vec{y} \text{ are terms,} \\ \text{undefined} & \text{else.} \end{cases}
\end{aligned}
\tag{3.27}
$$

Fig. 3.2 An unbalanced bigrammar for binary strings I

$$\begin{aligned}
\mathcal{K}^{\mu}(f_0)() &:= 0\\
\mathcal{K}^{\mu}(f_1)() &:= 1\\
\mathcal{K}^{\mu}(f_2)(\langle\vec{x},m\rangle) &:= \begin{cases} 2m & \text{if } m \in \mathbb{Z},\\ \text{undefined} & \text{else.}\end{cases}\\
\mathcal{K}^{\mu}(f_3)(\langle\vec{x},m\rangle) &:= \begin{cases} 2n+1 & \text{if } m \in \mathbb{Z},\\ \text{undefined} & \text{else.}\end{cases}\\
\mathcal{K}^{\mu}(f_4)(\langle\vec{x},m\rangle,\langle\vec{y},n\rangle) &:= \begin{cases} m+n & \text{if } m,n \in \mathbb{Z},\\ \text{undefined} & \text{else.}\end{cases}\\
\mathcal{K}^{\mu}(f_5)(\langle\vec{x},m\rangle,\langle\vec{y},n\rangle) &:= \begin{cases} m-n & \text{if } m,n \in \mathbb{Z},\\ \text{undefined} & \text{else.}\end{cases}\\
\mathcal{K}^{\mu}(f_6)(\langle\vec{x},m\rangle,\langle\vec{y},n\rangle) &:= \begin{cases} \top & \text{if } m,n \in \mathbb{Z} \text{ and } m = n,\\ \bot & \text{if } m,n \in \mathbb{Z} \text{ and } m \neq n,\\ \text{undefined} & \text{else.}\end{cases}
\end{aligned} \tag{3.28}$$

Fig. 3.3 An unbalanced bigrammar for binary strings II

Let me conclude with a few words on the algebraic treatment. A grammar $G = \langle\Omega,\mathcal{I}\rangle$ can also be viewed as a partial Ω-algebra defined over the space $E \times M$ (see Appendix A for definitions). Bigrammars have no straightforward algebraic equivalent. Exercises 3.10 and 3.11 will pursue this theme.

Exercise 3.1 It is possible to interpret the modes f_2 and f_3 by the string functions $\vec{x} \mapsto \mathtt{0}^\frown\vec{x}$ and $\vec{x} \mapsto \mathtt{1}^\frown\vec{x}$. Show that it is however impossible to use the meaning functions given above with these string functions.

Exercise 3.2 (Continuing the previous exercise.) Give a grammar that generates the language of equations using the string functions above. (Evidently, the functions on meanings must be quite different.)

Exercise 3.3 Let $G = \langle\Omega,\mathcal{I}\rangle$ be a grammar. Show that there is a bigrammar $G_\bullet = \langle\Omega,\mathcal{I}^{\varepsilon}_\bullet,\mathcal{I}^{\mu}_\bullet\rangle$ such that $(G_\bullet)^\times = G$ and such that for every $f \in F$, $\mathcal{I}^{\varepsilon}_\bullet(f)$ is total. (Dually, we can construct $G_\bullet$ such that $\mathcal{I}^{\mu}_\bullet(f)$ is total for every $f \in F$.)

Exercise 3.4 (Using the previous exercise.) Show by giving an example that we cannot expect both $\mathcal{I}^{\varepsilon}_\bullet(f)$ and $\mathcal{I}^{\mu}_\bullet(f)$ to be total. *Hint.* This should be totally straightforward.

3.3 Compositionality and Independence

In this section we shall look at the interdependence between the components of a sign. We shall look at ways of formulating the grammar in such a way that the exponents and meanings are completely independent. We have so far assumed that the modes are interpreted as functions on signs. As such they have the form

$$\mathcal{I}(f) = f^{\varepsilon} \times f^{\mu}, \tag{3.29}$$

with the functions defined as given in (3.17). If, however, we start with a bigrammar we simply put

$$f^{\varepsilon} := \mathcal{I}^{\varepsilon}(f), \qquad f^{\mu} := \mathcal{I}^{\mu}(f). \tag{3.30}$$

In this case, as we observed, (3.24) does not necessarily hold any more. Although we shall not mention this fact in the sequel, the reader is asked to be aware of the possibility that bigrammars can help to distribute the partiality between syntax and semantics, which is why we shall work mainly with bigrammars rather than grammars.

There are two senses in which the equation (3.29) can be required to hold. I call the first the *strict sense*: the equation is valid as stated above. This means that the equation specified is valid even if the relevant functions are applied to signs that are not in the language. The *extensional sense* requires that the equation only holds for the language of the grammar. This is formally expressed in (3.31).

$$\mathcal{I}(f) \restriction L(G) = (f^{\varepsilon} \times f^{\mu}) \restriction L(G) \tag{3.31}$$

Here, if $f : A^n \hookrightarrow B$ and $C \subseteq A$,

$$f \restriction C := \{\langle \vec{c}, f(\vec{c})\rangle : \vec{c} \in C^n\}. \tag{3.32}$$

These two viewpoints really are different. It is assumed that the grammatical formation rules are more general; they may be applied to words (and meanings) that do not exist in the language. For example, we may introduce new words into a language or create new idioms. What we find is that more often than not the morphological rules know how to deal with them. If the rules were just defined on the language as it is, we would have to artificially extend the interpretation of the modes as soon as new entries get introduced into the lexicon. Consider for example the nouns of Malay (cf. also the discussion in Example 3.8 below). Malay nouns reduplicate in the plural. Now suppose a new word, say, a loanword from English is introduced. Will it be reduplicated or will it be used with the English plural? Exactly this question is studied in the so-called "wug-test", where people are asked to form the plural of a word that is not English. If a speaker forms a plural of such a word it means that his or her morphological functions are more general; they operate on words that are not English, and they operate even in the absence of any semantics. Children face a similar situation. When they grow up they will have to guess how the plural of nouns is formed. It is not realistic to assume that they will simply learn the plural of each word individually. Rather, they will abstract a general rule that can be used on new words as well. And they can both understand what is a morphological plural and what is the concept behind plurality. And both seem to be independent. Notice that the idea of a human grammar as different from a formal grammar is irrelevant here. Formal languages often do display similar differences. And though the wug-test seems to indicate that there is a uniform rule of plural formation in English it is not clear that all people have the same abstract formation rule. Not only does individual variation exist (showing us extensional differences, that is, differences in the languages of the speakers); also it is quite conceivable that intensional variation exists. For example, it is conceivable that when presented with a nonexistent verbal root, German speakers will differ as to how they will inflect a new verb even when they completely agree on the inflection of existing verbs (though I am not aware of a positive result showing this).

Thus, we assume with some justification that the functions above may also be defined on signs outside of the language generated by the grammar. Nevertheless we shall study the behaviour of the functions in the intensional sense. This is because it is easy to return to the extensional sense by restricting the original functions to $L(G)$. Formally, this may be expressed as follows. We say that $G' = \langle \Omega, \mathcal{I}' \rangle$ is an **extensional variant** of $G = \langle \Omega, \mathcal{I} \rangle$ if $L(G') = L(G)$ and for every mode f, $\mathcal{I}'(f) \restriction L(G) = \mathcal{I}(f) \restriction L(G)$. Extensional variants cannot be distinguished from each other by looking at the language they generate; but they might be distinguishable by introducing "nonce signs".

Let us return to the equation (3.29) above. I shall rewrite it as follows:

$$\begin{aligned} &\mathcal{I}(f)(\langle e_0, m_0 \rangle, \cdots, \langle e_{\Omega(f)-1}, m_{\Omega(f)-1} \rangle) \\ &= \langle f^{\varepsilon}(\langle e_0, m_0 \rangle, \cdots, \langle e_{\Omega(f)-1}, m_{\Omega(f)-1} \rangle), \\ &\quad f^{\mu}(\langle e_0, m_0 \rangle, \cdots, \langle e_{\Omega(f)-1}, m_{\Omega(f)-1} \rangle) \rangle. \end{aligned} \tag{3.33}$$

We say that a bigrammar is compositional if f^{μ} does not depend on the e_i. This can be restated as follows. (For notions of independence for (partial) functions see Appendix A. For partial functions, independence is weak independence by default.)

Definition 3.5 A bigrammar G is **semicompositional** if, for every mode f, f^{μ} is (weakly) independent of the exponents of the signs. If the f^{μ} are strongly independent of the exponents, G is called **compositional**. G is **extensionally compositional** if it has an extensional variant that is compositional. An interpreted language L is **compositional** if there is a compositional bigrammar G such that $L = L(G)$.

Example 3.4 There are pairs of words whose meaning is roughly the same, of which one member is singular and the other in the plural (see Kac, Manaster-Ramer, and Rounds (1987)): examples are /`military`/:/`armed forces`/, /`forest`/:/`woods`/ and /`location`/: /`whereabouts`/. Consider a bigrammar that has these words as values of constants and a single unary operation that forms the regular plural. Semantically, each of the concepts has a plural (there is a notion of armies, forests and locations). However, depending on the exponent, the plural can or cannot be regularly formed. This grammar is therefore semicompositional but not compositional. Using the notation of Example 2.10, the term $p(f_{\text{forest}})$ is definite and interpreted by $\langle$`forests`, pl′(forest′)$\rangle$. However, $p(f_{\text{woods}})$ is not definite. It is however semantically definite. An example of a compositional bigrammar is the following. Switch the interpretation of p as follows: if the noun is in the singular, form the regular plural. If it is in the plural, leave the noun unchanged. The second grammar generates the pluralia tanta also in their plural meaning, so that, e.g., /`armed forces`/ means either army (singular meaning) or armies (plural meaning). ⚽

The notion of semicompositionality may easily be confused with compositionality. The difference is not in the value that the function yields: it is unique. The difference is whether the choice of certain expressions can make the semantic function undefined when it has a value for at least *some* expressions. In a compositional bigrammar this is excluded while a semicompositional still allows for that possibility.

We extend these notions to interpreted grammars as follows. For an interpreted grammar G, G is $\mathcal{P}$ if and only if $G^{\times}$ is $\mathcal{P}$ (see page 65 for notation). So, G is semicompositional if and only if $G^{\times}$ is. Notice that a language is compositional if and only if it has a compositional interpreted grammar.

If G is extensionally compositional or semicompositional then for every mode f there exists a partial function $f_*^{\mu} : M^{\Omega(f)} \hookrightarrow M$ such that

$$\mu(\mathcal{I}(f)(\sigma_0, \cdots, \sigma_{\Omega(f)-1})) \stackrel{\geq}{=} f_*^{\mu}(\mu(\sigma_0), \cdots, \mu(\sigma_{\Omega(f)-1})). \tag{3.34}$$

The sign $\stackrel{\geq}{=}$ means that the left- and right-hand sides are equal *if defined*; and moreover, the right-hand side is defined if the left-hand side is, but the converse need not hold. If G is compositional then also the left-hand side is defined if the right-hand side is, so full equality holds. In that case we can put

$$f_*^{\mu}(m_0, \cdots, m_{\Omega(f)-1}) := f^{\mu}(\langle e, m_0\rangle, \langle e, m_1\rangle, \cdots, \langle e, m_{\Omega(f)-1}\rangle), \tag{3.35}$$

where e is chosen arbitrarily. Since by assumption f^{μ} does not depend on the exponents, any choice of e will give the same result. Another definition is to take the full image of the function f under projection. Recall that an n-ary function g on signs is a subset of $(E \times M)^{n+1}$. For any such function put

$$\mu[g] := \{\langle \mu(\sigma_0), \cdots, \mu(\sigma_n)\rangle : \langle \sigma_0, \cdots, \sigma_n\rangle \in g\}. \tag{3.36}$$

Then we may alternatively define f_*^{μ} by

$$f_*^{\mu} := \mu[\mathcal{I}(f)]. \tag{3.37}$$

Independence from the exponents guarantees that this is a function. We see here more explicitly that f_*^{μ} is a partial function only on meanings. Suppose now that L is compositional; this means that there is a compositional grammar G such that $L = L(G)$. This means in turn that for every $\sigma \in L$ there is a term t such that $\sigma = \iota_G(t)$. If $t = f s_0 \cdots s_{\Omega(f)-1}$ then the meaning of $\iota_G(t)$ equals $f_*^{\mu}(\mu(\iota_G(s_0)), \cdots, \mu(\iota_G(s_{\Omega(f)-1})))$, which is to say that, given that the σ_i are the parts of σ, the meaning of σ is the result of applying the function f_*^{μ} to the meaning of its parts. However, notice that we have two senses of compositionality, the simple (intensional) and the extensional. For a language to be compositional we may require the existence of either an extensionally compositional grammar, or of a compositional grammar. For if an extensionally compositional grammar exists, there is a compositional variant, which by definition generates the same language.

Notice a further consequence. If G is extensionally compositional then we can produce an extensional variant in the following way. Put

$$\widehat{f^{\varepsilon}} := (\varepsilon \circ \mathcal{I}(f)) \restriction L(G). \tag{3.38}$$

This function is defined exactly on the signs of $L(G)$. Now take as $\widehat{f^{\mu}_{*}}$ any function extending f^{μ}_{*}. (In other words, $\widehat{f^{\varepsilon}}$ carries all the load in terms of undefinedness. In this case, $\widehat{f^{\mu}_{*}}$ may even be a total function.)

Example 3.5 Here is an example. Let $G = \langle \Omega, \mathcal{I} \rangle$ be a grammar containing a binary mode f and zeroary modes g_i, $i < 3$, where

$$\begin{aligned} \mathcal{I}(g_0)() &= \langle \texttt{ed}, \mathsf{past}' \rangle \\ \mathcal{I}(g_1)() &= \langle \texttt{laugh}, \mathsf{laugh}' \rangle \\ \mathcal{I}(g_2)() &= \langle \texttt{car}, \mathsf{car}' \rangle \end{aligned} \tag{3.39}$$

Here, I am assuming the following type assignment: $\mathsf{car}' : e \to t$, $\mathsf{laugh}' : e \to s \to t$ and $\mathsf{past}' : (e \to s \to t) \to (e \to s \to t)$.

$$\mathcal{I}(f)(\langle e, m \rangle, \langle e', m' \rangle) := \langle e^\frown e', m'(m) \rangle \tag{3.40}$$

Note that this is undefined if $m'(m)$ is undefined. This means that semantically the only meaningful combination is $\mathsf{past}'(\mathsf{laugh}')$. Now take the bigrammar $G^{\times} = \langle \Omega, \mathcal{I}^{\varepsilon}, \mathcal{I}^{\mu} \rangle$. Define a new bigrammar $\langle \Omega, \mathcal{K}^{\varepsilon}, \mathcal{K}^{\mu} \rangle$ as follows. $\mathcal{K}^{\mu}(f)$ is any total function extending $\mathcal{I}^{\mu}(f)$; for example, it also takes the pairs $\langle e, \mathsf{car}' \rangle$, $\langle e', \mathsf{past}' \rangle$ as arguments (whatever e and e') and returns some value. Then put

$$\mathcal{K}^{\varepsilon}(f)(\langle e, m \rangle, \langle e', m' \rangle) := \begin{cases} e^\frown e' & \text{if } e = /\texttt{laugh}/ \text{ and } e' = /\texttt{ed}/, \\ \text{undefined} & \text{else.} \end{cases} \tag{3.41}$$

It is not hard to check that $\mathcal{K}^{\varepsilon}(f) = \mathcal{I}^{\varepsilon}(f)$. This bigrammar therefore generates the same output language. The source of partiality has been shifted from the semantics to the syntax. ⚽

A particular choice that we may take for f^{μ}_{*} is $\mu[\mathcal{I}(f)]$. This is sufficient. Notice however that this may still be a partial function. Any function extending it will also do but nothing less.

In and of itself this seems to capture the notion of compositionality. However, it presupposes a notion of a part and mode of composition. There are two ways to understand "part" and "mode of composition". We may simply say that it is the grammar that defines what is part of what and what counts as a mode. Or we may say that the notion of part is not arbitrary. Not every grammar implements a correct notion of "part of". Not every grammar therefore uses a good notion of "mode of composition". In Kracht (2003) I have put the restrictions into the definition of compositionality. Here I shall keep them separate.

Signs are pairs; switching the order in the pair gives rise to the **dual** of the sign. Switching the order in the entire language defines the dual of the language. Notice that most technical notions do not distinguish between exponents and meanings, so they can be applied to both a language and its dual. The notion dual to compositionality is known as *autonomy*.

Definition 3.6 A bigrammar G is **semiautonomous** if for every mode f the function f^{ε} is weakly independent of the m_i. If f^{ε} are also strongly independent of the m_i, G is called **autonomous.** G is **extensionally autonomous** if it has an extensional variant that is autonomous. An interpreted language L is **autonomous** if there is an autonomous bigrammar G such that $L = L(G)$.

Semiautonomy says that the exponent of a complex sign is the result of applying a certain function to the exponent of its parts and that that function depends only on the leading symbol of the analysis term. One consequence is that for every mode f there exists a partial function $f^{\varepsilon}_{*} : E^{\Omega(f)} \hookrightarrow E$ such that

$$\varepsilon(\mathcal{I}(f)(\sigma_0, \cdots, \sigma_{\Omega(f)-1})) \stackrel{\geq}{=} f^{\varepsilon}_{*}(\varepsilon(\sigma_0), \cdots, \varepsilon(\sigma_{\Omega(f)-1})). \tag{3.42}$$

Again, if the left-hand side is defined then the right-hand side is as well but not conversely. In an autonomous grammar, also the converse holds.

Finally, we say our language is *independent* if both syntax and semantics can operate independently from each other.

Definition 3.7 A bigrammar is **independent** if it is both compositional and autonomous; it is **extensionally independent** if it is both extensionally compositional and extensionally autonomous. A language is **independent** if it has an independent bigrammar.

Thus G is independent if for every f there are functions f^{ε}_{*} and f^{μ}_{*} such that for all $\sigma_i = \langle e_i, m_i \rangle, i < n$:

$$\mathcal{I}(f)(\sigma_0, \cdots, \sigma_{\Omega(f)-1}) = \langle f^{\varepsilon}_{*}(e_0, \cdots, e_{\Omega(f)-1}), f^{\mu}_{*}(m_0, \cdots, m_{\Omega(f)-1})\rangle. \tag{3.43}$$

with the left-hand side defined if and only if the right-hand side is. (The functions f^{ε}_{*} and f^{μ}_{*} are defined as $\varepsilon[\mathcal{I}^{\varepsilon}(f)]$ and $\mu[\mathcal{I}^{\mu}(f)]$, respectively.) Another formulation is

$$\mathcal{I}(f) = (f^{\varepsilon}_{*} \circ \langle \overbrace{\varepsilon, \cdots, \varepsilon}^{\Omega(f)} \rangle) \times (f^{\mu}_{*} \circ \langle \overbrace{\mu, \cdots, \mu}^{\Omega(f)} \rangle) \tag{3.44}$$

or

$$\mathcal{I}(f)(\sigma_0, \cdots, \sigma_{\Omega(f)-1}) \qquad (3.45)$$
$$= \langle f_*^{\varepsilon}(\varepsilon(\sigma_0), \cdots, \varepsilon(\sigma_{\Omega(f)-1})), f_*^{\mu}(\mu(\sigma_0), \cdots, \mu(\sigma_{\Omega(f)-1}))\rangle.$$

It may be thought that for languages, extensional independence follows from extensional autonomy and extensional compositionality. However, this does not seem to be the case. I remark here that I have not been able to find an example of a language that is *not* (!) independent. If there are no restrictions on the functions that can be used, independence seems to be guaranteed.

Example 3.6 We construct various different grammars to show that autonomy and compositionality are independent notions. Let $A := \{\mathtt{a}\}$, $E := A^*$; $M := \mathbb{N}$. The signature is $\{f_0, f_1, f_2\}$, with f_0 zeroary and f_1 and f_2 both unary. We have

$$\begin{aligned} \mathcal{I}(f_0)() &:= \langle \varepsilon, 0\rangle \\ \mathcal{I}(f_1)(\langle \vec{x}, n\rangle) &:= \begin{cases} \langle \vec{x}^\frown\mathtt{a}, n+1\rangle & \text{if } |\vec{x}| = n, \\ \text{undefined} & \text{otherwise.} \end{cases} \\ \mathcal{I}(f_2)(\langle \vec{x}, n\rangle) &:= \begin{cases} \langle \vec{x}^\frown\mathtt{a}, n\rangle & \text{if } |\vec{x}| \geq n, \\ \langle \vec{x}, n+1\rangle & \text{otherwise.} \end{cases} \end{aligned} \qquad (3.46)$$

Call this grammar U. The action of the unary functions on the space $E \times M$ is shown in Fig. 3.4. U generates the language $D := \{\langle \vec{x}, n\rangle : n \leq |\vec{x}|\}$, as is easily verified; the entry point is the origin, and everything is in D that is reachable by following the arrows. Notice that the second clause of the definition for $\mathcal{I}(f_2)$ is never used inside D. Thus, we could have made $\mathcal{I}(f_2)(\langle \vec{x}, n\rangle)$ undefined if $n > |\vec{x}|$. This would give us an extensional variant of the original grammar. U is not autonomous: $\mathcal{I}(f_2)(\langle \mathtt{a}, 3\rangle) = \langle \mathtt{a}, 4\rangle$ but $\mathcal{I}(f_2)(\langle \mathtt{a}, 1\rangle) = \langle \mathtt{aa}, 1\rangle$. So to compute the exponent we need to know the meaning. It is not compositional either. For we have in addition to $\mathcal{I}(f_2)(\langle \mathtt{a}, 3\rangle) = \langle \mathtt{a}, 4\rangle$ also $\mathcal{I}(f_2)(\langle \mathtt{aaa}, 3\rangle) = \langle \mathtt{aaaa}, 3\rangle)$, so to compute the meaning we need to know the exponent.

Consider the following variants of $\mathcal{I}$, which agree on f_0 and f_1 with $\mathcal{I}$:

$$\begin{aligned} \mathcal{I}^a(f_2)(\langle \vec{x}, n\rangle) &:= \begin{cases} \langle \vec{x}^\frown\mathtt{a}, n\rangle & \text{if } |\vec{x}| \geq n, \\ \langle \vec{x}^\frown\mathtt{a}, n+1\rangle & \text{else.} \end{cases} \\ \mathcal{I}^c(f_2)(\langle \vec{x}, n\rangle) &:= \begin{cases} \langle \vec{x}^\frown\mathtt{a}, n\rangle & \text{if } |\vec{x}| \geq n, \\ \langle \vec{x}^\frown\mathtt{a}^\frown\mathtt{a}, n\rangle & \text{else.} \end{cases} \\ \mathcal{I}^{ac}(f_2)(\langle \vec{x}, n\rangle) &:= \langle \vec{x}^\frown\mathtt{a}, n\rangle \end{aligned} \qquad (3.47)$$

All of them only generate the language D. The grammar $U^{ac} := \langle \Omega, \mathcal{I}^{ac}\rangle$ is semiautonomous and semicompositional.

$U^c = \langle \Omega, \mathcal{I}^c\rangle$ is semicompositional but not semiautonomous. To see this, note that we have $\mu(\mathcal{I}^c(f_2)(\langle e, m\rangle)) = m$, which is independent of e; on the other hand

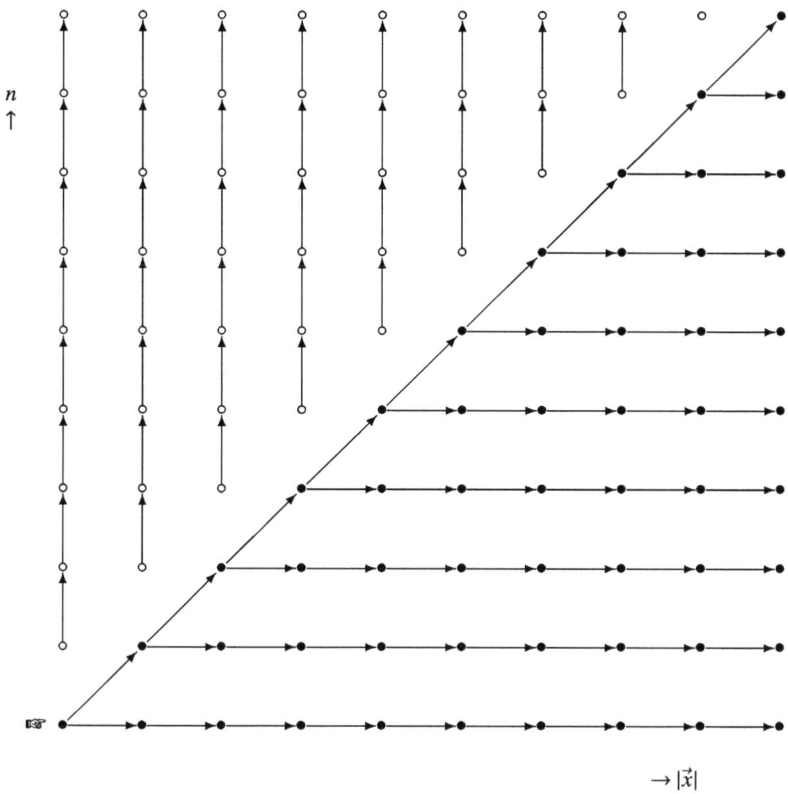

Fig. 3.4 The action of the grammar U

we have $\varepsilon(\mathcal{I}^c(f_2)(\langle \mathsf{aa}, 2\rangle)) = \mathsf{aaa} \neq \mathsf{aa} = \varepsilon(\mathcal{I}^c(f_2)(\langle \mathsf{aa}, 3\rangle))$. Similarly we find that $\langle U^a := \langle \Omega, \mathcal{I}^a\rangle$ is semiautonomous but not semicompositional. ⚽

Now, let $\mathcal{J}(f_0) := \mathcal{I}(f_0)$ and $\mathcal{J}(f_2) := \mathcal{I}(f_2)$. Put

$$\mathcal{J}(f_1)(\langle \vec{x}, n\rangle) := \langle \vec{x}^\frown \mathsf{a}, n+1\rangle. \tag{3.48}$$

Define $\mathcal{J}^a$, $\mathcal{J}^c$ and $\mathcal{J}^{ac}$ by changing the interpretation of f_2 as above. $\langle \Omega, \mathcal{J}^{ac}\rangle$ is independent, that is, autonomous and compositional. Similarly, $\mathcal{J}^a$ is autonomous and noncompositional while $\mathcal{J}^c$ is nonautonomous but compositional.

Finally, let us look at these concepts for bigrammars. If a bigrammar is autonomous then it is possible to define an extensional variant of the form $\langle \Omega, \mathcal{I}^\varepsilon_\circ, \mathcal{I}^\mu_\circ\rangle$ where $\mathcal{I}^\varepsilon_\circ(f)$ is total for every f. Namely, observe that there is a function g on exponents such that

$$\mathcal{I}^\varepsilon(f)(\vec{\sigma}) = g(e_0, \cdots, e_{\Omega(f)-1}). \tag{3.49}$$

Choose a total extension $g_\circ \supseteq g$.

$$\begin{aligned} \mathcal{I}^{\varepsilon}_{\circ}(f)(\vec{\sigma}) &:= g_{\circ}(e_0, \cdots, e_{\Omega(f)-1}) \\ \mathcal{I}^{\mu}_{\circ}(f) &:= \mathcal{I}^{\mu}(f) \restriction \mathrm{dom}(\mathcal{I}^{\varepsilon}(f)) \end{aligned} \tag{3.50}$$

Then $\mathcal{I}^{\varepsilon}_{\circ}(f)(\vec{\sigma})$ is defined if and only if $\vec{\sigma} \in \mathrm{dom}(\mathcal{I}^{\mu}_{\circ}(f)) = \mathrm{dom}(\mathcal{I}^{\varepsilon}(f)) \cap \mathrm{dom}(\mathcal{I}^{\mu}(f))$. And in this case

$$\begin{aligned} \langle \mathcal{I}^{\varepsilon}_{\circ}(f)(\vec{\sigma}), \mathcal{I}^{\mu}_{\circ}(f)(\vec{\sigma})\rangle &= \langle g_{\circ}(\vec{e}), \mathcal{I}^{\mu}(f)(\vec{\sigma})\rangle \\ &= \langle g(\vec{e}), \mathcal{I}^{\mu}(f)(\vec{\sigma})\rangle \\ &= \langle \mathcal{I}^{\varepsilon}(f)(\vec{\sigma}), \mathcal{I}^{\mu}(f)(\vec{\sigma})\rangle \end{aligned} \tag{3.51}$$

Example 3.7 From a grammar we can construct two bigrammars where the partiality is only in one component: one where all the exponent functions are total and another where the semantic functions are total. With a bit of luck the first grammar is autonomous and the second compositional. Here is an example. Let $A := \{\mathsf{a}\}$, $E := A^*$; $M := \mathbb{N}$. The signature is $\{f_0, f_1, f_2\}$, with f_0 zeroary and f_1 and f_2 both unary.

$$\begin{aligned} \mathcal{I}(f_0)() &:= \langle \varepsilon, 0\rangle \\ \mathcal{I}(f_1)(\langle \vec{x}, n\rangle) &:= \langle \vec{x}^\frown\mathsf{a}, n+1\rangle \\ \mathcal{I}(f_2)(\langle \vec{x}, n\rangle) &:= \begin{cases} \langle \vec{x}^\frown\mathsf{a}, n\rangle & \text{if } |\vec{x}| = n, \\ \text{undefined} & \text{else.} \end{cases} \end{aligned} \tag{3.52}$$

The definite terms are of the form $f_1^n f_0$ or $f_1^m f_2 f_1^n f_0$. The first bigrammar is as follows.

$$\begin{aligned} \mathcal{I}^{\ltimes}_{\varepsilon}(f_1)(\langle \vec{x}, n\rangle) &:= \vec{x}^\frown\mathsf{a} \\ \mathcal{I}^{\ltimes}_{\varepsilon}(f_2)(\langle \vec{x}, n\rangle) &:= \begin{cases} \vec{x}^\frown\mathsf{a} & \text{if } |\vec{x}| = n, \\ \text{undefined} & \text{else.} \end{cases} \end{aligned} \tag{3.53}$$

$$\begin{aligned} \mathcal{I}^{\ltimes}_{\mu}(f_1)(\langle \vec{x}, n\rangle) &:= n+1 \\ \mathcal{I}^{\ltimes}_{\mu}(f_2)(\langle \vec{x}, n\rangle) &:= n \end{aligned} \tag{3.54}$$

The second bigrammar is as follows.

$$\begin{aligned} \mathcal{I}^{\rtimes}_{\varepsilon}(f_1)(\langle \vec{x}, n\rangle) &:= \vec{x}^\frown\mathsf{a} \\ \mathcal{I}^{\rtimes}_{\varepsilon}(f_2)(\langle \vec{x}, n\rangle) &:= \vec{x}^\frown\mathsf{a} \end{aligned} \tag{3.55}$$

$$\begin{aligned} \mathcal{I}^{\rtimes}_{\mu}(f_1)(\langle \vec{x}, n\rangle) &:= n+1 \\ \mathcal{I}^{\rtimes}_{\mu}(f_2)(\langle \vec{x}, n\rangle) &:= \begin{cases} n & \text{if } |\vec{x}| = n, \\ \text{undefined} & \text{else.} \end{cases} \end{aligned} \tag{3.56}$$

The grammar $G^{\ltimes}$ is compositional but only semiautonomous; the grammar $G^{\rtimes}$ is autonomous but only semicompositional. The reason is this. In $G^{\ltimes}$ the functions $\mathcal{I}^{\ltimes}_{\mu}(f_i)$ do not depend on the exponent, they are total and always yield a unique value. On the other hand, $\mathcal{I}^{\ltimes}_{\varepsilon}(f_2)$ weakly depends on the meaning:

$$\mathcal{I}^{\ltimes}_{\varepsilon}(f_2)(\langle \texttt{aaa}, 2\rangle) \text{ is undefined,} \qquad \mathcal{I}^{\ltimes}_{\varepsilon}(f_2)(\langle \texttt{aaa}, 3\rangle) = \texttt{aaaa}. \tag{3.57}$$

Thus $G^{\ltimes}$ is indeed semiautonomous but compositional. Likewise for the other claim. However, it turns out that there is no bigrammar corresponding to G that is both autonomous and compositional. To see this, suppose $G^{\bowtie} = \langle \Omega, \mathcal{I}^{\bowtie}_{\varepsilon}, \mathcal{I}^{\bowtie}_{\mu}\rangle$ is such a grammar. Then for any given string $\vec{x}$ there is some n (namely $|\vec{x}|$) such that $\mathcal{I}^{\bowtie}_{\varepsilon}(f_2)(\langle \vec{x}, n\rangle)$ is defined. If the grammar is autonomous this means that for all m $\mathcal{I}^{\bowtie}_{\varepsilon}(f_2)(\langle \vec{x}, m\rangle)$ is defined. Hence the function $\mathcal{I}^{\bowtie}_{\varepsilon}(f_2)$ is total. Likewise we see that $\mathcal{I}^{\bowtie}_{\mu}(f_2)$ is total. It follows that $\mathrm{dom}(\mathcal{I}^{\bowtie}(f_2)) = \mathrm{dom}(\mathcal{I}(f_2))$ equals $E \times M$. But this is not the case in G. ⚽

The independence of form and meaning has interesting consequences also for the assessment of arguments concerning generative capacity. Both examples concern the problem whether or not there is copying in syntax.

Example 3.8 This and the next example deal with the problem of reduplication. In Malay, the plural of a noun is formed by reduplication: /`orang`/ means "man", /`orang-orang`/ means "men" (see also the discussion on page 52). Thus, the plural mode p in Malay is a unary mode and is interpreted as follows.

$$\mathcal{I}(p)(\langle e, m\rangle) := \begin{cases} \langle e^\frown\texttt{-}^\frown e, \mathsf{pl}'(m)\rangle & \text{if } e \text{ is a singular noun,} \\ \text{undefined} & \text{otherwise.} \end{cases} \tag{3.58}$$

Under this interpretation, there is a plural morpheme with no fixed exponent; the exponent of the morpheme depends on whatever the singular is. If Malay works like this, then the grammar is not context free in the sense that it has non context free rules. An alternative view however is to assume that Malay has a binary operation q with the following interpretation.

$$\mathcal{I}(q)(\langle e, m\rangle, \langle e', m'\rangle) := \begin{cases} \langle e^\frown\texttt{-}^\frown e', \mathsf{pl}'(m)\rangle & \text{if } e \text{ and } e' \text{ are nouns} \\ & \quad \text{and } e = e', \\ \text{undefined} & \text{otherwise.} \end{cases} \tag{3.59}$$

This means that each occurrence of the singular form is a true occurrence of a constituent. A third account is this. Malay has a binary mode r defined by

$$\mathcal{I}(r)(\langle e, m\rangle, \langle e', m'\rangle) := \begin{cases} \langle e^\frown\texttt{-}^\frown e', \mathsf{pl}'(m)\rangle & \text{if } e \text{ and } e' \text{ are nouns} \\ & \quad \text{and } m = m', \\ \text{undefined} & \text{otherwise.} \end{cases} \tag{3.60}$$

This looks similar to q but the difference is that the combinatorial restrictions are now semantic and syntactic rather than only syntactic. This has repercussions on how powerful we believe the syntax of Malay is. If we think Malay uses p then the syntax uses nonlinear polynomials, hence cannot be approximated by what is known as linear context free rewrite systems (LCFRS). If we think that Malay uses q then our theory is that the syntax is an LCFRS, even context free, since the number of nouns is finite. However, performing the substitution tests will reveal that there are as many form classes as there are nouns. Finally, if we think that Malay uses r we think that the syntax is context free *and* that there is essentially only one noun class. It is not easy to distinguish between these alternatives. Only if Malay has two nouns e and e' with identical meaning can we check whether Malay uses p, q or r (though it is in principle also possible to treat exceptions with extra modes as well). ⚽

The previous discussion uses grammars but it is clear how the bigrammars in question should be constructed.

Example 3.9 Manaster-Ramer (1986) discuss a construction of English in which a constituent is repeated verbatim:

`The North Koreans were developing nuclear weapons anyway, Iraq war or no Iraq war.` (3.61)

`*The North Koreans were developing nuclear weapons anyway, Iraq war or no Afghanistan war.` (3.62)

The meaning is something like: "independent of", "irrespective of". As Manaster-Ramer claims, the construction has the form $/\vec{x}$ `or no` $\vec{x}/$, where $\vec{x}$ is an NP (determinerless!). The construction $/\vec{x}$ `or no` $\vec{y}/$ where $\vec{x}$ and $\vec{y}$ are different does not have this meaning. On this basis, Manaster-Ramer argues that English is not context free. Basically, the idea is that there is a unary mode f defined as follows.

$$\mathcal{I}(f)(\langle e, m\rangle) := \begin{cases} \langle e^\frown\text{␣or␣no␣}^\frown e, \textsf{irrespective-of}'(m)\rangle & \text{if } e \text{ is an NP,} \\ \text{undefined} & \text{otherwise.} \end{cases} \qquad (3.63)$$

I put aside the alternative with a binary operation that checks for string identity. This construction is called the "X-or-no-X construction" by Pullum and Rawlins (2007). They observe that the second part of it need not be an exact copy. They take this as evidence that this is not a requirement imposed by the syntax but a semantic requirement. So the construction takes the form $/\vec{x}$ `or no` $\vec{y}/$, where $\vec{x}$ and $\vec{y}$ may be different but must be synonymous. I shall leave the issue of nonidentity aside and focus on the following point. What Pullum and Rawlins (2007) propose is that rather than checking syntactic identity, English works with a binary mode g defined by

$$\mathcal{I}(f)(\langle e, m\rangle, \langle e', m'\rangle) := \begin{cases} \langle e^\frown\text{␣or␣no␣}^\frown e, & \text{if } e, e' \text{ are NP} \\ \quad \textsf{irrespective-of}'(m)\rangle & \quad \text{and } m = m', \\ \text{undefined} & \text{otherwise.} \end{cases} \tag{3.64}$$

The problem is reminiscent of reduplication discussed earlier. Although Pullum and Rawlins (2007) show that the resulting language is not context free, their argument makes clear that there are two notions of generative capacity involved. One is the purely syntactic capacity and the other is the capacity to generate signs. Given a bigrammar $\langle \Omega, \mathcal{I}^\varepsilon, \mathcal{I}^\mu\rangle$ we may either look at the language generated by $\langle \Omega, \mathcal{I}^\varepsilon_*\rangle$ (pure syntax), or we may look at the language $\varepsilon[L(G)]$. The first is the set of all syntactically well-formed sentences, the second the set of all syntactically *and* semantically well-formed sentences.

The two analyses are not identical empirically. Suppose namely we have expressions that are synonymous for all we know (say /`Abelian group`/ and /`commutative group`/ then the two proposals make different claims about grammaticality. If syntactic identity is the key then using the expression

`Abelian group or no commutative group` (3.65)

cannot mean "irrespective of an abelian group", whereas if semantic identity counted, this would be perfect. I have not investigated this, though. ⚽

Under the assumption of independence it is possible to extend some of the results of formal language theory to the present setting. I give an instructive example. A CF string language has the following property:

Lemma 3.1 (Pumping Lemma) *Let L be a context free string language. Then there exists a number* c_L*, such that for every* $\vec{x} \in L$ *of length at least* c_L *there are strings* $\vec{u}, \vec{v}, \vec{w}, \vec{y}, \vec{z}$ *such that*

1. $\vec{x} = \vec{u}\,\vec{y}\,\vec{v}\,\vec{z}\,\vec{w}$;
2. $\vec{x}\,\vec{y} \neq \varepsilon$;
3. *for all* $n \in \mathbb{N}$: $\vec{u}\,\vec{y}^n\,\vec{v}\,\vec{z}^n\,\vec{w} \in L$.

For a proof see among others (Harrison, 1978). This theorem has many strengthenings and all of them could be used in its place below. To be able to state the extension properly, we need to look at two different equivalence relations induced by a bigrammar $\langle \Omega, \mathcal{I}^\varepsilon, \mathcal{I}^\mu\rangle$. Recall from Definition 2.23 the definition of a categorial equivalence. The first is the equivalence $\sim_{G^\varepsilon}$, where $G^\varepsilon := \langle G, \mathcal{I}^\varepsilon \times 1\rangle$, where $1(f)$ gives a unit value for every input (and is always defined). This equivalence relation gives rise to the syntactic categories only. Another is the equivalence $\sim_G$, induced by G itself. It is defined in the same way as Definition 2.23, the only difference being that the definition is applied to a bigrammar. We say that G is **syntactically well regimented** if $\sim_G = \sim_{G^\varepsilon}$. Intuitively, if a grammar is syntactically well regimented then the combinability of signs can be determined by looking at the exponents alone (which does *not* mean that the semantic functions have to be total). Or, $\mathcal{I}(f)(\vec{\sigma})$ is defined if only $\mathcal{I}^\varepsilon(f)(\vec{e})$ is defined.

Theorem 3.1 *Let L be an interpreted language that has a syntactically well regimented CF bigrammar. Then there is a c_L such that for all $\langle \vec{x}, m\rangle \in L$ where $\vec{x}$ has length of at least c_L there are strings $\vec{u}, \vec{v}, \vec{w}, \vec{y}, \vec{z}$, an element $n \in M$ and unary partial functions f, g on M such that*

1. $\langle \vec{x}, m\rangle = \langle \vec{u}\,\vec{y}\,\vec{v}\,\vec{z}\,\vec{w},\ f(p)\rangle$;
2. $\vec{x}\,\vec{y} \neq \varepsilon$;
3. *for all* $n \in \mathbb{N}$: $\langle \vec{u}\,\vec{y}^n\,\vec{v}\,\vec{z}^n\,\vec{w},\ f(g^n(p))\rangle \in L$.

The proof of the theorem proceeds basically in the same way as the proof of the original Pumping Lemma. Given a string $\vec{x}$ we find a decomposition of the string; furthermore, we know that the decomposition is in terms of constituents. In other words, we have terms $r(x_0)$, $s(x_0)$ and a constant term t such that

1. $\vec{x} = r^{\varepsilon}(s^{\varepsilon}(t^{\varepsilon}))$,
2. $\vec{y}\,\vec{v}\,\vec{z} = s^{\varepsilon}(t^{\varepsilon})$,
3. $\vec{v} = t^{\varepsilon}$.

Put $p := t^{\mu}$, $g(x_0) := s^{\mu}(x_0)$, and $f(x_0) := r^{\mu}(x_0)$. This defines the functions. The assumption of syntactic well regimentedness allows us to conclude that since the terms $r(s^n(t))$ are all orthographically definite, they are also semantically definite. Hence we have

$$\iota_G(r(s^n(t))) = \langle \vec{u}\vec{y}^n\vec{v}\vec{z}^n\vec{w},\ f(g^n(p))\rangle \in L. \tag{3.66}$$

Example 3.10 The assumption of the syntactic well regimentedness cannot be dropped. Here is an example. Let $E := \mathsf{v}^*$. According to Thue (1914) there is an infinite word $w_0w_1w_2\cdots$ over $\{\mathsf{a}, \mathsf{b}, \mathsf{c}\}$ such that no finite subword is immediately repeated. Let $M := \{w_0w_1\cdots w_{n-1} : n \in \mathbb{N}\}$. Our language is $\{\langle \mathsf{v}^n, w_0w_1\cdots w_{n-1}\rangle : n \in \mathbb{N}\}$. Here is a CF bigrammar for it: $\Omega(f_a) = \Omega(f_b) = \Omega(f_c) = 1$ and $\Omega(p) = 0$. The functions are defined as follows:

$$\begin{array}{llll}
\mathcal{I}^{\varepsilon}_*(p)() & := \varepsilon & \mathcal{I}^{\mu}(p)() & := \varepsilon \\
\mathcal{I}^{\varepsilon}_*(f_a)(\vec{x}) & := \vec{x}^\frown\mathsf{v} & \mathcal{I}^{\mu}_*(f_a)(\vec{x}) & := \begin{cases} \vec{x}^\frown\mathsf{a} & \text{if } \vec{x}^\frown\mathsf{a} \in M, \\ \text{undefined} & \text{else.} \end{cases} \\
\mathcal{I}^{\varepsilon}_*(f_b)(\vec{x}) & := \vec{x}^\frown\mathsf{v} & \mathcal{I}^{\mu}_*(f_b)(\vec{x}) & := \begin{cases} \vec{x}^\frown\mathsf{b} & \text{if } \vec{x}^\frown\mathsf{b} \in M, \\ \text{undefined} & \text{else.} \end{cases} \\
\mathcal{I}^{\varepsilon}_*(f_c)(\vec{x}) & := \vec{x}^\frown\mathsf{v} & \mathcal{I}^{\mu}_*(f_c)(\vec{x}) & := \begin{cases} \vec{x}^\frown\mathsf{c} & \text{if } \vec{x}^\frown\mathsf{c} \in M, \\ \text{undefined} & \text{else.} \end{cases}
\end{array} \tag{3.67}$$

Suppose that the assertion of Theorem 3.1 holds for L. Then with the notation as in the theorem we would have

$$\sigma := \langle \vec{u}\,\vec{y}^2\,\vec{v}\,\vec{z}^2\,\vec{w},\ f(g^2(p))\rangle \in L. \tag{3.68}$$

However, $g(\vec{x}) = \vec{x}\,\vec{e}$ for some string $\vec{e}$; and $f(\vec{x}) = \vec{x}\,\vec{q}$ for some $\vec{q}$. So, $f(g^2(p)) = p\,\vec{e}\,\vec{e}\,\vec{q}$. By assumption $\sigma \notin L$, since no string can repeat itself in a string from M. ⊛

The success of the previous counterexample rested in the fact that the same syntactic function is split into different semantic functions. I conjecture that if this were not the case Theorem 3.1 will also hold for L even if the grammar is not assumed to be syntactically well regimented. I simply conjecture that it can be shown that the grammar has that property anyway. This would constitute a case where the notions of compositionality based on identity of functions might actually be relevant. If compositionality is based on extensional identity of syntactic functions (see page 60) then Theorem 3.1 might hold without the assumption of syntactic well regimentedness. However, this still awaits proof.

I stress again that the diverse pumping lemmata discussed in the literature can be generalized to interpreted languages in the same way (Ogden's Lemma, the strengthened form of Manaster-Ramer, Moshier, and Zeitman (1992), the lemmata for simple literal movement grammars, see Groenink (1997) and so on). This is simply because they are all based on the identification of constituents, which are meaningful units of the language.

Exercise 3.5 Show how to generate the language of Example 3.7 using an independent grammar.

Exercise 3.6 Suppose that $L \subseteq E \times M$ is an unambiguous countable interpreted language. Show that L is extensionally autonomous. Show that the result holds also if we assume that there is a number k such that for every $e \in E$ there are at most k many m with $\langle e, m\rangle \in L$.

Exercise 3.7 Suppose that L is a monophone countable interpreted language. Show that L is extensionally compositional. *Note.* Show that if G is defined only on the signs from L, G is already extensionally compositional.

Exercise 3.8 Suppose that $L \subseteq E \times M$ is a countable interpreted language which is a partial bijection between E and M. Then L is independent.

Exercise 3.9 Let $L \subseteq E \times M$ be a language such that $\varepsilon[L]$ is finite. Show that L is independent. (Similarly, show that L is independent if $\mu[L]$ is finite.)

Exercise 3.10 The following exercise points at some algebraic connections. I refer to Appendix A for basic algebraic concepts. Let E and M be given. Given a signature Ω, we can think of a grammar as a partial Ω-algebra $\mathfrak{G} = \langle E \times M, I\rangle$. Now show the following. (a) G is autonomous if and only if the map ε is a homomorphism from $\mathfrak{G}$ onto some algebra $\mathfrak{E} = \langle E, J\rangle$ of exponents; can you identify the functions $J(f)$? (b) G is compositional if and only if μ is a homomorphism from $\mathfrak{G}$ onto some algebra $\langle M, K\rangle$ of meanings. Can you identify $K(f)$? *Hint.* (b) is dual to (a).

Exercise 3.11 (Continuing the previous exercise.) Show that if a bigrammar is independent then the algebra of signs that it generates is a direct product of its algebra of exponents and its algebra of meanings.

3.4 Categories

Following the tradition in linguistics, I have assumed in Kracht (2003) that signs are triples $\sigma = \langle e, c, m\rangle$, with e the exponent, m the meaning and c the **category** of σ. This is in line with Keenan and Stabler (2001), Pollard and Sag (1994), Mel'čuk (1993–2000), not to mention Categorial Grammar, for which categories are essential, and even recent LFG, which assumes a level of m-structures in addition to c-structure (syntax) and f-structure (semantics) and even a-structure (to deal with argument handling), see Falk (2001). However, from an abstract viewpoint we must ask if categories are really necessary. After all, each level that is added introduces new degrees of freedom and new ways to outplay restrictions in other levels. And, to add to that the categories are actually not directly observable. Chomsky (1993) assumes that language relates form with meaning. Whatever this says in practice for Generative Grammar (and in practice the syntactic categories reappear in the form part), the initial hypothesis is the same: start with a set of signs that contain only form and meaning. I am inclined to view categories as basically encoding restrictions that are the result of partiality in the operations (see Kracht (2006)). So, we can in principle do without them but they make the formulation somewhat more transparent. For example, in a context free grammar rather than making the string concatenation partial we may say that on the level of exponents there is only one function, concatenation, which is not partial; and that the partiality arises in the categories only. It turns out, though, that one needs to be extremely cautious in thinking that the different formulations are exactly the same. Time and again it appears that they are only the same in "normal" circumstances and that counterexamples to their equivalence exist. This section will elaborate on the theme of categories and prove some results only to abandon them later. One result is that in case the set of signs contains only finitely many categories they can be eliminated (Theorem 3.2), though we may be forced to pay a price.

The formal details are as follows. A **c-sign** is a triple $\gamma = \langle e, c, m\rangle$. The space of c-signs is a product $E \times C \times M$. The projections will be denoted as follows.

$$\varepsilon(\langle e, c, m\rangle) := e, \qquad \kappa(\langle e, c, m\rangle) := c, \qquad \mu(\langle e, c, m\rangle) := m. \tag{3.69}$$

Put $H := \varepsilon \times \mu$, that is,

$$H(\gamma) := \langle e, m\rangle. \tag{3.70}$$

A **c-language** is a set of c-signs. A **c-grammar** consists in a signature of modes $\langle F, \Omega\rangle$ plus an interpretation function $\mathcal{C}$, which for given f returns a partial function $(E \times C \times M)^{\Omega(f)} \hookrightarrow (E \times C \times M)$. As before, the concept we shall be working with is slightly different.

Definition 3.8 A **trigrammar** over $E \times C \times M$ is a quadruple $\langle \Omega, \mathcal{I}^{\varepsilon}, \mathcal{I}^{\kappa}, \mathcal{I}^{\mu}\rangle$, where Ω is a signature and $\mathcal{I}^{\varepsilon}(f) : (E \times C \times M)^{\Omega(f)} \to E$ an interpretation of f in E, $\mathcal{I}^{\kappa}(f) : (E \times C \times M)^{\Omega(f)} \to C$ an interpretation of f in C and $\mathcal{I}^{\mu}(f) : (E \times C \times M)^{\Omega(f)} \to M$ an interpretation of f in M.

From a trigrammar we form the corresponding c-grammar by putting

$$G_{\times} := \langle \Omega, \mathcal{I}^{\varepsilon} \times \mathcal{I}^{\kappa} \times \mathcal{I}^{\mu} \rangle. \tag{3.71}$$

The **c-language** of G, $L(G)$, is the set of c-signs generated by this grammar. This is defined inductively in the usual way.

A trigrammar is **autonomous** if the exponent of $\mathcal{I}(f)(\vec{\sigma})$ is strongly independent of the categories and meanings of the input signs; it is **compositional** if the meaning of $\mathcal{I}(f)(\vec{\sigma})$ is strongly independent of the exponent and category of the input signs. In addition to the notions of autonomy and compositionality we now have a third notion, which I call **categorial autonomy**. It says that the category of $\mathcal{I}(f)(\vec{\sigma})$ is strongly independent of the exponents and the meanings of the input signs. The trigrammar is **independent** if it is autonomous, compositional and categorially autonomous. In case of independence we can exchange the functions f^{ε}, f^{κ}, f^{μ} by their reductions $f^{\varepsilon}_{*} : E^{\Omega(f)} \to E$, $f^{\kappa}_{*} : C^{\Omega(f)} \to C$, $f^{\mu}_{*} : M^{\Omega(f)} \to M$, which are obtained by removing the other components.

Let $L = L(G)$ for some trigrammar G. The H-image of L is

$$\begin{aligned} H[L] &:= \{H(\gamma) : \gamma \in L\} \\ &= \{\langle e, m\rangle : \text{there is } c \in C : \langle e, c, m\rangle \in L\}. \end{aligned} \tag{3.72}$$

The question is whether there is an interpreted grammar for $H[L]$.

Theorem 3.2 *Let $G = \langle \Omega, \mathcal{C}\rangle$ be a c-grammar such that $L = L(G) \subseteq E \times C \times M$ for some finite C. Then there exists an interpreted grammar K such that $L(K) = H[L]$.*

Proof Let $\langle F, \Omega\rangle$ be the signature of G. For a natural number i let F_i be the set of f such that $\Omega(f) = i$. Define

$$F_n^{+} := \{f_{\vec{c}} : f \in F_n, \vec{c} \in C^n\}. \tag{3.73}$$

For example

$$\begin{aligned} F_0^{+} &= \{f_{\langle\rangle} : f \in F_0\}, \\ F_1^{+} &:= \{f_{\langle c\rangle} : f \in F_1, c \in C\}, \\ F_2^{+} &:= \{f_{\langle c,c'\rangle} : f \in F_2, c, c' \in C\}. \end{aligned} \tag{3.74}$$

As for the signature, we put

$$\Omega^{+}(f_{\vec{c}}) := \Omega(f). \tag{3.75}$$

We define the actions of the functions over this signature.

$$\begin{aligned}\mathcal{I}(f_{c_0,c_1,\cdots,c_{n-1}})(\langle e_0, m_0\rangle, \langle e_1, m_1\rangle, \cdots, \langle e_{n-1}, m_{n-1}\rangle)\\ := H(\mathcal{C}(f)(\langle e_0, c_0, m_0\rangle, \langle e_1, c_1, m_1\rangle, \cdots, \langle e_{n-1}, c_{n-1}, m_{n-1}\rangle))\end{aligned} \tag{3.76}$$

This can also be written as follows. Put $\sigma_i := \langle e_i, c_i, m_i\rangle$. Then

$$\mathcal{I}(f_{\vec{c}})(H(\sigma_0), H(\sigma_1), \cdots, H(\sigma_{n-1})) := H(\mathcal{C}(f)(\sigma_0, \sigma_1, \cdots, \sigma_{n-1})). \tag{3.77}$$

Here the left-hand side is defined if and only if the right-hand side is; and in this case the left-hand side is defined to be whatever the right-hand side is. This defines the grammar $K := \langle \Omega, \mathcal{I}\rangle$.

We shall show that $L(K) = H[L]$. First: $L(K) \supseteq H[L(G)]$. To this effect, let $\sigma \in L(G)$. We show that $H(\sigma) \in L(K)$. By assumption, there is a term t in the signature Ω such that $\iota_G(t) = \sigma$. We shall construct a term t^+ by induction on t and show that $\iota_K(t^+) = H(\iota_G(t)) = H(\sigma)$. Base case. $t = f$, where f is a constant. Then $f^+ := f_{\langle\rangle}$. Now, $\iota_K(f^+) = H(\iota_G(f))$, by construction. Inductive case. $t = f s_0 s_1 \cdots s_{n-1}$. $\Omega(f) = n > 0$. Let $\iota_G(s_i) = \langle e_i, c_i, m_i\rangle$. By induction hypothesis, for every $i < n$ there is a term s_i^+ such that $\iota_K\left(s_i^+\right) = H(\iota_G(s_i))$. Then $\mathcal{C}(f)$ is defined on the $\iota_G(s_i)$ and therefore $\mathcal{I}(f_{c_0,c_1,\cdots,c_{n-1}})$ is defined on $\langle e_i, m_i\rangle = \iota_K\left(s_i^+\right)$ and yields the value

$$\begin{aligned}\iota_K(t^+) &= \mathcal{I}(f_{\vec{c}})\left(\iota_K\left(s_0^+\right), \iota_K\left(s_1^+\right), \cdots, \iota_K\left(s_{n-1}^+\right)\right)\\ &= \mathcal{I}(f_{\vec{c}})(\langle e_0, m_0\rangle, \cdots, \langle e_{n-1}, m_{n-1}\rangle))\\ &= H(\mathcal{C}(f)(\langle e_0, c_0, m_0\rangle, \cdots, \langle e_{n-1}, c_{n-1}, m_{n-1}\rangle))\\ &= H(\mathcal{C}(f)(\iota_G(s_0), \iota_G(s_1), \cdots, \iota_G(s_{n-1})))\\ &= H(\iota_G(t))\\ &= H(\sigma)\end{aligned} \tag{3.78}$$

Second: $L(K) \subseteq H[L]$. Let $\sigma \in L(K)$. Then there is a term t such that $\iota_K(t) = \sigma$. Put t^- as follows:

$$(f_{\vec{c}} s_0 \cdots s_{\Omega(f)-1})^- := f s_0^- s_1^- \cdots s_{\Omega(f)-1}^-. \tag{3.79}$$

In particular, $(f_{\langle\rangle})^- = f$. We shall show that $H(\iota_G(t^-)) = \iota_K(t)$; for then put $\gamma := \iota_G(t^-)$. It follows that $H(\gamma) = \sigma$. The remaining proof is by induction on t. Base case. $\Omega(f_{\vec{c}}) = 0$. In this case $H(\iota_G(t^-)) = \iota_K(t)$, by definition. Inductive case. $n := \Omega(f) > 0$. Let $\iota_G\left(s_i^-\right) = c_i$ and $\vec{c} = \langle c_0, c_1, \cdots, c_{n-1}\rangle$. Then, using (3.77):

$$\begin{aligned}
H(\iota_G(t^-)) &= H\big(\iota_G\big(f s_0^- \cdots s_{n-1}^-\big)\big) \\
&= H\big(\mathcal{C}(f)\big(\iota_G\big(s_0^-\big), \cdots, \iota_G\big(s_{n-1}^-\big)\big)\big) \\
&= \mathcal{I}(f_{\vec{c}})\big(H\big(\iota_G\big(s_0^-\big)\big), H\big(\iota_G\big(s_1^-\big)\big), \cdots, H\big(\iota_G\big(s_{n-1}^-\big)\big)\big) \\
&= \mathcal{I}(f_{\vec{c}})(\iota_K(s_0), \iota_K(s_1), \cdots, \iota_K(s_{n-1})) \\
&= \iota_K(t)
\end{aligned} \tag{3.80}$$

This had to be shown. □

We shall write $H(G)$ for the grammar K, for future reference. Notice that the base cases are actually redundant in both parts; they are covered by the induction step!

This result is of some significance. It says that the categories are redundant. More precisely, they can be removed from the signs at the cost of introducing more modes of composition. The proof is completely general; it uses no assumptions on the grammar. This applies to CFGs but there are other cases too. Categorial grammars in principle use an infinite number of categories. However, mostly only a finite number of them is needed in a particular grammar. It may well be that the lexicon allows to produce only finitely many categories in any case. Such is the case in the Ajdukiewicz-Bar Hillel Calculus. The Lambek-Calculus is different in that we can create and use infinitely many categories (for example, if we have the product then we can form arbitrarily long categories). However, given that the Lambek-Calculus yields a context free language (see Pentus (1997)) it therefore enjoys a formulation using no categories whatsoever, by the above theorem.

It is worth pointing out why this theorem is actually not trivial. Suppose that a language has nouns and verbs and that these word classes are morphologically distinct. Suppose further that there are roots that can be used as nouns and verbs. English is such a language. Here are examples: /`dust`/, /`walk`/, /`leak`/ and so on, are examples of words that can be either nouns or verbs. Dictionaries see the matter as follows: the word /`leak`/ can be both a noun and a verb; if it is a noun it means something, say m, if it is a verb it means something else, say $\hat{m}$. Thus, dictionaries use categories; they say that the language contains two signs: ⟨`leak`, n, m⟩ and ⟨`leak`, v, $\hat{m}$⟩. For example, according to the Shorter Oxford English Dictionary (Onions, 1973), /`leak`/ as a verb means: "(1) to pass (*out*, *away*, *forth*) by a leak or leakage. (2) To let fluid pass in or out through a leak." The noun has this meaning "(1) A hole or fissure in a vessel containing or immersed in a fluid, which lets the fluid pass in or out of the vessel [...] (2) action of leaking or leakage." These two meanings are clearly distinct. The latter is a physical object (hole) while the former is a process.

If we eliminate the categories, we are left with the signs ⟨`leak`, m⟩ and ⟨`leak`, $\hat{m}$⟩. It seems that vital information is lost, namely that /`leak`/ means m *only if it is a noun*, and likewise that it means $\hat{m}$ *only if it is a verb*. On the other hand, we still know that /`leak`/ means m and $\hat{m}$. If we perform the construction above, the following will happen. The function that forms the past tense applies to the sign ⟨`leak`, v, $\hat{m}$⟩ but not to the sign ⟨`leak`, n, m⟩. It is the interpretation of some mode

f. This mode is now replaced among others by a mode f_v, which takes as input only the sign $\langle \texttt{leak}, \hat{m}\rangle$ and forms the sign $\langle \texttt{leaked}, \mathsf{past}'(\hat{m})\rangle$. It is not defined on $\langle \texttt{leak}, m\rangle$. Similarly the other functions are described.

Notice that the elimination of categories results in a redistribution of grammatical knowledge. The morphological (or syntactic) information is placed elsewhere. It used to be encoded in the categories of the signs. Now it is encoded in the domain of the newly introduced functions. For example, the domain of the function f_v forming the past tense of verbs is the set of pairs $\langle \vec{x}, m\rangle$ where $\vec{x}$ is a root and m the verbal meaning of that root. It is undefined on $\langle \vec{y}, m\rangle$ if $\vec{y}$ cannot be a verbal root or otherwise does not have the meaning m; it is not defined on $\langle \vec{x}, \hat{m}\rangle$ if $\hat{m}$ is not a meaning of the verbal root $\vec{x}$.

Although categories *can* be eliminated, this does not mean that they *should* be eliminated. One reason is purely practical: in evaluating a term, the computation may be much easier if we carried along category information, since the categories can be made to fit the partial nature of the functions. This is quite clear in Categorial Grammar, for example, which employs something that may be dubbed categorial well-regimentation; it means that the categories alone can tell whether a term is definite. To see whether a mode applies to certain signs it is enough to check the categories. If we used the above definition, we would have to recompute the category of the signs over and over. Additionally, we shall show below that the elimination of categories can have the effect of removing desirable properties from the grammar. Hence it may be desirable to keep the format in the usual way; it is however essential to know that categories are theoretically redundant.

As I just said, eliminating categories might come at a price. For example, we might lose compositionality of the grammar. To define compositionality for c-languages, we simply repeat Definition 3.5 almost verbatim. The following example now shows that compositionality and autonomy can be lost under reduction.

Example 3.11 Our example is based on the grammar of Example 3.7. We introduce a set $C = \{o, p\}$ of categories. For any given triple $\langle e, c, m\rangle$ we define

$$
\begin{aligned}
\mathcal{K}(f_1)(\langle e, c, m\rangle) &:= \begin{cases} \langle e^\frown \mathtt{a}, p, m+1\rangle & \text{if } c = p, \\ \text{undefined} & \text{else.} \end{cases} \\
\mathcal{K}(f_2)(\langle e, c, m\rangle) &:= \begin{cases} \langle e^\frown \mathtt{a}, o, m\rangle & \text{if } c = p, \\ \text{undefined} & \text{else.} \end{cases}
\end{aligned}
\tag{3.81}
$$

From this grammar we can define the following independent trigrammar. Let $(f_i)^\varepsilon_*(e) := e^\frown \mathtt{a}$, $(f_1)^\mu_*(m) := m + 1$, $(f_2)^\mu_*(m) := m$ and, finally, $(f_1)^\kappa : p \mapsto p, o \mapsto \downarrow$ (= undefined), $(f_2)^\kappa : p \mapsto o, o \mapsto \downarrow$. Call this trigrammar K. K is independent, its reduction via H is not; it also is neither autonomous (only extensionally autonomous) nor compositional (only extensionally compositional). For the reduction is exactly the grammar of Example 3.7. ⚽

Nevertheless, it is also possible to establish a positive result. Let L be a language. Say that it allows to **guess categories** if the following holds. There are functions

$p : E \to \wp(C)$ and $q : M \to \wp(C)$ such that if $\langle e, c, m\rangle \in L$ then $p(e) \cap q(m) = \{c\}$ and that if $\langle e, c, m\rangle \notin L$ then $p(e) \cap q(m) = \varnothing$. This means that if e and m are given then c is unique; and moreover, what can be inferred from e by itself and by m itself is enough to guess c.

Proposition 3.2 *Let L be an independent c-language that allows to guess categories. Suppose further that L has only finitely many categories. Then $H[L]$ is independent.*

Proof Let $p : E \to \wp(C)$ and $q : M \to \wp(C)$ be the guessing functions. Let G be an independent c-grammar for L. By assumption, for every mode f there are three functions f_*^ε, f_*^κ and f_*^μ such that

$$\begin{aligned}&\mathcal{I}(f)(\langle e_0, c_0, m_0\rangle, \cdots, \langle e_{n-1}, c_{n-1}, m_{n-1}\rangle)\\&\qquad = \langle f_*^\varepsilon(e_0, \cdots, e_{n-1}), f_*^\kappa(c_0, \cdots, c_{n-1}), f_*^\mu(m_0, \cdots, m_{n-1})\rangle.\end{aligned} \tag{3.82}$$

Proceed as in the proof of Theorem 3.2. We create modes of the form $f_{\vec{c}}$, where $\vec{c}$ is a sequence of categories of length $\Omega(f)$. Pick an n-ary mode. If $n = 0$ and $\mathcal{I}(f)() = \langle e, c, m\rangle$ let $\mathcal{I}(f_{\langle\rangle})() := \langle e, m\rangle$. Now suppose that $n > 0$. For each n-ary sequence of elements from C we introduce a new mode $f_{\vec{c}}$. We set

$$(f_{\vec{c}})^\varepsilon(e_0, \cdots, e_{n-1}) := \begin{cases} f_*^\varepsilon(e_0, \cdots, e_{n-1}) & \text{if for every } i < n\text{: } c_i \in p(e_i) \\ & \quad \text{and } f_*^\kappa(\vec{c}) \text{ is defined,} \\ \text{undefined} & \text{else.}\end{cases} \tag{3.83}$$

Likewise we put

$$(f_{\vec{c}})_*^\mu(m_0, \cdots, m_{n-1}) := \begin{cases} f_*^\mu(m_0, \cdots, m_{n-1}) & \text{if for every } i < n\text{: } c_i \in q(m_i) \\ & \quad \text{and } f_*^\kappa(\vec{c}) \text{ is defined,} \\ \text{undefined} & \text{else.}\end{cases} \tag{3.84}$$

This defines the grammar G^+ over the signature Ω^+. We show the following claim by induction over the length of the term: (a) if $\langle e, m\rangle$ is the value of a term t of length n then for the unique c such that $\langle e, c, m\rangle \in L$, $\langle e, c, m\rangle$ is the value of t^-; (b) if $\langle e, c, m\rangle$ is the value of a term t of length n then $\langle e, m\rangle$ is the value of some term u such that $u^- = t$. This will then establish the claim. Notice first that (a) is straightforward by construction, so we need to establish (b). For length 0 claim (b) is certainly true. Now let $t = f(u_0, \cdots, u_{n-1})$, where $n = \Omega(f)$, and let $\langle e_i, m_i\rangle$, $i < n$, be the value of u_i. Note right away that by assumption on L there can be only one such sequence and hence the set is either empty (no new sign generated) or contains exactly one member (by independence of the modes). Suppose first that for some $j < n$ there is no c such that $\langle e_j, c, m_j\rangle \in L$. Thus $p(e_j) \cap q(m_j) = \varnothing$. Then for every sequence $\vec{c}$ either $f_{\vec{c}}^\varepsilon(e_0, \cdots, e_{n-1})$ or $f_{\vec{c}}^\mu(m_0, \cdots, m_{n-1})$ is undefined. Hence none of the functions

$\mathcal{I}(f_{\vec{c}})$ are applicable on this input. Now suppose that for every i there is a g_i such that $\langle e_i, g_i, m_i\rangle \in L$. We have terms u_i^+ such that $\langle e_i, g_i, m_i\rangle$ is the value of u_i^+ for $i < n$. Then for $\vec{g} := \langle g_0, \cdots, g_{n-1}\rangle$ both $f_{\vec{g}}^{\varepsilon}(e_0, \cdots, e_{n-1})$ and $f_{\vec{g}}^{\mu}(m_0, \cdots, m_{n-1})$ are defined and they equal $f_*^{\varepsilon}(e_0, \cdots, e_{n-1})$ and $f_*^{\mu}(m_0, \cdots, m_{n-1})$, respectively. Since $f_*^{\kappa}(g_0, \cdots, g_{n-1})$ is also defined (by definition of the functions $f_{\vec{g}}^{\varepsilon}$ and $f_{\vec{g}}^{\mu}$) the following value exists:

$$\langle f_*^{\varepsilon}(e_0, \cdots, e_{n-1}), f_*^{\kappa}(g_0, \cdots, g_{n-1}), f_*^{\mu}(m_0, \cdots, m_{n-1})\rangle. \tag{3.85}$$

This is the value of $f_{\vec{g}}\left(u_0^+, \cdots, u_{n-1}^+\right)$, as is easily seen. (If $\vec{c} \neq \vec{g}$ then either of the functions $f_{\vec{c}}^{\varepsilon}(e_0, \cdots, e_{n-1})$ and $f_{\vec{c}}^{\mu}(m_0, \cdots, m_{n-1})$ is undefined). □

We close this section by some considerations concerning linguistic theories. First, the notion of a grammar as opposed to a bigrammar has the drawback of not distinguishing between syntactically well-formed input and semantically well-formed input. Or, to phrase this in the technical language of this book, in a grammar a term is semantically definite if and only if it is orthographically definite. It has a semantics if and only if it has an exponent. By using bigrammars we make these two notions independent. However, as much as this might be desirable, it creates problems of its own. For now we have to decide which of the components is to be blamed for the fact that a term has no value. We can see to it that it is the syntax, or we can see to it that it is the semantics. If we add categories, there is a third possibility, namely to have a term whose category does not exist. Linguistic theories differ in the way they handle the situation. Categorial Grammar is designed to be such that if a term is indefinite then it is categorially indefinite. That means, as long as a term has a category, it is also syntactically and semantically definite. This is *not* to say that there are no semantically indefinite terms. To the contrary, it was based on typed λ-calculus, so there were plenty of semantically ill-formed terms. But every time a term is semantically ill-formed it would automatically be categorially ill-formed. In LFG, each level has its own well-formedness conditions, so that one tries to explain the complexity of the output by factoring out which level is responsible for which output phenomenon. The theory is *modular*.

In Generative Grammar there is no separate level of categories. Technically, the syntax operates before semantics. Syntax operates autonomously from semantics. In the present formulation this just means that the syntactic functions do not respond to changes in the meaning (whence the name *autonomy* above). However, in our formulation there is no order in the way the terms are checked. The components of the complex sign are formed in parallel.

3.5 Weak and Strong Generative Capacity

Say that two CFGs G and G' are *weakly equivalent* if they generate the same string language; and that they are *strongly equivalent* if they assign the same structure to the strings. The question arises what we think to be the structure of the sentence.

It turns out that "same structure" depends on personal conviction. It could be, for example, identical topology over the string, or identical tree structure, so that only relabelling is allowed. (See Miller (1999) for an excellent discussion.) Typically, it is assumed that structure means tree structure. To say that a language is strongly context free is to assume that the language is given as a set of labelled (ordered) trees. It is not enough to just consider sets of strings.

In standard linguistic literature it is assumed that syntactic structure is independent of semantic structure. Of course this is an illusion, for all tests assume that when we manipulate certain sentences syntactically we are also manipulating their semantics. For example, when we consider whether /can/ is a noun and we coordinate it with, say, /tray/ to get /can and tray/, we are assuming that we are dealing with it under the same semantics that we have chosen initially (/can/ in the sense of metal object, not the auxiliary). And this should show in the semantics of the coordinate expression. Hence, no syntactic test really can be performed without a semantics. Hence, we shall in this section pursue a different route to "structure", namely this: we shall explore the idea that structure is in fact epiphenomenal, driven by the need to establish a compositional grammar for the language.

We have defined the associated string language $\varepsilon[L]$ of an interpreted language to be the set of all strings that have a meaning in L. We can likewise define for a grammar G the associated string grammar G^{ε}, which consists just in the functions f^{ε} for $f \in F$. Since f^{ε} may depend on the meanings of the input signs, this makes immediate sense only for an autonomous bigrammar. Recall that for such a grammar the functions f_*^{ε} are defined on $E^{\Omega(f)}$ with values in E. Even in this case, however, it may happen that $L(G^{\varepsilon}) \neq \varepsilon[L]$ precisely because there might be terms that are orthographically but not semantically definite. (In general, only $\varepsilon[L] \subseteq L(G^{\varepsilon})$ holds.)

Recall from previous discussions that in grammars the domains of f^{μ} and f^{ε} are identical. In this case some of the distinctions that are of interest in this section cannot be made, such as the distinction between weak dependency of f^{ε} on exponents and the weak dependency of f^{μ} on the exponents. Therefore, in this chapter we shall discuss bigrammars and not grammars. Recall also from Section 2.3 the discussion of context freeness. There we have defined context freeness of a string grammar intrinsically. The results in this section use the term the "context free" in this sense. The results are often more general, applying to concatenative grammars as well. I occasionally point out where results can be generalized.

Definition 3.9 Let L be an interpreted language and $\mathcal{C}$ a class of string grammars. L is **weakly** $\mathcal{C}$ if the associated string language $\varepsilon[L]$ has a grammar in $\mathcal{C}$. L is $\mathcal{C}$ if it has a weakly autonomous bigrammar whose associated string grammar is in $\mathcal{C}$. L is **autonomously** $\mathcal{C}$ if it has a strongly autonomous bigrammar whose associated string grammar is in $\mathcal{C}$.

Example 3.12 An example of an interpreted language that is weakly but not autonomously CF. Let

$$L := \left\{ \langle \mathtt{a}^n, i \rangle : n \in \mathbb{N}, i < 2^{2^n} \right\}. \tag{3.86}$$

Given a string $\vec{x}$ of length n the number of terms that unfold to $\vec{x}$ is at most exponential in n. This means that there is a number p such that if $|\vec{x}| = n$ then the number of parses is bounded by 2^{pn}, provided that n exceeds some number k. This means that the number of meanings for the string $\vec{x}$ cannot exceed 2^{pn}, if $k < n$. However, in L $\vec{x}$ has 2^{2^n} meanings and for all n such that $2^n > p$ we have $2^{2^n} > 2^{pn}$. ⚽

Theorem 3.3 *Let L be unambiguous. Then if L is weakly $\mathcal{C}$ it is also autonomously $\mathcal{C}$.*

Proof By assumption, there is a function $b : E \to M$ such that $\langle e, m\rangle \in L$ iff $m = b(e)$ (in set theory, L *is* that function b). Also, by assumption there is a string grammar $G = \langle \Omega, \mathcal{I}\rangle$ for $\varepsilon[L]$, which is in $\mathcal{C}$. Now put

$$\begin{aligned}\mathcal{I}^{\varepsilon}(f)(\langle e_0, m_0\rangle, \cdots, \langle e_{\Omega(f)n-1}, m_{\Omega(f)-1}\rangle) &:= \mathcal{I}(f)(e_0, \cdots, e_{\Omega(f)-1}) \\ \mathcal{I}^{\mu}(f)(\langle e_0, m_0\rangle, \cdots, \langle e_{\Omega(f)-1}, m_{\Omega(f)-1}\rangle) &:= b(\mathcal{I}(f)(e_0, \cdots, e_{\Omega(f)-1}))\end{aligned} \tag{3.87}$$

The bigrammar $G^+ := \langle \Omega, \mathcal{I}^{\varepsilon}, \mathcal{I}^{\mu}\rangle$ is obviously strongly autonomous. Moreover, it generates L. By construction, if it generates $\langle e, m\rangle$ then (1) $e \in L(G) = E$ and (2) $m = b(e)$. Moreover, if $\langle e, m\rangle \in L$ then $m = b(e)$ and $e \in L(G)$. It follows that $\langle e, m\rangle \in L(G^+)$. □

We can strengthen this as follows.

Theorem 3.4 *Let L be unambiguous and monophone. Then if L is weakly $\mathcal{C}$ it is also strongly $\mathcal{C}$.*

Proof By the previous theorem, L is autonomous. So f_*^{ε} is independent of the meanings. The art is in defining the semantic functions. By assumption, choosing $E := \varepsilon[L]$ and $M := \mu[L]$, there is a bijection $\pi : E \to M$ such that $L = \{\langle e, \pi(e)\rangle : e \in \varepsilon[L]\}$. With the help of this bijection put

$$f_*^{\mu}(m_0, \cdots, m_{\Omega(f)-1}) := \pi\left(f_*^{\varepsilon}\left(\pi^{-1}(m_0), \cdots, \pi^{-1}(m_{\Omega(f)-1})\right)\right). \tag{3.88}$$

This defines a grammar that is compositional. □

Notice that most interesting languages fail to be monophone. Hence the notions based on string grammars are not as interesting as they appear. A more interesting notion is provided by restricting the set of grammars to weakly independent bigrammars. In this case the semantic functions are required to act independently of the string functions. This means that the added semantic functions must give a unique value independently of the strings. It is however possible to tailor the *domain* of the semantic functions using the exponents. If the latter option is unavailable, we talk of superstrong generative capacity. It means that the semantic functions do not need to see the exponents nor even know when they should be undefined.

Definition 3.10 Let L be a language and $\mathcal{C}$ a class of string grammars. L is **strongly** $\mathcal{C}$ if it has a weakly independent bigrammar whose associated string grammar is in $\mathcal{C}$. L is **superstrongly** $\mathcal{C}$ if it has an independent bigrammar whose associated string grammar is in $\mathcal{C}$.

We shall see below an example of a language that is weakly CF but neither superstrongly nor strongly CF and an example of a language that is strongly CF but not superstrongly CF. Notice that by definition CFGs are strongly autonomous, so the distinction between strong and superstrong turns on the possibility to have a weakly compositional or compositional CFG, respectively.

Example 3.13 (See also Janssen (1997).) This example shows that weakly equivalent grammar classes may not be strongly equivalent. A CFG G is **left regular** if it only has rules of the form $A \to Bx$, $A \to \varepsilon$, or $A \to x$, A and B nonterminals and x a terminal symbol. G is **right regular** if it only has rules of the form $A \to xB$, $A \to \varepsilon$ or $A \to x$, A and B nonterminals and x a terminal symbol. Let $\mathcal{CL}$ be the class of left regular grammars and $\mathcal{CR}$ the class of right regular grammars. The language we look at is the language of binary strings and their ordinary denotations: $A := \{\mathtt{0}, \mathtt{L}\}$. For nonempty $\vec{x} \in A^*$ we put

$$\begin{aligned} n(\mathtt{0}) &:= 0 \\ n(\mathtt{L}) &:= 1 \\ n(\vec{x}\mathtt{0}) &:= 2n(\vec{x}) \\ n(\vec{x}\mathtt{L}) &:= 2n(\vec{x}) + 1 \end{aligned} \tag{3.89}$$

Finally,

$$L := \{\langle \vec{x}, n(\vec{x})\rangle : \vec{x} \in A^+\}. \tag{3.90}$$

This language is weakly left regular and weakly right regular. It is super strongly left regular but not strongly right regular. Here is a left regular strongly autonomous bigrammar (couched as a grammar). $F := \{f_0, f_1, f_2, f_3\}$, $\Omega(f_0) = \Omega(f_1) = 0$, $\Omega(f_2) = \Omega(f_3) = 1$.

$$\begin{aligned} \mathcal{I}(f_0)() &:= \langle \mathtt{0}, 0\rangle \\ \mathcal{I}(f_1)() &:= \langle \mathtt{L}, 1\rangle \\ \mathcal{I}(f_2)(\langle \vec{x}, n\rangle) &:= \langle \vec{x}^\frown\mathtt{0}, 2n\rangle \\ \mathcal{I}(f_3)(\langle \vec{x}, n\rangle) &:= \langle \vec{x}^\frown\mathtt{L}, 2n+1\rangle \end{aligned} \tag{3.91}$$

There is however no independent right regular bigrammar for this language. Suppose to the contrary that there is such a bigrammar. It has zeroary functions (to reflect the terminal rules) and unary functions. The latter reflect the nonterminal rules. Hence, they must have the form

$$f^\varepsilon(\langle \vec{x}, n\rangle) = \vec{y}^\frown\vec{x} \tag{3.92}$$

where $\vec{y}$ is a single symbol.

I now give a combinatorial argument that is worth remembering. Consider the following strings:

$$\mathtt{L0}, \mathtt{L00}, \mathtt{L000}, \mathtt{L0000}, \cdots \tag{3.93}$$

These strings must be obtained by adding /L/ to a string consisting in zeroes. We do not know which function is responsible for adding the /L/ in the individual cases (we may have any number of modes) but what we do know is that there is one mode f such that $\mathcal{I}(f)$ creates two of them, say /L000/ and /L0000000/. By definition, it creates them from the strings /000/ and /0000000/, respectively. Now, these strings have the same meaning, namely 0. If the grammar is compositional, f^μ is independent of the exponent. However, we must now have $f^\mu(0) = 8$, as well as $f^\mu(0) = 128$, a contradiction.

$$\begin{aligned} \mathcal{I}(f)(\langle 000, 0\rangle) &= \langle \mathrm{L000}, 8\rangle &&= \langle f^\varepsilon(000), f^\mu(0)\rangle \\ \mathcal{I}(f)(\langle 0000000, 0\rangle) &= \langle \mathrm{L0000000}, 128\rangle &&= \langle f^\varepsilon(0000000), f^\mu(0)\rangle \end{aligned} \tag{3.94}$$

⚽

This argument is pretty robust, it precludes a number of strategies. For example, making syntactic or semantic functions partial will obviously not improve matters.

The example is useful also because it shows the following. Suppose that $\mathcal{C}$ and $\mathcal{D}$ are classes of string grammars such that every string language that is $\mathcal{C}$ is also $\mathcal{D}$. Then it does not necessarily hold that a language that is superstrongly $\mathcal{C}$ is also superstrongly $\mathcal{D}$. For in the above example, we have two classes of grammars that generate the same set of string languages but they are not identical when it comes to interpreted languages.

The proof in the previous example is somewhat less satisfying since CFGs also use categories, though it works in this case as well. In order to include categories we have to switch to c-languages. We shall not introduce special terminology here to keep matters simple. Basically, if L is a language of c-signs it is called weakly CF if the associated string language is CF. It is called CF if there is an independent c-grammar for it whose string *and* category part taken together is CF.

Example 3.14 We continue Example 3.13. Given the same language L we show that there is no independent right regular c-language L' whose projection to $A^* \times M$ is L. This is to say, allowing *any* classification L' of string-meaning pairs into finitely many categories, there is no independent right regular c-grammar for L'. The argument is basically the same. We look at unary functions. If f is unary, it has the form

$$\mathcal{I}(\langle \vec{x}, \gamma, n\rangle) = \langle f_*^\varepsilon(\vec{x}), f_*^\kappa(\gamma), f_*^\mu(n)\rangle \tag{3.95}$$

for some f_*^ε, f_*^κ and f_*^μ. Furthermore, $f_*^\varepsilon(\vec{x}) = \vec{y}^\frown\vec{x}$. Look at the signs $\sigma_p := \langle \mathrm{L0}^p, \gamma_p, 2^p\rangle$ ($p \in \mathbb{N}$). Let t_p be an analysis term of σ_p. Either $t_p = f$ for some zeroary f, or $t_p = fs_p$ for some unary f. In the latter case, $f_*^\varepsilon(\vec{x}) = \mathrm{L0}^k{}^\frown\vec{x}$ for some k that depends only on f and so s_p unfolds to $\langle 0^{p-k}, \delta_p, 0\rangle$. Now we look at f_*^μ. We have $f_*^\mu(0) = 2^p$. It follows that if $q \neq p$ then t_q does not have the form fs_q. There are however only finitely many functions. ⚽

Notice that for the argument to work we did not have to assume that there are only finitely many categories. For the argument requires only (weak!) independence of the meaning functions from the exponents and the categories.

Example 3.15 An example to show that strong and superstrong CF languages are distinct. Consider the number expressions of English. We may for simplicity assume that the highest simple numeral is /million/. To keep this example small we add just the following words: /one/, /ten/, /hundred/, /thousand/. It will be easy to expand the grammar to the full language. Number expressions are of the following kind: they are nonempty sequences

$$\vec{x}_0{}^\frown(\texttt{million}_\sqcup)^{p_0}{}^\frown\vec{x}_1{}^\frown(\texttt{million}_\sqcup)^{p_1}{}^\frown\cdots{}^\frown(\vec{x}_{n-1}{}^\frown\texttt{million}_\sqcup)^{p_{n-1}} \tag{3.96}$$

where $p_0 > p_1 > \cdots > p_{n-1}$ and the $\vec{x}_i$ are expressions not using /million/, which are nonempty sequences of the following form.

$$\begin{aligned}((\texttt{one}_\sqcup \mid \texttt{ten}_\sqcup \mid \texttt{one}_\sqcup\texttt{hundred}_\sqcup)\texttt{thousand}_\sqcup)?\\ (\texttt{one}_\sqcup \mid \texttt{ten}_\sqcup \mid \texttt{one}_\sqcup\texttt{hundred}_\sqcup)?\end{aligned} \tag{3.97}$$

This language is not weakly CF. It does not satisfy the Pumping Lemma (see Exercise 3.13). It can therefore not be superstrongly CF. However, it is strongly CF. Here is a grammar for it. Call a **block** an expression containing /million/ only at the end. Say that $\vec{x}$ is **m-free** if it does not contain any occurrences of /million/ and that it is **t-free** if it is m-free and does not contain any occurrences of /thousand/. The grammar is given in Table 3.1. It has two modes of composition: "additive" concatenation and "multiplicative" concatenation. Since the language is unambiguous,

Table 3.1 Number names

$$\mathcal{I}(f_0)() := \langle\texttt{one}, 1\rangle$$
$$\mathcal{I}(f_1)() := \langle\texttt{ten}, 10\rangle$$
$$\mathcal{I}(f_2)() := \langle\texttt{hundred}, 100\rangle$$
$$\mathcal{I}(f_3)() := \langle\texttt{thousand}, 1000\rangle$$
$$\mathcal{I}(f_4)() := \langle\texttt{million}, 1,000,000\rangle$$

$$\mathcal{I}(a)(\langle\vec{x}, m\rangle, \langle\vec{y}, n\rangle) := \begin{cases} \langle\vec{x}^\frown{}_\sqcup{}^\frown\vec{y}, m+n\rangle & \text{if } \vec{x} \text{ is a block and } m > n \\ & \text{or } \vec{x} \text{ m-free but not t-free,} \\ & \quad \text{and } \vec{y} \text{ is t-free,} \\ \text{undefined} & \text{else.} \end{cases}$$

$$\mathcal{I}(m)(\langle\vec{x}, m\rangle, \langle\vec{y}, n\rangle) := \begin{cases} \langle\vec{x}^\frown{}_\sqcup{}^\frown\vec{y}, mn\rangle & \text{if } \vec{x} \text{ is a block and } \vec{y} = \texttt{million} \\ & \text{or } \vec{x} = \texttt{one} \text{ and} \\ & \quad \vec{y} = \texttt{hundred}, \texttt{thousand} \\ & \text{or } \vec{x} = \texttt{one}_\sqcup\texttt{hundred}, \\ & \quad \vec{y} = \texttt{thousand}, \\ \text{undefined} & \text{else.} \end{cases}$$

we can formulate a bigrammar using string functions that are total and semantic functions that are partial. Now define

> $A(\vec{x}, \vec{y}, m, n)$ if and only if either (a) $\vec{x}$ is a block and $m > n$ or (b) $\vec{x}$ is m-free but not t-free and $\vec{y}$ is t-free.

Also define

> $B(\vec{x}, \vec{y}, m, n)$ if and only if either (a) $\vec{x}$ is a block and $\vec{y}$ = `million` or (b) $\vec{x}$ = one and $\vec{y} \in$ {`hundred`, `thousand`} or (c) $\vec{x}$ = one␣`hundred` and $\vec{y}$ = `thousand`. (See Fig. 3.1).

Then define the modes as follows.

$$\begin{aligned}
a^{\varepsilon}(\langle\vec{x}, m\rangle, \langle\vec{y}, n\rangle) &:= \vec{x}^{\frown}\text{␣}^{\frown}\vec{y} \\
a^{\mu}(\langle\vec{x}, m\rangle, \langle\vec{y}, n\rangle) &:= \begin{cases} m+n & \text{if } A(\vec{x}, \vec{y}, m, n), \\ \text{undefined} & \text{else.} \end{cases} \\
m^{\varepsilon}(\langle\vec{x}, m\rangle, \langle\vec{y}, n\rangle) &:= \vec{x}^{\frown}\text{␣}^{\frown}\vec{y} \\
m^{\mu}(\langle\vec{x}, m\rangle, \langle\vec{y}, n\rangle) &:= \begin{cases} mn & \text{if } B(\vec{x}, \vec{y}, m, n), \\ \text{undefined} & \text{else.} \end{cases}
\end{aligned} \tag{3.98}$$

Thus, the semantic functions are weakly independent of the exponents but not strongly independent.

Variations can be played on this theme. First, if we introduce the word /`zero`/ and allow the use of expressions such as /`zero`␣(`million`␣)^k/ then the semantic condition "$m > n$" in $A(\vec{x}, \vec{y}, m, n)$ must be replaced by a syntactic condition involving the number k. In this case we may however say that the semantic functions are total while the syntactic functions are restricted and so the language is not really CF. ⚽

Example 3.16 Here is another example, see Radzinski (1990). In Chinese, yes-no questions are formed by iterating the VP. I reproduce the syntax of Chinese in English. To ask whether John went to the shop you say

`John went to the shop not went to the shop?` (3.99)

The recipe is this. Given a subject $\vec{x}$ and a VP $\vec{y}$, the yes-no question is formed like this

$$\vec{x}\text{␣}\vec{y}\text{␣}\texttt{not}\text{␣}\vec{y}\texttt{?} \tag{3.100}$$

The data for Chinese are not without problems but I shall ignore the empirical complications here and pretend that the above characterization is exact. One analysis proceeds via copying. An alternative analysis is the following. Observe that in Chinese, disjunctive statements are formed like this. To say that subject $\vec{x}$ $\vec{y}$s or $\vec{z}$s you may simply say

$$\vec{x}\text{␣}\vec{y}\text{␣}\vec{z}\texttt{.} \tag{3.101}$$

In particular, a disjunction between $\vec{y}$ and *not* $\vec{z}$ is expressed like this:

$$\vec{x}\text{␣}\vec{y}\text{␣}\mathtt{not}\text{␣}\vec{z}. \tag{3.102}$$

In this case it is required that $\vec{z} \neq \vec{y}$. This suggests that we may also form the yes-no question by concatenation, which however is partial. It is possible to construct a weakly CF bigrammar but not a strongly CF one. ⚽

I shall now return to the question whether ambiguity can be removed from a language. The question is whether there is a transform of a language into an unambiguous language and how that affects the possibility of generating it with a given class of grammars. It shall emerge that there are languages that are inherently structurally ambiguous. This means the following. Given a language L that is unambiguous, every derivation of a given exponent must yield the same meaning. Thus, as one says, all structural ambiguity is *spurious*.

Definition 3.11 Let G be a grammar. A G**-ambiguity** is a pair (t, t') of nonidentical terms such that $\iota_G(t) = \langle e, m\rangle$ and $\iota_G(t') = \langle e, m'\rangle$ for some e, m and m'. In this case we call e **structurally ambiguous in** G. The ambiguity (t, t') is **spurious** if $m = m'$. Also, (t, t') is a **lexical ambiguity**, where $t \approx_0 t'$, which is defined as follows:

$$\begin{gathered} f \approx_0 g \text{ if } \Omega(f) = \Omega(g) = 0 \\ f s_0 \cdots s_{n-1} \approx_0 f t_0 \cdots t_{n-1} \text{ if } n > 0,\ f = g \text{ and } s_i \approx_0 t_i \text{ for all } i < n \end{gathered} \tag{3.103}$$

An ambiguity that is not lexical is called **structural**.

Alternatively, an ambiguity is a pair (t, u) where $t^\varepsilon = u^\varepsilon$. Let L be a language. Then define the functional transform of L in the following way. For e we put $e^\circ := \{m : \langle e, m\rangle \in L\}$.

$$L^\S := \{\langle e, e^\circ\rangle : e \in \varepsilon[L]\}. \tag{3.104}$$

The functional transform of L is such that every e has exactly one meaning, which is the (nonempty) set of meanings that e has in L.

Example 3.17 We let $A := \{\mathtt{p}, \mathtt{0}, \mathtt{1}, \neg, \wedge, \vee\}$. $F := \{f_0, f_1, f_2, f_3, f_4, f_5\}$, $\Omega(f_0) := 0$, $\Omega(f_1) := \Omega(f_2) := \Omega(f_3) := 0$, $\Omega(f_4) := \Omega(f_5) := 2$. Meanings are sets of functions from $V := \{\mathtt{0}, \mathtt{1}\}^*$ to $\{t, f\}$. We define UBool as the language generated by the following CFG G_U. For a variable $\mathtt{p}\vec{x}$, $[\mathtt{p}\vec{x}] = \{\beta : \beta(\vec{x}) = t\}$. Given $U = [\mathtt{p}\vec{x}]$, it is possible to recover $\vec{x}$. Given U, let $\dagger U$ be the unique $\vec{x}$ for which $[\vec{x}] = U$. The set of all valuations is denoted by Val.

$$\begin{aligned}
\mathcal{I}(f_0)() &:= \langle \mathtt{p}, [\varepsilon] \rangle \\
\mathcal{I}(f_1)(\langle \vec{x}, U \rangle) &:= \langle \vec{x}^\frown \mathtt{0}, [(\dagger U)^\frown \mathtt{0}] \rangle \\
\mathcal{I}(f_2)(\langle \vec{x}, U \rangle) &:= \langle \vec{x}^\frown \mathtt{1}, [(\dagger U)^\frown \mathtt{1}] \rangle \\
\mathcal{I}(f_3)(\langle \vec{x}, U \rangle) &:= \langle \neg^\frown \vec{x}, \mathrm{Val} - U \rangle \\
\mathcal{I}(f_4)(\langle \vec{x}, U \rangle, \langle \vec{y}, V \rangle) &:= \langle \vec{x}^\frown \wedge^\frown \vec{y}, V \cap U \rangle \\
\mathcal{I}(f_5)(\langle \vec{x}, U \rangle, \langle \vec{y}, V \rangle) &:= \langle \vec{x}^\frown \vee^\frown \vec{y}, V \cup U \rangle
\end{aligned} \tag{3.105}$$

Notice that this language is like natural language in being highly ambiguous: there are no brackets. Thus, the expression /¬p0∧p/ can be read in two ways: it has the analysis terms $f_3 f_4 f_1 f_0 f_0$, with negation having scope over conjunction and $f_4 f_3 f_1 f_0 f_0$, with conjunction having scope over negation. Clearly, the meanings are different. ⚽

Let us now try to see whether we can define a CFG for UBool§. We shall keep the string part of G_U from Example 3.17. Look at the strings /p$\vec{x}$∧¬p$\vec{x}$/, where $\vec{x} \in \{\mathtt{0}, \mathtt{1}\}^*$. As they are uniquely readable and they have no satisfying valuation, their meaning in UBool§ is $\{\varnothing\}$. On the other hand, /p$\vec{x}$∧¬p$\vec{x}$∨p$\vec{y}$/ has three analyses corresponding to the following bracketed strings:

$$/((\mathtt{p}\vec{x}\wedge(\neg\mathtt{p}\vec{x}))\vee\mathtt{p}\vec{y})/,\ /(\mathtt{p}\vec{x}\wedge(\neg(\mathtt{p}\vec{x}\vee\mathtt{p}\vec{y})))/,\ /(\mathtt{p}\vec{x}\wedge((\neg\mathtt{p}\vec{x})\vee\mathtt{p}\vec{y}))/ \tag{3.106}$$

Thus the meaning is $\{[\vec{y}], [\vec{x}] \cap [\vec{y}], \varnothing\}$. Let us now look at one particular analysis.

$$\mathcal{J}(f_5)(\langle \mathtt{p}\vec{x}\wedge\neg\mathtt{p}\vec{x}, \{\varnothing\}\rangle, \langle \mathtt{p}\vec{y}, [\vec{y}]\rangle) = \langle \mathtt{p}\vec{x}\wedge\neg\mathtt{p}\vec{x}\vee\mathtt{p}\vec{y}, \{[\vec{y}], [\vec{x}] \cap [\vec{y}], \varnothing\}\rangle \tag{3.107}$$

In this analysis, there are infinitely many results for this pair of inputs, so this is a case of a grammar that cannot be strongly compositional. There is a possibility, though, of making the result undefined for this analysis term. Another analysis is this.

$$\begin{aligned}
&\mathcal{J}(f_4)(\langle \mathtt{p}\vec{x}, [\vec{x}]\rangle, \langle \neg\mathtt{p}\vec{x}\vee\mathtt{p}\vec{y}, \{(\mathrm{Val} - [\vec{x}]) \cup [\vec{y}], \mathrm{Val} - ([\vec{x}] \cup [\vec{y}])]\}\rangle) \\
&\qquad = \langle \mathtt{p}\vec{x}\wedge\neg\mathtt{p}\vec{x}\vee\mathtt{p}\vec{y}, \{[\vec{y}], [\vec{x}][\vec{y}], \varnothing\}\rangle
\end{aligned} \tag{3.108}$$

Here, the arguments provide enough information to compute the result. Thus, it is conceivable that an independent grammar exists.

Notice that we have so far only shown that there can be no compositional CFG that uses the structure that the formulae ordinarily have. It is not ruled out that some unconventional structure assignment can actually work. In fact, for this language no compositional CFGs exist. As a warm-up for the proof let us observe the following. Let φ be a formula that is composed from variables using only conjunction. Then although φ may be ambiguous, all the ambiguity is spurious: it has one meaning only. It is the set of assignments that make all occurring variables true. Notice additionally that neither the order nor the multiplicity of the variables matters. Thus the following have identical meaning: /p∧p0∧p1/, /p1∧p0∧p1∧p/, /p0∧p∧p1∧p1/. Next we consider formulae of the form $\alpha\vee\varphi$, where α is a variable and φ is of the previous form. An example is /p0∨p∧p1∧p1∧p2/. We assume that α does not occur in φ and that all occurrences of the same variable are adjacent. Up to spurious ambiguity this formula has the following bracketing (conjunction binding stronger than disjunction):

$$\begin{aligned}&(\mathtt{p0\vee p\wedge p1\wedge p1\wedge p2})\\&(\mathtt{p0\vee p})\mathtt{\wedge p1\wedge p1\wedge p2}\\&(\mathtt{p0\vee p\wedge p1})\mathtt{\wedge p1\wedge p2}\\&(\mathtt{p0\vee p\wedge p1\wedge p1})\mathtt{\wedge p2}\end{aligned} \tag{3.109}$$

The general form is $(\alpha \vee \chi) \wedge \rho$, and its satisfying valuations make either $\alpha \wedge \rho$ or $\chi \wedge \rho$ true. α is a single variable. It is easy to see that it makes no difference whether a variable occurs twice or more, while it may matter whether it occurs once or twice. If υ occurs once, it has a choice to be in χ or in ρ. How often it occurs in either of them does not matter. If υ occurs twice, it may additionally occur both in χ and ρ. However, even in this case there is no difference. Assuming that υ does not occur in α, χ or ρ, here are the choices if it occurs just once:

$$(\alpha \vee \chi) \wedge \upsilon \wedge \rho, (\alpha \vee \chi \wedge \upsilon) \wedge \rho \tag{3.110}$$

Here are the choices if it occurs twice:

$$(\alpha \vee \chi) \wedge \upsilon \wedge \upsilon \wedge \rho, (\alpha \vee \chi \wedge \upsilon) \wedge \upsilon \wedge \rho, (\alpha \vee \chi \wedge \upsilon \wedge \upsilon) \wedge \rho. \tag{3.111}$$

The first reading of (3.111) is the same as the first reading of (3.110), the last reading of (3.111) the same as the last reading of (3.110). The middle reading is synonymous with the first. (This argument requires χ to be nonempty.) For the purpose of the next theorem say that a bigrammar $\langle \Omega, \mathcal{I}^{\varepsilon}, \mathcal{I}^{\mu}\rangle$ is a concatenation bigrammar if $\langle \Omega, \mathcal{I}^{\varepsilon}_{*}\rangle$ is a concatenation grammar. (Notice that the meaning functions can be partial, too and that their partiality is not counted in the definition, since we take the string reduct of the grammar.)

Theorem 3.5 UBool§ *has no independent concatenation bigrammar. Hence,* UBool§ *is not strongly CF and also not superstrongly CF.*

Proof The proof will establish that there is no strongly independent concatenative grammar that has no syncategorematic symbols. We leave the rest of the proof to the reader. The grammar uses the alphabet of the language, the meanings as specified and a set C of categories. The functions on the exponents are total. Partiality exists in the semantics. It will emerge from the proof, however, that introducing partiality will not improve the situation. We shall show that for given n there is an exponential number of formulae that have to be derived from a polynomially bounded family of formulae via a one step application. This is impossible. If the modes are partial, this remains impossible since it gives us less definite terms not more. Superstrongly CFGs do not allow any dependency of the meaning on the strings. Thus, for every mode f and $\sigma_i = \langle e_i, m_i \rangle$, $i < \Omega(f)$, we have

$$\mathcal{I}(f)(\sigma_0, \cdots, \sigma_{\Omega(f)-1}) = \langle f^{\varepsilon}(e_0, \cdots, e_{\Omega(f)-1}), f^{\mu}(\sigma_0, \cdots, \sigma_{\Omega(f)-1}) \rangle. \tag{3.112}$$

Let us look at the following kinds of expressions, where $V = \mathbf{p}(\mathbf{0} \mid \mathbf{1})^*$ is the set of variables:

$$V \vee (V \wedge)^+ V \vee V \tag{3.113}$$

For ease of understanding, we shall first ignore the internal structure of variables and present them as units. The more concrete structure of our formulae is as follows, in ordinary notation:

$$\varphi = p_0 \vee p_2 \wedge p_4(\wedge p_4) \wedge p_5(\wedge p_5) \cdots p_{n+3}(\wedge p_{n+3}) \wedge p_3 \vee p_1 \tag{3.114}$$

Let us say that φ has a **cut** at i if the letter p_i is repeated twice. Let I be the set of indices i such that p_i occurs in φ; let R be a subset of I. Then by φ_R denote the formula that is like φ having a cut exactly at those i that are in R. We show first the following claim.

Claim. Let $R, S \subseteq [4, n+3] = [4, 5, \cdots, n+3]$. If $R \neq S$ then the meaning of φ_R in UBool§ is different from that of φ_S.

Let us look at the possible readings of such a formula. Pick a variable $v = p_i$. Bracketings are of several forms.

The first set is where the scopes of the disjunctions are nested: we consider the case where the first disjunct takes scope over the second (the other case is dual). (Here, $\wedge$ binds stronger than $\vee$. γ_1 may be empty; δ_2 may not be.)

(Form 1) $(p_0 \vee \gamma_1 \wedge (\gamma_2 \wedge p_i \wedge \delta \vee p_1))$ or $(p_0 \vee \gamma_1 \wedge (\gamma_2 \wedge p_i \wedge p_i \wedge \delta \vee p_1))$
(Form 2) $(p_0 \vee \gamma \wedge p_i \wedge \delta_1 \wedge (\delta_2 \vee p_1))$ or $(p_0 \vee \gamma \wedge p_i \wedge p_i \wedge \delta_1 \wedge (\delta_2 \vee p_1))$
(Form 3) $(p_0 \vee \gamma \wedge p_i \wedge (p_i \wedge \delta \vee p_1))$

The two variants of Form (1) and (2) are equivalent. Form (3) is equivalent with Form (2) with $\delta = \delta_2$. Let us now consider the case where the scopes of the disjunction signs do not intersect. We get the following list of forms, where it is assumed that γ, δ_1 and δ_2 do not contain p_i.

(Form A) $(p_0 \vee \gamma \wedge p_i) \wedge \delta_1 \wedge (\delta_2 \vee p_1)$ or $(p_0 \vee \gamma \wedge p_i \wedge p_i) \wedge \delta_1 \wedge (\delta_2 \vee p_1)$;
(Form B) $(p_0 \vee \gamma_1) \wedge \gamma_2 \wedge (p_i \wedge \delta \vee p_1)$ or $(p_0 \vee \gamma_1) \wedge \gamma_2 \wedge (p_i \wedge p_i \wedge \delta \vee p_1)$;
(Form C) $(p_0 \vee \gamma_1) \wedge \gamma_2 \wedge p_i \wedge \delta_1 \wedge (\delta_2 \vee p_1)$
or $(p_0 \vee \gamma_1) \wedge \gamma_2 \wedge p_i \wedge p_i \wedge \delta_1 \wedge (\delta_2 \vee p_1)$;

(Form D) $(p_0 \vee \gamma_1) \wedge \gamma_2 \wedge p_i \wedge (p_i \wedge \delta \vee p_1)$;
(Form E) $(p_0 \vee \gamma \wedge p_i) \wedge p_i \wedge \delta_1 \wedge (\delta_2 \vee p_1)$; and
(Form F) $(p_0 \vee \gamma \wedge p_i) \wedge (p_i \wedge \delta \vee p_1)$.

(We allow δ_i and γ_j to be empty.) The two variants of Forms (A), (B) and (C) are equivalent. Forms (D), (E) and (F) only exist if the formula has a cut at i. Thus, it is enough if we show that one of them has no equivalent formula of either of (A), (B) and (C). It is easily seen that Form (D) is equivalent to Form (C) with $\delta_2 = \delta$. Similarly, Form (E) is equivalent to Form (C) with $\gamma_1 = \gamma$. Finally, we turn to Form (F):

$$\begin{aligned} &(p_0 \vee \gamma \wedge p_i) \wedge (p_i \wedge \delta \vee p_1) \\ = &(p_0 \wedge p_i \wedge \delta) \vee (p_0 \wedge p_1) \vee (\gamma \wedge p_i \wedge p_i \wedge \delta) \vee (\gamma \wedge p_i \wedge p_1) \end{aligned} \tag{3.115}$$

Form (F) has a disjunct of the form $p_0 \wedge p_1$. This is only the case with Forms (1) and (2), (A) with δ_1 empty and (B) with γ_2 empty. Form (F) implies $(\neg p_0) \to \gamma$, as well as $(\neg p_1) \to \delta$. In Form (1), we therefore must have $\gamma_1 = \gamma$ and in Form (2) $\delta_2 = \delta$. Form (F) implies $\neg(p_0 \wedge p_1) \to p_i$. This is not a consequence of Forms (1) and (2), (A) or (B). Thus, Form (F) is not equivalent to any of the previous forms.

It follows that if the formula has a cut at i, it has a reading different from the formula obtained by removing this cut by removing one occurrence of p_i. Now, i was completely arbitrary. Thus the claim is established.

Now consider an analysis term of φ_R. The immediate constituents of φ_R cannot contain two disjunction symbols. They can only contain one. In this case, however, the cuts present in φ_R are not reflected in the semantics. To conclude the argument, let us assume that the analysis term of φ_R is $f s_0 \cdots s_{\Omega(f)-1}$. We shall look at all possible analysis terms for the φ_S, $S \subseteq [4, n+3]$. We look at (3.112) and count how many meanings we can compose in this way. The syntactic function is total. Let k^* be the maximal arity of functions and $p := \operatorname{card} C$ the number or nonterminal symbols. Choose a decomposition into parts; each part has a meaning that is determined just by the subset of $[i, j] \subseteq [2, n+3]$ of indices for variables that occur in it (and whether or not it contains p_0, p_1). For the category there is a choice of p symbols. The meanings must exhaust the set $[2, n+3]$. They can overlap in a single number (since sometimes p_i can occur twice). There are in total at most $(2p)^{k^*}\binom{n+2}{k^*-1}$ ways to cut φ_R into maximally k^* parts of different category and different meaning. The combinations of category and meaning do not depend on R. We have

$$(2p)^{k^*}\binom{n+2}{k^*-1} < (2p(n+2))^{k^*} \tag{3.116}$$

Out of such parts we must form in total 2^n different meanings to get all the φ_S, using our modes. Assume that we have μ modes. If n is large enough, however, $\mu(2p(n+2))^{k^*} < 2^n$. □

The proof has just one gap and it consists in the question of variables. The variables cannot be simple and need to be constructed as well using some modes. It is not difficult to see that here again just a polynomial number of choices exist, too few to generate the entire number of formulae that are needed. (See also Exercise 3.14 below.)

There is an interesting further question. Consider in place of the meaning e° another one; given that meanings are propositions we can form the disjunctions of all the possible meanings.

$$\begin{aligned} e^\vee &:= \bigvee\{m : \langle e, m\rangle \in L\} \\ L^\vee &:= \{\langle e, e^\vee\rangle : e \in \varepsilon[L]\} \end{aligned} \tag{3.117}$$

This leads to the language UBool$^\vee$. It is not clear whether this language is (super)strongly CF.

Exercise 3.12 Prove Theorem 3.3. Prove that the theorem can be strengthened to languages where a string has boundedly many meanings.

Exercise 3.13 The Pumping Lemma says that if a string language L is CF then there is a number k such that for every string $\vec{x} \in L$ of length $> k$ there is a decomposition $\vec{x} = \vec{u}\vec{y}\vec{v}\vec{z}\vec{w}$ such that for all n (including $n = 0$): $\vec{u}\vec{y}^n\vec{v}\vec{z}^n\vec{w} \in L$. (See Section 3.4.) Show that the language in Example 3.15 does not satisfy the Pumping Lemma.

Exercise 3.14 Look again at UBool. Call a **formula** a string of ε[UBool] that contains /p/. (The remaining strings are **indices**.) Subformulae are (occurrences) of formulae in the ordinary sense (for example, they are the parts defined by G_U in Example 3.17). We shall gain some insight into the structure of parts of a formula. Show the following. *Let $\vec{x}$ be a formula and $\vec{y}$ be a substring that is a formula. Then there is an index $\vec{z}$ such that $\vec{y}\vec{z}$ is a subformula of $\vec{x}$.* Thus, any context free grammar that generates the set of formulae proceeds basically like G_U modulo appending some index at the end of a formula.

Exercise 3.15 Use the previous exercise to show that there is no strongly independent context free grammar avoiding syncategorematic rules for UBool§.

Exercise 3.16 Let L be a language with finite expressive power (that is, with $\mu[L]$ finite). Then if L is weakly $\mathcal{C}$, it is strongly $\mathcal{C}$. Give an example of a language that is weakly $\mathcal{C}$ but not superstrongly $\mathcal{C}$. *Remark.* For the proof to go through we need some trivial assumptions on $\mathcal{C}$. I propose to assume that membership in $\mathcal{C}$ depends only on the fact that all $\mathcal{I}(f)$ have a certain property $\mathcal{P}$.

3.6 Indeterminacy in Interpreted Grammars

This section is largely based on Kracht (2008), though the proof of the central theorem has been greatly simplified. We have considered in Section 2.4 the notion of an indeterminate grammar. I shall now pick up that theme again, fulfilling my earlier promise to show that if we are serious about compositionality then indeterminacy is not an option.

Definition 3.12 Let E and M be sets of exponents and meanings, respectively. An **indeterminate interpreted grammar over** $E \times M$ is a pair $\langle \Omega, \mathcal{I} \rangle$, where Ω is a signature and for every $f \in F, \mathcal{I}(f) \subseteq (E \times M)^{\Omega(f)+1}$. The **language** generated by G, in symbols $L(G)$, is defined to be the least set S such that for every $f \in F$ and all $\sigma_i \in E \times M, i < \Omega(f)$ and $\tau \in E \times M$:

$$\text{If for all } i < \Omega(f), \sigma_i \in S \text{ and if } \langle \sigma_0, \cdots, \sigma_{\Omega(f)-1}, \tau \rangle \in \mathcal{I}(f), \text{ then } \tau \in S. \tag{3.118}$$

This is the broadest notion, allowing to form signs from signs. Now, as before we have to replace grammars by bigrammars. The definition is completely analogous. Instead of a pair of functions f^ε and f^μ we have a pair of relations

$$\begin{aligned} f^\varepsilon &\subseteq (E \times M)^{\Omega(f)} \times E, \\ f^\mu &\subseteq (E \times M)^{\Omega(f)} \times M. \end{aligned} \tag{3.119}$$

This is called an indeterminate (interpreted) grammar. G is **autonomous** if the exponent of the output sign is independent of the meanings. We can explicate this as follows. For every f and $\sigma_i = \langle e_i, m_i \rangle$ and $\sigma_i' = \langle e_i, m_i' \rangle \in E \times M$ (where $i < \Omega(f)$)

$$\text{if } \langle \vec{\sigma}, e \rangle \in f^\varepsilon \text{ then } \langle \vec{\sigma}', e \rangle \in f^\varepsilon. \tag{3.120}$$

This can be restricted to the language generated by the grammar but we refrain from introducing too many fine distinctions. Dually, **compositionality** is defined. Let us draw some consequences. If G is indeterminate, we say that the indeterminacy of G is **semantically spurious** if for all $\sigma_i \in L(G)$, $i < \Omega(f) + 1$, if $\langle \sigma_0, \cdots, \sigma_{\Omega(f)-1}, \langle e, m \rangle \rangle \in \mathcal{I}(f)$ and $\langle \sigma_0, \cdots, \sigma_{\Omega(f)-1}, \langle e, m' \rangle \rangle \in \mathcal{I}(f)$ then $m = m'$. This means that G restricted to its own language actually has a semantically functional equivalent (the exponents may still be indeterminate even inside the language). **Syntactically spurious indeterminacy** is defined dually.

Proposition 3.3 *Let L be unambiguous and assume that G is an indeterminate interpreted grammar for L. Then the indeterminacy of G is semantically spurious.*

The proof is straightforward. If we generate two signs $\langle e, m \rangle$ and $\langle e, m' \rangle$ from the same input (in fact from any input), then $m = m'$.

Thus, G is already autonomous (at least extensionally). For an unambiguous grammar it may still be possible to write an indeterminate compositional (and hence independent) grammar. In the remainder of this section we study boolean logic and give both a positive and a negative example. Recall from Example 2.22 boolean logic in Polish Notation and the unbracketed notation as given in Example 3.17. Here we shall give yet another formulation, this time with obligatory bracketing. The details are similar to those in Example 3.17. The only difference is that the alphabet also contains the symbols /(/ and /)/ and that the formation rules insert these brackets every time a new constituent is being formed:

$$\begin{aligned}
\mathcal{I}(f_0)() &:= \langle \mathsf{p}, [\varepsilon]\rangle \\
\mathcal{I}(f_1)(\langle \vec{x}, U\rangle) &:= \langle \vec{x}^\frown \mathsf{0}, [\dagger(U)^\frown \mathsf{0}]\rangle \\
\mathcal{I}(f_2)(\langle \vec{x}, U\rangle) &:= \langle \vec{x}^\frown \mathsf{1}, [\dagger(U)^\frown \mathsf{1}]\rangle \\
\mathcal{I}(f_3)(\langle \vec{x}, U\rangle) &:= \langle (^\frown\neg^\frown\vec{x}^\frown), \mathrm{Val} - U\rangle \\
\mathcal{I}(f_4)(\langle \vec{x}, U\rangle, \langle \vec{y}, V\rangle) &:= \langle (^\frown\vec{x}^\frown\wedge^\frown\vec{y}^\frown), V \cap U\rangle \\
\mathcal{I}(f_5)(\langle \vec{x}, U\rangle, \langle \vec{y}, V\rangle) &:= \langle (^\frown\vec{x}^\frown\vee^\frown\vec{y}^\frown), V \cup U\rangle
\end{aligned} \tag{3.121}$$

We call this language Bool. This grammar defines the semantics of a formula to be a set of valuations. There is a different semantics, which is based on a particular valuation β and which is defined as follows.

$$\beta(\varphi) = \begin{cases} 1 & \text{if } \beta \in [\varphi], \\ 0 & \text{else.} \end{cases} \tag{3.122}$$

Example 3.18 Let B be the string language of boolean expressions. Pick a valuation β and let

$$L := \{\langle \varphi, \beta(\varphi)\rangle : \varphi \in B\}. \tag{3.123}$$

Consider an indeterminate string grammar $G = \langle F, \Omega\rangle$ for it, for example the grammar from Exercise 2.22. Put $F_2 := \{f^0, f^1 : f \in F\}$ and let $\Omega^2(f^0) := \Omega^2(f^1) := \Omega(f)$. Finally, put

$$\begin{aligned}
\mathcal{I}(f^0) := \{\langle\langle e_i, m_i\rangle : i < \Omega(f)+1\rangle : \langle e_i : i < \Omega(f)+1\rangle \in \mathcal{I}(f), \\
\beta(e_{\Omega(f)}) = 0, m_{\Omega(f)} = 0\}, \\
\mathcal{I}(f^1) := \{\langle\langle e_i, m_i\rangle : i < \Omega(f)+1\rangle : \langle e_i : i < \Omega(f)+1\rangle \in \mathcal{I}(f), \\
\beta(e_{\Omega(f)}) = 1, m_{\Omega(f)} = 1\}.
\end{aligned} \tag{3.124}$$

So the relations are split into two variants, where the first set contains the tuples whose last member is a formula that is true under the valuation and the second relation collects the other tuples. This is an indeterminate interpreted grammar. Call it G^2. It might be that the newly created symbols are actually interpreted by functions but this does not have to be the case. A case in point is Example 2.22, the grammar for Polish Notation. A given string of length n may possess up to n adjunction sites, thus making the resulting grammar G^2 indeterminate again. Consider for example the string /∧p∧p∧pp/. Assume that $\beta(\mathsf{p}) = 1$. Then the value of that formula is also 1. The string /∧p/ can be adjoined at several places, marked here with ∘:

$$\circ\wedge\circ\mathsf{p}\circ\wedge\circ\mathsf{p}\circ\wedge\circ\mathsf{p}\circ\mathsf{p} \tag{3.125}$$

In all cases the resulting formula has value 1 but it is clear that we do not even need to know this. There are more than two output strings, so some of them must have the same truth value. ⚽

That the semantics is finite is used essentially in the proof. The example is of course quite dissatisfying; the functions are undefined depending on what the meaning of the string is. On the other hand, there may be a way to circumvent the dependency on semantics, which is to say, the fact that the meaning figures in the definition of the functions may just be an artefact of the way we defined them. However, there are different examples to show that indeterminacy is not such a good idea.

In what is described below I shall look into the possibility of defining a compositional adjunction grammar for the language of boolean expressions, where φ has as its meaning the set of all assignments that make it true. The rest of this section is devoted to the proof of the following theorem.

Theorem 3.6 *There is no independent tree adjunction bigrammar (and hence no compositional tree adjunction grammar) for* Bool *in which all meaning functions are total.*

Independence is of course essential. Since Bool is unambiguous, there can also be no compositional grammar, for autonomy can be guaranteed at no cost: the dependency of the exponents on the meanings is eliminable since we can recover the meaning from the exponent.

Before we can embark on the proof, we have to make some preparations.

Definition 3.13 Let $L \subseteq E \times M$ be an interpreted language and $D \subseteq E$. Then $L \upharpoonright D := L \cap (D \times M)$ is the D-**fragment** of L. If $E = A^*$ and $D = B^*$ then we also write $L \upharpoonright B$ in place of $L \upharpoonright B^*$.

The case where we restrict to a subalphabet is the one that we shall use here. We shall study the following fragments of Bool:

$$\begin{aligned} \mathrm{Var} &:= \mathrm{Bool} \upharpoonright \{\mathtt{p}, \mathtt{0}, \mathtt{1}\} \\ \mathrm{Bool}^{\wedge} &:= \mathrm{Bool} \upharpoonright \{\mathtt{(}, \mathtt{)}, \mathtt{0}, \mathtt{1}, \mathtt{p}, \wedge\} \\ \mathrm{Bool}^{\neg} &:= \mathrm{Bool} \upharpoonright \{\mathtt{(}, \mathtt{)}, \mathtt{0}, \mathtt{1}, \mathtt{p}, \neg\} \end{aligned} \tag{3.126}$$

Now assume G is a grammar for L. Then for every f, let

$$\begin{aligned} f^{\varepsilon} \upharpoonright D &:= f^{\varepsilon} \restriction (D \times M) \\ f^{\mu} \upharpoonright D &:= f^{\mu} \restriction (D \times M) \end{aligned} \tag{3.127}$$

Finally,

$$f \restriction D := (f^{\varepsilon} \upharpoonright D) \times (f^{\mu} \upharpoonright D). \tag{3.128}$$

For this to be well defined we need to show that the functions stay inside $D \times M$. For a string $\vec{x}$ and a symbol a, let $\sharp_a(\vec{x})$ denote the number of occurrences of a in $\vec{x}$.

For $E = A^*$, $f : E^n \to E$ is **pseudoadditive** if for every $a \in A$: either $\sharp_a(\vec{x}_i) = 0$ for all $i < n$ and then $\sharp_a(f(\vec{x}_0, \cdots, \vec{x}_{n-1})) = 0$ or

$$\sharp_a(f(\vec{x}_0, \vec{x}_1, \cdots, \vec{x}_{n-1})) \geq \sum_{i<n} \sharp_a(\vec{x}_i). \tag{3.129}$$

If equality holds, f is called **additive**. A grammar is additive if every function is. (A combination of Structure Preservation and Syncategorematicity Prohibition guarantees additivity, actually.) Now suppose further that our grammar is additive and that $D = B^*$. Then if all the $\vec{x}_i$ are in B^*, so is $f^\varepsilon(\vec{x}_0, \cdots, \vec{x}_{n-1})$. Hence we have a grammar

$$\begin{aligned} (\mathcal{I} \upharpoonright B)(f) &:= \mathcal{I}(f) \upharpoonright B \\ G \upharpoonright B &:= \langle \Omega, \mathcal{I} \upharpoonright B \rangle \end{aligned} \tag{3.130}$$

Now, $G \upharpoonright B$ generates a subset of L, by construction. Moreover, by induction on the term t we can show that if $\iota_G(t) \in (B^* \times M)$ then $\iota_{G\upharpoonright B}(t) = \iota_G(t)$. It follows that $G \upharpoonright B$ generates *exactly* $G \upharpoonright B$.

Proposition 3.4 *Suppose that G is an additive compositional bigrammar for L. Then $G \upharpoonright B$ is an additive compositional bigrammar for $L \upharpoonright B$.*

Thus if G is an adjunction grammar so is $G \upharpoonright B$.

Example 3.19 We look in some detail at the fragment Var. Syntactically, we may generate this language by admitting adjunction anywhere except before the letter /p/. Yet, for every weakly compositional grammar G there can only be a bounded number of adjunction sites for most variables. Consider, for example, the adjunction string $\langle 1, \varepsilon \rangle$ and the variable

$$\mathtt{p000000}\cdots\mathtt{0} \tag{3.131}$$

For simplicity we fix the adjunction sites to be of the form $\langle \mathtt{p}\vec{x}, \vec{y}, \varepsilon \rangle$. Depending on $\vec{x}$ we get a different variable. Thus, for any given rule only one of the adjunction sites from $\{\langle \mathtt{p0}^m, \mathtt{0}^{k-m}, \varepsilon \rangle : m \leq k\}$ may be chosen for the rule. One way to achieve this is to only use adjunction strings of the form $\langle \vec{x}, \varepsilon \rangle$ and adjunction sites of the form $\langle \mathtt{p}, \vec{y}, \varepsilon \rangle$. ⚽

Example 3.20 Another place where caution needs to be exercised when doing adjunction is the following. Let φ be a formula consisting in variables and their negations. Suppose that φ contains a variable and its negation, as in

$$\mathtt{(p01\wedge(\neg p01))} \tag{3.132}$$

Then no valuation satisfies φ. In other words, we have $\langle\varphi, \varnothing\rangle \in$ Bool. Consider now what happens if we adjoin to one of them some string. Then one of the occurrences disappears and the formula may suddenly have valuations that satisfy it. Let us adjoin /1/, for example:

$$\texttt{(p101}\wedge\texttt{(}\neg\texttt{p01))} \tag{3.133}$$

Any valuation mapping /p101/ to 1 and /p01/ to 0 satisfies this formula. Suppose that G is compositional. (Weakness does not add anything interesting here.) As G has only boundedly many rules, there can only be boundedly many values computed from any given meaning. Thus, if G has k rules, $\text{card}(\{f^{\mu}(\varnothing) : f \in G\}) \leq k$. It follows that adjunction can target only a restricted set of contradicting variables. ⚽

Adjoining binary strings to variable names is a good case to show that the independence of syntax and semantics is actually useless for practical applications. In the case of adjoining other strings, their adjunction is actually syntactically heavily restricted, see Kracht (2008).

Let me now prove the central theorem. Assume that we have an independent adjunction bigrammar G for Bool$^{\wedge}$. Let ρ be the number of rules of G and κ be the maximum number of symbol occurrences added by any rule. A tree is called **binary** if it only contains occurrences of /0/ and /1/. Choose a formula of the following form.

$$\varphi = \texttt{(p}\vec{x}_0\wedge\texttt{(p}\vec{x}_1\wedge\texttt{(p}\vec{x}_2\cdots\wedge\texttt{p}\vec{x}_{2\rho+2}\texttt{)}\cdots\texttt{)))} \tag{3.134}$$

The length of the $\vec{x}_i$ is subject to the following restriction. (a) $|\vec{x}_i| > (2\rho + 3)\kappa$ and (b) for $i < j < 2\rho + 3$: $||\vec{x}_i| - |\vec{x}_j|| > \kappa$.

Let φ be derived by G. Then it contains at most $2\rho + 2$ occurrences of trees with symbols other than /0/ and /1/. (It is not hard to see that for every occurrence of /p/ one occurrence of /∧/, of /(/ and /)/ must be added as well and similarly for the other nonbinary symbols.) Thus, by Condition (a), each of the $\vec{x}_i$ contains occurrences added by a binary tree. Thus, in each of the variables we can somewhere adjoin a binary tree. There are $2\rho + 3$ variables. As a single adjunction can manipulate up to two variables, we have $\rho + 1$ different adjunction sites for binary trees, each manipulating a different set of variables. As we have ρ many rules, two of the adjunction sites must yield the same output semantically. (At this point totality enters; for it says that whenever adjunction is syntactically licit there is a corresponding semantic output.) Hence two of them must yield the same syntactic output. Now, adjunction at $\vec{x}_i$ can only enlarge the index by κ many symbols, which by Condition (b) does not make it the same length as any other $\vec{x}_j$, for $j \neq i$. Thus the sets of variables obtained by adjoining at different sites are different. So is their semantics. We have $\rho + 1$ sites and at most ρ different results. Contradiction.

Example 3.21 I give a letter by letter translation of Bool into English:

$$\begin{aligned} t(\mathtt{p}) &= /\mathtt{Jack\ sees\ a\ boy}/ \\ t(\mathtt{(}) &= \varepsilon \\ t(\mathtt{)}) &= \varepsilon \\ t(\mathtt{0}) &= /\mathtt{who\ sees\ a\ girl}/ \\ t(\mathtt{1}) &= /\mathtt{who\ sees\ a\ boy}/ \\ t(\wedge) &= /\mathtt{who\ sees\ no\ one\ and}/ \\ t(\vee) &= /\mathtt{who\ sees\ no\ one\ or}/ \\ t(\neg) &= /\mathtt{it\ is\ not\ the\ case\ that}/ \end{aligned} \tag{3.135}$$

Now define the functions s as follows.

$$\begin{aligned} s(\varepsilon) &:= /\mathtt{who\ sees\ no\ one.}/ \\ s(a^\frown\vec{x}) &:= t(a)^\frown\Box^\frown s(\vec{x}) \end{aligned} \tag{3.136}$$

This gives us, for example,

$$\begin{aligned} s(\mathtt{(p0\wedge(\neg p))}) = /&\mathtt{Jack\ sees\ a\ boy\ who\ sees\ a\ girl\ who\ sees} \\ &\mathtt{no\ one\ and\ it\ is\ not\ the\ case\ that} \\ &\mathtt{Jack\ sees\ a\ boy\ who\ sees\ no\ one.}/ \end{aligned} \tag{3.137}$$

Consider the set $B := \{j\} \cup \{b\vec{x} : \vec{x} \in (\mathtt{0} \mid \mathtt{1})^*\} \cup \{g\vec{x} : \vec{x} \in (\mathtt{0} \mid \mathtt{1})^*\}$. Here j is Jack, $b\vec{x}$ is the boy number $\vec{x}$ and $g\vec{x}$ the girl number $\vec{x}$. Let $U \subseteq (\mathtt{0} \mid \mathtt{1})^*$. Define $R(U)$ as follows.

$$R(U) := \begin{cases} \{\langle b\mathtt{0}\vec{x}, g\vec{x}\rangle : \vec{x} \in (\mathtt{0} \mid \mathtt{1})^*\} \\ \cup\{\langle g\mathtt{0}\vec{x}, g\vec{x}\rangle : \vec{x} \in (\mathtt{0} \mid \mathtt{1})^*\} \\ \cup\{\langle b\mathtt{1}\vec{x}, b\vec{x}\rangle : \vec{x} \in (\mathtt{0} \mid \mathtt{1})^*\} \\ \cup\{\langle g\mathtt{1}\vec{x}, b\vec{x}\rangle : \vec{x} \in (\mathtt{0} \mid \mathtt{1})^*\} \\ \cup\{\langle j, b\vec{x}\rangle : \vec{x} \in U\} \end{cases} \tag{3.138}$$

What can be shown is that the translation of $/\mathtt{p}\vec{x}/$ is true in $\langle B, j, R(U)\rangle$ (with $R(U)$ interpreting the relation of seeing and j interprets the constant "Jack") iff $\vec{x} \in U$. Thus we have a translation into English that preserves synonymy. Though the argument is not complete (for the reason that the English examples do away with brackets and so introduce ambiguity), it does serve to transfer Theorem 3.6 to English. ⚽

Exercise 3.17 Recall the definition of $G_\times$ and $G^\times$ from page 65. Extend these definitions to indeterminate grammars. Construct an indeterminate grammar G for which $(G^\times)_\times \neq G$.

Exercise 3.18 Write a compositional adjunction grammar for Var.

Exercise 3.19 Let G be additive. Show that if $\iota_G(t) \in (B^* \times M)$ then $\iota_{G \upharpoonright B}(t) = \iota_G(t)$.

3.7 Abstraction

At the end of this chapter I shall return to a problem that has been central in the development of modern linguistics: the definition of the *unit*. Units are *abstract* objects and are related to concrete things via *realizations*. As de Saussure already insisted, the linguist almost always deals with abstract objects. The letter /b/, the sound [b], the genitive case—all these things are abstractions from observable reality. Thus, on the one hand the sign $\langle$/`mountain`/, $\lambda x.\mathsf{mountain}'(x)\rangle$ is the only thing that can be said to belong to *langage* as de Saussure defined it, on the other hand it does not exist, unlike particular utterances of the word /`mountain`/ and particular mountains (the concept of mountainhood is an abstract object, the only thing we take to exist in the physical sense are individual mountains). An utterance of /`mountain`/ stands to the sequence of phonemes of /`mountain`/ in the same way as a particular mountain stands to $\lambda x.\mathsf{mountain}'(x)$. In both cases the first is the concrete entity the second the abstract one, the one that is part of language. The picture in Fig. 3.5 illustrates this. The main aim of this section is to give some mathematical background to the idea of abstracting units. Before I do so, I shall point out that there is no consensus as to how abstract language actually is. In earlier structuralism it was believed that only the abstract object was relevant. It was often suggested that only the contrast matters and that the actual content of the contrasting items was irrelevant.

This view was applied to both phonology and semantics. It was thought that nothing matters to linguistics beyond the contrast, or feature, itself. It would then

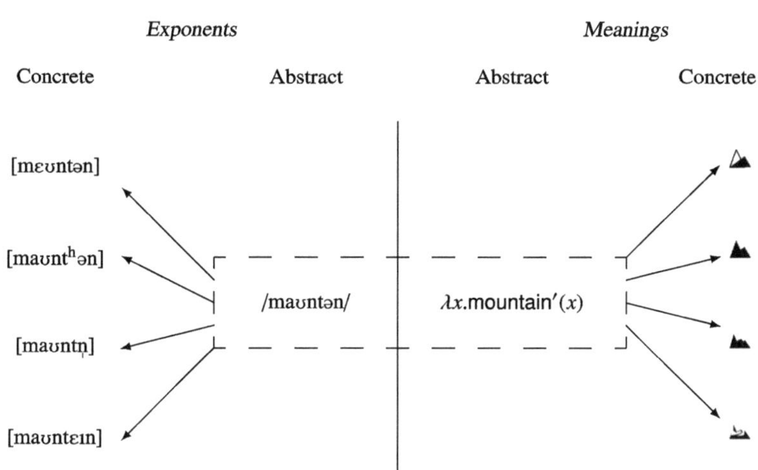

Fig. 3.5 Abstract signs

seem that the contrast between [p] and [b] could from the abstract viewpoint not be distinguished from the contrast between [p] and [t]; the labels "voicing" or "labial" are meaningless to phonology. Similarly, the meaning contrast between "short" and "tall" is formally indistinguishable from the contrast between "cold" and "hot"; all that can be said is that the contrasting items are different. This position—though not without merits, as we shall see—is nowadays not so popular. One reason among many is that it cannot explain how languages can change in a quasi continuous way and yet be underlyingly discrete. Additionally, it gives us no insight into why languages are the way they are, particularly when it comes to the certain bias that they display (for example to devoice consonants in coda). Also, the precise content matters more often in language than structuralists were willing to admit. (The same predicament with respect to natural kinds and induction is discussed in Gärdenfors (2004)). The idea that we propose here is that the continuous change is the effect of a continuously changing surface realization of abstract units. The contrasts are a matter of the underlying abstract language and they get projected to the surface via realization maps.

The picture that emerges is this. There are in total four domains:

1. concrete exponents (utterances),
2. abstract exponents (phonological representations),
3. concrete meanings (objects, things),
4. abstract meanings (semantic representations).

There are many-to-one maps from the concrete to the corresponding abstract domains. We take the pairing between concrete exponents and concrete meanings as given; these are the data. The pairing between abstract exponents and abstract meanings is postulated and likewise the correspondence concrete-to-abstract. In this scenario it becomes clear why we can have on the one hand agreement about the extensional language, say, English and yet disagreement about what the nature of representations is. Moreover, it becomes clear why it is that different people possess the same language yet possess a different grammar.

We take the notion of (concrete) language in the purely extensional sense: a set of pairs between utterances and concrete relata. For concreteness, we shall just assume the relata to be things. Thus let us be given a set U of **utterances** and a set R of (physical) **relata**, that is, objects of the world. Language in the extensional sense is a subset of $U \times R$. A pair $\langle u, r\rangle$ is in L if and only if u *means* r in that language. Thus, if a particular object h, say a house, can be referred to by a particular utterance h', e. g., of /house/, then $\langle h', h\rangle$ is a member of English. Some people may worry that R is potentially too big (something like the universal class) but from a methodological point of view nothing much is lost if we suitably restrict R. (In set theory one usually considers models of bounded size, the bound being suitably high. In a subsequent step one looks at the dependency of the result of the size of the bound.)

Both sets U and R are structured. The intrinsic structure of R is much harder to establish, so we just look at U. To simplify matters again, we assume that U consists in occurrences of sound bits (but see Scollon and Wong Scollon (2003) for an eloquent argument why this is wrong). Then we may be justified in assuming that only the intrinsic physical quality really matters, in other words: we can shift u in time (and place) without affecting its signalling potential. Thus, from now on we deal not with actual utterances but with what we call "sound bits". Sound bits are what you store in a file on a computer to play it to someone (or yourself) any time you want. This is nowadays used a lot in talking machines (as are installed in GPS systems, dialog systems, trains or elevators). Now let $\odot$ be the append operation on sound bits. Such an operation can easily be realised on a computer, and this technique is also widely used in technical applications. $\odot$ restricted to U becomes a partial operation. This is because there are phonotactic restrictions on the combinations of sounds. Given this operation $\odot$ it is possible to segment sound bits into smaller units. In this way an utterance h' can be segmented into a sequence of more primitive utterances, which are instances of some sound bits corresponding to the basic sounds of English. Ideally, they correspond to the sounds [h], the diphthong [aʊ] and [s]; or maybe the diphthong is disected into [a] and [ʊ]. So, we propose a set P of primitive sound bits. The set P is an alphabet and $\odot$ the concatenation. P^* is the closure of P under $\odot$. Further, U is a subset of P^*. P is the set of **phones**. The choice of P is to some extent arbitrary; for example, in phonetics, an affricate is seen as a sequence of stop plus fricative (see for example (IPA, 1999)) but in phonology the affricates are often considered phonemes (= indecomposable). Similar problems are created by diphthongs. Although segmentation is a problem area, we shall not go into it here and instead move on to sketch the method of abstraction.

Both utterances and relata are concrete entities. My utterance u of /house/ at 11:59 today is certainly a concrete entity. We can record it and subsequently analyse it to see if, for example, I really pronounced it in a proper English way or whether one can hear some German accent in it. Technically, each time you have the computer or tape recorder play u again you have a different utterance. Yet, we believe that *this* difference is merely temporal and that the relevant physical composition (pitch, loudness etc.) is all that is needed to make the two identical for the purpose of linguistics. That is to say, there is, hidden in the methodology at least, an underlying assumption that if u and u' are acoustically the same they are also linguistically the same. However, in our definitions we need not make any such assumption. If u cannot be reproduced since it is unique, so be it. If acoustic features really *are* sufficient this will actually be a result of the inquiry. Similarly, this building opposite of me is concrete; I can ask English speakers whether it qualifies to be called u (by playing them a copy of u). Again there is a question whether calling this building a house today means that you will do so tomorrow; and if not why that is. If the difference in time is large enough (some decades) we cannot be sure that we are dealing with the same language again. If asking a different person we are not sure that s/he uses the words just like the one we asked before. And so on. Again, such difficulties do not affect so much the principles of the methodology described below; they mainly delimit its factual applicability in concrete situations. However, once we know what the theoretical limitations of this methodology are—independently of its practical limitations—we can know better how to apply it.

The first tool in abstraction is the method of **oppositions**. We say that u and u' are **first degree L-equivalent**, in symbols, $u \sim_L u'$, if for all $r \in R$: $\langle u, r\rangle \in L \Leftrightarrow$

$\langle u', r\rangle \in L$. Notice that this definition applies to entire utterances and it tells us whether or not two particular utterances denote the same thing. Similarly, we say of two relata r and r' whether they are **first degree L-equivalent** if for all $u \in U$: $\langle u, r\rangle \in L \Leftrightarrow \langle u, r'\rangle \in L$. It is possible to factor out first-degree equivalence in the following way: let

$$[u]_1 := \{u' : u' \sim_L u\}, \qquad [r]_1 := \{r' : r' \sim_L r\}. \tag{3.139}$$

Finally, put

$$L_1 := \{\langle [u]_1, [r]_1\rangle : \langle u, r\rangle \in L\}. \tag{3.140}$$

Proposition 3.5 *Let $u' \sim_L u$ and $r' \sim_L r$. Then $\langle [u]_1, [r]_1\rangle \in L_1$ if and only if $\langle u', r'\rangle \in L$.*

Proof Assume that $\langle [u]_1, [r]_1\rangle \in L_1$. Then $\langle u, r\rangle \in L$, by definition. Since $u' \sim_L u$, we also have $\langle u', r\rangle \in L$; and since $r' \sim_L r$ we have $\langle u', r'\rangle \in L$. This reasoning can be reversed. □

We can formalise this as follows.

Definition 3.14 Let U and R be sets, $L \subseteq U \times R$ a language. Let $f : U \to V$ and $g : R \to S$ be maps such that the following holds:

1. If $f(u) = f(u')$ then $u \sim_L u'$.
2. If $g(r) = g(r')$ then $r \sim_L r'$.

Then with $L' := \{\langle f(u), g(r)\rangle : \langle u, r\rangle \in L\}$ the triple $\langle f, g, L'\rangle$ is called an **abstraction of L**.

In particular, with the maps $\varphi : u \mapsto [u]_1$ and $\psi : r \mapsto [r]_1$ the triple $\langle \varphi, \psi, L_1\rangle$ is an abstraction of L. This is the maximal possible abstraction. Its disadvantage is that it is not "structural". Consider a somewhat less aggressive compression that works as follows. Assume a representation of utterances as sequences of phones (so, $U \subseteq P^*$ for some P). Define $p \approx_L p'$ if for all $u \odot p \odot u'$:

$$\text{If } u \odot p \odot u', u \odot p' \odot u' \in U \text{ then } u \odot p \odot u' \sim_L u \odot p' \odot u'. \tag{3.141}$$

This can be phrased mathematically as follows: $\approx_L$ is the largest weak congruence on $\langle U, \odot\rangle$ that is contained in $\sim_L$ (cf. Appendix A).

Standardly, the congruence $\approx_L$ is used to define the **phonemes**. We say that p and p' are **allophones** of the same phoneme. Even though p and p' may not be exchangeable in every context, if they are, exchanging them causes no difference in meaning. In principle this method can also be applied to sequences of sounds (or strings) but this is only reluctantly done in phonology. One reason is that phonology likes the explanation for variability and equivalence to be phonetic: a combination of two sounds is "legal" because it can easily be pronounced, illegal because its pronunciation is more difficult. Yet, with a different segmentation we can perform similar abstractions. Suppose we propose two units, say /good/ and /bett/, which occur in the gradation of the adjective "good". In the positive we find /good/ while in the comparative we find /bett/. Thus, given that gradation proceeds by adding /∅/ in the positive and /er/ in the comparative we can safely propose that the two are equivalent. All it takes is to assume that only /good/ can be concatenated with /∅/ and only /bett/ with /er/. There are two reasons why this is not a phonological but a morphological fact. The first is that there is no phonological law motivated by other facts that supports this equivalence. The other is that we can assign meanings to all the four parts; furthermore, we shall assume that /good/ and /bett/ have identical meaning and with this the facts neatly fall out. One problem however remains in all these approaches: they posit *nonexistent parts*. To be exact: they are nonexistent as utterances in themselves; however, they do exist as parts of genuine utterances. This contradicts our earlier assumption that the set of valid forms of the language are only those that are first members of a pair $\langle u, r\rangle$. For now we accept forms that are not of this kind. Notice that the phonological abstraction did not require the units to be meaningful and proceeded just by comparing alternatives to a sound in context. The abstract units (phonemes) are not required to be in the language, nor are their parts. Thus the abstracted image L_1 is of a new kind, it is a language (**langue**) in de Saussure's sense. It is certainly possible to do morphology along similar lines.

The language L can be identified with *parole*, while *langue* is L_1. However, we should be aware of the fact that while L is unique (given by experience), L_1 is not. The most trivial way in which we can make a different abstraction is by using different abstract relata.

Definition 3.15 Let $\mathcal{A} = \langle \varphi, \psi, L_1\rangle$ and $\mathcal{B} = \langle \eta, \theta, L_2\rangle$ be abstractions of L. We call $\mathcal{A}$ and $\mathcal{B}$ **equivalent** if

① $\mathrm{dom}(\varphi) = \mathrm{dom}(\eta)$ and $\mathrm{dom}(\psi) = \mathrm{dom}(\theta)$,
② there is a bijection $i : L_1 \to L_2$ such that $\eta \times \theta = i \circ (\varphi \times \psi)$.

Put $U = \mathrm{dom}(\varphi)$ and $R = \mathrm{dom}(\psi)$. Then we have the following situation.

$$\begin{array}{ccc} U \times R & \xrightarrow{\varphi \times \psi} & L_1 \\ & \searrow_{\eta \times \theta} & \downarrow i \\ & & L_2 \end{array} \tag{3.142}$$

By definition there is an inverse map $j : L_2 \to L_1$. Finally, given a grammar $G = \langle \Omega, \mathcal{I}\rangle$ for $L = E \times M$ and an abstraction $\mathcal{A} = \langle \varphi, \psi, L'\rangle$ we can define the abstracted grammar $G/\mathcal{A} := \langle \Omega, \mathcal{I}^{\mathcal{A}}\rangle$ for L' via $\mathcal{A}$ as follows. For a sign $\sigma = \langle e, m\rangle \in E \times M$ let $\sigma^{\mathcal{A}} := \langle \varphi(e), \psi(m)\rangle$, the abstraction of σ. Then for a function symbol f define

$$\mathcal{I}^{\mathcal{A}}(f)\left(\sigma_0^{\mathcal{A}}, \cdots, \sigma_{\Omega(f)-1}^{\mathcal{A}}\right) := (\mathcal{I}(f)(\sigma_0, \cdots, \sigma_{\Omega(f)-1}))^{\mathcal{A}}. \tag{3.143}$$

This is a familiar definition in mathematics; given an equivalence of elements we define the functions over the equivalence classes by picking representatives. This definition is sound only if the definition is actually independent of the choice of representatives. Otherwise the grammar becomes indeterminate.

Example 3.22 Here is an instructive example. Suppose

$$L = \{\langle \mathsf{a}, m\rangle, \langle \mathsf{b}, m\rangle, \langle \mathsf{c}, p\rangle, \langle \mathsf{ac}, n\rangle, \langle \mathsf{bc}, n'\rangle\}. \tag{3.144}$$

The grammar consists in the following operations:

$$\begin{aligned}
\mathcal{I}(f_0)() &:= \langle \mathsf{a}, m\rangle \\
\mathcal{I}(f_1)() &:= \langle \mathsf{b}, m\rangle \\
\mathcal{I}(f_2)() &:= \langle \mathsf{c}, p\rangle \\
\mathcal{I}(f_3)(\langle e, m\rangle, \langle e', m'\rangle) &:= \begin{cases} \langle \mathsf{ac}, n\rangle & \text{if } e = \mathsf{a}, e' = \mathsf{c}, \\ \langle \mathsf{bc}, n'\rangle & \text{if } e = \mathsf{b}, e' = \mathsf{c}, \\ \text{undefined} & \text{else.} \end{cases}
\end{aligned} \tag{3.145}$$

/a/ and /b/ are L-equivalent. Put

$$L_1 = \{\langle \alpha, m\rangle, \langle \gamma, p\rangle, \langle \alpha\gamma, n\rangle, \langle \alpha\gamma, n'\rangle\}. \tag{3.146}$$

Let $\varphi : \mathsf{a}, \mathsf{b} \mapsto \alpha, \mathsf{c} \mapsto \gamma$ and 1_M the identity on $M = \{m, p, n, n'\}$; then $\mathcal{A} := \langle \varphi, 1_M, L_1\rangle$ is an abstraction. However, the grammar is not deterministic. Basically, the output of $\mathcal{I}^{\mathcal{A}}(f_3)(\langle \alpha, m\rangle, \langle \gamma, p\rangle)$ must be both $\langle \alpha\gamma, n\rangle$ and $\langle \alpha\gamma, n'\rangle$. ⚽

It is important to note that the example does not show the impossibility of delivering a grammar. It just shows that the original grammar cannot necessarily be used as a canonical starting point. In general, (3.143) is a proper definition only if the congruence induced by φ and ψ is strong. Formally, the congruence induced by an abstraction is $\theta_{\mathcal{A}}$, where

$$\langle x, y\rangle \;\theta_{\mathcal{A}}\; \langle u, v\rangle \quad :\Leftrightarrow \quad \varphi(x) = \varphi(u) \text{ and } \psi(y) = \psi(v). \tag{3.147}$$

However, the condition is far too strong to be useful. A far more interesting case is when the congruence $\theta_{\mathcal{A}}$ is only weak. In this case the function is not independent of the choice of representatives; however, it is only weakly dependent. We will then say that $\mathcal{I}^{\mathcal{A}}(f)$ is simply the image of $\mathcal{I}(f)$ under φ and ψ. Then in place of (3.143) we say that $\mathcal{I}^{\mathcal{A}}(\vec{\sigma})$ is defined if there are τ_i, $i < \Omega(f)$, such that $\tau_i \;\theta_{\mathcal{A}}\; \sigma_i$ for all $i < \Omega(f)$ and $\mathcal{I}(f)(\vec{\tau})$ is defined. And in that case

$$\mathcal{I}^{\mathcal{A}}(f)\left(\sigma_0^{\mathcal{A}}, \cdots, \sigma_{\Omega(f)-1}^{\mathcal{A}}\right) := (\mathcal{I}(f)(\tau_0, \cdots, \tau_{\Omega(f)-1}))^{\mathcal{A}}. \tag{3.148}$$

Otherwise $\mathcal{I}^{\mathcal{A}}(\vec{\sigma})$ is undefined.

Example 3.23 There are two sounds in the phoneme /ɹ/, namely the voiced [ɹ] and the voiceless [ɹ̥]. They are mapped onto the same phoneme via φ. Now, in onset position, the combination [pɹ] does not exist in English, neither does the combination [bɹ̥]. Only the combination [pɹ̥] and the combination [bɹ] are possible. Consider the operation $\odot$ of concatenation. [b] $\odot$ [ɹ] is defined; [b] $\odot$ [ɹ̥] is not. However, φ([ɹ]) $=$ φ([ɹ̥]). Thus, congruences associated with the standard phonemicization maps are generally only weak congruences. ⚽

Likewise, a grammar for the abstracted language does not give rise to a grammar of the original language. In fact it may even be impossible to give one.

It is instructive to see that the combinatory restrictions on sounds do not necessarily determine a strong congruence. In fact, they rarely do. This has consequences worth pointing out. The most important one concerns the standard definition of a phoneme. In the classical definition, two sounds are members of the same phoneme if they can be replaced for each other in any context without affecting meaning. It is clear that this must be read in the sense that replacing s for s' either yields a nonexistent form or else a form that has the same meaning. Otherwise, [ɹ] and [ɹ̥] might not be in the same phoneme for lack of intersubstitutability. However, that might not be enough to secure adequate phonemicization. For it also turns out that the definition requiring the substitutability of *single* occurrences is also not enough if we have weak congruences.

Example 3.24 Let $L := \{\langle \texttt{aa}, m\rangle, \langle \texttt{bb}, m\rangle\}$. In this situation it seems justified to postulate a single phoneme α with $\varphi(\texttt{a}) = \varphi(\texttt{b}) = \alpha$. The test that uses single substitutions indeed succeeds: we can replace /a/ by /b/ at any of the places and the result is either undefined or has the same meaning. The abstracted language is $\{\langle \alpha\alpha, m\rangle\}$.

Now look instead at the language $L' := \{\langle \texttt{aa}, m\rangle, \langle \texttt{bb}, n\rangle\}$. Here the definition based on single substitutions gives wrong results: if we change /a/ to /b/ once we get /ab/, which is *not* in the language. But if we change both occurrences we get /bb/, which however has different meaning. The abstracted language is the same. This cannot be correct. ⚽

As the previous example showed, it is not enough to do a single replacement. It is not easy to come up with a sufficiently clear natural example. Vowel harmony could be a case in point. Recall that vowel harmony typically requires all vowels of a word to come from a particular set of vowels. In Finnish, for example, they may only be from {ä, e, i, ö, y} or from {a, e, i, o, u}. Consider now a bisyllabic word containing two occurrences of /ä/. Exchanging one of them by /a/ results in a nonharmonic string, which is therefore not a word. However, exchanging two or more occurrences may yield a proper word of Finnish. (Notice however that there are plenty of words that contain only one nonneutral vowel and so the logic of this argument is not perfect. For the latter kind of words it may be enough to exclude those phonemicizations that are improper for the other words too.)

Chapter 4
Meanings

MEANINGS are the topic of this chapter. More precisely, it is abstract meanings that we want to characterize. Unlike what is ordinarily assumed we do not consider the structure of the space of meanings and the functions on them a matter of arbitrary convention. Like with exponents we must ask what meanings actually are and how they can be manipulated.

4.1 "Desyntactified" Meanings

The present chapter is about what meanings *are*. Given the discussion of Section 3.7 we have two kinds of meanings to worry about: concrete meanings and abstract meanings. We shall for the most part consider a calculus of concrete meanings but most of the results are actually independent of which of the two we study. Though much has been made of Putnam's dictum that meanings (that is, concrete meanings) cannot be in a speaker's head (Putnam (1975), see also Gärdenfors (2004)), the question whether or not that is so is actually peripheral to the question we are raising, namely, what meanings are and how they can be manipulated. It threatens to focus the debate on questions of factual knowledge rather than principle. Whether or not my concept of gold is the same as that of another person and who has the right concept is a question of factual detail. What matters in this book is what kind of object that concept of mine is and how I use it; and similarly for any other person. Language is therefore subjective, I make no attempt at constructing a language for a community of speakers. Communication is effected only via common expressions and must rely on intersubjective identity (or near identity) in their meaning.

We have said that meanings are given at the outset. It therefore seems to be needless to ask what meanings are, we just look at them. However, there is a larger issue in the background that I cannot adequately treat in this book. The issue is that we cannot access concrete meanings as such; the only thing we can access is particular judgements. We have difficulties saying exactly what defines the concept "book" whereas we seem to be completely reliable in our judgement whether this or that thing is a book. And so there is a legitimate question as to whether the data we can access are the ones we actually need.

While sentences are concrete since we can make them appear on tape or on paper, meanings are not directly observable. There is a long intellectual tradition to assume

M. Kracht, *Interpreted Languages and Compositionality*, Studies in Linguistics and Philosophy 89, DOI 10.1007/978-94-007-2108-1_4,
© Springer Science+Business Media B.V. 2011

that meanings are structured (see King (2007) for a recent exposition). This position is adopted not only in philosophy but also in cognitive linguistics. Unfortunately, it is in practice hard to assess which particular structure the meaning of a given sentence has. In absence of a priori arguments the methodology should be to try to discover that structure from the given data. For it very often happens that our intuitions on meanings are obscured by our own language. What appears to be a semantic fact often enough is just a syntactic (or morphological) fact in disguise. In this way semantics is often infected with syntax. To counteract this trend I shall try to "desyntactify" meanings. (See Erdélyi Szabó, Kálmán, and Kurucz (2007) for a more radical proposal of desyntactification.) In particular, below I shall identify some traits of semantic representations that I consider of purely syntactic nature: hierarchy, order and multiplicity. Hierarchy shows up in the notion of a functional *type*; some meanings are functions that can take objects of certain lower types as arguments. This introduces an asymmetry into meanings that I claim does for the most part not exist in the meanings themselves. Order shows up in the notion of a *tuple*. Predicate logic explicates the meanings of formulae as relations, or sets of tuples. But where exactly the idea of a first member in a tuple or a second member is to be found in the actual denotation is unclear. Finally, although we can repeat a variable, we cannot repeat the same object. It follows that repetition may exist in syntax but not in semantics. We shall look at these problem areas in more detail.

Frege is one of the proponents of the idea that there are "unsaturated" expressions. For example, a function is unsaturated; it yields a value only when given an argument. The function $x^2 + 5$, in conventional notation, does not denote a number. We only get a number when we assign to x some value, say 3. Likewise, Frege argues, many words do not by themselves express a complete thought. They need certain argument places to be filled before this is the case. In this view, the phrase /`Ate.`/ is unsaturated: it lacks a specification of the subject. Thus, only /`John ate.`/ is complete. It is precisely this idea that has been exploited in Montague Grammar and Categorial Grammar. Both of them diagnose this as a syntactic failure that is essentially a type mismatch. Unfortunately, it is unclear whether the incompleteness of /`Ate.`/ is at all a semantic fact. There is an alternative line of analysis, which treats meanings as intrinsically complete (that is, propositional) and instead views the unacceptability of sentences such as /`Ate.`/ as a purely syntactic fact of English. On this view, /`Ate.`/ means "someone was eating something". There are several reasons why this is a better idea for natural languages. The main one is that the correspondence between semantic arguments and syntactic positions is at best weak. The notion of eating involves both a subject and an object (and a time point, for that matter). An event of eating is constituted minimally by something being eaten and someone eating it. In order to pin down the exact meaning we need to know who ate what when. As it happens, /`eat`/ can also be used without an object. The standard approach (even in syntactic theory) has been to assume that in this case the sentence contains an empty object. Also, there are ways to convey the same meaning and yet use a fully grammatical construction, such as /`There is eating.`/. What is or is not obligatorily expressed in a sentence varies greatly between languages. Some languages allow the subject to be dropped, for example. Finally and relatedly, the analogy with functions is misleading in one important respect: while the argument to the function is an object, that is, a thing, the syntactic subject does not necessarily supply one. For should we assume that /`John or Mary`/ denotes an object that we can feed to the verb, say in /`John or Mary ate.`/? Similarly, /`Someone ate.`/ contains a quantifier in subject position, something that is analysed not as an argument to the verb but rather as a functor. In my view, a syntactic argument serves to specify the identity of some object in question. This specification can be incomplete and thus the function once again lacks any specific value.

Montague has been impressed by the idea that syntactic requirements are at the heart of semantic nature and has consequently endorsed the view that meanings are objects of a typed universe of functions. To implement this we may either choose a universe of the typed λ-calculus or some version of typed combinatory logic. A type is a term of the language with a single binary symbol → (you might want more type constructors but this does not change the argument). There is a set of basic types, for example e and t, and one formation rule: If α and β are types, so is $\alpha \to \beta$. Each type α is associated with a set M_α of denotations. It is generally required that $M_\alpha \cap M_\beta = \varnothing$ whenever $\alpha \neq \beta$. This means that every object has at most one type. Furthermore, we require

$$M_{\alpha\to\beta} := (M_\beta)^{M_\alpha} := \{f : M_\alpha \to M_\beta\}. \tag{4.1}$$

This means that we only need to fix the sets M_b for basic b.

At its core Montague Grammar uses only two modes of combination: forward application and backward application.

$$\begin{aligned} \mathtt{A}_{>}(\langle \vec{x}, m\rangle, \langle \vec{y}, n\rangle) &= \langle \vec{x}^\frown{\sqcup}^\frown\vec{y}, m(n)\rangle \\ \mathtt{A}_{<}(\langle \vec{x}, m\rangle, \langle \vec{y}, n\rangle) &= \langle \vec{x}^\frown{\sqcup}^\frown\vec{y}, n(m)\rangle \end{aligned} \tag{4.2}$$

For $\mathtt{A}_{>}(\langle \vec{x}, m\rangle, \langle \vec{y}, n\rangle)$ to be defined m must be a function that can take n as its argument. This means that there are α and β such that m is of type $\alpha \to \beta$ and n of type α. The result is then an object of type β.

Montague Grammar inherits from λ-calculus a number of traits; one is that functions cannot take several arguments simultaneously. A function can only take one argument at a time. This can be eliminated either by allowing simultaneous abstraction or by adding a pair constructor (as in the Lambek Calculus). However, linguists have supported the idea that functions take their arguments one by one. For this means that syntax is binary branching. This has been one of the central arguments in favour of Categorial Grammar. Thus, if we have a predicate with several arguments, we bring it into the desired form by "Currying", a procedure abstracting the arguments one by one. Additionally, it assumes that when two constituents are concatenated to form a new constituent, the meaning of the result is already determined, at least in the basic calculus. Namely, if two constituents can at all be put together into a single constituent then one of them will have type $\alpha \to \beta$ and the other the type α; the result will therefore be of type β. The idea that constituent formation adds nothing to the meaning is also known as *lexicalism*. In this section I shall propose that rather than using functions we should use relations; and that we should also abandon lexicalism.

The idea of higher order types makes sense only if it is unequivocally clear what is argument and what is function. For if it is an intrinsic property of the meaning of a verb that it takes something as its argument there should be no doubt about this at all. Precisely this, however, has been a problematic issue for Montague Grammar. For on the one hand a singular proposition like "John is sick" is taken to be one where the verb denotes a semantic function taking the subject as its argument. On the other hand, quantified expressions have been argued to be structured in the opposite way: /`everyone`/ denotes a function in /`Everyone is sick.`/. In order to avoid this mismatch, Montague decided to raise the denotation of /`John`/ so that it becomes a function over functions. But that was a technical manoeuver. It was clearly not motivated from semantic considerations but rather from syntactic uniformity. From here, it is a small step towards the type changing operations, which have been used extensively in Landmann (2004). However, they threaten to undermine the idea that we have an intuitive grasp over the semantics of expressions.

Worse, it appears that the idea of the meaning of the syntactic subject as denoting the argument that is supplied to the function is generally unworkable. We can only say that the subject expression predicates *of* that argument. Modern semantics has basically adopted that latter view. However, if that is so, the whole function-argument asymmetry becomes arbitrary. And if we are free to view the subject at one moment as the argument to the verb and at another moment as the function I conclude that the distinction should be dropped altogether. Indeed, some philosophers and linguists have pursued a different semantics. One avenue is event semantics, which has been introduced to overcome not only the rigidity of the typing but also that of predicate logic itself (see Parsons (1994)). (The need to free semantics from syntactic "impositions" is also felt in Minimal Recursion Semantics (see Copestake et al. (2005)). However, the latter is driven purely by concerns of practicability and compensates for the lack of syntactic information by introducing labels. Such approaches, though widespread in computational linguistics do nothing to answer the questions that I have in mind here: namely whether semantics is independent of syntax.) Yet not everyone may be convinced. Therefore, to settle the matter we need empirical criteria. Additionally we need to see if there is a way to replace the typed universe with something else. For if there is not, then this in itself would weaken our position.

The preceding discussion can also be seen in a different light. Even if we grant that the meaning of /`eat`/ is a function there might be a question as to how that function is used in actual semantics. One camp holds that expressions are basically closed expressions. There are no free variables. One exponent of this view is P. Jacobson. The opposing view is that there is such a thing as free variables and there is no need to quantify them away. Proposals to this effect have been made in Kamp (1981) and Staudacher (1987), among others. The disadvantage of closed expressions is that they make pronominal reference difficult (if not impossible). (But see Jacobson (1999, 2000, 2002) for an opposing view.)

As a consequence, DRT went the opposite way, namely not to abstract away arguments but use formulae instead, with or without free variables. This however comes at a price. For if variables are no longer quantified away we must take proper care of them. There is a standard procedure to eliminate functions from predicate logic. Likewise we shall show here that an approach based on functions can be replaced by one that uses open propositions. An open proposition is a proposition that still needs certain variables to be filled. (These are exactly the "incomplete thoughts".) Open propositions are the denotations of formulae. A formula is an expression of the form $\varphi(x_0, x_1, \cdots, x_{n-1})$ of type t (= truth value), where x_i, $i < n$, are variables of any type. Thus, given an assignment of objects of appropriate type to the variables this expression will yield a truth value. A notable change to previous conceptions of truth, however, is that we consider an open proposition true exactly when it has a satisfying assignment. Thus, /eat/ becomes true exactly when someone is eating something at some moment. This is opposite to the standard conception in logic where an open proposition is considered true if there is no falsifying assignment; so /eat/ would be true if everyone eats everything at every moment. In our approach free variables are inherently existential, in standard predicate logic they are inherently universal. We should note that one problem that besets the free variable approach is that the choice of the actual variable inserted matters for the interpretation of the formula. However, it is patently clear that whether we use x_8 or x_{11} is a matter of convenience. (Fine (2007) has addressed this issue and came to the conclusion that meanings are relational. I will briefly discuss his proposal in Section 4.6.) Thus we have to devise a method to interpret such formulae and manipulate them in such a way that it does not make reference to the actual names of the variables. It is often thought that algebraic semantics has provided a solution to this problem, for example in the proposal by Quine. Here, meanings are relations and there is no talk of variable names. Yet, now we need to talk about positions in a relation, which are not in semantics either. We must namely also make explicit use of substitutions based on indices (see Ben Shalom (1996)). So this does not fully answer the complaint.

There is a well-known procedure to convert all meanings into open propositions. If m is a meaning of type α, $\alpha \neq t$, then replace it with $x = m$, where x is of type α. Consequently, signs of the form $\langle \vec{x}, m \rangle$ are now replaced by signs of the form $\langle \vec{x}, x = m \rangle$. Now consider the rule of application:

$$\mathtt{A}{>}(\langle \vec{x}, m \rangle, \langle \vec{y}, n \rangle) = \langle \vec{x}^\frown\text{␣}^\frown\vec{y}, m(n) \rangle \tag{4.3}$$

In the new semantics it becomes:

$$\mathtt{U}{>}(\langle \vec{x}, u = m \rangle, \langle \vec{y}, v = n \rangle) = \langle \vec{x}^\frown\text{␣}^\frown\vec{y}, u = m \wedge v = n \wedge w = u(v) \rangle. \tag{4.4}$$

This is however not always satisfactory. It introduces the idea of applying m to n through the construction; and the construction still speaks of applying m to n. There is an alternative, which runs as follows.

$$\mathtt{U}{>}(\langle \vec{x}, u = m(w) \rangle, \langle \vec{y}, v = n \rangle) = \langle \vec{x}^\frown\text{␣}^\frown\vec{y}, u = m(w) \wedge v = n \wedge w = v \rangle \tag{4.5}$$

This rule simply conjoins the two meanings and unifies certain variables. The unification, by the way, is the semantic contribution of the rule itself and cannot—on pain of reintroducing the same problematic meanings—be pushed into the meanings of the elements themselves. If $m(w)$ is a function and has to be applied then we also have to feed to $m(w)$ these additional arguments. In this way we can see to it that the generalized rule is as follows.

$$\mathsf{U}^{ij}_{>}(\langle \vec{x}, \varphi(\vec{u})\rangle, \langle \vec{y}, \chi(\vec{v})\rangle) = \langle \vec{x}^\frown {\sqcup}^\frown \vec{y}, \varphi(\vec{u}) \wedge \chi(\vec{v}) \wedge u_i = v_j\rangle \tag{4.6}$$

Eliminating the equation we can alternatively write

$$\mathsf{U}^{ij}_{>}(\langle \vec{x}, \varphi(\vec{u})\rangle, \langle \vec{y}, \chi(\vec{v})\rangle) = \langle \vec{x}^\frown {\sqcup}^\frown \vec{y}, \varphi(\vec{u}) \wedge [u_i/v_j]\chi(\vec{v})\rangle. \tag{4.7}$$

Thus we have the following result: the meaning of a complex constituent is a conjunction of the meaning of its parts with some fixed open formula. This is a welcome result. For it says that every meaning is propositional and merging two constituents is conjunction—modulo the addition of some more constraints.

The standard rendering in predicate logic suffers from defects, too. Consider the meaning of /eat/ again. It has, as we agreed, three slots: that of the subject, the object and the time point. When we want to specify any one of the arguments we must know which one that is. If we want to say who is eating we must be able to connect the subject expression with the appropriate subject slot in the predicate. In predicate logic this mechanism is ensured through a linear notation. That there is eating of a sandwich by Steven at noon today is rendered in relational notation as follows.

$$\text{eat}(\text{Steven}, x, 12:00) \wedge \text{sandwich}(x) \tag{4.8}$$

Recall that we agreed to read this existentially: it means that there is a value, say s1, for x that is a sandwich and such that Steven eats it at 12:00. The order of the three arguments, "Steven", "x" and "12:00" is syntactic: the linear alignment in the formula allows to assign them a particular slot in the relation. One may disagree and claim that it is not the notation that achieves this but rather the denotation: /eat/ denotes a three place relation, which in turn is a set of triples. If this is so then we must ask what reality there is to these triples. In predicate logic, it turns out, they have *no reality*. Compare the following pieces of notation:

$$p(x, y, z) \qquad p(\langle x, y, z\rangle) \tag{4.9}$$

On the left we have a ternary predicate p and three arguments. On the right we have a unary predicate p being applied to a single argument, the triple $\langle x, y, z\rangle$. Standard models for predicate logic do not assume that triples exist. It is true that the interpretation of relation symbols is given in the form of sets of tuples but these objects are not part of the domain. Technically, it is possible to install a domain for such tuples; however, that seems to be a mere technical trick we are pulling. The fundamental question to be asked is namely what makes the arguments come in that particular order as opposed to another. I do not know of any reason to put the subject first. But what is the significance of being the first member in the sequence anyway? I know of no answer to that question. At best, the significance is not objective but rather an artefact of the way we code meanings in predicate logic; this in turn is simply a effect of the language we speak. I am sure that speakers of an OSV language would use a different encoding. But what difference would that make in terms of the meaning as opposed to the encoding? In fact, Dixon (1994) translates Dyirbal verbs in active morphology by their passive counterparts in English. Mel'čuk (1988) goes one step further and says that in Dyirbal the syntactic subject is the object of the corresponding English verb.

Now, if it is possible to systematically exchange the first and the second position in the predicate logic encoding, then we know that what counts is not the actual position. Rather, what is first in one notation is second in the other and vice versa. Thus, if the meanings had these positions in them it should not be possible to exchange the positions in this way. This avenue is to be explored. Suppose we have a language just like English except that in transitive constructions all objects and subjects are exchanged. Such a language is not so outlandish: it would be the consistent ergative counterpart of English. Call this language *Erglish*. Thus, for Dixon, Dyirbal is Erglish though with somewhat different pronunciation. The question is: to what extent can semantics tell the difference between English and Erglish? The answer is: it precisely depends on whether it can tell the difference between being subject and being object. Unless there is a semantic difference, these languages look semantically exactly the same. It therefore appears that if subjects and objects are different we ought to define our semantic rules in terms of this semantic difference rather than using arbitrary labels.

Kit Fine has argued in Fine (2000) that from a metaphysical point of view we should better renounce the idea of a positionalist view of relations. The calculus of concepts below is an attempt to provide such an account. (For a more sophisticated theory of relations see Leo (2010).) It will do more than this, as we believe there is more to the problem. Ultimately, we want to say that a property is true not of a sequence (as in predicate logic) nor of a multiset but rather of a *set* of objects under a particular way of relating the members to a slot. This means that we shall also eliminate *repetitions* in the sequence. It will follow that the concept of self-loving is different from the concept of loving someone else in that the first is unary and the second is binary.

4.2 Predicate Logic

Standard semantic theories assume that meanings are adequately described using predicate logic, first or higher order. Therefore, in this section I shall describe two semantics for (many sorted) predicate logic. This section does not introduce predicate logic as an interpreted language; we leave that topic to Section 5.1. In this section we shall concentrate on standard predicate logic and clarify the basic terminology and definitions.

We assume that basic objects are sortal; we have, for example, *objects*, *time points*, *degrees*, *events*, *situations*, *regions*, *worlds*, *truth values* and so on. For each sort we assume that the meanings associated with it come from a particular set. Thus we assume that we have a primitive set S of **sorts**. Each sort $s \in S$ is interpreted by a set M_s. Thus we have a family of sets $\mathcal{M} := \{M_s : s \in S\}$. Standardly, it is assumed that the sets M_s and M_t are disjoint whenever $s \neq t$. A **relational type** is a member of S^*, that is, it is a string of sorts. For a relational type $\vec{s}$, an **object of type** $\vec{s}$ is an element of the set $M_{\vec{s}}$, which is defined inductively as follows.

$$\begin{aligned} M_{\langle\rangle} &:= \{\varnothing\} \\ M_{\langle s\rangle} &:= M_s \\ M_{\vec{s}\cdot t} &:= M_{\vec{s}} \times M_t \end{aligned} \tag{4.10}$$

Finally, a **relation of type** $\vec{s}$ is a set of objects of type $\vec{s}$. The type $\langle\rangle$ is of special importance. It corresponds to the set $\{\varnothing\}$. This set has two subsets: $0 := \varnothing$ and $1 := \{\varnothing\}$. These sets will function as our truth values: 1 is for "true" and 0 for "false". This is achieved by somewhat unorthodox means. A predicate is true in a model if it has a satisfying tuple (see Definition 4.1). Otherwise it is false. Thus, it is true if its extension is not empty and false otherwise. So, denotations of predicates of type $\vec{s}$ are subsets of $M_{\vec{s}}$. Applied to $\vec{s} = \langle\rangle$ this gives the desired correspondence.

I also mention that functions are treated basically as relations; a function of type $\langle s_0, s_1, \cdots, s_n\rangle$ is interpreted as follows. Its arguments are of sort s_i, $i < n$ and the value is of sort s_n. It is known that we can eliminate functions from a first-order signature (see Monk (1976)) and so for simplicity we shall assume that there are no functions.

A **first-order** (**sortal**) **signature** over a set S of sorts is a pair $\tau = \langle \text{Rel}, \tau\rangle$ such that Rel is a finite set, the set of **relation symbols** and $\tau : \text{Rel} \to S^*$ an assignment of relational types to relation symbols. All signatures will be finite. The alphabet of PL_τ consists in the following symbols

1. variables x_i^s, where $i \in \mathbb{N}$ and $s \in S$;
2. relation symbols R of type $\tau(R)$;
3. propositional connectives $\wedge, \vee, \to, \neg$;
4. for each $i \in \mathbb{N}$ and each sort $s \in S$ the quantifiers $\exists x_i^s$ and $\forall x_i^s$.

PL_τ is infinite even if τ is finite. This will require creating a new type, that of an *index*. Indices are generated from a finite alphabet. From these symbols we can form formulae in the following way:

1. If $\vec{s} = \tau(R)$ and $\vec{x}$ is a sequence of variables of type $\vec{s}$ then $R(\vec{x})$ is an **atomic formula**.
2. If φ and χ are formulae, so are $\neg\varphi$, $\varphi \wedge \chi$, $\varphi \vee \chi$ and $\varphi \to \chi$.
3. If φ is a formula and x_s^i a variable then $(\exists x_i^s)\varphi$ and $(\forall x_i^s)\varphi$ is a formula.

Notice that formulae have no type (or, more accurately, are all of the same type). For each $s \in S$ there is an identity $=^s$, which we normally write $=$. Identity is sortal; $x_i^t =^s x_j^u$ is true only if $t = u = s$ (that is, if the sorts are identical). A τ**-structure** is a pair $\mathscr{M} = \langle \mathcal{M}, \mathcal{I}\rangle$, where $\mathcal{M} = \{M_s : s \in S\}$ and for every relation symbol

$R, \mathcal{I}(R)$ is a relation of type $\tau(R)$ over $\mathcal{M}$, that is, $\mathcal{I}(R) \subseteq M_{\tau(R)}$. An **assignment** into $\mathscr{M}$ or a **valuation** is defined as a function β from the set of variables into $\bigcup \mathcal{M} := \bigcup_{s \in S} M_s$ such that for every $s \in S$: $\beta(x_i^s) \in M_s$. The pair $\langle \mathscr{M}, \beta \rangle$ is called a **τ-model**. Ordinarily, a formula $\varphi(x_0, x_1, \cdots, x_{n-1})$ with variables x_i of type s_i is interpreted as a relation of type $\vec{s} := \langle s_0, s_1, \cdots, s_{n-1} \rangle$. We shall take a detour via the assignments. Write $[\varphi]_{\mathscr{M}}$ for the set of assignments making a formula φ true. It is defined inductively. For a given assignment β, write $\beta' \sim_{x_i^s} \beta$ if for all $t \neq s$ and all $j \neq i$: $\beta'\left(x_j^t\right) = \beta\left(x_j^t\right)$. Ass denotes the set of all assignments.

$$\begin{aligned}
[R(\vec{y})]_{\mathscr{M}} &:= \{\beta : \langle \beta(y_0), \beta(y_1), \cdots, \beta(y_{n-1}) \rangle \in \mathcal{I}(R)\} \\
[\neg\varphi]_{\mathscr{M}} &:= \text{Ass} - [\varphi]_{\mathscr{M}} \\
[\varphi \wedge \chi]_{\mathscr{M}} &:= [\varphi]_{\mathscr{M}} \cap [\chi]_{\mathscr{M}} \\
[\varphi \vee \chi]_{\mathscr{M}} &:= [\varphi]_{\mathscr{M}} \cup [\chi]_{\mathscr{M}} \\
[\varphi \to \chi]_{\mathscr{M}} &:= (\text{Ass} - [\varphi]_{\mathscr{M}}) \cup [\chi]_{\mathscr{M}} \\
[(\exists x_i^s)\varphi]_{\mathscr{M}} &:= \{\beta : \text{there is } \beta' \sim_{x_i^s} \beta : \beta' \in [\varphi]_{\mathscr{M}}\} \\
[(\forall x_i^s)\varphi]_{\mathscr{M}} &:= \{\beta : \text{for all } \beta' \sim_{x_i^s} \beta : \beta' \in [\varphi]_{\mathscr{M}}\}
\end{aligned} \tag{4.11}$$

This formulation makes predicate logic amenable to the treatment of this book. Standardly, however, one prefers a different formulation. Let β be a valuation and φ a formula. Then say that φ is **true in $\mathscr{M}$ under the assignment** β and write $\langle \mathscr{M}, \beta \rangle \vDash \varphi$, if $\beta \in [\varphi]_{\mathscr{M}}$. This notion is defined inductively by

$$\begin{aligned}
\langle \mathscr{M}, \beta \rangle &\vDash \varphi(\vec{x}) && :\Leftrightarrow \beta(\vec{x}) \in \mathcal{I}(R) \\
\langle \mathscr{M}, \beta \rangle &\vDash \neg\varphi && :\Leftrightarrow \text{ not } \langle \mathscr{M}, \beta \rangle \vDash \varphi \\
\langle \mathscr{M}, \beta \rangle &\vDash \varphi \wedge \chi && :\Leftrightarrow \langle \mathscr{M}, \beta \rangle \vDash \varphi \text{ and } \langle \mathscr{M}, \beta \rangle \vDash \chi \\
\langle \mathscr{M}, \beta \rangle &\vDash \varphi \vee \chi && :\Leftrightarrow \langle \mathscr{M}, \beta \rangle \vDash \varphi \text{ or } \langle \mathscr{M}, \beta \rangle \vDash \chi \\
\langle \mathscr{M}, \beta \rangle &\vDash \varphi \to \chi && :\Leftrightarrow \langle \mathscr{M}, \beta \rangle \nvDash \varphi \text{ or } \langle \mathscr{M}, \beta \rangle \vDash \chi \\
\langle \mathscr{M}, \beta \rangle &\vDash (\exists y)\varphi && :\Leftrightarrow \text{ for some } \beta' \sim_y \beta\text{: } \langle \mathscr{M}, \beta' \rangle \vDash \varphi \\
\langle \mathscr{M}, \beta \rangle &\vDash (\forall y)\varphi && :\Leftrightarrow \text{ for all } \beta' \sim_y \beta\text{: } \langle \mathscr{M}, \beta' \rangle \vDash \varphi
\end{aligned} \tag{4.12}$$

For a formula φ the set of **free variables**, $\text{fr}(\varphi)$, is defined as follows.

$$\begin{aligned}
\text{fr}(R(\vec{y})) &:= \{y_i : i < \text{length}(\tau(R))\} \\
\text{fr}(\neg\varphi) &:= \text{fr}(\varphi) \\
\text{fr}(\varphi \wedge \chi) &:= \text{fr}(\varphi) \cup \text{fr}(\chi) \\
\text{fr}(\varphi \vee \chi) &:= \text{fr}(\varphi) \cup \text{fr}(\chi) \\
\text{fr}(\varphi \to \chi) &:= \text{fr}(\varphi) \cup \text{fr}(\chi) \\
\text{fr}((\exists y)\varphi) &:= \text{fr}(\varphi) - \{y\} \\
\text{fr}((\forall y)\varphi) &:= \text{fr}(\varphi) - \{y\}
\end{aligned} \tag{4.13}$$

Proposition 4.1 (Coincidence Lemma) *Let β and β' be valuations such that for all $y \in \mathrm{fr}(\varphi)$ $\beta(y) = \beta'(y)$. Then $\langle \mathscr{M}, \beta \rangle \vDash \varphi$ iff $\langle \mathscr{M}, \beta' \rangle \vDash \varphi$. Alternatively, $\beta \in [\varphi]_{\mathscr{M}}$ iff $\beta' \in [\varphi]_{\mathscr{M}}$.*

A **theory** (or **deductively closed set**) in the signature τ is a set of formulae $T \subseteq L_\tau$ such that

for every formula φ and every formula χ: if $\varphi \to \chi \in T$ and $\varphi \in T$, then $\chi \in T$.

There is a calculus for predicate logic, whose nature we shall not elucidate (however, see Monk (1976) or Rautenberg (2006)). It defines in syntactic terms a relation $\Delta \vdash \varphi$ between sets Δ of formulae and a single formula φ. If $\Delta \vdash \varphi$, we say that φ is **derivable** from Δ. With respect to this calculus, we say that T is **consistent** if for $\bot := (\exists x_0^s) \neg (x_0^s = x_0^s)$ (any choice of s) we do *not* have $T \vdash \bot$.

Theorem 4.1 (Completeness of Predicate Logic) *For every consistent theory T there is a model $\mathscr{M}$ and a valuation β such that for all $\delta \in T$: $\langle \mathscr{M}, \beta \rangle \vDash \delta$.*

An alternative to sets of assignments are finitary relations. Since this gets us closer to our final interpretation (via concepts), let us see how this approach might go. We assume that we have a slightly different enumeration of the variables as before. Instead of enumerating the variables of each sort separately, we enumerate *all* variables in one infinite list. The set of variables of all sorts is $\mathrm{Var} := \{x_i : i \in \mathbb{N}\}$. Each of the x_i has its sort, s_i, which we leave implicit in the notation. For every formula φ we define the meaning to be a relation $(\!|\varphi|\!)_{\mathscr{M}}$. Before we specify the precise nature of this relation we shall introduce an idea by Kleene. Let the syntactic objects be pairs $(\varphi, \vec{x})$, where φ is a formula and $\vec{x}$ a sequence of variables. Then we let its denotation be the set of all tuples $\vec{a}$ of the same type as $\vec{x}$ such that there is a valuation that satisfies φ and sends x_i to a_i. For example, $(x_0 + x_1 = x_3, x_0)$ is a syntactic object and denotes over the natural numbers the set $\{\langle i \rangle : i \in \mathbb{N}\}$; $(x_0 + x_1 = x_3, x_0, x_3)$ is a syntactic object and it denotes the set $\{\langle i, j \rangle : i \leq j\}$. Finally, $(x_0 + x_1 = x_3, x_0, x_3, x_1)$ denotes the set $\{\langle i, j, k \rangle : i + k = j\}$. Call a syntactic object $(\varphi, \vec{x})$ **complete** if every free variable of φ is in $\vec{x}$. (We may or may not disallow repetition of variables.) It is possible to give a compositional semantics for complete syntactic objects (see the exercises).

The problem with predicate logic is that our strings are not pairs of formulae and variables. But there is in fact no need to assume that. Namely, all we need to assume is a canonical linear order on the variables. We then assume that the meaning of the formula φ is what the meaning of $(\varphi, \vec{x})$ is, where $\vec{x}$ is a specific set containing the set of free variables of φ in canonical order. The sequence we choose here is $\langle x_0, x_1, \cdots, x_{n-1} \rangle$ where x_{n-1} is the highest free variable of φ. (Notice that the variables x_i with $i < n - 1$ need not occur free in φ.) Thus the relation codes the assignment of the first n variables x_i, $i < n$, in the following way. For a valuation β we define the partialization $\beta_n := \beta \restriction \mathrm{Var}_n$, where $\mathrm{Var}_n = \{x_i : i < n\}$ for some n. We translate the valuation γ into a sequence

$$(\beta_n)^{\heartsuit} := \langle \beta_n(x_i) : i < n \rangle \in \mathsf{X}_{i<n} M_{s_i}. \tag{4.14}$$

Let $\ell(\varphi)$ be the largest number such that $x_{\ell(\varphi)-1} \in \mathrm{fr}(\varphi)$. Then put

$$(\!|\varphi|\!)_{\mathcal{M}} := \{(\beta_{\ell(\varphi)})^{\heartsuit} : \beta \in [\varphi]_{\mathcal{M}}\}. \tag{4.15}$$

Clearly,

$$(\!|\varphi|\!)_{\mathcal{M}} \subseteq \mathsf{X}_{i<n} M_{s_i}. \tag{4.16}$$

Now, instead of defining $(\!|\varphi|\!)_{\mathcal{M}}$ via the set of satisfying valuations we can also give an inductive definition. Let $R^{\to k}$ be the expansion of R to a k-ary relation. This is defined as follows. (a) $R^{\to 0} := R$. (b) If k is less than the length of R then $R^{\to k+1} := R$. (c) If k is at least the length of R then $R^{\to k+1} := (R^{\to k}) \times M_{s_k}$, where s_k is the sort of x_k. For a tuple $\vec{a}$ let $[i : b]\vec{a}$ denote the result of replacing a_i by b. $\vec{a} \cdot b$ denotes $\vec{a}$ with b added at the end. Given a relation R of length n, put

$$\mathsf{C}_i.R := \begin{cases} R & \text{if } i \geq n, \\ \{\vec{a} : \text{there is } b \in M_{s_i} \text{ such that } \vec{a} \cdot b \in R\} & \text{if } i = n-1, \\ \{\vec{a} : \text{there is } b \in M_{s_i} \text{ such that } [i : b]\vec{a} \in R\} & \text{else.} \end{cases} \tag{4.17}$$

Notice that in case $i = n - 1$ the relation gets contracted. Cylindrification yields a relation of length $n - 1$ in this case. Finally, let Ω^k be the total relation of length k.

$$\begin{aligned} (\!|R(x_{i_0}, \cdots, x_{i_{n-1}})|\!)_{\mathcal{M}} &:= \{\vec{a} : \langle a_{i_0}, \cdots, a_{i_{n-1}}\rangle \in \mathcal{I}(R)\} \\ (\!|\neg\varphi|\!)_{\mathcal{M}} &:= \Omega^{\ell(\varphi)} - (\!|\varphi|\!)_{\mathcal{M}} \\ (\!|\varphi \wedge \chi|\!)_{\mathcal{M}} &:= (\!|\varphi|\!)_{\mathcal{M}}^{\to \ell(\chi)} \cap (\!|\chi|\!)_{\mathcal{M}}^{\to \ell(\varphi)} \\ (\!|\varphi \vee \chi|\!)_{\mathcal{M}} &:= (\!|\varphi|\!)_{\mathcal{M}}^{\to \ell(\chi)} \cup (\!|\chi|\!)_{\mathcal{M}}^{\to \ell(\varphi)} \\ (\!|\varphi \to \chi|\!)_{\mathcal{M}} &:= \left(\Omega^{\ell(\chi)} - (\!|\varphi|\!)_{\mathcal{M}}^{\to \ell(\chi)}\right) \cup (\!|\chi|\!)_{\mathcal{M}}^{\to \ell(\varphi)} \\ (\!|(\exists x_i)\varphi|\!)_{\mathcal{M}} &:= \mathsf{C}_i.(\!|\varphi|\!)_{\mathcal{M}} \end{aligned} \tag{4.18}$$

Example 4.1 It is worthwhile to mention a few facts about how we intend to use this for natural language. First, we assume that the denotation of expressions is a relation of some sort. To make this come about, we must eliminate all functions and constants. This technique is known (see Monk (1976)). We show some cases. The denotation of /John/ is the set of things being identical to John; we can represent this by the formula $x = \mathrm{j}$, where j is the constant denoting John. There is no saturation; merge corresponds to conjunction. The sentence "John left." contains two pieces whose meaning we can paraphrase as "someone is John" and "someone left". The syntagma adds the meaning that the two people are the same. ⚽

In order to implement the previous idea it is necessary to revise our notion of satisfaction.

Definition 4.1 We write $\mathscr{M} \vDash \varphi(\vec{x})$ and say that $\varphi(\vec{x})$ is **true** in $\mathscr{M}$ if there is some valuation β such that $\langle \beta(x_i) : i < n \rangle \in (\!|\varphi|\!)_{\mathscr{M}}$.

For comparison we shall say a few words about the type theoretic interpretation chosen by Montague. Instead of using "flat" types (which we call sorts) he introduces a hierarchy as follows (compare also Section 4.1). A **functional type** is (a) either a basic type or (b) a sequence $\rightarrow s_0 s_1$ where s_0 and s_1 are functional types. We use variables α, β to denote functional types and also write $\alpha \rightarrow \beta$ rather than using Polish Notation, to keep within the standard notation. We associate with $\alpha \rightarrow \beta$ the set of all functions from M_α to M_β. Montague uses e for *objects* and t for *truth values*. A relational type $\langle s_0, s_1, \cdots, s_{n-1} \rangle$ is coded as the functional type

$$s_0 \rightarrow (s_1 \rightarrow (\cdots \rightarrow (s_{n-1} \rightarrow t))) \tag{4.19}$$

This allows to dispense with the original "flat" types.

Exercise 4.1 Prove the Coincidence Lemma (Proposition 4.1).

Exercise 4.2 Spell out a compositional approach to the semantics of complete syntactic objects. (You may consult Section 5.1 on this but the solution should be clear anyhow.)

Exercise 4.3 Show that there is no compositional semantics for syntactic objects in general. (So, dropping the completeness requirement will not work.)

Exercise 4.4 Give an example to show why the semantics $(\!|\varphi|\!)_{\mathscr{M}}$ cannot simply be based on the pairs $(\varphi, \vec{x})$ where $\vec{x}$ is exactly the set of free variables of φ in canonical order.

4.3 Concepts

Standard semantic theories assume that meanings are adequately described using predicate logic, first or higher order. In this section, however, I shall sketch a different theory of meaning, which is based on *concepts*. A concept is a set of relations that are in some sense variants of each other. A relation is a variant of another relation if it can be obtained either by permutation of its arguments or by contracting or expanding it. A precise definition is as follows.

Let $\vec{s} = \langle s_0, s_1, \cdots, s_{n-1} \rangle$ be a type and $\pi : n \rightarrow n$ be a permutation. Then $\pi(\vec{s}) := \langle s_{\pi(0)}, s_{\pi(1)}, \cdots, s_{\pi(n-1)} \rangle$ is a **permutation** of $\vec{s}$. If $t \in S$ then $\vec{s} \cdot t$ is an **expansion** of $\vec{s}$. Given a relation R of type $\vec{s}$, define

$$\pi[R] := \{\pi(\vec{x}) : \vec{x} \in R\}. \tag{4.20}$$

This is a relation of type $\pi(\vec{s})$. A relation R' is said to be a **permutation** of R if and only if it is of the form $\pi[R]$ for some permutation π. Furthermore, let

$$E(R) := \{\langle x_0, x_1, \cdots, x_{n-1}, x_{n-1} \rangle : \langle x_0, x_1, \cdots, x_{n-1} \rangle \in R\}. \tag{4.21}$$

This is a relation of type $\vec{s} \cdot s_{n-1}$. A relation R' is said to be a **diagonal expansion** of R if and only if it has the form $E(R)$. Finally, set

$$P_t(R) := R \times M_t. \tag{4.22}$$

This is a relation of type $\vec{s} \cdot t$. A relation is said to be a **product expansion of** R (with type t) if and only if it has the form $P_t(R)$.

Definition 4.2 R' is an **immediate variant** of R if and only if R' is either a permutation of R or R' is a diagonal expansion of R or R is a diagonal expansion of R' or R' is a product expansion of R or R is a product expansion of R'. R' is a **variant** of R if there is a series $\langle R_i : i < n+1 \rangle$ such that $R_0 = R$, $R_n = R'$ and for each $i < n$, R_{i+1} is an immediate variant of R_i. We write $R \sim R'$ if R' is a variant of R.

The relation of variance is an equivalence relation. It is clearly transitive and reflexive (choose $n = 0$ in the definition), and it is symmetric because it is the transitive and reflexive closure of a symmetric relation.

Example 4.2 Let $S := \{\ell, n\}$, $M_\ell := \{a, b, c\}$ and $M_n := \{0, 1\}$. The relation $R = \{\langle a, 0\rangle, \langle b, 1\rangle\}$ is of type $\langle \ell, n\rangle$. It has a nonidentical permutation $R' = \{\langle 0, a\rangle, \langle 1, b\rangle\}$. This is also known as the **converse** of R and written $R^{\smile}$. The diagonal expansion of R is $E(R) := \{\langle a, 0, 0\rangle, \langle b, 1, 1\rangle\}$. The diagonal expansion of R' is $E(R') = \{\langle 0, a, a\rangle, \langle 1, b, b\rangle\}$. ⚽

Even though the diagonal expansion repeats only the last column, R has many more variants. Write

$$E_i(R) := \{\langle x_0, x_1, \cdots, x_{n-1}, x_i\rangle : \langle x_0, x_1, \cdots, x_{n-1}\rangle \in R\}. \tag{4.23}$$

Then $E_i(R)$ is a variant of R. Namely, let $\pi = (i\ n-1)$ (see Appendix A for notation) and $\pi' = (i\ n)$. These are the permutations that exchange the items number i and $n-1$ in the case of π and i and n in the case of π'. Then

$$E_i(R) = \pi'[E(\pi[R])]. \tag{4.24}$$

We say that R' is a **generalized diagonal expansion** of R if $R' = E_i(R)$ for some i. Likewise, the generalized product expansion is defined by

$$P_t^i(R) := \{\langle x_0, x_1, \cdots, x_{n-1}, x_n\rangle : \langle x_0, x_1, \cdots, x_{i-1}, x_{i+1}, \cdots, x_n\rangle \in R, x_i \in M_t\}. \tag{4.25}$$

Notice the following. The identity relation of type $\langle s, s\rangle$ is defined as

$$\{\langle x, x\rangle : x \in M_s\}. \tag{4.26}$$

This is a diagonal expansion of type s of the total relation M_s of type $\langle s\rangle$. This in turn is a product expansion of the relation $M_{\langle\rangle} = \{\varnothing\} = 1$. Thus the identity relation is a variant of the "true" relation. This has consequences we shall look at in more detail later.

Definition 4.3 A **concept** is a set of relations of the form $[\![R]\!] := \{R' : R' \sim R\}$. Concepts are denoted by small Gothic letters: $\mathfrak{c}$, $\mathfrak{d}$. For a set M (or a structure $\mathscr{M}$), the set of concepts over M ($\mathscr{M}$) is denoted by $\mathrm{Conc}(M)$ ($\mathrm{Conc}(\mathscr{M})$).

Notice that this is well-defined since variance is an equivalence relation. In principle we should write $[\![R]\!]_{\mathscr{M}}$ since the concept depends on the structure; however, I shall mostly drop the reference to the structure since it will always be clear from the context. There are two special concepts: the *verum* concept, denoted by $\mathfrak{t}$ and the *falsum* concept, denoted by $\mathfrak{f}$. We have

$$\mathfrak{t} := [\![\{\varnothing\}]\!], \qquad \mathfrak{f} := [\![\varnothing]\!]. \tag{4.27}$$

We employ the following convention. For a set M we take M to be the same as $1 \times M$, where $1 = \{\varnothing\}$. Thus, if M_s is the domain of elements of type s, since M_s and $1 \times M_s$ count as the same, the set (= relation) M_s is a variant of 1. This is to be kept in mind. $M^1 = \{\langle x\rangle : x \in M\}$ is technically different from M but considered here the same object.

Example 4.3 Let us look at a universe consisting in just one element, a. The concept generated by the empty relation is of course just the set $\{\varnothing\}$. This is the falsum concept. The verum concept is the concept of the form $\mathfrak{t} = [\![\{\varnothing\}]\!]$. These are the only concepts. Let R be a nonempty relation. Then it has the form $\{\langle a, a, \cdots, a\rangle\}$. Any two such sets are variants of each other. For example, $\{\langle a, a, a\rangle\}$ is a variant of $\{\langle a, a\rangle\}$ (being both a diagonal and a product expansion), which in turn is a variant of $\{\langle a\rangle\}$. The latter is a variant of 1. Thus, every nonempty relation is a variant of every other nonempty relation but not a variant of the empty relation. So, $\mathrm{Conc}(\{a\}) = \{\mathfrak{t}, \mathfrak{f}\}$. ⚽

Example 4.4 We shall describe the concepts over a two element universe $M := \{a, b\}$ (only one sort, with extension M). We shall only look at concepts generated by at most binary relations. The zeroary relations are $\varnothing$ and $\{\varnothing\}$, generating the concepts $\mathfrak{t}$ and $\mathfrak{f}$. The unary relations are $\varnothing$, $\{\langle a\rangle\}$, $\{\langle b\rangle\}$, $M = \{\langle a\rangle, \langle b\rangle\}$. The first and the last are variants of zeroary relations, so we effectively have only two new members, $\{\langle a\rangle\}$ and $\{\langle b\rangle\}$. Next we turn to binary relations. Here is a list of all 16:

$$\begin{array}{ll}
R_1 := \varnothing & R_9 := \{\langle a, b\rangle, \langle b, a\rangle\} \\
R_2 := \{\langle a, a\rangle\} & R_{10} := \{\langle a, b\rangle, \langle b, b\rangle\} \\
R_3 := \{\langle a, b\rangle\} & R_{11} := \{\langle b, a\rangle, \langle b, b\rangle\} \\
R_4 := \{\langle b, a\rangle\} & R_{12} := \{\langle a, a\rangle, \langle a, b\rangle, \langle b, a\rangle\} \\
R_5 := \{\langle b, b\rangle\} & R_{13} := \{\langle a, a\rangle, \langle a, b\rangle, \langle b, b\rangle\} \\
R_6 := \{\langle a, a\rangle, \langle a, b\rangle\} & R_{14} := \{\langle a, a\rangle, \langle b, a\rangle, \langle b, b\rangle\} \\
R_7 := \{\langle a, a\rangle, \langle b, a\rangle\} & R_{15} := \{\langle a, b\rangle, \langle b, a\rangle, \langle b, b\rangle\} \\
R_8 := \{\langle a, a\rangle, \langle b, b\rangle\} & R_{16} := \{\langle a, a\rangle, \langle a, b\rangle, \langle b, a\rangle, \langle b, b\rangle\}
\end{array} \tag{4.28}$$

R_1 and R_{16} are variants of $\varnothing$ and $\{\varnothing\}$, respectively. R_2 and R_5 are diagonal expansions of $\{\langle a\rangle\}$ and $\{\langle b\rangle\}$, respectively. R_3 and R_4 are permutations of each other. R_6 is $\{\langle a\rangle\} \times M$, so it is a variant of $\{\varnothing\}$; R_7 is a permutation of R_6. R_8 is the identity on M, hence in turn a variant of verum. R_9 is symmetric; it generates a concept different from the previous. R_{10} and R_{11} are diagonal expansions of unary relations. R_{12}, R_{13} and R_{15} are essentially new, while R_{14} is a variant of R_{13}. Thus, up to variance, there are only six relations: R_3, R_6, R_9, R_{12}, R_{13} and R_{15}. ⚽

Notice that the empty set is the empty n-ary relation for every n. It thus plays multiple roles. This is not so for concepts. The empty concept has length 0 (see below for a definition). The empty binary relation generates the empty concept, just as any other empty relation, since they are the same set.

It is to be noted that the identity concept is nothing but verum, a welcome consequence of the calculus. For it is the diagonal relation $\Delta_M := \{\langle a, a\rangle : a \in M\}$. This set is the diagonal expansion of M, which is a product expansion of 1. Hence identity is a variant of 1 and therefore generates the concept $\mathfrak{t}$. This reflects the fact that self-identity is trivially true of everything. To say that an object is identical to itself is to issue a mere triviality. For this it does not matter whether or not we take identity to be sortal. For example, the sortal diagonal $\Delta_s := \{\langle a, a\rangle : a \in M_s\}$ is a diagonal expansion of M_s, which is an expansion of 1.

Let us now investigate the structure of the concept space somewhat.

Definition 4.4 The **length** of a relation R is the length of any member of R. Let $\mathfrak{c}$ be a concept. A relation $R \in \mathfrak{c}$ is **minimal** in $\mathfrak{c}$ if it is of minimal length among all members of $\mathfrak{c}$. The **length** of $\mathfrak{c}$ is the length of any minimal member of $\mathfrak{c}$. The length of $\mathfrak{c}$ is denoted by $\ell(\mathfrak{c})$.

Minimal relations obviously exist; moreover, they are in an important sense unique. For the purpose of the next proof, say in a relation R column i is **independent** if for every tuple $\vec{a} \in R$ and $b \in M_s$ of the appropriate sort s we have $[i : b]\vec{a} \in R$. Say that column i is a replica of column j if the columns have the same sort s and for every tuple $\vec{a} \in R$ we have $a_i = a_j$.

Proposition 4.2 *Let R and R' be minimal members of a concept $\mathfrak{c}$. Then R is a permutation of R'.*

Proof We assume here that M_s has at least two members for each sort. (This just eliminates trivial cases; for a one-element set is always redundant in a minimal member.) Let R be a minimal relation of length n. Call an n-**sequence** a sequence $\vec{o}$ over the set $\{\star_0, \star_1, \cdots, \star_{n-1}\} \cup \{\mathrm{o}_s : s \in S\}$. $\vec{o}$ is **full** if every $\star_i$, $i < n$, occurs at least once. For each $s \in S$ choose some $y_s \in M_s$. Let $\vec{o}$ be of length k. Given $\vec{a} \in R$ we can assign an element $\vec{o}(\vec{a})$ as follows.

$$\vec{o}(\vec{a}) = \langle o_0(\vec{a}), o_1(\vec{a}), \cdots, o_{k-1}(\vec{a})\rangle \tag{4.29}$$

where

$$o_i(\vec{a}) := \begin{cases} a_j & \text{if } o_i = \star_j, \\ y_s & \text{if } o_i = \circ_s. \end{cases} \tag{4.30}$$

By induction, we shall assign an n-sequence to all variants R' of R. These sequences will be full, as can easily be checked. Moreover, inductively it is checked that $\vec{o}$ is an embedding of R into R' (fullness is essential here). When R' is minimal, its sequence is of length n, consisting in the $\star_i$ in some permutation. So R' is a permutation of R. And this then concludes the proof.

R is assigned the sequence $\langle \star_0, \star_1, \cdots, \star_{n-1}\rangle$. Assume that R' has the sequence $\vec{o}$ and that R'' is an immediate variant of R'. Case 1. R'' is a permutation of R' via π. Assign to R'' the sequence $\pi(\vec{o})$. If $\vec{o}$ is full then so is $\pi(\vec{o})$. The map $\pi(\vec{o})$ is an embedding. Case 2. R'' is a diagonal expansion of R'. Then assign to R'' the sequence $\vec{o} \cdot o$, where o is the last member of $\vec{o}$. If $\vec{o}$ is full so is the sequence $\vec{o} \cdot o$. Case 3. R'' is a product expansion of R' by sort s. Then assign to R'' the sequence $\vec{o} \cdot \circ_s$. If $\vec{o}$ is full so is $\vec{o} \cdot \circ_s$. Case 4. R' is a product expansion of R'' by sort s. Two cases need to be considered. The first is that $\vec{o} = \vec{m} \cdot \circ_s$. Then assign $\vec{m}$ to R''. The second case is where the last member is $\star_i$ for some $i < n$. This case never arises. For either $\vec{m}$ contains $\star_i$ and then the last column is a replica, contradicting its independence. Or $\vec{m}$ does not contain $\star_i$. And this would mean that the ith column of R is independent of the other columns. In other words, R would not be minimal. Contradiction. So, $\vec{m}$ is full and defines an embedding. Case 5. R' is a diagonal expansion of R''. Then either $\vec{o} = \vec{m} \cdot \star_i$ for some $i < n$ or $\vec{o} = \vec{m} \cdot \circ_s$ for some $s \in S$. R'' will be assigned the sequence $\vec{m}$ in both cases. $\vec{m}$ is also full, since the last member of $\vec{o}$ also occurs in $\vec{m}$ if it is of the form $\star_i$. Suppose the last member is $\star_i$ for some $i < n$. Again, being an expansion of R'' the last column is either independent of the other columns (which would contradict the minimality of R) or it repeats some other column of R'', say column h. Then o_h is either $\circ_s$ or $\star_j$. In the second case the jth column of R would be a replica of the ith column, so R is not minimal, unless $j = i$. But then $\vec{m}$ is full. In the first case column k is independent of the ith column of R and so cannot depend on the last column. □

The proof reveals that the concept allows to define the generating relation up to a permutation on condition that the generating relation is nonreducible, that is, cannot be obtained from another relation by expansion.

Lemma 4.1 *Let R, R' be minimal members of $\mathfrak{c}$. If $R \subseteq R'$ then $R = R'$.*

Proof Suppose that $R \subseteq R'$. By the previous theorem, $R' = \pi[R]$ for some permutation π. So, $R \subseteq \pi[R]$. From this we derive $\pi^i[R] \subseteq \pi^{i+1}[R]$ for any i and by transitivity, $R \subseteq \pi^i[R]$ for any i. Now, since there is a k such that π^k is the identity, we can also derive $\pi^{k-1}[R] \subseteq \pi^k[R] = R$ and reasoning backwards establish that $\pi^i[R] \subseteq R$ for all $i < k$. It follows that $R' = \pi[R] \subseteq R$. □

We can use this to define the type of a concept. Suppose $\mathfrak{c}$ is a concept and that $R \in \mathfrak{c}$ is minimal. Then R has a type $\vec{s}$. This is a sequence. It defines a multiset $\S(\vec{s})$ in the following way: the sort s is contained in $\S(\vec{s})$ exactly as many times as it is contained in $\vec{s}$. Thus we say that $\S(\vec{s})$ is the **type** of $\mathfrak{c}$.

We define the following subsumption relation on concepts.

$$\mathfrak{c} \leq \mathfrak{d} :\Leftrightarrow (\forall R \in \mathfrak{c})(\exists S \in \mathfrak{d})(R \subseteq S) \tag{4.31}$$

Notice that $R \subseteq S$ means that the relations are of same length and type. It turns out that just one pair of sets is sufficient to establish an order between the concepts.

Lemma 4.2 $\mathfrak{c} \leq \mathfrak{d}$ *if and only if there is* $R \in \mathfrak{c}$ *and* $S \in \mathfrak{d}$ *such that* $R \subseteq S$.

Proof From left to right is clear. So assume that there exists $R \in \mathfrak{c}$ and $S \in \mathfrak{d}$ such that $R \subseteq S$. Let π be a permutation. Then $\pi[R] \subseteq \pi[S]$. Also, $R \times M \subseteq S \times M$ and $E(R) = E(S)$. So for any permutation and expansion of R there is a corresponding set in $\mathfrak{d}$. If however R is itself an expansion of T then $T = \mathsf{C}_i.R$ for some i. Now, $\mathsf{C}_i.R \subseteq \mathsf{C}_i.S$. Hence for all $R' \sim R$ there is a $S' \sim S$ such that $R' \subseteq S'$. □

Proposition 4.3 $\leq$ *is an ordering relation. That is to say for all* $\mathfrak{c}$, $\mathfrak{d}$ *and* $\mathfrak{e}$*:*

① $\mathfrak{c} \leq \mathfrak{c}$.
② *If* $\mathfrak{c} \leq \mathfrak{d}$ *and* $\mathfrak{d} \leq \mathfrak{e}$ *then* $\mathfrak{c} \leq \mathfrak{e}$.
③ *If* $\mathfrak{c} \leq \mathfrak{d}$ *and* $\mathfrak{d} \leq \mathfrak{c}$ *then* $\mathfrak{c} = \mathfrak{d}$.

Proof ① is clear. For ②, suppose $R \in \mathfrak{c}$. Then by assumption there is $S \in \mathfrak{d}$ such that $R \subseteq S$; again by assumption there is a $T \in \mathfrak{e}$ such that $S \subseteq T$. So, $R \subseteq T$ for some $T \in \mathfrak{e}$. It follows that $\mathfrak{c} \leq \mathfrak{e}$. For ③ let R be minimal in $\mathfrak{c}$. Assume first that there is a minimal $S \in \mathfrak{d}$ such that $R \subseteq S$. Then by assumption there is a $R' \in \mathfrak{c}$ such that $S \subseteq R'$. Since $R \subseteq R'$ and both are of the same length, R' is not only minimal (by Proposition 4.2), we also have $R = R'$, by Lemma 4.1. It follows that $R = S$ and $\mathfrak{c} = \mathfrak{d}$. Now suppose that there is no minimal S such that $R \subseteq S$. Then $\mathfrak{d}$ has smaller length than $\mathfrak{c}$, for there is at least one S of length $\ell(\mathfrak{c})$ in $\mathfrak{d}$. Hence $\ell(\mathfrak{d}) < \ell(\mathfrak{c})$. Now pick a minimal $S \subseteq \mathfrak{d}$. There is no $R \in \mathfrak{c}$ for which $S \subseteq R$, contrary to assumption. □

The concatenation of concepts plays the role of conjunction.

Definition 4.5 Suppose that $\mathfrak{c} = [\![R]\!]$ and $\mathfrak{d} = [\![S]\!]$. Then we define

$$\mathfrak{c} * \mathfrak{d} := [\![S \times R]\!]. \tag{4.32}$$

This definition does not depend on representatives. We omit the proof. Notice that even if R is minimal in $\mathfrak{c}$ and S is minimal in $\mathfrak{d}$, $R \times S$ need not be minimal in $\mathfrak{c} * \mathfrak{d}$. This is easily seen if $\mathfrak{c} = \mathfrak{d}$.

Proposition 4.4 $*$ *is a semilattice operation on* $\mathrm{Conc}(M)$*. This means that for all* $\mathfrak{c}$, $\mathfrak{d}$ *and* $\mathfrak{e}$*:*

① $\mathfrak{c} * \mathfrak{c} = \mathfrak{c}$.
② $\mathfrak{c} * \mathfrak{d} = \mathfrak{d} * \mathfrak{c}$.
③ $\mathfrak{c} * (\mathfrak{d} * \mathfrak{e}) = (\mathfrak{c} * \mathfrak{d}) * \mathfrak{e}$.

Proof Let $\mathfrak{c} = [\![R]\!]$, $\mathfrak{d} = [\![S]\!]$ and $\mathfrak{e} = [\![T]\!]$. Then, as $R \times R \sim R$ (using a series of diagonal expansions), we have $[\![R \times R]\!] = [\![R]\!] = \mathfrak{c}$. Further, since $R \times S \sim S \times R$ (using a suitable permutation) we have $\mathfrak{c} * \mathfrak{d} = \mathfrak{d} * \mathfrak{c}$. Finally, $(\mathfrak{c} * \mathfrak{d}) * \mathfrak{e} = [\![(R \times S) \times T]\!] = [\![R \times (S \times T)]\!] = \mathfrak{c} * (\mathfrak{d} * \mathfrak{e})$. □

The concatenation is a kind of conjunction. It represents the conjunction without any identification. In fact we can show that under the ordering $\leq$ defined above, $*$ is exactly the greatest lower bound.

Proposition 4.5 *$*$ is the greatest lower bound in $\langle \mathrm{Conc}(M), \leq \rangle$. This means that*

- $\mathfrak{c} * \mathfrak{d} \leq \mathfrak{c}$ *and* $\mathfrak{c} * \mathfrak{d} \leq \mathfrak{d}$;
- *for every $\mathfrak{e}$ such that $\mathfrak{e} \leq \mathfrak{c}$ and $\mathfrak{e} \leq \mathfrak{d}$ we also have $\mathfrak{e} \leq \mathfrak{c} * \mathfrak{d}$.*

Proof The first assumption follows from the second. Assume therefore $\mathfrak{e} \leq \mathfrak{c}$ and $\mathfrak{e} \leq \mathfrak{d}$ for some $\mathfrak{e}$. Pick $R \in \mathfrak{e}$. There is then $S \in \mathfrak{c}$ and $T \in \mathfrak{d}$ such that $R \subseteq S$ and $R \subseteq T$. Let R be of length n. Define the set $R^{\bowtie}$ as follows.

$$R^{\bowtie} := \{\langle a_0, \cdots, a_{n-1}, a_0, \cdots, a_{n-1} \rangle : \langle a_0, \cdots, a_{n-1} \rangle \in R\} \tag{4.33}$$

$R^{\bowtie} \sim R$ (by repeated generalized diagonal expansion). Moreover, $R^{\bowtie} \subseteq S \times T$. By Lemma 4.2, $\mathfrak{e} \leq \mathfrak{c} * \mathfrak{d}$. □

There is no natural definition of disjunction, since this needs identification of columns. We leave it to the next section to go deeper into the topic of identification of columns across concepts.

As we have explained in Section 4.1, we claim that natural language meanings are not sets of assignments but rather concepts. For a formula φ of predicate logic we put

$$«\varphi»_{\mathcal{M}} := [\![(\!|\varphi|\!)_{\mathcal{M}}]\!]_{\mathcal{M}}. \tag{4.34}$$

Recall that $(\!|\varphi|\!)_{\mathcal{M}}$ delivers a relation (a subset of $\prod_{i<\ell(\varphi)} M_{s_i}$) based on the set of free variables of φ. In the sequel, we shall drop multiple references to the model whenever possible. Thus $[\![(\!|\varphi|\!)_{\mathcal{M}}]\!]_{\mathcal{M}}$ will often be simplified to $[\![(\!|\varphi|\!)]\!]_{\mathcal{M}}$, dropping innermost occurrences.

We can give a somewhat more compact version of this set. Notice namely that $(\!|\varphi|\!)_{\mathcal{M}}$ was based on a set that may properly include the set $\mathrm{fr}(\varphi)$. For if x_i is not free but there is $j > i$ such that x_j is free in φ, then φ does not depend on x_i but nevertheless the ith component of $(\!|\varphi|\!)_{\mathcal{M}}$ records the values of x_i. It is thus easily seen that there are sets $A \subseteq \prod_{j<i} M_{s_j}$ and $B \subseteq \prod_{i<j<\ell(\varphi)} M_{s_j}$ such that

$$(\!|\varphi|\!)_{\mathcal{M}} \subseteq A \times M_{s_i} \times B. \tag{4.35}$$

There is a set $C \subseteq A \times B$ such that

$$(\!|\varphi|\!)_{\mathcal{M}} = \{\vec{x} \cdot y \cdot \vec{z} : \vec{x} \cdot \vec{z} \in C, y \in M_{s_i}\}. \tag{4.36}$$

By the laws of concepts,

$$[\![(\!|\varphi|\!)_{\mathcal{M}}]\!]_{\mathcal{M}} = [\![C \times M_{s_i}]\!]_{\mathcal{M}} = [\![C]\!]_{\mathcal{M}}. \tag{4.37}$$

Thus, we can actually eliminate from $(\!|\varphi|\!)_{\mathcal{M}}$ all columns referring to variables that are not free in φ.

However, one should not be misled to think that it is exactly the free variables whose values need to be recorded for the formation of the concept. For sometimes variables occur free but nevertheless make no significant contribution to the formula. For example, for the formula $\chi := \varphi(\vec{y}) \wedge x_k^s = x_k^s$ we get $\mathrm{fr}(\chi) = \mathrm{fr}(\varphi) \cup \{x_k^s\}$. If $k \geq \ell(\varphi)$ we have

$$(\!|\varphi|\!)_{\mathcal{M}} \neq (\!|\chi|\!)_{\mathcal{M}}. \tag{4.38}$$

On the other hand we have

$$[\varphi]_{\mathcal{M}} = [\chi]_{\mathcal{M}}. \tag{4.39}$$

since both formulae are satisfied by the same assignments. We have $«\chi»_{\mathcal{M}} = «\varphi»_{\mathcal{M}}$. Thus the addition of "trivial" variables has no effect on the concept.

Let us finally turn to elementarily definable concepts. Suppose that R has the form $(\!|\varphi(x_0, \cdots, x_{n-1})|\!)_{\mathcal{M}}$ for some $\varphi(x_0, \cdots, x_{n-1})$. In this case R is said to be **definable**. Then

① $\pi[R] = (\!|\varphi(x_{\pi(0)}, \cdots, x_{\pi(n-1)}|\!)_{\mathcal{M}}$.
② $R \times M = (\!|\varphi(x_0, \cdots, x_{n-1}) \wedge x_n = x_n|\!)_{\mathcal{M}}$.
③ $E(R) = (\!|\varphi(x_0, \cdots, x_{n-1}) \wedge x_{n-1} = x_n|\!)_{\mathcal{M}}$.

Hence, if one minimal member of a concept is definable, all members of the concept are definable.

Proposition 4.6 *Let* $\mathfrak{c}$ *be a concept and* $R, S \in \mathfrak{c}$. *Then* R *is definable if and only if* S *is.*

Proof It remains to be shown that if $E(R)$ or $R \times M$ is definable, so is R. To this end, let $(\!|\varphi(x_0, \cdots, x_n))|\!)_{\mathcal{M}} = E(R)$. Then $(\!|\exists x_n.\varphi(x_0, \cdots, x_n))|\!)_{\mathcal{M}} = R$. Similarly, if $(\!|\varphi(x_0, \cdots, x_n))|\!)_{\mathcal{M}} = R \times M$ then $(\!|\exists x_n.\varphi(x_0, \cdots, x_n))|\!)_{\mathcal{M}} = R$. □

Thus the variants of a relation can be obtained by adding some equation or existentially quantifying a relation. But there is more. Notice, for example, that the concept does not depend on the way we number the y_i. The relation will be a permutation of the original relation, which by definition is a variant of it. Additionally, let $\chi(y_1, y_0) := \varphi(y_0, y_1)$. Then $«\chi»_{\mathcal{M}} = «\varphi»_{\mathcal{M}}$. It is therefore the case that

$$«x_0^e < x_1^e»_{\mathcal{M}} = «x_0^e > x_1^e»_{\mathcal{M}}. \tag{4.40}$$

In other words, for objects of sort e the concept of "being smaller than" is the same concept as "being bigger than". This looks like a contradiction but it is not. The idea is that although the concept contains both relations, in the formation of complex formulae just one of them is being used at a time. This is achieved by the so-called *linking aspect*, to which we now turn.

Exercise 4.5 Show that $\mathfrak{c} \leq \mathfrak{d}$ does not hold if $\ell(\mathfrak{c}) < \ell(\mathfrak{d})$. However, give examples where $\ell(\mathfrak{d}) > \ell(\mathfrak{c})$ and still $\mathfrak{c} \leq \mathfrak{d}$.

Exercise 4.6 Show that «$\varphi(x_0, x_1) \wedge x_0 = x_1$» $\leq$ «$\varphi(x_0, x_1)$» need not hold.

Exercise 4.7 Show that if $R \subseteq S$ then $\mathsf{C}_i.R \subseteq \mathsf{C}_i.S$ and $E(R) \subseteq E(S)$.

4.4 Linking Aspects and Constructional Meanings

The previous section has introduced the concatenation of concepts, which turned out to be the greatest lower bound in the space of concepts ordered by $\leq$. However, when we spell this out in terms of defining formulae we get something slightly different.

Proposition 4.7 *Let φ and χ be formulae. Let s be an injective substitution such that* $\mathrm{fr}(\varphi) \cap \mathrm{fr}(s(\chi)) = \varnothing$. *Then*

$$«\varphi» * «\chi» = «\varphi \wedge s(\chi)». \tag{4.41}$$

The proof is easy and left as an exercise. We just point out an example to show why it is generally not the case that «φ» $*$ «ψ» $=$ «$\varphi \wedge \psi$». Let $\varphi = x_0 < x_1$ and $\psi = x_1 < x_0$. Then $\varphi \wedge \psi$ is unsatisfiable, hence «$\varphi \wedge \psi$» is the null or falsum concept. On the other hand, the concatenation is not empty, so cannot be the null concept. According to the theorem above it is «$x_0 < x_1 \wedge x_2 < x_3$».

This is a welcome result. Vermeulen (1995) has made the point that the merge operation for merging DRSs should not be as proposed in Zeevat (1989), namely simply taking all variables at face value. Recall that the Zeevat-merge was defined like this, where $\langle V, \Gamma\rangle$ and $\langle W, \Delta\rangle$ are pairs of variable sets and sets of formulae:

$$\langle V, \Gamma\rangle \bullet \langle W, \Delta\rangle := \langle V \cup W, \Gamma \cup \Delta\rangle. \tag{4.42}$$

One of the problems that this faces is accidental capture.

$$\langle\{x\}, \varnothing\rangle \bullet \langle\varnothing, \{\varphi(x)\}\rangle = \langle\{x\}, \{\varphi(x)\}\rangle \tag{4.43}$$

The left-hand sides read "$\exists x$" and "$\varphi(x)$", respectively and the right-hand side "$\exists x.\varphi(x)$". Such results can only be obtained by intelligent variable handling. On occasion, though, we really *do* want variables to be identified. This is the case with the phrase /a dog/, which is the concatenation of /a/ and /dog/, which translate as $\langle\{x\}, \varnothing\rangle$ and $\langle\varnothing, \{\mathsf{dog}(x)\}\rangle$, respectively. The result we want is $\langle\{x\}, \{\mathsf{dog}(x)\}\rangle$.

To get this effect, Vermeulen (1995) introduces *names*. Variables are optionally paired with a name, which can be anything, even an index and the variables that have the same name will be identical after merge.[1] Let $[x \mapsto 1]$ be the function mapping the variable x to 1. Then with these stipulations we get

$$\langle [x \mapsto 1], \langle \{x\}, \varnothing \rangle \rangle \bullet \langle [x \mapsto 1], \langle \varnothing, \{\mathsf{dog}(x)\} \rangle \rangle = \langle [x \mapsto 1], \langle \{x\}, \{\mathsf{dog}(x)\} \rangle \rangle, \tag{4.44}$$

$$\langle [x \mapsto 1], \langle \{x\}, \varnothing \rangle \rangle \bullet \langle [x \mapsto 2], \langle \varnothing, \{\mathsf{dog}(x)\} \rangle \rangle = \langle [x \mapsto 1; y \mapsto 2], \langle \{x\}, \{\mathsf{dog}(y)\} \rangle \rangle. \tag{4.45}$$

In this system the names of the variables are insignificant. Variables can be renamed inside a representation as long as distinct variables are mapped to distinct variables. Yet, the names of the variables are significant in the same way as the variable was in the Zeevat-merge. Thus we have not made much progress, because the names cannot be part of the meaning.

What we need to find is a definition of merge that does not assume that the functions are part of the representation. Instead, we must be able to define them on the basis of the concept itself. We show how to transform Vermeulen's approach. First, we simplify it by using numbers in place of names. It is clear that the names can be absolutely anything, since the only thing that matters for merge is whether names are equal or different. Now think of each number as naming a position in a tuple. Then instead of using names to associate with the variable, we associate positions in a tuple and the positions are simply numbers. Same number means then that the variable will be associated with the same position in a tuple. This leads directly to the idea of simply associating a relation with a concept. So the idea is basically this. Assume that f and g are functions from concepts to relations such that $f(\mathfrak{c}) \in \mathfrak{c}$ for every $\mathfrak{c}$. Then put

$$\mathfrak{c} \circledwedge^{f,g} \mathfrak{d} := [\![f(\mathfrak{c}) \cap g(\mathfrak{d})]\!]. \tag{4.46}$$

This is well-defined just in case $f(\mathfrak{c})$ and $g(\mathfrak{d})$ are relations of the same type. Write $\mathfrak{c} \circledwedge^{f} \mathfrak{d}$ in place of $\mathfrak{c} \circledwedge^{f,f} \mathfrak{d}$.

Example 4.5 Transitive verbs can be coordinated to form transitive verbs. The meaning of `/fry and eat/` is again a 2-concept as witnessed by `/fry and eat a sausage/`. Let $f = g$ both be such that they assign to the 2-concept $«\mathsf{fry}'(x_0, x_1)»_{\mathscr{M}}$ the set $(\!| \mathsf{fry}'(x_0, x_1) |\!)_{\mathscr{M}}$ and similarly to $«\mathsf{eat}'(x_0, x_1)»_{\mathscr{M}}$ the set $(\!| \mathsf{eat}'(x_0, x_1) |\!)_{\mathscr{M}}$. Then on the basis of this choice,

[1] The actual referent systems operated with a pair of such injections but we can safely ignore that complication.

$$\begin{aligned}&«\mathsf{fry}'(x_0, x_1)»_{\mathscr{M}} \oslash^{f,g} «\mathsf{eat}'(x_0, x_1)»_{\mathscr{M}} \\ =&[\![(\!|\mathsf{fry}'(x_0, x_1)|\!)_{\mathscr{M}} \cap (\!|\mathsf{eat}'(x_0, x_1)|\!)_{\mathscr{M}}]\!]_{\mathscr{M}} \\ =&[\![(\!|\mathsf{fry}'(x_0, x_1) \wedge \mathsf{eat}'(x_0, x_1)|\!)_{\mathscr{M}}]\!]_{\mathscr{M}} \\ =&«\mathsf{fry}'(x_0, x_1) \wedge \mathsf{eat}'(x_0, x_1)»_{\mathscr{M}}\end{aligned} \tag{4.47}$$

It is however also possible to coordinate concepts of different length, for example /`hit and run`/. Here, /`hit`/ denotes a 2-concept and /`run`/ a 1-concept. In this connection, /`hit`/ functions in the same way as /`hit someone`/. To make this work we need to select for $«\mathsf{run}'(x_0)»_{\mathscr{M}}$ not the set $(\!|\mathsf{run}'(x_0)|\!)_{\mathscr{M}}$ but the set $(\!|\mathsf{run}'(x_0)|\!)_{\mathscr{M}} \times M$. Intersect this with the set $(\!|\mathsf{hit}'(x_0, x_1)|\!)_{\mathscr{M}}$ and one gets the set $(\!|\mathsf{hit}'(x_0, x_1)|\!)_{\mathscr{M}} \cap (\!|\mathsf{run}'(x_0)|\!)_{\mathscr{M}}$ of pairs $\langle x, y\rangle$ such that x hits y and runs. This is as desired. ⚽

As concepts are defined (uniquely) by their minimal members, a special variant of this approach is to assume that f and g always pick out minimal members. Such functions are called *linking aspects*.

Definition 4.6 A **linking aspect** is a partial function Y defined on some set of concepts such that $Y(\mathfrak{c})$ is a member of $\mathfrak{c}$. Y is **minimal** if $Y(\mathfrak{c})$ is a minimal member of $\mathfrak{c}$ for every $\mathfrak{c}$.

A particular way to define a linking aspect is by means of critical sets.

Definition 4.7 Let $\mathfrak{c}$ be a concept, R a minimal member of $\mathfrak{c}$. A **critical set for** R is a set A such that for all minimal $Q \in \mathfrak{c}$: if $A \subseteq Q$ then $Q = R$.

Instead of mapping concepts to relations we can map them to critical sets. Let V be such a map. Then given $\mathfrak{c}$, $Y_V(\mathfrak{c})$ is defined to be the unique minimal member of $\mathfrak{c}$ containing $V(\mathfrak{c})$.

Example 4.6 Take the concept defined by $<$ on the natural numbers. It has two minimal members: $\{\langle i, j\rangle : i < j\}$ and $\{\langle i, j\rangle : i > j\}$. The pair $\langle 0, 1\rangle$ is in the first and not the second. Therefore $\{\langle 0, 1\rangle\}$ is a critical set. Similarly, suppose that John is taller than Phil. Then the concept denoted by "is taller than" has two minimal relations, only one of which contains $\langle$John, Phil$\rangle$. Therefore, $\{\langle$John, Phil$\rangle\}$ is a critical set. ⚽

For an n-ary relation S let $\Pi(S)$ be the following partition of n: $C \in \Pi(S)$ iff for all $\vec{x} \in S$ and all $i, j \in C$, $x_i = x_j$. It is not hard to see that A is critical for R iff $\Pi(A) = \Pi(R)$. Now, $\Pi(\varnothing) = \{n\}$. We now define a sequence $\vec{x}_i \in R$ as follows. Put $A_i := \{\vec{x}_j : j < i\}$. If $\Pi(A_i) \neq \Pi(R)$ then let $\vec{x}_i \in R$ be chosen such that one of the sets from $\Pi(\{\vec{x}_i\})$ is not a join of partition sets from $\Pi(A_i)$. Such an element must exist if $\Pi(A_i) \neq \Pi(R)$. In that case, $\Pi(A_{i+1}) \neq \Pi(A_i)$. Since the size of the partition sets must decrease with every step it is easy to see that we can take only $n - 1$ steps; that is, we need to choose at most $n - 1$ $\vec{x}_i$.

Proposition 4.8 *Let $\mathfrak{c}$ be of length n. Then for every minimal $R \in \mathfrak{c}$ there is a critical set of cardinality at most $n - 1$.*

This dramatically improves the bound given by Dorr (2004) of $n! - 1$. This is the best possible result. (We leave a proof of this claim to the exercises.)

Example 4.7 To see that it is not at all a weird idea to consider conjunction to be ambiguous let us look at the notion of a syntactic pivot. In English the following sentence implies that John fell:

`John kissed the woman and fell.` (4.48)

We say that /`John`/ is the **pivot** in the coordination. This is ordinarily attributed to the fact that we have a VP coordination and /`John`/ is the subject of both. There are languages in which the same coordination will imply that the woman fell. Such languages are invariably ergative (see Dixon (1994)); however, it is not the case that ergative languages all function in this way. Thus we need to distinguish between ergativity in case marking and ergativity in pivot choice. Similarly, some languages indicate whether or not a clause uses the same subject. Thus it explicitly marks part of the linking aspect to be used. ⚽

Example 4.8 The linking aspect is responsible for dealing with pronouns.

`John saw the thief in his office.` (4.49)

The pronoun /`his`/ may denote either John or the thief or a third person. In the present case we can paraphrase its meaning by "belonging to someone". Thus, the phrase /`in his office`/ has the meaning "in the office belonging to someone". We can interpret this someone as John, the thief or leave it unidentified. Again, for this we need different linking aspects if we insist that the only operation we want to use is conjunction. ⚽

Linking aspects give great flexibility in handling coordination. Every concept can be treated independently from the other. This might not be so desirable and leads to results that may be surprising.

Example 4.9 It is possible to define reflexivization of 2-concepts through concept conjunction. Namely, put $f(1) = \{\langle x, x\rangle : x \in M\}$ (this is not a linking aspect, in fact choosing a minimal aspect here cannot work as the minimal member of the truth concept is of length 0). Then let $\mathfrak{c}$ be a 2-concept with minimal member R.

$$\mathfrak{c} \owedge^f 1 = [\![R \cap \{\langle x, x\rangle : x \in M\}]\!]. \tag{4.50}$$

⚽

Example 4.10 Let $M = \{a, b, c, d\}$. There are $\mathfrak{c}$ and f such that $\mathfrak{c} \owedge^f 1 \neq (\mathfrak{c} \owedge^f 1) \owedge^f 1$. Namely, let $R = \{\langle a, a, a\rangle, \langle a, a, b\rangle, \langle a, b, a\rangle, \langle a, b, b\rangle, \langle a, a, c\rangle\}$, $\mathfrak{c} = [\![R]\!]$. Further, let $f(1) = \{\langle x, x\rangle : x \in M\} \times M$ and $f(\mathfrak{c}) = R$. Then

$$\mathfrak{c} \owedge^f 1 = [\![\{\langle a, a, a\rangle, \langle a, a, b\rangle, \langle a, a, c\rangle\}]\!] = [\![\{\langle a, a\rangle, \langle a, b\rangle, \langle a, c\rangle\}]\!]. \tag{4.51}$$

Finally, put $f(\llbracket\{\langle a,a\rangle,\langle a,b\rangle,\langle a,c\rangle\}\rrbracket) := \{\langle a,a\rangle,\langle a,b\rangle,\langle a,c\rangle\}$ and we get

$$\begin{aligned}(\mathfrak{c} \circledast^f 1) \circledast^f 1 =& (\llbracket\{\langle a,a\rangle,\langle a,b\rangle,\langle a,c\rangle\}\rrbracket) \circledast^f 1 \\ =& \llbracket\{\langle a\rangle\}\rrbracket.\end{aligned} \tag{4.52}$$

⚽

$\circledast^{Y,Z}$ is unfortunately somewhat inflexible. When we merge $\mathfrak{c}$ and $\mathfrak{d}$ via Y and Z, this is defined only if $Y(\mathfrak{c})$ and $Z(\mathfrak{d})$ have same length. Thus if $Y(\mathfrak{e})$ has different length as $Y(\mathfrak{d})$, then only one of $\mathfrak{c} \circledast^{Y,Z} \mathfrak{d}$ and $\mathfrak{c} \circledast^{Y,Z} \mathfrak{e}$ is defined. A better version is as follows. Let U be a function from pairs of concepts to pairs of relations such that if $U(\mathfrak{c},\mathfrak{d}) = (R,S)$ then $R \in \mathfrak{c}$ and $S \in \mathfrak{d}$. Then put

$$\mathfrak{c} \circledast^U \mathfrak{d} := \llbracket R \cap S \rrbracket, \qquad \text{where } U(\mathfrak{c},\mathfrak{d}) = (R,S). \tag{4.53}$$

This function offers more flexibility than might be needed in natural languages but that is another matter. We conclude with a useful characterization of the logical strength of these operations.

Proposition 4.9 *Let* $\mathfrak{c} = «\varphi(\vec{x})»$ *and* $\mathfrak{d} := «\psi(\vec{y})»$ *with* $\vec{x}$ *and* $\vec{y}$ *disjoint. Then there is a formula* χ*, which is a conjunction of equations of the form* $x_i = y_j$ *such that* $(\mathfrak{c} \circledast^U \mathfrak{d}) = «\varphi(\vec{x}) \wedge \psi(\vec{y}) \wedge \chi»$.

I conclude this section with a characterization of the constructional meanings. By an constructional meaning I mean such a meaning that is not provided through a lexical entry but is rather defined by the grammar. In Montague Grammar there was no need to talk about admissible meanings. If a constituent is formed, its meaning is completely determined by the meaning of its two parts. The introduction of concepts, however, has not only made it possible to use different linking aspects (and so to get different resulting meanings). The introduction of linking aspects was actually also necessitated since linking of arguments places is not unique. Additionally, the introduction of new intermediate variables has the drawback of introducing discourse objects where sometimes none should exist. Thus, we also need a mechanism to remove them. Section 4.7 will introduce a way to do this without removing them. Here we shall revert to the standard way, namely quantification. Thus we generalize the operation (4.53) once more. Let H be a set of numbers. Define for a relation R the operation $\mathsf{C}_H.R$ as follows.

$$\begin{aligned}\mathsf{C}_{\varnothing}.R :=& R \\ \mathsf{C}_H.R :=& \mathsf{C}_{H-\{i\}}.\mathsf{C}_i.R\end{aligned} \tag{4.54}$$

In the equations above we assume that i is actually in H. (This is not strictly required but makes the definition well-founded.) The general scheme of constructional meaning is now this.

$$\mathfrak{c} \circledast^{U,H} \mathfrak{d} := \llbracket \mathsf{C}_H.(R \cap S) \rrbracket, \qquad \text{where } U(\mathfrak{c},\mathfrak{d}) = (R,S). \tag{4.55}$$

Exercise 4.8 Prove Proposition 4.7.

Exercise 4.9 Show that the bound of Proposition 4.8 cannot be improved.

Exercise 4.10 Show that $\mathfrak{c} \circledS^{Y} \mathfrak{c} = \mathfrak{c}$ and that $\mathfrak{c} \circledS^{Y,Z} \mathfrak{c} = \mathfrak{c} \circledS^{Z,Y} \mathfrak{c}$. Show that $(\mathfrak{c} \circledS^{Y,Z} \mathfrak{c}) = \mathfrak{c}$ does not generally hold.

Exercise 4.11 Show that $\mathfrak{c} \circledS^{Y} \mathfrak{d} = \mathfrak{d} \circledS^{Y} \mathfrak{c}$. Give an example to show that in general $\mathfrak{c} \circledS^{Y,Z} \mathfrak{d} = \mathfrak{d} \circledS^{Y,Z} \mathfrak{c}$ is false.

4.5 Concepts and Pictures

Up to now it looked as if concepts were a complicated sort of relations. However, the intention is that in reality things are the other way around: that relations are a complicated sort of concept. In this section I would like to sketch a very different approach to concepts using *pictures*; moreover, I shall show that concepts are not at all difficult to use. The approach is just one among many and only illustrates the way things might go. We shall assume throughout that basic relations are *symmetric* so that questions of ordering between the argument places are irrelevant.

We want to define all sentence meanings as certain sets of pictures; a picture in turn is an array of coloured dots. Hence we construe pictures as functions from arrays into the set of colours. A simple approach would be to say that an array is a certain subset of, say, $\mathbb{N}^2$ (if the picture is planar) or $\mathbb{N}^3$ (for spatial pictures). However, we prefer a slightly more abstract definition. We start with a set L, the set of **locations**. A **space** is a pair $\mathscr{S} = \langle L, A\rangle$ where $A \subseteq \binom{L}{2}$ is a relation, the **adjacency relation**. Here, $\binom{L}{2}$ is the set of 2-element subsets of L. In what is to follow, relations will be identified through the two-element subsets rather than pairs. We define L^+ to be the transitive closure of L. (It follows that L^+ is symmetric and reflexive (if $\operatorname{card} L > 1$).) We assume that any two points are related via L^+. This means that $\mathscr{S}$ is **connected**.

Let us assume that L is a subset of $\mathbb{N}^2$ and that $\{(x_0, x_1), (y_0, y_1)\} \in A$ iff $|x_1 - x_0| + |y_0 + y_1| = 1$. This means that either (a) $x_1 = x_0$ and $y_1 = y_0 \pm 1$, or (b) $y_1 = y_0$ and $x_1 = x_0 \pm 1$. Say that ℓ' is a **neighbour** of ℓ if $\{\ell', \ell\} \in A$. It follows that any $\ell \in L$ has at most 4 neighbours. We shall assume that no points have exactly zero or one neighbour; this excludes some trivial sets. From this we can define three sets of points (see Fig. 4.1):

1. **corners**: have exactly two neighbours;
2. **sides**: have exactly three neighbours;
3. **interior points**: have exactly four neighbours.

If ℓ is interior, let n_0, n_1, n_2 and n_3 be its neighbours. We say that n_1 is **across** from n_0 if there is exactly one p such that (1) $\{n_0, p\}, \{p, n_1\} \in A$ and (2) p is not a corner. There is a exactly one point that is across from n_0; let n_1 be across from n_0 and n_3 across from n_2. In the space $\mathscr{S}$, the relation of acrossness can be used to define lines: a **line** is a maximal connected subset $G \subseteq L$ such that for any three

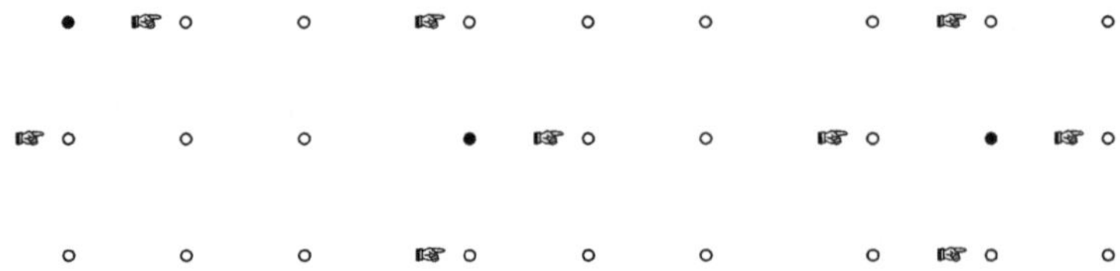

Fig. 4.1 Types of points

points p, q, r such that $\{p, q\}, \{q, r\} \in A$ p is across from r. It is easy to see that if p and q are neighbours, there is a unique line that contains them. In the plane $\mathbb{N} \times \mathbb{N}$, lines are subsets that are either horizontal or vertical. The vertical lines are parallel to each other, so are the horizontal lines. So we say that two lines G and G' are **parallel** if $G \cap G' = \varnothing$. If G and G' are not parallel, then we require that $\text{card}(G \cap G') = 1$. In the plane, if G and G' are parallel and H is not parallel to G, then it is also not parallel to G'. Now pick any line H and let $\mathcal{H} := \{H' : H \cap H' = \varnothing\}$. This defines the set of horizontal lines; pick another line V and put $\mathcal{V} := \{H : H \cap V = \varnothing\}$. This defines the set of vertical lines. Any line is either horizontal or vertical.

I stress that there is no way to say in advance which line is horizontal; the map $\bowtie: (x, y) \mapsto (y, x)$ maps L onto some different set $L^{\bowtie}$ preserving the adjacency but interchanging horizontal and vertical lines. Furthermore, by symmetry of A, the directions "up" and "down" cannot be distinguished; likewise, the directions "left" and "right". To fix them, we need to introduce extra structure. A **coordinate frame** is a triple $\mathcal{C} = \langle o, r, u\rangle$ in L such that $\{o, r\}, \{o, u\} \in A$ and u is not across from r. The line containing o and r defines $\mathcal{H}$ and the line containing o and u defines the set $\mathcal{V}$. Now pick an interior point p. It has four neighbours, q_0 through q_3. Which one of them is "up" from p? First, there is exactly one line in $\mathcal{V}$ through p and it contains, say, q_0. It also contains one more neighbour or p, say p_1. Then either q_0 is "up" from p or q_1 is. To settle the problem which is which we need to introduce more notions. First, the **distance** $d(x, y)$ between x and y is n if n is the smallest number such that there is a sequence $\langle x_i : i < n + 1\rangle$ with $x_0 = x$, $x_n = y$ and for all $i < n$ $\{x_i, x_{i+1}\} \in A$. p is **between** q and r, in symbols $B(r, p, q)$ if p, q and r are on a line and $d(r, p), d(r, q) < d(p, q)$. Using betweenness it is finally possible to define what it is for two pairs (p, q) and (p', q') to be oriented the same way. This is left as an exercise. It follows that q_0 is up from p iff (p, q_0) is equioriented with (o, u).

Pictures are pairs $\langle \mathscr{S}, f\rangle$, where $f : L \to C$ is a function assigning each location a colour. For simplicity we assume we have just two colours: black and white. Black represents the points of matter; white points represent nonmatter or "air". In this case, in place of f we may just name the set of black points. This is a well known type of representations. For example, printers prints pictures by means of little dots of ink placed at certain points of a grid. Letters can be sufficiently clearly represented using a 5 by 7 grid (see Fig. 4.2). Thus we represent "matter" with a subset of the locations. A **picture** is a pair $\mathcal{P} = \langle \mathscr{S}, B\rangle$ where $\mathscr{S}$ is a space and

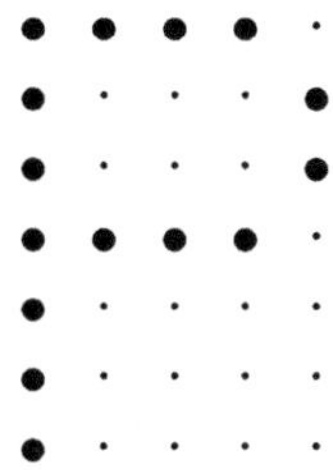

Fig. 4.2 Pictures by pixels

$B \subseteq L$. We shall continue to assume that $\mathscr{S}$ is a rectangular subset of $\mathbb{N} \times \mathbb{N}$. An **object** in $\mathscr{P}$ is a maximally connected subset of B. Here, $C \subseteq B$ is connected if for any two points $p, q \in C$ we have $\{p, q\} \in (A \cap \binom{B}{2})^+$. (In plain words: there is a sequence of pairwise adjacent points inside B.) $\mathscr{O}(\mathscr{S})$ is the set of objects of $\mathscr{S}$. Objects are therefore defined through their location. An **object schema** is a picture $\mathscr{P} = \langle\langle P, N\rangle, C\rangle$ containing a single object. We may for simplicity assume that the picture is a minimal rectangle around the object. Then we may say that $\mathscr{S}$ **contains** an object of type $\mathscr{P}$ if there is a function $f : P \to L$ such that (a) $\{x, y\} \in N$ iff $\{f(x), f(y)\} \in A$ and (b) $f[C]$ is an object of $\mathscr{S}$. The function f is also said to be a **realization** of $\mathscr{P}$ in $\mathscr{S}$. The same object of $\mathscr{S}$ can realize an object schema in different ways. This is exactly the case if it possesses internal symmetry.

Obviously, this is the most simple of all scenarios. We define an object schema as an arrangement of pixels and then declare any pixel schema that has identical arrangements (up to flipping it upside down or left-to-right) as an instantiation of that object schema. Evidently, however, we may easily complicate the matter by allowing more fancy embeddings: those that keep distance ratios intact (thus allowing to shrink or magnify the picture) or those that rotate the picture. This makes full sense only if pictures are defined over the real plane but nothing essential hinges on this, except that there is no more adjacency relation and we have to work with the topology and the metric. Let us remain with the scenario as developed so far. It is then quite easy to see how object schemata can be learnt. We need to be shown a single instance. Properties of objects (the denotations of common nouns) are inferred from their instances. It is not our concern to see how this can be done; this is the domain of cognitive science. Basically, it is done by inferring a set from some of its members (for example by constructing so-called Voronoi cells, see Gärdenfors (2004)).

The way such learning can take place in language is as follows. Let Paul be our language learner. Paul is shown a picture containing a single object, say, a football and is told that it is a ball. Thus, Paul will get the following data.

⟨/`This is a ball.`/, ⟩ (4.56)

To the left we have an utterance, to the right a picture. That the utterance is paired with a specific picture is of some importance. Now, Paul will have to do some inference here to arrive at the fact that /`ball`/ denotes the object schema 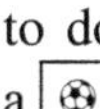 rather than the picture. Once this is achieved, however, he is able to identify the concept denoted by /ball/. In a similar fashion he will learn other unary concepts such as “flag”, “hut”, “tent”, “telephone” and so on.

The next step from here is to learn the meaning of relational concepts. Let us take the concept “to the left of”. Unlike the denotation of common nouns, it is not identifiable by means of a single picture, since it is a relation between objects. How then can it be learned? The answer is that it is learned in basically the same way. Paul is presented with a picture and a sentence:

⟨`/The scissor is to the left of the ball./`, [✂ ⚽]⟩. (4.57)

This picture allows to establish an association between the phrase /the scissor/ and the object to the left (since it is the only scissor) and between the phrase /the ball/ and the object to the right. This requires only knowledge of the meaning of the expressions. Similarly, Paul will encounter the following pair:

⟨`/The square is to the left of the heart./`, [□ ♡]⟩. (4.58)

He may come to realize that the concept “left of” is independent of the shape and size of the objects involved and that it is about the location of the objects with respect to each other. In this case it can be represented just like an object schema, using a set of pictures. The burden is then entirely on the kinds of maps (“deformations”) that one is allowed to use to embed such pictures in others. It is not our main concern to do this; rather we wish to point out that the learning of the concept “left of” is no more complex using concepts than it is using relations.

How then is “right of” learnt? Basically the same way. It could be using the following data.

⟨`/The ball is to the right of the scissor./`, [✂ ⚽]⟩ (4.59)

Here we can appreciate for the first time that concepts really *are* simpler. The picture shown is namely absolutely the same. However, in conventional representations we would write (4.59) as

$$\mathsf{right}'(\iota x.\mathsf{ball}'(x), \iota x.\mathsf{scissor}'(x)). \tag{4.60}$$

By contrast, the meaning of (4.57) would be rendered as

$$\mathsf{left}'(\iota x.\mathsf{scissor}'(x), \iota x.\mathsf{ball}'(x)). \tag{4.61}$$

The two formulae are not the same. The positional regime in the formulae forbids us from treating them the same. To get an identical encoding we need to translate “right” systematically as “left” and invert the linking. This is what the concepts do anyway. Paul will learn that whatever is to the left of the occurrence of /right/ will be on the right in the picture of what is to the right of the occurrence of /right/.

I should point out that it is certainly not necessary that the meaning of (4.57) is exactly the same as (4.59). In this case /`right`/ denotes a different concept than /`left`/. We shall worry no further about that possibility. It should however be said that there can be concomitant differences in the choice between (4.57) and (4.59) stemming from different sources. I mention here that constructions of the form "X is in location Y" generally indicate that Y is more stable, less movable, or bigger than X (see Talmy (2000)).

`The bicycle is to the left of the house.` (4.62)

`?The house is to the right of the bicycle.` (4.63)

Again, this issue seems to be orthogonal to the one at hand. (Notice also that (4.63) is not *false*, just inappropriate.)

We shall now test Paul's knowledge of English. We give him the picture (4.64)

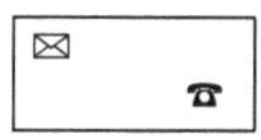
(4.64)

and ask him:

`Is the letter to the left of the phone?` (4.65)

Paul will perform the following steps:

① Compare the two arguments of /`left`/ in (4.65) in (4.57). The comparison on the basis of form alone yields that /`the scissor`/ must be associated with /`the letter`/ and /`the ball`/ with /`the phone`/.
② Take the picture of (4.57) and do the following replacement: replace the scissor by the letter and the ball by the phone.
③ Compare the resulting picture with the one given:

 *versus:* 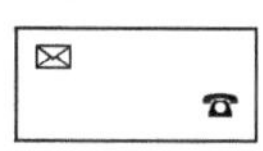

④ If there is an admissible deformation to take us from left to right for the concept "left" then the answer is "yes".

Thus, the entire burden is still in learning the correct meaning of the geometry of "left". Learning the associations with syntactic arguments is very easy by comparison. Moreover, a semantics based on relations offers no advantage.

We have deliberately picked the concept "left". Unlike concepts denoted by verbs, geometric notions do not allow to pick out one of the arguments by means of intrinsic properties. For example, the sentence "John is pushing the cart." is true because it is John who exerts force on the cart and not conversely. Likewise, it is known that directionals modify the mover in an event and no other constituent. Thus "John threw the banana out of the window." means that John threw the banana and *it* went out of the window. If John decides to jump out of the window while tossing the banana onto the kitchen table, that does not make the sentence true. The mechanism for learning such concepts is essentially the same. However, while the linking in relational nouns and adjectives has to be learned on a case by case basis, the linking on verbs sometimes allows to make big abstractions. This just means that the knowledge of how linking is to be effected becomes more abstract.

Let us finally turn to another complication, namely passive, or relation change in general.

`John throws the banana out of the window.` (4.66)

`The banana is thrown out of the window.` (4.67)

It is obvious that to learn English correctly consists in realizing that there are different verb forms, namely active and passive and that what they signal is that the linking has to be different in the two cases. From this point on there are two choices: Paul might start acquiring *two* different linkings for the verbs, one active and one passive; or Paul might develop a recipe of deriving the linking in the passive sentences from the linking in active sentences. How he goes about this is to a large degree a question of how the languages are structured (in other words: how systematic the active passive change really is).

I close this section with a few remarks about what we have done. We have described sentences as properties of pictures. There was therefore only one entity in semantics: that of a picture. To describe how it is that we arrive at the interpretation of a sentence, however, we complicated the ontology. If a sentence has subjects, something must correspond to them. Thus we introduced individuals, concepts and so on into the semantics. However, ontologically these were considered derived objects. We constructed a function that will derive from a picture $\mathscr{P}$ the set of its objects $\mathscr{O}(\mathscr{P})$. The next object we introduced are the object schemes; an object scheme P is a picture $\mathscr{Q}$ together with a family F of admissible embeddings. An object $o \in \mathscr{O}(\mathscr{P})$ has a property P if there is an admissible embedding $f : \mathscr{Q} \to \mathscr{P}$ such that the image of the black points is exactly o.

Exercise 4.12 Define the relation of "having same orientation" using betweenness in a plane. *Hint.* Start by defining it for pairs of points on the same line. Then show it can be projected to other, parallel lines.

4.6 Ambiguity and Identity

We have shown earlier that sentences are ambiguous and this is either because the words have several meanings or because a given exponent has several derivations. In view of ambiguity we must reassess our notion of what it is that makes a sentence true. Under the standard definitions in logic we declare a sentence true if it denotes the value 1 or the true concept, whichever. However, if a sentence is ambiguous this creates a difficulty. Consider the word /`crane`/. It has two meanings: it denotes a kind of bird and a kind of machine. This means that the lexicon contains two signs, where crane_1 is the concept of bird cranes and crane_2 is the concept of machine cranes.

$$\text{BCR} := \langle \texttt{crane}, \mathsf{crane}_1 \rangle \tag{4.68}$$
$$\text{MCR} := \langle \texttt{crane}, \mathsf{crane}_2 \rangle \tag{4.69}$$

Consider now the following sentence.

`Cranes weigh several tons.` (4.70)

This sentence has two derivations. Unless partiality strikes, in a structure term containing BCR we can replace BCR by MCR and the new term unfolds to a sign with the same exponent (but different meaning).

(4.70) is false if we interpret /`cranes`/ as talking about birds (that is, if we take the structure term to contain BCR rather than MCS) but true in the other understanding of the word. It is the other way around with

`Cranes can fly.` (4.71)

This creates a tension between the notion of "true given an understanding" and "true simpliciter". We shall propose (not uncontroversially) that a sentence is true simpliciter if it has a structure term under which it is true. This is a matter of convention but for the case at hand not far off the mark. It then is the case that both (4.70) and (4.71) are true.

Now what about negated sentences? Here we must distinguish between two kinds of negations. There is an inner negation and an outer negation. The inner negation produces a negated sentence, while the outer negation denies the truth of the sentence. Let us look at negation formed by /`it is not the case that`/.

`It is not the case that cranes weigh several tons.` (4.72)

If taken as outer negation, this sentence is false (because (4.70) is true). If taken as inner negation, it is true. To see this, let us imagine that we do not have the word /`cranes`/ but in fact two: /$\texttt{cranes}_1$/, denoting the birds and /$\texttt{cranes}_2$/, denoting a kind of machines. Then (4.70) is true if either of the following sentences is true:

$\texttt{Cranes}_1$ `weigh several tons.` (4.73)
$\texttt{Cranes}_2$ `weigh several tons.` (4.74)

(4.70) is false if *both* (4.73) and (4.74) are false. It is possible though to negate both of them individually:

`It is not the case that` $\texttt{cranes}_1$ `weigh several tons.` (4.75)
`It is not the case that` $\texttt{cranes}_2$ `weigh several tons.` (4.76)

The first is true while the second is false. In English, where the two concepts are denoted by the same word, (4.75) and (4.76) are both expressed by (4.72). Since (4.76) is true, so is therefore (4.72).

I should say, however, that the notion of outer negation cannot be implemented in the present system without major changes. For if outer negation is a sign in its own right, its meaning is a quantifier over structure terms. However there is no way to get such a quantifier. It is not clear to me whether or not outer negation can be expressed in embedded sentences. If it cannot be expressed, the present theory can obviously be adapted rather straightforwardly; but if it can be expressed, then the adaptations are indeed major. They would require namely a grammar that uses the language transform $L^{\S}$ of L rather than L itself (see page 95 for a discussion of $L^{\S}$).

The previous discussion can be used to shed light on identity statements as well. Consider the sentence

$$\texttt{The morning star is the evening star.} \tag{4.77}$$

This is true if and only if the star that is the morning star is the same star as the evening star. It happens to be the case that they actually *are* the same. If John however is unaware of this, then he believes that (4.77) is false and that (4.78) is true.

$$\texttt{The morning star is not the evening star.} \tag{4.78}$$

This problem has been extensively dealt with in philosophy. I shall not go into that discussion. Rather, I shall discuss how our definitions change the way in which this puzzle must be discussed.

Example 4.11 Let $M = \{x\}$. Furthermore, we shall assume that our language has the following basic signs.

$$\begin{aligned} \mathcal{I}(f_0) &:= \langle \texttt{the morning star}, \{x\} \rangle \\ \mathcal{I}(f_1) &:= \langle \texttt{the evening star}, \{x\} \rangle \end{aligned} \tag{4.79}$$

And let it have one mode:

$$\mathcal{I}(f_2)(\langle e_0, m_0\rangle, \langle e_1, m_1\rangle) := \langle e_0{}^\frown\texttt{\textvisiblespace is\textvisiblespace}{}^\frown e_1, m_0 \oslash m_1\rangle. \tag{4.80}$$

Here, $\oslash$ is defined as intersection of two 1-concepts by intersecting their minimal members. Let L_1 be the language defined by all definite terms. It is

$$\begin{aligned} L_1 := \{&\langle \texttt{the morning star}, (\!|\{x\}|\!)_M\rangle, \langle \texttt{the evening star}, (\!|\{x\}|\!)_M\rangle, \\ &\langle \texttt{the morning star is the morning star}, 1\rangle, \\ &\langle \texttt{the morning star is the evening star}, 1\rangle, \\ &\langle \texttt{the evening star is the morning star}, 1\rangle, \\ &\langle \texttt{the evening star is the evening star}, 1\rangle\} \end{aligned} \tag{4.81}$$

Now let $N = \{v, w\}$. We assume the same signature but instead the following interpretation:

$$\begin{aligned}\mathcal{K}(f_0) &:= \langle \texttt{the morning star}, \{v\}\rangle \\ \mathcal{K}(f_1) &:= \langle \texttt{the evening star}, \{w\}\rangle \\ \mathcal{I}(f_2)(\langle e_0, m_0\rangle, \langle e_1, m_1\rangle) &:= \langle e_0^\frown \texttt{␣is␣}^\frown e_1, m_0 \circledS m_1\rangle\end{aligned} \tag{4.82}$$

Let L_2 be the language defined by this interpretation. Then

$$\begin{aligned}L_2 := \{&\langle \texttt{the morning star}, (\!\{v\}\!)_M\rangle, \langle \texttt{the evening star}, (\!\{w\}\!)_M\rangle, \\ &\langle \texttt{the morning star is the morning star}, 1\rangle, \\ &\langle \texttt{the morning star is the evening star}, 0\rangle, \\ &\langle \texttt{the evening star is the morning star}, 0\rangle, \\ &\langle \texttt{the evening star is the evening star}, 1\rangle\}\end{aligned} \tag{4.83}$$

We have the following result: there are *two* languages, not one, whose corresponding string language is the same and we even have two string identical grammars. Nevertheless, qua interpreted languages, L_1 and L_2 are different. ⚽

The example has the following moral. Two languages cannot be the same if the models are not the same. Thus, to say that John and Paul speak the same language—in the sense of interpreted language, which we take to be the default—requires that their interpretations are the same. If Paul is convinced that the morning star is the evening star and John thinks they are different then Paul and John do not speak the same language. In order for them to speak the same language we require that not only the expressions are the same, we also require that the expressions have the same meaning. And "same" must be taken in a strict sense: both John and Paul would be required to take the expressions /`the morning star`/ to denote the same thing and likewise /`the evening star`/. But they do not. There are in fact two reasons why two people can fail to share the same language. One is as just described: they disagree on the truth value of some sentences. Another more subtle case is described in the next example.

Example 4.12 L_3 is like L_1 except that y takes the place of x. Thus, for example,

$$\begin{aligned}L_3 := \{&\langle \texttt{the morning star}, (\!\{y\}\!)_M\rangle, \langle \texttt{the evening star}, (\!\{y\}\!)_M\rangle, \\ &\langle \texttt{the morning star is the morning star}, 1\rangle, \\ &\langle \texttt{the morning star is the evening star}, 1\rangle, \\ &\langle \texttt{the evening star is the morning star}, 1\rangle, \\ &\langle \texttt{the evening star is the evening star}, 1\rangle\}\end{aligned} \tag{4.84}$$

Now let $P = \{y\}$. We assume the same signature but instead the following interpretation:

$$\begin{aligned} \mathcal{L}(f_0) &:= \langle \texttt{the morning star}, \{y\}\rangle \\ \mathcal{L}(f_1) &:= \langle \texttt{the evening star}, \{y\}\rangle \\ \mathcal{L}(f_2)(\langle e_0, m_0\rangle, \langle e_1, m_1\rangle) &:= \langle e_0^\frown \texttt{␣is␣}^\frown e_1, m_0 \circledS m_1\rangle \end{aligned} \tag{4.85}$$

The grammars $\langle \Omega, \mathcal{I}\rangle$ and $\langle \Omega, \mathcal{L}\rangle$ are naturally equivalent. ⚽

The languages L_1 and L_3 are different, yet in an abstract sense identical. Now picture the case where George speaks L_3. We would like to say that George and Paul speak the same language but we cannot. In fact, this is as it should be. Notice that we must distinguish (for natural language) two notions of language. There is a private language, where expressions are interpreted as objects or constructs in a speaker; and a public language where expressions are interpreted with real objects (if applicable). We think for example that the public meaning of /`the morning star`/ is Venus, as is the public meaning of /`the evening star`/. The private language of an individual speaker needs to be "connected" to the public language in the correct way. This is similar in the distinction between phonemes and sounds. While two speakers can share the same phonemic system it may turn out that the two systems are differently realized in terms of sounds. And likewise it may happen that while Paul thinks that the morning star is the evening star and both happen to be Venus, it may also happen that George thinks that the morning star and the evening star are Mars. The private languages of Paul and George are different for the trivial reason that the internal objects of both Paul and George must be different; but we can easily establish a correspondence between them, an isomorphism, that makes them the same. And so the private languages of Paul and George are the same up to isomorphism, yet their public languages are different. The puzzle is thus resolved by appeal to different *de lingua* beliefs, to use a phrase of Fiengo and May (2006). The idea of Fiengo and May (2006) is roughly that what is behind many puzzles of identity is that speakers hold different beliefs concerning the referents of expressions. In the theory proposed here, this is cashed out as follows. The **abstract language** is a language where meanings are identifiable up to equivalence (as established in Section 3.7). Any two speakers can speak the same abstract language, so the abstract language is not the private language. Neither is it the public language. For that, we also need to **ground** a language by providing translations into real world objects. Abstract language behaviour can be established using logical connections between sentences, while concrete language behaviour can be established by asking people about meanings in terms of observable facts.[2] This is just a sketch of a solution but it serves as a formal explification of Fiengo and May (2006) who actually think that

[2] This is evidently a simplified scenario. The visible facts may not be the same across speakers, thus accounting for a different layer of confusion. But it is important to note that the distinction between what is abstract in a language and what is not is real. In a sense, the fact that Tully is Cicero is not part of the abstract language.

many sentences also express what they call a *de lingua belief*. A de lingua belief is a belief about what expressions denote. If the present theory is correct, it is a belief about the public language.

One puzzle that Fiengo and May discuss at length is the Paderewski puzzle by Kripke. It goes roughly as follows. Max goes to a concert by a musician named Paderewski and comes to believe that he is a great musician. Later he visits a political rally by a person named Paderewski. He comes to think that the latter person is actually a bad musician. So he holds two beliefs.

`Paderewski is a great musician.` (4.86)

`Paderewski is a bad musician.` (4.87)

It so turns out that the two people are one and the same. The philosophical problems arise from the fact that under certain views of reference Max holds inconsistent beliefs. Both Fine (2007) and Fiengo and May (2006) discuss this problem. Again we need not go into the philosophical detail here. What interests us is what may linguistically be said to be going on. The idea is that for Pavel, who knows (or believes) that both persons are the same, /`Paderewski`/ is unambiguous. For Max it is not. So, the language of Max has two signs, say, $\langle$`Paderewski`, $\{x\}\rangle$ and $\langle$`Paderewski`, $\{y\}\rangle$, while the language of Pavel only has one such sign, say $\langle$`Paderewski`, $\{v\}\rangle$. Thus, for Max the expression /`Paderewski`/ is ambiguous, for Pavel it is not. Given our notion of truth for ambiguous sentence, it is correct for Max to hold both (4.86) and (4.87) true. There is no logical problem, since the sentence is simply ambiguous. This contrasts with the idea of Fiengo and May (2006) who think that names are not expressions. They can only occur in the form $[_1$`Paderewski`$]$, where the brackets are used to keep track of different objects. In the theory proposed here there is no sense in disambiguation on the syntactic level. This must be done in the semantics. Consequently, also the two occurrences of the name in the sentence

`Paderewski is Paderewski.` (4.88)

cannot simply be told apart by indexation so that one can distinguish between, for example,

$\texttt{Paderewski}_1$ `is` $\texttt{Paderewski}_1$. (4.89)

and

$\texttt{Paderewski}_1$ `is` $\texttt{Paderewski}_2$. (4.90)

The reason, again, is that there is no indication at the surface. Instead, in order to be clear, Max must use some expression that makes the referent unique. Notice that Max also agrees to the (inner!) negation of (4.88):

`Paderewski is not Paderewski.` (4.91)

The difference between this approach and Fiengo and May (2006) is brought out also by the way in which Pavel can make Max aware that he is wrong about Paderewski. For it is not enough for him to point out (4.91), for that is what is also true for Max. Rather he must use a sentence that would not be true for Max, for example

`There is only one Paderewski.` (4.92)

The problem is that Pavel cannot make himself understood to Max by using the name simpliciter. He must in order to discriminate his beliefs from Max's beliefs use sentences that come out differently. What Fiengo and May (2006) have in mind is that Pavel can also use a certain version of (4.88), for example

`But Max, Paderewski` *`IS`* `Paderewski.` (4.93)

But again, how is Max to interpret this if he cannot see which of the Paderewskis is pointed to on each of the occasions?

Exercise 4.13 In Example 4.11 the word `/is/` is syncategorematic. Show that this syncategorematic use can be eliminated from the grammar.

4.7 Profiling

As I have indicated at many places there is a difference between what is commonly referred to as model theoretic semantics and the more popular representational semantics. It has not always been openly admitted by semanticists that the representations involved in many brands of formal semantics do not use meanings in the sense of truth conditions but rather are just pieces of notation. Such is the case with DRT, Minimal Recursion Semantics, semantics used in connection with TAGs, underspecification semantics, continuations and so on. If meanings only contain truth conditions, then all these semantics could not ever claim to implement a compositional approach to meaning. However, such argumentation misses a point. For one line of defence is still open and should be considered: that it is not the only objective of semantics to account for truth conditional meanings but *also* to account for internal meanings. Thus I believe that the justification for using such representations cannot be found in the truth conditions that they formulate. Rather, it must be in the fact that these objects are essentially what humans use. Whether that is so and which one it is that we use is an empirical question and will have to be left to empirical research. However, I shall just add a few remarks about the necessity of considering internal meanings. If we take, for example, the notion of a dog to be the set of all dogs, then that object is not the kind of object we can have in our head. We may say instead that the meaning is a particular algorithm (for recognising dogs); but even that has a similar consequence. The algorithm turns out to be abstract, too. The particular procedure that one person uses to differentiate dogs from other animals might be different from that of some other person in certain insignificant ways. We will then still say that the two people have the same algorithm, though its implementations, that is, the concrete procedures, are different.

The crucial fact about the concreteness of meanings is that to understand whether or not two concrete meanings m and m' instantiate the same abstract meaning must be decided by explicit manipulation of the representations. This is the same in logic, where we distinguish between two formulae representing the same truth condition. Since truth conditions are too big to be stored directly we rely instead on a calculus that manipulates representations up to truth conditional equivalence. This picture undermines much of what I have said so far about semantics since it moves us away from a static notion of meaning and towards a dynamic semantics based on reasoning whose objects are symbolic in nature. I shall not continue this line since it is too early to tell how such an account may go.

It so turns out, however, that human languages are still different. There are certain things that have been argued to exist in internal representations for which there is no obvious external correlate. One such thing is profiling. Profiling is the way in which objects in an array are distinguished from each other, by making one more prominent than the others. We can explain the difference between "left" and "right", for example, in terms of profiling. While they both denote the same concept, the profile of "left" is inverse of that of "right". How can this be understood? In the pictures we can simply add a pointer to the profiled entity. If we denote concepts by formulae then we can use underlining to do the same: thus, «$\mathsf{left}'(x, \underline{y})$» and «$\mathsf{left}'(\underline{x}, y)$» are concepts in which different elements are profiled. If we use concepts, we reserve, say, the first column for the profiled element and restrict permutation in such a way that it does not permute the first column with any other. There is a temptation to think of profiling as just another instance of a sort. But we have to strictly distinguish the two. The two objects involved in the relation "left" (and "right") are not sortally distinct. Moreover, one and the same object can at the same time be to the left of an object and to the right of another. This cannot happen if a different profile means a different sort. However, from the standpoint of combining meanings profiling has the same effect, namely to enhance the possibilities of combining two concepts.

In the first part of this section I shall outline a formalism for such meanings. In the second half I show how this gets used in practice.

Let S be a set of sorts. So far we have construed concepts as sets of relations. The minimal members of a relation had to be of similar type. Now we think of the relations of a concept to be divided into subparts, each corresponding to a particular profile. We allow individual sorts to be profiled independently.

Definition 4.8 Let P be a set of profiles and M a set. A **P-profiled relation over M** is a pair $\mathcal{R} = \langle \vec{p}, R \rangle$ where R is a relation and $\vec{p} \in P^*$ of length identical to the length of R.

The relation R contains vectors $\langle x_0, x_1, \cdots, x_{n-1} \rangle$. When paired with the sequence $\langle p_0, p_1, \cdots, p_{n-1} \rangle$ this means that x_i will have the profile p_i. Since the profile is paired with the entire relation, the profile p_i is also given to y_i in

$\langle y_0, y_1, \cdots, y_{n-1}\rangle \in R$ in $\mathcal{R}$. One may or may not want to impose requirements on the profiling. For example, suppose there is a label saying that the element is in focus; this label we do not want to be distributed to more than one column. I will not pursue this here.

A profiled concept is a set of profiled relations. The details are similar to those of Section 4.3. Moreover, I add here that referent systems of Vermeulen (1995) can be seen as profiled concepts. The profiled concept generated by $\mathcal{R}$, also written $[\![\mathcal{R}]\!]_{\mathscr{M}}$, is the least set closed both ways under the following operations.

① $\pi[\langle\vec{p}, R\rangle] := \langle\pi(\vec{p}), \pi[R]\rangle$, π a permutation of the set $|\vec{p}| = \{0, 1, \cdots, |\vec{p}|-1\}$;
② $E_{s,q}(\langle\vec{p}, R\rangle) := \langle\vec{p}\cdot q, R \times M_s\rangle$;
③ $D_i(\langle\vec{p}, R\rangle) := \langle\vec{p}\cdot p_i, \{\vec{x}\cdot x_i : \vec{x} \in R\}\rangle$.

Notice that when duplicating a column we must also duplicate the corresponding profile. It is therefore quite possible to have two identical columns, as long as they have different profiles. Notice that full columns are discarded regardless of their profile.

The **deprofiling** of $\langle\vec{p}, R\rangle$, $\delta(\langle\vec{p}, R\rangle)$, is simply R. Similarly, we define the deprofiling of a profiled concept.

$$\delta([\![\mathcal{R}]\!]) := \{S : \text{there is } \vec{q}\text{: } \langle\vec{q}, R\rangle \in [\![\mathcal{R}]\!]\} \tag{4.94}$$

So, $\delta(\mathcal{C}) = \delta[\mathcal{C}]$. The following gives the justification for this definition. Its proof is left as an exercise.

Proposition 4.10 *$\delta([\![\mathcal{R}]\!])$ is a concept.*

There is a converse operation of introducing a profiling. While we could do that on a concept-by-concept basis, there are more interesting methods.

Definition 4.9 Let Y be a linking aspect and $f : \mathbb{N} \to P$ a function. Then define the profiled concept $f^Y(\mathfrak{c})$ as follows.

$$f^Y(\mathfrak{c}) := [\![\langle f \restriction \text{card}(Y(\mathfrak{c})), Y(\mathfrak{c})\rangle]\!] \tag{4.95}$$

In this definition, assume that $\text{card}(Y(\mathfrak{c})) = n$. Then $f \restriction \text{card}(Y(\mathfrak{c}))$ is the restriction of f to $n = \{0, \cdots, n-1\}$. This is then viewed as the sequence $\langle f(0), f(1), \cdots, f(n-1)\rangle$. The idea is that all we need to specify is the way in which the positions are profiled; the rest is done by the linking aspect, which lines up the columns of the relation in a particular way.

The crucial difference between profiled concepts and ordinary concepts is that we can use the profiles to define the linking; and that we can also change the profile if necessary (unlike the typing). In principle, since the profiling is arbitrary, we consider two profiled concepts as basically identical if they have the same profile.

Definition 4.10 Two profiled concepts $\mathcal{C}$ and $\mathcal{D}$ are said to be **homologous** if $\delta(\mathcal{C}) = \delta(\mathcal{D})$.

Any change from a profiled concept to a homologous profiled concept is thus considered legitimate. There are various methods to define such a change for the entire space of concepts. Here is one.

Definition 4.11 Let S be a set of sorts and P a set of profiles. A **reprofiling** is a family $\{\rho_s : s \in S\}$ of maps $\rho_s : P \to P$. The reprofiling of a profiled relation $\mathcal{R} = \langle \vec{p}, R \rangle$ of type $\vec{s}$ is the relation $\rho(\mathcal{R}) := \langle \rho_R\{\vec{p}\}, R \rangle$ which is defined as follows.

$$\begin{aligned} \rho_R\{p_i\} &:= \rho_{s_i}(p_i) \\ \rho_R\{\vec{p}\} &:= \langle \rho_R\{p_i\} : i < |\vec{p}| \rangle \end{aligned} \tag{4.96}$$

Notice that the type of the relation is recoverable from the relation itself (in contrast to its profile). So the reprofiling assigns to elements of type s and profile p the new profile $\rho_s(p)$, whereas the type remains the same.

Proposition 4.11 *Let $\mathcal{C}$ be a profiled concept and $\rho = \{\rho_s : s \in S\}$ a reprofiling. Then $\rho[\mathcal{C}]$ is a profiled concept.*

Again the proof is straightforward.

The simplification introduced by profiling is considerable. Suppose for example we want to conjoin two concepts. Then we can only do this if we have a linking aspect. However, linking aspects are in general not finitely specifiable. Thus, unlike syntactic rules, the semantic combination rules based on concepts are arbitrarily complex. In Section 5.3 I shall give an example of a grammar for a fragment of English that essentially uses linking aspects only for the basic entries of the lexicon. If one wants to treat language in its full complexity one will be forced to do either of two things: make the linking aspect dynamic, that is, to be computed on the side; or introduce profiling. In this section I shall explore the second option.

Now that we have profiled concepts we may actually take advantage of the profiling in defining combinations of concepts. Our example here concerns the definition of linking aspects.

Example 4.13 Arbitrarily embedded relative clauses.

```
a dog that saw a cat that chased a mouse that ate      (4.97)
    a cheese
```

Let $D = \{d_i, c_i, m_i, h_i : i \in \mathbb{N}\}$ be the domain. There is only one sort. Let us define three binary relations:

$$\begin{aligned} E &:= \{\langle m_0, h_0 \rangle\} \cup \{\langle d_i, h_{i+1} \rangle : i \in \mathbb{N}\} \\ C &:= \{\langle c_i, m_i \rangle : i \in \mathbb{N}\} \cup \{\langle c_i, d_{i+1} \rangle : i \in \mathbb{N}\} \\ S &:= \{\langle d_i, c_i \rangle : i \in \mathbb{N}\} \cup \{\langle m_i, d_{2i} \rangle : i \in \mathbb{N}\} \end{aligned} \tag{4.98}$$

$$\begin{aligned}
\mathcal{I}(g_0)() &:= \langle \texttt{a}, «\top» \rangle \\
\mathcal{I}(g_1)() &:= \langle \texttt{that}, «\top» \rangle \\
\mathcal{I}(f_0)() &:= \langle \texttt{dog}, [\![\{d_i : i \in \mathbb{N}\}]\!] \rangle \\
\mathcal{I}(f_1)() &:= \langle \texttt{cat}, [\![\{c_i : i \in \mathbb{N}\}]\!] \rangle \\
\mathcal{I}(f_2)() &:= \langle \texttt{mouse}, [\![\{m_i : i \in \mathbb{N}\}]\!] \rangle \\
\mathcal{I}(f_3)() &:= \langle \texttt{cheese}, [\![\{h_i : i \in \mathbb{N}\}]\!] \rangle \\
\mathcal{I}(f_4)() &:= \langle \texttt{saw}, [\![S]\!] \rangle \\
\mathcal{I}(f_5)() &:= \langle \texttt{chased}, [\![C]\!] \rangle \\
\mathcal{I}(f_6)() &:= \langle \texttt{ate}, [\![E]\!] \rangle
\end{aligned} \tag{4.99}$$

There will be one mode of composition, which is binary. Let Y be the following linking aspect. For every unary concept it picks the unique minimal member and is defined on three binary concepts only, where $Y(\mathfrak{c})$ is that relation which contains $V(\mathfrak{c})$, where V assigns the following critical sets to the concepts:

$$\begin{aligned}
[\![E]\!] &\mapsto \{\langle m_0, h_0\rangle\} \\
[\![C]\!] &\mapsto \{\langle c_0, m_0\rangle\} \\
[\![S]\!] &\mapsto \{\langle d_0, c_0\rangle\}
\end{aligned} \tag{4.100}$$

(Recall $V(\mathfrak{c})$ is a set such that exactly one minimal member of $\mathfrak{c}$ contains $V(\mathfrak{c})$. $Y(\mathfrak{c})$ is defined to be that set.)

Now, $\gamma(e, e')$ is defined if and only if either of the following holds:

① $e = /\texttt{a}/$ and e' begins with /cheese/, /mouse/, /dog/, or /cat/.
② $e \in \{/\texttt{ate}/, /\texttt{saw}/, /\texttt{chased}/\}$ and e' starts with /a␣/.
③ $e = /\texttt{that}/$ and e' starts with /chased␣/, /saw␣/ or /ate␣/.
④ $e \in \{/\texttt{cat}/, /\texttt{mouse}/, /\texttt{dog}/, /\texttt{cheese}/\}$ and e' starts with /that␣/.

$$\mathcal{I}(m)(\langle e, m\rangle, \langle e', m'\rangle) := \begin{cases} \langle e^\frown {\sqcup}^\frown e', m \circledcirc^Y m'\rangle & \text{if } \gamma(e, e'), \\ \text{undefined} & \text{else.} \end{cases} \tag{4.101}$$

So, the syntax is right regular. Without specifying too much detail let me note the first steps in the derivation.

$$\begin{aligned}
&\langle \texttt{cheese}, [\![\{h_i : i \in \mathbb{N}\}]\!] \rangle \\
&\langle \texttt{a cheese}, [\![\{h_i : i \in \mathbb{N}\}]\!] \rangle \\
&\langle \texttt{ate a cheese}, [\![\{\langle d_i, h_{i+1}\rangle : i \in \mathbb{N}\} \cup \{\langle m_0, h_0\rangle\}]\!] \rangle \\
&\langle \texttt{that ate a cheese}, [\![\{\langle d_i, h_{i+1}\rangle : i \in \mathbb{N}\} \cup \{\langle m_0, h_0\rangle\}]\!] \rangle \\
&\langle \texttt{mouse that ate a cheese}, [\![\{\langle m_0, h_0\rangle\}]\!] \rangle \\
&\langle \texttt{a mouse that ate a cheese}, [\![\{\langle m_0, h_0\rangle\}]\!] \rangle
\end{aligned} \tag{4.102}$$

At this point we get stuck; for we must now be able to combine two binary concepts. If we combine them the wrong way, instead of interpreting /`a cat that chased a mouse that ate a cheese`/ we interpret /`a cat that chased a cheese that ate a mouse`/. As the embedding depth of relative clauses is unbounded there is no recipe for defining the linking aspect using critical sets as long as they do not exhaust the entire relation. So, we have to use a linking aspect instead. ⚽

Example 4.14 We come to the first repair strategy. Leave everything as is with one exception. In the interpretation of m, quantify away the lower elements, always retaining a 1-concept. M is the domain of the model.

$$\mathcal{I}(m)(\langle e, m\rangle, \langle e', m'\rangle) \\ := \begin{cases} \langle e^\frown \sqcup ^\frown e', [\![\mathsf{C}_1.(Y(m) \cap (M \times Y(m')))]\!]\rangle & \text{if } \gamma(e, e') \text{ and } m \text{ is binary,} \\ \langle e^\frown \sqcup ^\frown e', m \circledS^Y m'\rangle & \text{if } \gamma(e, e') \text{ and } m \text{ is unary,} \\ \text{undefined} & \text{else.} \end{cases} \tag{4.103}$$

The derivation now goes as follows.

$$\begin{aligned} &\langle \texttt{cheese}, [\![\{h_i : i \in \mathbb{N}\}]\!]\rangle \\ &\langle \texttt{a cheese}, [\![\{h_i : i \in \mathbb{N}\}]\!]\rangle \\ &\langle \texttt{ate a cheese}, [\![\{d_i : i \in \mathbb{N}\} \cup \{m_0\}]\!]\rangle \\ &\langle \texttt{that ate a cheese}, [\![\{d_i : i \in \mathbb{N}\} \cup \{m_0\}]\!]\rangle \\ &\langle \texttt{mouse that ate a cheese}, [\![\{m_0\}]\!]\rangle \\ &\langle \texttt{a mouse that ate a cheese}, [\![\{m_0\}]\!]\rangle \end{aligned} \tag{4.104}$$

The step from the second to the third line is the crucial bit. We invoke the linking aspect on both concepts. The right-hand side is unary, so we get the unique minimal member. The left-hand side is the concept associated with one of the verbs and by using the critical sets we align them such that the first column is the subject and the second is the object. We identify the object with the unary relation and quantify it away.

Thus, when we have processed one embedding we are back to a unary concept and can continue:

$$\begin{aligned} &\langle \texttt{chased a mouse that ate a cheese}, [\![\{c_0\}]\!]\rangle \\ &\langle \texttt{that chased a mouse that ate a cheese}, [\![\{c_0\}]\!]\rangle \\ &\langle \texttt{cat that chased a mouse that ate a cheese}, [\![\{c_0\}]\!]\rangle \\ &\langle \texttt{a cat that chased a mouse that ate a cheese}, [\![\{c_0\}]\!]\rangle \end{aligned} \tag{4.105}$$

The problem with this approach is that the intermediate objects are gone and cannot be referred to any more (say, with /`the mouse that ate a cheese`/). ⚽

Example 4.15 The second strategy uses profiling. Let $P := \{t, b\}$. The rule of combination is this. We assume that the subjects of verbs are assigned the profile t; all other arguments are assigned b. When a verb is combined with an object, the object position is identified with the object with profile t, upon which the profile of this element is set to b. On the assumption that only one column has label t, we define the following linking algorithm. Assume that $\langle t \cdot \vec{b}_1, R\rangle \in \mathcal{C}$ is of length m and $\langle x \cdot \vec{b}_2, S\rangle \in \mathcal{D}$ of length n. Then we put

$$R \overline{\otimes} S := \{x \cdot \vec{y} \cdot \vec{z} : x \cdot \vec{y} \in R \text{ and } x \cdot \vec{z} \in S\}. \tag{4.106}$$

This is almost like the Cartesian product, except that we take only the tuples that share the same first element and eliminate its second occurrence. With respect to the profile, we proceed slightly differently. On the assumption that $\langle t \cdot \vec{b}_1, R\rangle \in \mathcal{C}$ and $\langle t \cdot \vec{b}_2, \mathcal{D}\rangle \in \mathcal{D}$ we put

$$\mathcal{C} \otimes^t \mathcal{D} := [\![\langle t \cdot \vec{b}_1 \cdot \vec{b}_2, R \overline{\otimes} S\rangle]\!]_{\mathscr{M}}. \tag{4.107}$$

This is defined only if either (a) both the concepts are at least unary or (b) both profiles contain exactly one t. We extend this definition to the truth concept $\mathcal{T}$ by putting

$$\mathcal{T} \otimes^t \mathcal{D} := \mathcal{D} \otimes^t \mathcal{T} := \mathcal{D}. \tag{4.108}$$

All nouns denote concepts where the one minimal relation has profile t. And so we put

$$\mathcal{I}(m)(\langle e, m\rangle, \langle e', m'\rangle) := \begin{cases} \langle e^\frown {\llcorner\!\lrcorner}^\frown e', m \otimes^t m'\rangle & \text{if } \gamma(e, e'), \\ \text{undefined} & \text{else.} \end{cases} \tag{4.109}$$

We denote the column with label t by underlining. The derivation begins as follows.

$$\begin{aligned} &\langle \texttt{cheese}, [\![\{\underline{h_i} : i \in \mathbb{N}\}]\!]\rangle \\ &\langle \texttt{a cheese}, [\![\{\underline{h_i} : i \in \mathbb{N}\}]\!]\rangle \\ &\langle \texttt{ate a cheese}, [\![\{\langle \underline{d_i}, h_{i+1}\rangle : i \in \mathbb{N}\} \cup \{\langle \underline{m_0}, h_0\rangle\}]\!]\rangle \\ &\langle \texttt{that ate a cheese}, [\![\{\langle \underline{d_i}, h_{i+1}\rangle : i \in \mathbb{N}\} \cup \{\langle \underline{m_0}, h_0\rangle\}]\!]\rangle \\ &\langle \texttt{mouse that ate a cheese}, [\![\{\langle \underline{m_0}, h_0\rangle\}]\!]\rangle \\ &\langle \texttt{a mouse that ate a cheese}, [\![\{\langle \underline{m_0}, h_0\rangle\}]\!]\rangle \end{aligned} \tag{4.110}$$

We have only one privileged member. We continue the derivation.

$$\langle \texttt{chased a mouse that ate a cheese}, [\![\{\langle \underline{c_0}, m_0, h_0\rangle\}]\!]\rangle$$
$$\langle \texttt{that chased a mouse that ate a cheese}, [\![\{\langle \underline{c_0}, m_0, h_0\rangle\}]\!]\rangle$$
$$\langle \texttt{cat that chased a mouse that ate a cheese}, [\![\{\langle \underline{c_0}, m_0, h_0\rangle\}]\!]\rangle \quad (4.111)$$
$$\langle \texttt{a cat that chased a mouse that ate a cheese}, [\![\{\langle \underline{c_0}, m_0, h_0\rangle\}]\!]\rangle$$

The next step is to merge with /saw/:

$$\langle \texttt{saw a cat that chased a mouse that ate a cheese}, [\![\{\langle \underline{d_0}, c_0, m_0, h_0\rangle\}]\!]\rangle \quad (4.112)$$

And so on. Thus, the relations are growing in length but retain only one distinguished member. ⚽

The idea of profiling is not new. In formal semantics, referent systems (see Vermeulen (1995)) formalize a variant of profiling. Also Centering Theory implements a notion of profiling (see for example Bittner (2006) and references therein).

Exercise 4.14 Prove Proposition 4.10.

Chapter 5
Examples

IN this chapter we shall look at some examples. The first example will be standard predicate logic. It will be shown that if semantics is based on concepts and not on relations then there must be a limit on the number of free variables. The second example will be a fragment (Montague size) of English. Finally, we shall indicate how the present approach allows to get insights into sentence structure.

5.1 Predicate Logic

This chapter is devoted to applications as well as examples. We begin by presenting standard predicate logic. In this section we shall give a grammar for predicate logic together with two standard interpretations. One interprets formulas as sets of valuations the other as relations. Then we shall turn to concept based interpretations. This will then be applied to natural language. Later in the chapter we shall show how the present assumptions on semantics (and syntax) allow to predict facts about sentential structure.

Recall from Section 4.2 the basic facts about predicate logic and its structures. In contrast to that section we do not deal with sorts; they do not add anything of significance. We start with a signature $\langle \text{Rel}, \tau \rangle$, Rel a finite set of relation symbols and $\tau : \text{Rel} \to \mathbb{N}$. We shall as usual write τ in place of $\langle \text{Rel}, \tau \rangle$. The alphabet is then the following set: $A := \{\texttt{(}, \texttt{)}, \texttt{,}, \texttt{0}, \texttt{1}, \texttt{x}, \texttt{→}, \neg, \vee, \wedge, \exists, \forall\} \cup \text{Rel}$. We assume that there are no function symbols. The arity of $R \in \text{Rel}$ is given by $\tau(R)$. We shall first describe informally the formation rules of well-formed expressions and their meanings and then present a grammar of the interpreted language. The interpretation is based on a fixed structure $\mathscr{M} = \langle M, \mathfrak{I} \rangle$, where M is a set and $\mathfrak{I}$ a function sending a relation symbol R to a set $\mathfrak{I}(R) \subseteq M^{\tau(R)}$. A **valuation** is a function from the set of variables to M. The set of all valuations is denoted by Val.

In Section 4.2 we have provided meanings only for formulae. However, our alphabet is finite and we need an infinite array of variables. So we must generate the set of variables from a finite base. This means, however, that we need to give some meaning to the variables. An **index** is a member of $(\texttt{0}|\texttt{1})^*$, that is, a possibly empty string of /0/ and /1/. The meaning of an index is the index itself. A **variable** is a sequence $\vec{v} := /\texttt{x}\vec{y}$, where $\vec{y}$ is an index. The meaning of the variable is

M. Kracht, *Interpreted Languages and Compositionality*, Studies in Linguistics and Philosophy 89, DOI 10.1007/978-94-007-2108-1_5,
© Springer Science+Business Media B.V. 2011

the function $\vec{v}^* : \beta \mapsto \beta(\vec{v})$. An **atomic formula** is an expression of the form $/R^\frown(^\frown\vec{v}_0^\frown,^\frown\vec{v}_1^\frown\cdots^\frown,^\frown\vec{v}_{\tau(R)-1}{}^\frown)/$, where the $\vec{v}_i$ are variables. Its meaning is the set $m(R) := \{\beta : \langle m(\vec{v}_0)(\beta), m(\vec{v}_1)(\beta), \cdots, m(\vec{v}_{\tau(R)-1})(\beta)\rangle \in \mathfrak{I}(R)\}$. Complex formulae are of the form $/(\neg\varphi)/$, $/(\varphi\wedge\chi)/$, $/(\varphi\vee\chi)/$, $/(\varphi\rightarrow\chi)/$, $/(\exists\mathtt{x}\vec{v})\varphi/$, $/(\forall\mathtt{x}\vec{v})\varphi/$, where $\vec{v}$ is an index and φ and χ are formulae. The meaning of formulae has been spelled out earlier in Section 4.2. Thus the full language is L_τ.

$$\begin{aligned} L_\tau := \quad & \{\langle \vec{y}, \vec{y}\rangle : \vec{y} \in (0|1)^*\} \\ & \cup\{\langle \mathtt{x}\vec{v}, \mathtt{x}\vec{y}^*\rangle : \vec{y} \in (0|1)^*\} \\ & \cup\{\langle \varphi, [\varphi]_{\mathscr{M}}\rangle : \varphi \in \mathrm{PL}_\tau\} \end{aligned} \tag{5.1}$$

(See (4.11) for a definition of $[\cdot]_{\mathscr{M}}$.) Now we shall present a grammar for L_τ. We shall use the following modes:

$$F := \{f_\varnothing, f_0, f_1, f_v, f_\neg, f_\wedge, f_\vee, f_\rightarrow, f_\exists, f_\forall\} \cup \{f_R : R \in \mathrm{Rel}\}. \tag{5.2}$$

The signature is $\Omega : f_\varnothing \mapsto 0$, $f_1 \mapsto 1$, $f_2 \mapsto 1$, $f_v \mapsto 1$, $f_\neg \mapsto 1$, $f_\wedge \mapsto 2$, $f_\vee \mapsto 2$, $f_\rightarrow \mapsto 2$, $f_\exists \mapsto 2$, $f_\forall \mapsto 2$, $f_R \mapsto \tau(R)$, where $R \in \mathrm{Rel}$. First, we shall define the modes that build up the variables. We put $e^*(\beta) := \beta(e)$. The function e^* is defined on valuations and applies the valuation to the variable e.

$$\begin{aligned} \mathcal{C}(f_\varnothing) &:= \langle \varepsilon, \varepsilon\rangle \\ \mathcal{C}(f_0)(\langle e, m\rangle) &:= \begin{cases} \langle e^\frown 0, m^\frown 0\rangle & \text{provided that } e \text{ is an index,} \\ \text{undefined} & \text{else.} \end{cases} \\ \mathcal{C}(f_1)(\langle e, m\rangle) &:= \begin{cases} \langle e^\frown 1, m^\frown 1\rangle & \text{provided that } e \text{ is an index,} \\ \text{undefined} & \text{else.} \end{cases} \\ \mathcal{C}(f_v)(\langle e, m\rangle) &:= \begin{cases} \langle \mathtt{x}^\frown e, (\mathtt{x}^\frown m)^*\rangle & \text{provided that } e \text{ is an index,} \\ \text{undefined} & \text{else.} \end{cases} \end{aligned} \tag{5.3}$$

The last rule seems dangerous since it seemingly converts any object m into a function m^* on assignments. However, the other rules can only generate the pairs $\langle \vec{y}, \vec{y}\rangle$ and so $m = e$.

Next we turn to relations. Let R be a relation:

$$\begin{aligned} & \mathcal{C}(f_R)(\langle e_0, m_0\rangle, \cdots, \langle e_{\tau(R)-1}, m_{\tau(R)-1}\rangle) \\ & := \begin{cases} \langle R^\frown(^\frown e_0^\frown,^\frown\cdots^\frown,^\frown e_{\tau(R)-1}{}^\frown), \{\beta : \langle m_0(\beta), \cdots, m_{\tau(R)-1}(\beta)\rangle \in \mathfrak{I}(R)\}\rangle \\ \qquad \text{if the } e_i \text{ are variables,} \\ \text{undefined else.} \end{cases} \end{aligned} \tag{5.4}$$

Finally we introduce the modes for the connectives. No difficulties arise with the booleans:

$$\mathcal{C}(f_\neg)(\langle e, m\rangle) := \begin{cases} \langle (^\frown\neg^\frown e^\frown), \mathrm{Val} - m\rangle & \text{if } e \text{ is a formula,} \\ \text{undefined} & \text{else.} \end{cases}$$

$$\mathcal{C}(f_\wedge)(\langle e_0, m_0\rangle, \langle e_1, m_1\rangle) := \begin{cases} \langle (^\frown e_0^\frown\wedge^\frown e_1^\frown), m_0 \cap m_1\rangle \\ \qquad \text{if } e_0 \text{ and } e_1 \text{ are formulae,} \\ \text{undefined else.} \end{cases}$$

$$\mathcal{C}(f_\vee)(\langle e_0, m_0\rangle, \langle e_1, m_1\rangle) := \begin{cases} \langle (^\frown e_0^\frown\vee^\frown e_1^\frown), m_0 \cup m_1\rangle \\ \qquad \text{if } e_0 \text{ and } e_1 \text{ are formulae,} \\ \text{undefined else.} \end{cases} \tag{5.5}$$

$$\mathcal{C}(f_\rightarrow)(\langle e_0, m_0\rangle, \langle e_1, m_1\rangle) := \begin{cases} \langle (^\frown e_0^\frown\rightarrow^\frown e_1^\frown), (\mathrm{Val} - m_0) \cup m_1\rangle \\ \qquad \text{if } e_0 \text{ and } e_1 \text{ are formulae,} \\ \text{undefined else.} \end{cases}$$

Finally the quantifiers. They are introduced by binary modes, one responsible for the handling of the variable and the other responsible for the scope. The definition is somewhat tricky. We assume that M has at least two elements, say a and b. Given a variable $\vec{y}$, let $\beta_a^{\vec{y}}$ be the valuation that assigns a to $\vec{y}$ and b to every other variable. If m has the form v^* for some variable v then we can find the index of this variable by looking at the unique $\vec{y}$ such that $\vec{y}^*\left(\beta_a^{\vec{y}}\right) = a$. We denote the variable with meaning m by $\zeta(m)$.

$$\begin{aligned} &\mathcal{C}(f_\exists)(\langle e_0, m_0\rangle, \langle e_1, m_1\rangle) \\ &:= \begin{cases} \langle (^\frown\exists^\frown e_0^\frown)^\frown e_1, \{\beta' : \text{exists } \beta \sim_{\zeta(m_0)} \beta' : \beta \in m_1\}\rangle \\ \qquad \text{if } e_0 \text{ is a variable and } e_1 \text{ a formula,} \\ \text{undefined else.} \end{cases} \end{aligned} \tag{5.6}$$

If M contains just one element then we put

$$\mathcal{C}(f_\exists)(\langle e_0, m_0\rangle, \langle e_1, m_1\rangle) := \begin{cases} \langle (^\frown\exists^\frown e_0^\frown)^\frown e_1, m_1\rangle \\ \qquad \text{if } e_0 \text{ is a variable and } e_1 \text{ a formula,} \\ \text{undefined else.} \end{cases} \tag{5.7}$$

The universal quantifier is quite similar. This finishes the definition of the grammar. Let us notice that this grammar is actually independent. The functions on the exponents and the functions on the meanings are independently formulated. In this case what needs to be checked is that the domains for these functions (which are partial) are independently specifiable. As we have spelled out the grammar, the functions on the exponents are partial and the conditions on the modes are spelled out as conditions on the exponents. Hence this is unproblematic. Now, the functions on the meaning are de facto partial. Yet in case the functions on the exponents are defined, the meanings can also be composed and therefore no supplementary condition needs to be added.

Intermission 2 One may have noticed that the grammar adds syncategorematic symbols other than brackets. In fact, all occurrences of logical and relation symbols are syncategorematic. This is unavoidable given the language L_τ. For if /`r`/ is a unary relation symbol /`r(x)`/ is a formula but the only part of it that is an expression is /`x`/, while /`r`/ itself is not. This is a common dilemma. Montague has basically opted to make logical words in natural language syncategorematic. The price is that we cannot explain the meaning of /`John walks and Pete talks.`/ in terms of the meaning of /and/ and the constituent sentences. Rather, /and/ merely signals the application of a rule whose effect is to coordinate the sentences. ⚽

I should mention here that Fine (2003) has claimed that there is no compositional semantics for predicate logic. The above grammar suggests that this is false. Indeed, what Fine has in mind is a different language of predicate logic by which we do not use variables that consist in, say, a letter and an index. Rather, he has in mind a semantics where the name of the variable is arbitrary and not fixed in any way in advance (like it is in mathematical logic, for example); this corresponds to the factual *use* of predicate logic in everyday discourse, even in logic. Careful texts admit that what they are using are not actual variables but metavariables. (To my knowledge, the book (Monk, 1976) is a rare exception in actually using *variables* rather than metavariables.) If we want to give a semantics of predicate logic in terms of metavariables we must change the definitions rather substantially. Notice that the same issue arises in connection with programming languages. It used to be the case that variables had to have a specific format to make them distinct from other expressions. In many modern programming languages this is no longer required. Any expression that is not predefined can be used. Since the programmer is also free to define a host of other things, it turns out that it is highly context dependent whether or not a given sequence of letters actually denotes a variable.

There is certainly more than one way in which we can implement the semantics of predicate logic. Thus, L_τ is one in many other formulations of predicate logic. Another way is described in Section 4.5. Let $\mathscr{S} := \langle \mathscr{M}, \beta \rangle$ be a model. Based on the model $\mathscr{S}$, we perform a reduction of the formulae in the following way: write $\varphi \equiv_{\mathscr{S}} \chi$ if

$$\langle \mathscr{M}, \beta \rangle \vDash \varphi \leftrightarrow \chi . \tag{5.8}$$

This is an equivalence relation. Moreover, it is a congruence with respect to the standard boolean operations. This means that for $\circ \in \{\vee, \wedge, \rightarrow\}$:

$$\frac{\varphi \equiv_{\mathscr{S}} \chi}{(\neg\varphi) \equiv_{\mathscr{S}} (\neg\chi)} \qquad \frac{\varphi_1 \equiv_{\mathscr{S}} \chi_1 \quad \varphi_2 \equiv_{\mathscr{S}} \chi_2}{(\varphi_1 \circ \varphi_2) \equiv_{\mathscr{S}} (\chi_1 \circ \chi_2)} \tag{5.9}$$

However, it is checked that the following does *not* hold.

$$\frac{\varphi \equiv_{\mathscr{S}} \chi}{(\exists \mathtt{x}_i)\varphi \equiv_{\mathscr{S}} (\exists \mathtt{x}_i)\chi} \tag{5.10}$$

Similarly, given just $\mathscr{M}$, write $\varphi \equiv_{\mathscr{M}} \chi$ if for all β

$$\langle \mathscr{M}, \beta \rangle \vDash \varphi \leftrightarrow \chi . \tag{5.11}$$

This is equivalent to saying that for all β:

$$\langle \mathscr{M}, \beta \rangle \vDash \varphi \Leftrightarrow \langle \mathscr{M}, \beta \rangle \vDash \chi . \tag{5.12}$$

This in turn is the same as $[\varphi]_{\mathscr{M}} = [\chi]_{\mathscr{M}}$. Finally, the denotation of a formula is not the set $[\varphi]_{\mathscr{M}}$ but rather the set $\{\chi : \varphi \equiv_{\mathscr{M}} \chi\}$. This time not only the laws (5.9) hold (with $\equiv_{\mathscr{M}}$ replacing $\equiv_{\mathscr{S}}$) but we also have

$$\frac{\varphi \equiv_{\mathscr{M}} \chi}{(\exists \mathtt{x}_i)\varphi \equiv_{\mathscr{M}} (\exists \mathtt{x}_i)\chi} \tag{5.13}$$

I seize the opportunity to broaden the scope of the semantics somewhat. Let W be a set, the set of **worlds**. For every $w \in W$ assume a model $\mathscr{M}(w) = \langle \mathcal{M}(w), \mathfrak{I}(w), \beta(w) \rangle$. This gives us an indexed family $\mathscr{W} := \{\mathscr{M}(w) : w \in W\}$ of models. We write $\varphi \equiv_{\mathscr{W}} \chi$ if for all $w \in W$: $\varphi \equiv_{\mathscr{M}(w)} \chi$. The laws (5.9) hold but (5.10) need not hold.

The rationale behind this is that the family $\mathscr{W}$ represents the space of all possibilities. We say that φ is **necessary** (in $\mathscr{W}$) if $\varphi \equiv_{\mathscr{W}} \top$. (Here, $\top$ is any tautology, say, $(\forall \mathtt{x})\mathtt{x}=\mathtt{x}$.) φ is **possible** if $\varphi \not\equiv_{\mathscr{W}} \bot$. Let Λ be a first-order logic in the chosen signature τ. Then for every formula $\varphi \in L_\tau$ two choices arise: either it is inconsistent, that is, its negation is in Λ; or it is consistent, in which case there is a structure $\mathscr{M}$ and a valuation β such that $\langle \mathscr{M}, \beta \rangle \vDash \varphi$. (See Section 4.2.) We can sharpen this somewhat. Say that a theory T is **maximally consistent** if T is consistent but there is no consistent U properly containing T. Let W be the set of maximally consistent sets and $\langle \mathscr{M}(w), \beta(w) \rangle$ be a model such that for every $\delta \in w$: $\langle \mathscr{M}(w), \beta(w) \rangle \vDash \delta$. With this choice of $\mathscr{W}$ we have that $\varphi \equiv_{\mathscr{W}} \chi$ if and only if $\varphi \leftrightarrow \chi$ is a theorem of predicate logic. In this model, φ is a necessary if it is logically true; and possible if logically consistent.

Definition 5.1 A structure $\mathscr{S} = \{\langle \mathscr{M}(w), \beta(w) \rangle : w \in W\}$ is **canonical** for a logic L if φ is necessary in $\mathscr{S}$ if and only if φ is L-equivalent to $\top$, impossible in $\mathscr{S}$ if and only if φ is L-equivalent to $\bot$ and possible otherwise.

This construction and result can be extended to other logics extending predicate logic. A particular case are *meaning postulates*.

Example 5.1 It is standardly assumed that /`bachelor`/ and /`unmarried man`/ are synonymous (ignoring presuppositions). There are two ways to implement this logically. One is to insert two unary predicate symbols, /`r`/ and /`m`/ and *define*

$$\texttt{b(x)} := \texttt{((}\neg\texttt{r(x))}\wedge\texttt{m(x))}. \tag{5.14}$$

This is basically a metalinguistic convention: it says that the string /b/ (which is not a relation symbol of our language), when followed by /$\texttt{(x}\vec{v}\texttt{)}$/ is to be replaced by the sequence on the right, where /x/ is replaced by /$\texttt{x}\vec{v}$/. Another way is to introduce three one place relation symbols, /b/, /m/ and /r/ and add the *meaning postulates*

$$\begin{aligned}&\texttt{(}\forall\texttt{x)(b(x)}\texttt{→((}\neg\texttt{r(x))}\wedge\texttt{m(x)))},\\ &\texttt{(}\forall\texttt{x)(((}\neg\texttt{r(x))}\wedge\texttt{m(x))}\texttt{→b(x))}.\end{aligned} \tag{5.15}$$

This means that our logic—call it L^+—is no longer predicate logic but a stronger logic. It is the least logic containing predicate logic and the two formulae of (5.15). The canonical structure for this logic consists in all models of the canonical structure for predicate logic in the new signature minus all the models where (5.15) does not hold. ⚽

Another point of extension is modal logic. Introduce a relation $\lhd$ on the set W. Then pick $w \in W$ and write

$$\langle \mathscr{W}, w\rangle \vDash \varphi :\Leftrightarrow \langle \mathscr{M}(w), \beta(w)\rangle \vDash \varphi. \tag{5.16}$$

Introduce a unary $\Box$ operator on formulae and define

$$\langle \mathscr{W}, w\rangle \vDash (\Box\varphi) \text{ for all } u\text{: if } w \lhd u \text{ then } \langle \mathscr{W}, u\rangle \vDash \varphi. \tag{5.17}$$

This is the way in which Montague Semantics analyses propositional attitudes and tense, for example. We shall not have much to say on this topic, though. An alternative approach to intensionality is to add a new *sort*, that of a world and make predicates relative to worlds.

Exercise 5.1 Spell out a grammar for the language $\{\langle\varphi, (\!|\varphi|\!)_{\mathscr{M}}\rangle : \varphi \in L_\tau\}$, adding interpretations for indices and variables as given in this section.

Exercise 5.2 Let L^+ be the logic of Example 5.1. Let A be the set of formulae in (5.15). Say that a theory T is L^+_τ-consistent if $T \cup A$ is consistent. Use the Completeness Theorem to derive that there is a canonical structure $\mathscr{S}$ for L^+.

Exercise 5.3 Define the following order on indices:

$$\varepsilon, \texttt{0}, \texttt{1}, \texttt{00}, \texttt{01}, \texttt{10}, \texttt{11}, \texttt{000}, \ldots \tag{5.18}$$

So, $\vec{x}$ comes before $\vec{y}$, in symbols $\vec{x} \lessdot \vec{y}$, if and only if either $\vec{x}$ is shorter than $\vec{y}$ or $\vec{x}$ and $\vec{y}$ are of equal length and the binary number of $\vec{x}$ is less than that of $\vec{y}$. Describe an algorithm to calculate from a number k the string $\vec{x}$, where $\vec{x}$ has position k in the order $\lessdot$. Describe also the algorithm of the inverse to this mapping.

5.2 Concept Based Predicate Logic

In this section we shall explore the question whether there exists a compositional grammar for predicate logic based on concepts. It will turn out that such grammar only exists if we restrict the language to a fragment based on finitely many variables. Whether or not the language is sorted is of no importance. Thus we ignore sorts and look at the following language:

$$\mathrm{CL}_\tau := \{\langle\varphi, «\varphi»_{\mathcal{M}}\rangle : \varphi \in \mathrm{PL}_\tau\}. \tag{5.19}$$

There is a trivial grammar for this language. Simply use the formation rules f_*^ε of the previous section and define the meaning functions f^μ by

$$f^\mu(\langle e_0, m_0\rangle, \cdots, \langle e_{\Omega(f)-1}, m_{\Omega(f)-1}\rangle) := «f_*^\varepsilon(\vec{e})»_{\mathcal{M}}. \tag{5.20}$$

Thus

$$\mathcal{I}(f)(\langle e_0, m_0\rangle, \cdots, \langle e_{\Omega(f)-1}, m_{\Omega(f)-1}\rangle) := \langle f_*^\varepsilon(\vec{e}), «f_*^\varepsilon(\vec{e})»_{\mathcal{M}}\rangle \tag{5.21}$$

In plain words: we first form the exponent (which we can do since the grammar of the previous section is autonomous) and then compute the meaning directly from the exponent. The problem is that this grammar is not compositional. The question therefore is whether we can give a compositional grammar for the language of concepts.

As stated above, this depends on whether or not we have only boundedly many variables. Therefore, let us assume first that we use only formulae that contain the variables x_0 through x_{n-1}. We call this language PL_τ^n. This is the set of all formulae from PL_τ such that any occurring variable is contained in $\{x_i : i < n\}$. (It is of course not necessary that the variables are called x_0 through x_{n-1}. Any other set of variables with cardinality n will do.) Now fix a structure $\mathcal{M} = \langle M, \mathfrak{I}\rangle$. We put

$$«\varphi»_{\mathcal{M}} := [\![(\!|\varphi|\!)_{\mathcal{M}}]\!]_{\mathcal{M}}. \tag{5.22}$$

We shall present an independent grammar for

$$\mathrm{CL}_\tau^n = \left\{\langle\varphi, «\varphi»_{\mathcal{M}}\rangle : \varphi \in \mathrm{PL}_\tau^n\right\}. \tag{5.23}$$

Define $C := \left\{«\varphi»_{\mathcal{M}} : \varphi \in \mathrm{PL}_\tau^n\right\}$, the expressive power of CL_τ^n. It is clear that no relation of length $> n$ can be minimal for any member of C. This is because there are only n different free variables to choose from, so they generate only n-ary relations. However, C not only contains concepts of length n but concepts of length $k < n$ as well.

Let $f : C \to \mathrm{PL}_\tau^n$ be a function such that $\mathfrak{c} = «f(\mathfrak{c})»_{\mathcal{M}}$. Thus, f picks for each concept a formula defining it. For an arbitrary $\chi \in \mathrm{PL}_\tau^n$ the **type** $\mathrm{tp}(\chi)$ is a subset of Π_n, the set of permutations of n (see Appendix A). It is defined by

$$\pi \in \mathrm{tp}(\chi(\vec{x})) :\Leftrightarrow \mathcal{M} \vDash \chi(x_{\pi^{-1}(0)}, \cdots, x_{\pi^{-1}(n-1)}) \leftrightarrow f(«\chi(\vec{x})»_{\mathcal{M}}). \tag{5.24}$$

We may write each formula as $\varphi(x_0, \cdots, x_{n-1})$ even if some of the variables do not appear in it. A formula may thus have several types, since nonoccurring variables can be permuted freely (also it may happen that a relation is symmetric in some columns). Let $[y_0/z_0, \cdots, y_{n-1}/z_{n-1}]\delta$ denote the result of substituting, for each $i < n$ simultaneously, all free occurrences of z_i in δ by y_i. Given a type π and a concept $\mathfrak{c}$ we define

$$f_\pi(\mathfrak{c}) := [x_{\pi(i)}/x_i : i < n] f(\mathfrak{c}). \tag{5.25}$$

Together with (5.24) this gives us for every $\varphi \in \mathrm{CL}^n_\tau$ and $\pi \in \mathrm{tp}(\varphi)$:

$$\mathcal{M} \vDash \varphi \leftrightarrow f_\pi(«\varphi»_{\mathcal{M}}). \tag{5.26}$$

Example 5.2 Here is an example. Suppose we have a binary relation symbol /r/ and we are looking at the language PL^2_τ. The variables are called /x0/ (written here x_0) and /x1/ (written here x_1). Let $\mathfrak{c} := «\mathtt{r(x0,x1)}»_{\mathcal{M}}$. Then we also have

$$\mathfrak{c} = «\mathtt{r(x1,x0)}»_{\mathcal{M}} \tag{5.27}$$

Let $f(\mathfrak{c}) = \mathtt{r(x0,x1)}$. Then the type of /r(x0,x1)/ is the identity permutation, written (). However, the type of /r(x1,x0)/ is the permutation $\pi = (0\ 1)$. For we have

$$f_\pi(\mathfrak{c}) = [\mathtt{x1/x0, x0/x1}]\mathtt{r(x0,x1)} = \mathtt{r(x1,x0)}. \tag{5.28}$$

And so we evidently have

$$\mathcal{M} \vDash \mathtt{r(x1,x0)} \leftrightarrow f_\pi(«\mathtt{r(x1,x0)}»_{\mathcal{M}}). \tag{5.29}$$

Similarly for $n > 2$. A particular case to look at is where we have more variables than occur free in the formula, for example, PL^4_τ. Here the type of /r(x0,x1)/ consist both in () and in (2 3), because the action on nonoccurring variables is irrelevant. Similarly, the types of /r(x1,x0)/ are (0 1) and (0 1)(2 3). ⚽

This finishes the preparations. We are ready to spell out the modes. They are given in Fig. 5.1. In the definition, the following functions are being used. For the existential quantifier we introduce the following functions.

$$\exists^i_\pi(\mathfrak{c}) := «(\exists \mathtt{x}_i) f_\pi(\mathfrak{c})»_{\mathcal{M}} \tag{5.30}$$

For the universal quantifier we use

$$\forall^i_\pi(\mathfrak{c}) := «(\forall \mathtt{x}_i) f_\pi(\mathfrak{c})»_{\mathcal{M}} \tag{5.31}$$

with $i < n$ and $\pi \in \Pi_n$. Now for the booleans.

$$\begin{aligned} N(\mathfrak{c}) &:= «(\neg f(\mathfrak{c}))»_{\mathscr{M}} \\ A_{\pi;\rho}(\mathfrak{c},\mathfrak{d}) &:= «(f_\pi(\mathfrak{c})\vee f_\rho(\mathfrak{d}))»_{\mathscr{M}} \\ C_{\pi;\rho}(\mathfrak{c},\mathfrak{d}) &:= «(f_\pi(\mathfrak{c})\wedge f_\rho(\mathfrak{d}))»_{\mathscr{M}} \\ I_{\pi;\rho}(\mathfrak{c},\mathfrak{d}) &:= «(f_\pi(\mathfrak{c})\rightarrow f_\rho(\mathfrak{d}))»_{\mathscr{M}} \end{aligned} \tag{5.32}$$

The modes are as follows: for every relation symbol R and every map $\tau : n \to n$ (not necessarily injective) we pick a 0-ary mode f_τ^R. For every $i < n$ and every $\pi \in \Pi_n$ we pick a unary mode $f_{i,\pi}^{\exists}$ and a unary mode $f_{i,\pi}^{\forall}$. There will be a unary mode $f^{\neg}$ and for every $\pi, \rho \in \Pi_n$ (not necessarily distinct) binary modes $f_{\pi,\rho}^{\wedge}$, $f_{\pi,\rho}^{\vee}$ and $f_{\pi,\rho}^{\rightarrow}$. This defines the set F_n and the signature Ω_n. The interpretation $\mathcal{J}_n$ is shown in Fig. 5.1. α ranges over (not necessarily bijective or even injective) functions from n to n and i over elements from n.

$$\begin{aligned}
\mathcal{J}_n\left(f_\alpha^R\right) &:= \langle R^\frown(^\frown\mathbf{x}_{\alpha(0)}{}^\frown,{}^\frown\cdots{}^\frown,{}^\frown\mathbf{x}_{\alpha(a(R)-1)}{}^\frown), \\
&\qquad «R^\frown(^\frown\mathbf{x}_{\alpha(0)}{}^\frown,{}^\frown\cdots{}^\frown,{}^\frown\mathbf{x}_{\alpha(a(R)-1)}{}^\frown)»_{\mathscr{M}}\rangle \\
\mathcal{J}_n(f^{\neg})(\langle e,m\rangle) &:= \langle(^\frown\neg^\frown e^\frown), N(m)\rangle \\
\mathcal{J}_n\left(f_{i,\pi}^{\exists}\right)(\langle e,m\rangle) &:= \begin{cases} \langle(^\frown\exists^\frown\mathbf{x}_i{}^\frown)^\frown e, \exists_\pi^i(m)\rangle & \text{if } \pi\in\mathrm{tp}(e), \\ \text{undefined} & \text{else.}\end{cases} \\
\mathcal{J}_n\left(f_{i,\pi}^{\forall}\right)(\langle e,m\rangle) &:= \begin{cases} \langle(^\frown\forall^\frown\mathbf{x}_i{}^\frown)^\frown e, \forall_\pi^i(m)\rangle & \text{if } \pi\in\mathrm{tp}(e), \\ \text{undefined} & \text{else.}\end{cases} \\
\mathcal{J}_n\left(f_{\pi,\rho}^{\vee}\right)(\langle e,m\rangle,\langle e',m'\rangle) &:= \begin{cases} \langle(^\frown e^\frown\vee^\frown e'^\frown), A_{\pi,\rho}(m,m')\rangle & \text{if } \pi\in\mathrm{tp}(e) \\ & \text{and } \rho\in\mathrm{tp}(e'), \\ \text{undefined} & \text{else.}\end{cases} \\
\mathcal{J}_n\left(f_{\pi,\rho}^{\wedge}\right)(\langle e,m\rangle,\langle e',m'\rangle) &:= \begin{cases} \langle(^\frown e^\frown\wedge^\frown e'^\frown), C_{\pi,\rho}(m,m')\rangle & \text{if } \pi\in\mathrm{tp}(e) \\ & \text{and } \rho\in\mathrm{tp}(e'), \\ \text{undefined} & \text{else.}\end{cases} \\
\mathcal{J}_n\left(f_{\pi,\rho}^{\rightarrow}\right)(\langle e,m\rangle,\langle e',m'\rangle) &:= \begin{cases} \langle(^\frown e^\frown\rightarrow^\frown e'^\frown), I_{\pi,\rho}(m,m')\rangle & \text{if } \pi\in\mathrm{tp}(e) \\ & \text{and } \rho\in\mathrm{tp}(e'), \\ \text{undefined} & \text{else.}\end{cases}
\end{aligned} \tag{5.33}$$

Fig. 5.1 The modes for CL_τ^n

Theorem 5.1 *The grammar* $G_n = \langle\Omega_n, \mathcal{J}_n\rangle$ *is independent, context free and* $L(G_n) = \mathrm{CL}_\tau^n$.

Proof It is easy to see that G_n is independent. The functions on the concepts are defined and the functions on the exponents are partial, with conditions that are completely independent of the meaning. (This is because the concept of a formula is uniquely determined anyway, so any mention of meaning of a sign can be eliminated.) It remains to be shown that the grammar generates CL_τ^n. This is done by induction. The inductive claim is that for every formula φ there is a term t such that $\iota(t) = \langle \varphi, «\varphi»_{\mathscr{M}} \rangle$. The base case is

$$\varphi = R(\mathtt{x}_{j_0}, \cdots, \mathtt{x}_{j_{a(R)-1}}). \tag{5.34}$$

Put $i(k) := j_k$ if $k < a(R)$ and $i(k) := 0$ else. Then

$$\varphi = R(\mathtt{x}_{i(0)}, \cdots, \mathtt{x}_{i(a(R)-1)}) \tag{5.35}$$

and so

$$\mathcal{I}\left(f_i^R\right) = \langle \varphi, «\varphi»_{\mathscr{M}} \rangle. \tag{5.36}$$

I perform only two of the inductive steps. Suppose for example that the formula has the form $/(e \vee e')/$. By inductive hypothesis there are analysis terms t and t' that unfold to $\langle e, m \rangle$ and $\langle e', m' \rangle$, respectively. Let π be a type of e and ρ a type of e'. (Every formula has at least one type.) By inductive hypothesis, $m = «e»_{\mathscr{M}}$ and $m' = «e'»_{\mathscr{M}}$. Then $f^{\vee}_{\pi,\rho} t t'$ is defined and has exponent $/(e \vee e')/$. For the meaning we have by definition

$$\begin{aligned} & A_{\pi,\rho}(m, m') \\ =& «(f_\pi(m) \vee f_\rho(m'))»_{\mathscr{M}} \\ =& «(e \vee e')»_{\mathscr{M}} \end{aligned} \tag{5.37}$$

Next we deal with $f^{\exists}_{i,\pi}$. Suppose we have generated the sign $\langle e, m \rangle$ using the term t. The induction hypothesis is that $m = «e»_{\mathscr{M}}$. Assume that e has type π. Then from (5.26) we get

$$\mathscr{M} \vDash (\exists \mathtt{x}_i)e \leftrightarrow (\exists \mathtt{x}_i) f_\pi(«e»_{\mathscr{M}}) \tag{5.38}$$

and so

$$«(\exists \mathtt{x}_i)e»_{\mathscr{M}} = «(\exists \mathtt{x}_i) f_\pi(«e»_{\mathscr{M}})»_{\mathscr{M}} = \exists^i_\pi(m) \tag{5.39}$$

Then $f^{\exists}_{i,\pi}$ can be applied to the sign and we get

$$\mathcal{J}_n\left(f^{\exists}_{i,\pi}\right)(\langle e, m \rangle) = \langle (^\frown \exists ^\frown \mathtt{x}_i ^\frown) ^\frown e, \exists^i_\pi(m) \rangle. \tag{5.40}$$

This completes the proof. □

The formulation of the semantics did not use linking aspects. They could in principle also be used but it was easier to perform a definition by returning to the language CL^n_τ. We were taking advantage of the fact that CL^n_τ is unambiguous. In general, it is not possible to eliminate the linking aspects by splitting the functions on the exponents.

Let us discuss now the case where we have infinitely many variables. As I noted in Intermission 2, the language with infinitely many variables has the disadvantage that it must insert nontrivial syncategorematic symbols. Let us ignore this problem. Let us consider the language with $\mathrm{Rel} = \{\mathtt{r}\}$ and $\tau(\mathtt{r}) = 2$. The model is $\mathscr{N} = \langle \mathbb{N}, \mathfrak{I}\rangle$, with $\mathfrak{I}(\mathtt{r}) = \{\langle i, i+1\rangle : i \in \mathbb{N}\}$. We have three modes, $f_\varnothing$ (zeroary), f_1 and f_0 (unary). Their interpretation is as follows (recall the definition of the verum concept $\mathfrak{t}$ as $[\![\{\varnothing\}]\!]$).

$$\mathfrak{I}(f_\varnothing)() := \langle \mathtt{x}, \mathfrak{t}\rangle \tag{5.41}$$

$$\mathfrak{I}(f_0)(\langle e, m\rangle) := \begin{cases} \langle e^\frown \mathtt{0}, m\rangle & \text{if } e \text{ is a variable,} \\ \text{undefined} & \text{else.} \end{cases} \tag{5.42}$$

$$\mathfrak{I}(f_1)(\langle e, m\rangle) := \begin{cases} \langle e^\frown \mathtt{1}, m\rangle & \text{if } e \text{ is a variable,} \\ \text{undefined} & \text{else.} \end{cases} \tag{5.43}$$

Notice that we have this time generated variables from variables, to show that alternatives to introducing indices are possible. In fact, we are now generating the following language:

$$\mathrm{CL}_\tau \cup \{\langle \mathtt{x}\vec{u}, \mathfrak{t}\rangle : \vec{u} \in (\mathtt{0}|\mathtt{1})^*\}. \tag{5.44}$$

This language has two types of expressions: formulae and variables. The interpretation of variables is their range and therefore the "truth". Now we introduce the relation symbol by means of a binary mode:

$$\begin{aligned} &f_r(\langle e, m\rangle, \langle e', m'\rangle) \\ &:= \begin{cases} \langle \mathtt{r}(^\frown e^\frown, ^\frown e'^\frown), \text{«}\{\langle i, i+1\rangle : i \in \mathbb{N}\}\text{»}_{\mathscr{N}}\rangle & \text{if } e \neq e' \text{ are variables,} \\ \langle \mathtt{r}(^\frown e^\frown, ^\frown e'^\frown), \text{«}\varnothing\text{»}_{\mathscr{N}}\rangle & \text{if } e = e' \text{ are variables,} \\ \text{undefined} & \text{else.} \end{cases} \end{aligned} \tag{5.45}$$

Define the following formulae.

$$\begin{aligned} \varphi_0 &:= \mathtt{r(x,x0)} \\ \varphi_1 &:= \mathtt{(r(x,x0)\land r(x1,x00))} \\ \varphi_2 &:= \mathtt{((r(x,x0)\land r(x1,x00))\land(r(x01,x10)\land r(x11,x000)))} \\ \varphi_3 &:= \mathtt{(((r(x,x0)\land r(x1,x00))\land(r(x01,x10)} \\ &\quad \mathtt{\land r(x11,x000)))\land((r(x001,x010)} \\ &\quad \mathtt{\land r(x011,x100))\land(r(x101,x110)\land r(x111,x0000))))} \end{aligned} \tag{5.46}$$

Also, define the following sets:

$$S_n := \{\langle i, i+1, \cdots, i+n-1\rangle : i \in \mathbb{N}\}. \tag{5.47}$$

For example, S_1 is $\mathbb{N}$, S_2 consists in the pairs $\langle 0, 1\rangle$, $\langle 1, 2\rangle$, $\langle 2, 3\rangle$ and so on and S_3 consists in the triples $\langle 0, 1, 2\rangle$, $\langle 1, 2, 3\rangle$, $\langle 2, 3, 4\rangle$ and so on. The meaning of φ_0 is $[\![S_2]\!]_{\mathcal{N}}$, the meaning of φ_1 is $[\![S_2 \times S_2]\!]_{\mathcal{N}}$. The set of formulae we are interested in is a bit larger; it consists in all substitution instances of the φ_n. The following is easy to see.

Lemma 5.1 *Let χ be a substitution instance of φ_n. Either χ is unsatisfiable in $\mathcal{N}$ or «χ»$_{\mathcal{N}}$ is the concept generated by a nontrivial product $\mathsf{X}_{k<p} S_{n(k)}$ for some numbers $n(k) > 1$.*

Proof Clearly, some formulae are unsatisfiable, for example

$$\texttt{((r(x,x0)}\wedge\texttt{r(x0,x1))}\wedge\texttt{(r(x,x1)}\wedge\texttt{r(x,x1)))}. \tag{5.48}$$

Now, let $x \prec y$ if and only if χ contains the clause $\texttt{r}(x,y)$. Say that x is of height 0 if there is no y such that $y \prec x$; and of height $n+1$ if there is a y of height n such that $y \prec x$. Now we shall characterise all satisfying assignments. Suppose that $x \prec y, y'$ and β a satisfying assignment; then $\beta(y) = \beta(x) + 1$ and $\beta(y') = \beta(x) + 1$, from which $\beta(y) = \beta(y')$. Similarly, if $x, x' \prec y$ then $\beta(x) = \beta(x')$. Let $\approx_0$ be the identity. And let $x \approx_{n+1} x'$ if for some y, y' such that $y \approx_n y'$ either (a) $y \prec x$ and $y' \prec x'$ or (b) $x \prec y$ and $x' \prec y'$; $x \approx x'$ is the union of all $\approx_n$. This is an equivalence relation. For $\approx$-equivalence classes A and B write $A \prec B$ if there are $x \in A$ and $y \in B$ such that $x \prec y$. The relation $\prec$ is linear on the classes. For assume $A \prec B, B'$. Then there are $x, x' \in A$ and $y \in B$, $y' \in B'$ such that $x \prec y$ and $x' \prec y'$. Since $x \approx x'$, we have $y \approx y'$, by definition of $\approx$. Hence $B = B'$. Similarly we can show that if $A, A' \prec B$ then $A = A'$. A valuation is now constructed as follows. For each class A that has no $\prec$-predecessor, pick a representative and assign to it any value. Then the values of the members of A must all be the same. Suppose that the values to members of A are known and are all identical to k; let $A \prec B$. Then the value of every member of B is $k + 1$. By this recipe, the valuation is completely determined. Now let us turn to the concept defined by χ. It is clear that when we pass to the concept all equivalence classes of $\approx$ can be shrunk to one. All factors of the form S_1 can be dropped. This gives the product representation. □

In particular, consider the following substitution instances.

$$\begin{aligned}
\vartheta_0 &:= \texttt{r(x,x0)} \\
\vartheta_1 &:= \texttt{(r(x,x0)}\wedge\texttt{r(x0,x1))} \\
\vartheta_2 &:= \texttt{((r(x,x0)}\wedge\texttt{r(x0,x1))}\wedge\texttt{(r(x1,x00)}\wedge\texttt{r(x00,x01)))} \\
\vartheta_3 &:= \texttt{(((r(x,x0)}\wedge\texttt{r(x0,x1))}\wedge\texttt{(r(x1,x00)} \\
&\qquad \wedge\texttt{r(x00,x01)))}\wedge\texttt{((r(x01,x10)} \\
&\qquad \wedge\texttt{r(x10,x11))}\wedge\texttt{(r(x11,x000)}\wedge\texttt{r(x000,x001))))}
\end{aligned} \tag{5.49}$$

The meaning of these formulae is exactly $[\![S_{2^n+1}]\!]_{\mathcal{N}}$.

If $\dot{g} = \langle g(0), \cdots, g(k-1)\rangle$ is a vector of numbers, we put $S_{\dot{g}} := \mathsf{X}_{i<k} S_{g(i)}$. Let us look at the possible ways to assemble such formulae. We shall show that there is no way in which this sublanguage can be generated by a compositional context free interpreted grammar. This shall suffice for the following reason. The sublanguage is closed under taking subformulae; so if there is a grammar for the full language it must generate these formulae by means of other formulae of this kind. Hence if this is impossible, no grammar for the entire language exists.

Basically, for any context free grammar, the modes of composition must be to assemble some formulae and add some bounded material.

$$\begin{aligned}\mathcal{I}(f)(\langle e_0, m_0\rangle, \cdots, \langle e_{n-1}, m_{n-1}\rangle) \\ := \langle \vec{x}_0{}^\frown e_0{}^\frown \vec{x}_1{}^\frown \cdots {}^\frown \vec{x}_{n-1}{}^\frown e_{n-1}{}^\frown \vec{x}_n, h_f(m_0, \cdots, m_{n-1})\rangle\end{aligned} \tag{5.50}$$

We may assume that $m_i = [\![S_{\dot{g}(i)}]\!]_{\mathcal{N}}$ and that $h_f(m_0, \cdots, m_{n-1}) = [\![S_{\dot{g}(n)}]\!]_{\mathcal{N}}$, where $\dot{g}(0), \cdots, \dot{g}(n)$ are vectors of natural numbers. In this way, the function h can be coded by the assignment

$$h_f^\spadesuit : \langle \dot{g}(0), \cdots, \dot{g}(n-1)\rangle \mapsto \dot{g}(n). \tag{5.51}$$

Now the following can easily be verified.

Lemma 5.2 *Suppose that n_i are numbers and that $h_f^\spadesuit(n_0, \cdots, n_{k-1})$ also is a number. Then $h_f^\spadesuit(n_0, \cdots, n_{k-1})$ can be any number between* $\max\{n_i : i < k\}$ *and* $\left(\sum_{i<k} n_i\right) - (k-1)$.

We now turn to an investigation of the morphology.

Lemma 5.3 *Assume that $\mathcal{I}(f)$ is as in* (5.50). *Then for given e' there is at most one vector $\vec{e} = \langle e_i : i < \Omega(f)\rangle$ such that $f^\varepsilon(\vec{e}) = e'$.*

Proof Let $n = \Omega(f)$. Assume that $f^\varepsilon(\vec{e}) = f^\varepsilon(\vec{c})$ for some vector $\vec{c} = \langle c_i : i < n\rangle$. Then we have

$$\vec{x}_0 e_0 \vec{x}_1 e_1 \vec{x}_2 \cdots \vec{x}_{n-1} e_{n-1} \vec{x}_n = \vec{x}_0 c_0 \vec{x}_1 c_1 \vec{x}_2 \cdots \vec{x}_{n-1} c_{n-1} \vec{x}_n. \tag{5.52}$$

From this it follows that

$$e_0 \vec{x}_1 e_1 \vec{x}_2 \cdots \vec{x}_{n-1} e_{n-1} \vec{x}_n = c_0 \vec{x}_1 c_1 \vec{x}_2 \cdots \vec{x}_{n-1} c_{n-1} \vec{x}_n. \tag{5.53}$$

Suppose first that e_0 and c_0 are formulae. It is a property of this language that no prefix of a formula is a formula. Hence $e_0 = c_0$, since neither can be a prefix of the other. Therefore

$$\vec{x}_1 e_1 \vec{x}_2 \cdots \vec{x}_{n-1} e_{n-1} \vec{x}_n = \vec{x}_1 c_1 \vec{x}_2 \cdots \vec{x}_{n-1} c_{n-1} \vec{x}_n. \tag{5.54}$$

Now assume that e_0 is not a formula. Then it is a variable and so of the form $\mathbf{x}\vec{u}$, where $\vec{u}$ is a binary string. In this case, since also e_1 is either a variable or a formula, $\vec{x}_1$ must contain a prefix that finishes the occurrence of the variable that e_0 begins. It does the same with c_0; thus, $e_0 = c_0$. Similarly, if c_0 is not a formulae. Thus, we get (5.54) in all cases.

Repeat this argument $n - 1$ times. □

Finally, let $\langle \vec{u}, \vec{v} \rangle$ be an occurrence of $\vec{x}$ in $\vec{z} = \vec{u}\vec{x}\vec{v}$. The **embedding depth** of this occurrence of $\vec{x}$ is defined as the number of opening brackets minus the number of closing brackets in $\vec{u}$. Notice that in φ_n every atomic subformula has embedding depth n.

Lemma 5.4 *Let χ be a formula with an occurrence of depth d in φ_n. Then χ is a substitution instance of φ_{n-d}.*

Proof By induction on $n - d$. Let $n = d$. Since no formula has embedding depth $> n$, the formula is atomic and so a substitution instance of φ_0. Now let the claim be shown for $n - d$. We show it for $n - d + 1$. Let us be given an occurrence $\langle \vec{u}, \vec{v} \rangle$ of χ. Then χ begins with an opening bracket (since no atomic formula has embedding depth $n - d + 1$). Thus, it is easily seen that $\chi = (\vec{z}_0 \wedge \vec{z}_1)$, where $\vec{z}_0$ and $\vec{z}_1$ are subformulae of embedding depth $n - d$. By inductive hypothesis, they are substitution instances of φ_{n-d}. Then χ is a substitution instance of φ_{n-d+1}. □

Thus, with $\mathcal{I}$ defined as in (5.50) let μ_f be the largest of the bracket balances of $\vec{x}_0\vec{x}_1 \cdots \vec{x}_i, i < n$. Now, if $f_*^{\varepsilon}(e_0, \cdots, e_{n-1}) = \varphi_n$, we conclude that the embedding depth of the occurrences of the e_i in φ_n are less than or equal to $n - \mu_f$. By choosing n large enough we can make the e_i to be of any minimal length we want.

Let now G be any context free compositional interpreted grammar for the language. Define

$$\mu_G := \max\{\mu_f : f \in F\}, \qquad \alpha_G := \max\{\Omega(f) : f \in F\}. \tag{5.55}$$

Make n large enough so that $n^* := 2^{n-\mu_G} + 1 > \alpha_G + \text{card}\, F$. For every $f \in F$, let $\dot{v}_f := h_f^{\spadesuit}(n^*, \cdots, n^*)$. By choice of n^* there is a number j^* between n^* and $2n^* - 1$ which is not of the form $\dot{v}_f$. (If $\dot{v}_f$ is not a number, that is anyhow the case.) Next let ψ_k be the substitution into $\vartheta_{n-\mu_G}$ such that the names of the variables are shifted by k in the order $\lessdot$ (see Exercise 5.3). Since this shift is injective, the meaning of ψ_k is the same as that of $\vartheta_{n-\mu_G}$, which is $[\![S_{2n^*}]\!]$. Now we define the following sequence of formulae:

$$\begin{aligned} \chi^\circ(0) &:= \psi_0 & \chi^\bullet(0) &:= \psi_{j^*-n^*} \\ \chi^\circ(n+1) &:= (^\frown\chi^\circ(n)^\frown\wedge^\frown\chi^\circ(n)^\frown) & \chi^\bullet(n+1) &:= (^\frown\chi^\bullet(n)^\frown\wedge^\frown\chi^\bullet(n)^\frown) \end{aligned} \tag{5.56}$$

Finally, let $\zeta := (\chi^\circ(\mu_G)\wedge\chi^\bullet(\mu_G))$. Its meaning is $[\![S_{j^*}]\!]$. (For $\chi^\circ(\mu_G)$ contains the first n^* variables, and $\chi^\bullet(\mu_G)$ contains this set shifted by $j^* - n^*$ (which is a number $< n^*$).) Their conjunction therefore contains the first j^* variables.

We show that $\langle \zeta, «\zeta»_{\mathcal{N}} \rangle$ cannot be generated in G. Assume that it is the value of the term $f t_0 \cdots t_{n-1}$. Then ζ has a decomposition as follows.

$$\zeta = \vec{x}_0 e_0 \vec{x}_1 e_1 \vec{x}_2 \cdots \vec{x}_{n-1} e_{n-1} \vec{x} \tag{5.57}$$

As we have seen, the e_i must be subformulae. Now, we may assume that $e_i \neq \zeta$ (or else $\zeta = e_0$ and then we must obviously find a way to generate e_0 using another function). And so the e_i are subformula of either $\chi^\circ(\mu_G)$ or of $\chi^\bullet(\mu_G)$. As they are of embedding depth at most μ_G they have the form $\chi^\circ(d)$ or $\chi^\bullet(d)$ for some d. Hence their meaning is $[\![S_{n^*}]\!]$. The denotation of the term $f t_0 \cdots t_{n-1}$ is of the form $[\![S_k]\!]$ where $k = h_f^\spadesuit(n^*, \cdots, n^*)$. However, ζ has the meaning $[\![S_{j^*}]\!]$, which is not of this form. This completes the proof.

Theorem 5.2 *There are models and signatures for which* CL_τ *has no compositional interpreted context free grammar.*

It is perhaps worthwhile saying something about the significance of this result. In generative grammar it has been observed that there are constituents that serve as a bottleneck in syntax, called *phases*. In the earlier fragment of Chomsky (1986), the CP- and DP-constituents had the property that, unlike VPs, they could not be adjoined to arbitrarily. While the existence of phases has always been a mystery, here we find an indication as to why such bottlenecks must exist. Since we argued that meanings are not standard meanings, such as sets of valuations or relations but rather concepts, there is a limit on how many elements we can have in storage. One way of calibrating the idea of storage is to calculate the number of free variables occurring in a formula.

Exercise 5.4 The function for concept negation did not depend on the type of the formula, while the disjunction, conjunction and implication depended on the types of both arguments. A closer analysis reveals that for an n-ary boolean operator the concept function depends on all n types; it is however enough to assume functions that depend only on $n-1$ arguments. Can you give a general solution how to lift an n-ary operator to concepts using $n-1$ type parameters rather than n? Perform this reduction for $A_{\pi;\rho}$, $C_{\pi;\rho}$ and $I_{\pi;\rho}$. Can you see why negation is independent of the type of its unique argument?

Exercise 5.5 What happens if we allow functions in the primitive vocabulary of predicate logic?

Exercise 5.6 Modify the above proof of Theorem 5.2 to the case where the language is as follows (cf. the definition of L_τ of the previous section):

$$\mathrm{CL}_\tau \cup \{\langle \vec{v}, \vec{v} \rangle : \vec{v} \in (\mathtt{0}|\mathtt{1})^*\} \tag{5.58}$$

Exercise 5.7 Show that Theorem 5.2 would also hold if we allowed to introduce an arbitrary finite set of categories. (Assuming, of course, that the grammar is independent in all three components.)

Exercise 5.8 Here is a variation on the formulae defined above. Define η_n as follows.

$$\begin{aligned}
\eta_0 &:= \texttt{r(x,x0)} \\
\eta_1 &:= \texttt{(r(x,x0)}\wedge\texttt{r(x1,x00))} \\
\eta_2 &:= \texttt{((r(x,x0)}\wedge\texttt{r(x1,x00))}\wedge\texttt{r(x01,x10))} \\
\eta_3 &:= \texttt{(((r(x,x0)}\wedge\texttt{r(x1,x00))}\wedge\texttt{r(x01,x10))}\wedge\texttt{r(x11,000))}
\end{aligned} \tag{5.59}$$

Show that no compositional context free interpreted grammar exists that generates all the pairs $\langle s(\eta_n), «s(\eta_n)»\rangle$, where s is a substitution (together with all pairs $\langle \mathtt{x}\vec{v}, [\![\{\varnothing\}]\!]_{\mathscr{N}}\rangle$).

5.3 A Fragment of English

In this section we discuss a small fragment of English to show how one can overcome the limitations of concepts. We shall consider various strategies to define the composition via linking aspects. One strategy is to use thematic roles. The idea is that in an event of some sort the participants can be distinguished by some property that they have as opposed to the others. For example, the standard, relation based, meaning of the verb /`hit`/ may—in standard notation—be a relation $\mathsf{hit}'(t, w, x, y)$ where t is a time point, w is a possible world or situation and x and y are things. In this case it is already possible to distinguish the variable t from the others due to the fact that all variables are sortal. A time variable can never be identical to a world variable or an entity variable; and the things that these variables denote are completely separate, too. Likewise w is uniquely identifiable through its sort. Only x and y are sortally identical. Nevertheless, we can distinguish them by observing that in an act of hitting there is one participant that exerts force on the other. It is this one that performs an action, while the other can be completely at rest. Thus, there is a formula $\alpha(t, w, x)$ such that in our standard model $\mathscr{M}$

$$\mathscr{M} \models \mathsf{hit}'(t, w, x, y) \to \alpha(t, w, x), \qquad \mathscr{M} \not\models \mathsf{hit}'(t, w, x, y) \to \alpha(t, w, y). \tag{5.60}$$

This is essentially the theory proposed by Wechsler (1995). Wechsler uses modal notation, so it would look more like

$$\mathscr{M} \models \Box(\mathsf{hit}'(x, y) \to \alpha(x)), \qquad \mathscr{M} \not\models \Box(\mathsf{hit}'(x, y) \to \alpha(y)). \tag{5.61}$$

(Notice that using modal operators means that we have to suppress the variables on which the modality is based, here time and world.) But these differences are superficial. Let us suppose that something like (5.60) holds. However, as the model we are using is characteristic (all that is logically true is true in it, all that is not logically true is false in it), we should rather require the following (with $\pi_{(23)}$ the permutation interchanging the third and the fourth column).

$$
\begin{aligned}
(\!|\mathsf{hit}'(t, w, x, y)|\!)_{\mathcal{M}} &\subseteq (\!|\alpha(t, w, x)|\!)_{\mathcal{M}} \times M_{\mathrm{e}} \\
\pi_{(23)}[(\!|\mathsf{hit}'(t, w, x, y)|\!)_{\mathcal{M}}] &\nsubseteq (\!|\alpha(t, w, x)|\!)_{\mathcal{M}} \times M_{\mathrm{e}}
\end{aligned}
\tag{5.62}
$$

The formula $\alpha(t, w, x)$ does not suffer from the same combinatorial ambiguity. Thus, the concept $«\alpha(t, w, x)»_{\mathcal{M}}$ has only *one* minimal member in its type. The task of picking out the correct representative has become trivial. So, we pick the minimal member R and then return to $\mathsf{hit}'(t, w, x, y)$. The concept has two minimal members, say S and T. According to the above, we have $R \times M_{\mathrm{e}} \subseteq S$ and $R \times M_{\mathrm{e}} \nsubseteq T$ or $R \times M_{\mathrm{e}} \nsubseteq S$ and $R \times M_{\mathrm{e}} \subseteq T$. Thus, there is a way to find out which minimal member to pick.

Example 5.3 There are three sorts, e, w and t. Assume that $M_{\mathrm{e}} = \{a, b, c\}$, $M_{\mathrm{w}} = \{w_0, w_1\}$ and $M_{\mathrm{t}} = \{t_0, t_1\}$.

$$
\begin{aligned}
(\!|\alpha(t, w, x)|\!)_{\mathcal{M}} =&\{\langle t_0, w_0, a\rangle, \langle t_0, w_0, b\rangle, \langle t_0, w_0, c\rangle, \langle t_0, w_1, a\rangle, \\
&\langle t_1, w_0, b\rangle, \langle t_1, w_0, c\rangle\}
\end{aligned}
\tag{5.63}
$$

$$
\begin{aligned}
(\!|\mathsf{hit}'(t, w, x, y)|\!)_{\mathcal{M}} =&\{\langle t_0, w_0, a, a\rangle, \langle t_0, w_0, a, b\rangle, \langle t_0, w_0, b, a\rangle, \\
&\langle t_0, w_0, a, c\rangle, \langle t_1, w_0, c, a\rangle, \langle t_1, w_0, c, b\rangle\}
\end{aligned}
\tag{5.64}
$$

In this model (5.62) is satisfied. Let us now consider all permutations of the relations where the time variable is first, the world variable is second and the object variables third. There is only one such permutation for $(\!|\alpha(t, w, x)|\!)_{\mathcal{M}}$, where there are two for $(\!|\mathsf{hit}'(t, w, x, y)|\!)_{\mathcal{M}}$, namely:

$$
\begin{aligned}
T_0 :=&\{\langle t_0, w_0, a, a\rangle, \langle t_0, w_0, a, b\rangle, \langle t_0, w_0, b, a\rangle, \\
&\langle t_0, w_0, a, c\rangle, \langle t_1, w_0, c, a\rangle, \langle t_1, w_0, c, b\rangle\}, \\
T_1 :=&\{\langle t_0, w_0, a, a\rangle, \langle t_0, w_0, b, a\rangle, \langle t_0, w_0, a, b\rangle, \\
&\langle t_0, w_0, c, a\rangle, \langle t_1, w_0, a, c\rangle, \langle t_1, w_0, b, c\rangle\}.
\end{aligned}
\tag{5.65}
$$

Now, T_0 can be distinguished from T_1 by the fact that T_1 contains $\langle t_1, w_0, a, c\rangle$, which is not contained in the set $(\!|\alpha(t, w, x)|\!)_{\mathcal{M}} \times M_{\mathrm{e}}$.

$$
\begin{aligned}
(\!|\alpha(t, w, x)|\!)_{\mathcal{M}} \times M_{\mathrm{e}} = \{&\langle t_0, w_0, a, a\rangle, \langle t_0, w_0, a, b\rangle, \langle t_0, w_0, a, c\rangle, \\
&\langle t_0, w_0, b, a\rangle, \langle t_0, w_0, b, b\rangle, \langle t_0, w_0, b, c\rangle, \langle t_0, w_0, c, a\rangle, \\
&\langle t_0, w_0, c, b\rangle, \langle t_0, w_0, c, c\rangle, \langle t_0, w_1, a, a\rangle, \langle t_0, w_1, a, b\rangle, \\
&\langle t_0, w_1, a, c\rangle, \langle t_1, w_0, b, a\rangle, \langle t_1, w_0, b, b\rangle, \langle t_1, w_0, b, c\rangle, \\
&\langle t_1, w_0, c, a\rangle, \langle t_1, w_0, c, b\rangle, \langle t_1, w_0, c, c\rangle\}
\end{aligned}
\tag{5.66}
$$

Notice that looking at truth conditions rather than accidental facts is essential, that is to say, the intensionality does real work here. For in w_0 at t_0 every object has property α. If we had to define our minimal member only here, there would be no way to distinguish the arguments. For example, suppose that at w_0 and t_0, everybody is such that he or she is moving and exerting some force. Still it should not follow that everybody is hitting someone. They could, for example, push a car uphill. Thus, we need to make reference to other worlds. It is clear that in the entire space of worlds there must be one where the concepts really *is* nonsymmetrical, otherwise (5.62) could not be used to discriminate the arguments. ⚽

We shall display a primitive trigrammar. It has five modes: $F = \{f_0, f_1, f_2, f_3, f_4\}$. $\Omega(f_0) := \Omega(f_1) := \Omega(f_2) := 0$, $\Omega(f_3) := \Omega(f_4) := 2$. For the purpose of the next definition, let $\sigma = \langle e, c, m\rangle$ and $\sigma' = \langle e', c', m'\rangle$. Further, let d^k_{ij} be the relation $\{\langle a_0, \cdots, a_{k-1}\rangle : a_i = a_j\}$. (This relation is only defined if sorts match. For simplicity we suppress mentioning sorts.) Y is a linking aspect that extends the aspect as in the previous example. What is important below is only that it orders the arguments like this: time, world, patient, actor. Let $\sigma = \langle e, c, m\rangle$ and $e' = \langle e', c', m'\rangle$.

$$\begin{aligned}
\mathcal{D}(f_0)() &:= \langle \texttt{John}, \text{NP}, \{a\}\rangle \\
\mathcal{D}(f_1)() &:= \langle \texttt{Paul}, \text{NP}, \{b\}\rangle \\
\mathcal{D}(f_2)() &:= \langle \texttt{hits}, \text{V}, «\mathsf{hit}'(t, w, x, y)»_{\mathscr{M}}\rangle \\
\mathcal{D}(f_3)(\sigma, \sigma') &:= \begin{cases} \langle e^\frown\Box^\frown e', \text{VP}, [\![\mathsf{C}_2.\mathsf{C}_4.\big(Y(m) \times Y(m') \cap d^5_{24})]\!]_{\mathscr{M}}\rangle \\ \qquad \text{if } c = \text{V and } c' = \text{NP}, \\ \text{undefined else.} \end{cases} \\
\mathcal{D}(f_4)(\sigma, \sigma') &:= \begin{cases} \langle e'^\frown\Box^\frown e^\frown ., \text{S}, [\![\mathsf{C}_0.\mathsf{C}_1.\mathsf{C}_2.\mathsf{C}_3.\big(Y(m) \times Y(m') \cap d^4_{23})]\!]_{\mathscr{M}}\rangle \\ \qquad \text{if } c = \text{VP and } c' = \text{NP}, \\ \text{undefined else.} \end{cases}
\end{aligned} \tag{5.67}$$

The resulting meaning of a sentence is true if there is a time point and world such that the sentence is true in that world at that time. Let us see how that works. The sentence /`John hits Paul.`/ can be generated only as the exponent of $f_4 f_3 f_2 f_1 f_0$. Let us do this step by step.

$$\begin{aligned}
\iota_G(f_3 f_2 f_1) &= \mathcal{D}(f_3)(\langle \texttt{hits}, \text{V}, R\rangle, \langle \texttt{Paul}, \text{NP}, \{b\}\rangle) \\
&= \langle \texttt{hits}^\frown\Box^\frown\texttt{Paul}, \text{VP}, «\mathsf{C}_2.\mathsf{C}_4.\Big(Y(m) \times Y(m') \cap d^5_{24}\Big)»_{\mathscr{M}}\rangle \\
&= \langle \texttt{hits Paul}, \text{VP}, «\{\langle t_0, w_0, a\rangle, \langle t_1, w_0, c\rangle\}»_{\mathscr{M}}\rangle
\end{aligned} \tag{5.68}$$

Here is how the concept in the last step is derived. First, we apply the linking aspect Y to the concept of hitting, whereupon we get

$$\begin{aligned}
Y(m) =\{&\langle t_0, w_0, a, a\rangle, \langle t_0, w_0, b, a\rangle, \langle t_0, w_0, a, b\rangle, \\
&\langle t_0, w_0, c, a\rangle, \langle t_1, w_0, a, c\rangle, \langle t_1, w_0, b, c\rangle\}.
\end{aligned} \tag{5.69}$$

Also, $Y(m') = \{b\}$, since there is nothing to order. We take the product:

$$\begin{aligned} Y(m) \times Y(m') = &\{\langle t_0, w_0, a, a, b\rangle, \langle t_0, w_0, b, a, b\rangle, \langle t_0, w_0, a, b, b\rangle, \\ &\langle t_0, w_0, c, a, b\rangle, \langle t_1, w_0, a, c, b\rangle, \langle t_1, w_0, b, c, b\rangle\}. \end{aligned} \tag{5.70}$$

Next we intersect with the set d^5_{24}. That is to say we take the subset of all vectors $\langle x_0, x_1, x_2, x_3, x_4\rangle$ such that $x_2 = x_4$.

$$Y(m) \times Y(m') \cap d^5_{24} = \{\langle t_0, w_0, b, a, b\rangle, \langle t_1, w_0, b, c, b\rangle\} \tag{5.71}$$

Finally, we remove the third and fifth column.

$$\mathsf{C}_2.\mathsf{C}_4.Y(m) \times Y(m') \cap d^5_{24} = \{\langle t_0, w_0, a\rangle, \langle t_1, w_0, c\rangle\} \tag{5.72}$$

And then we form the concept, which just means that we basically forget the order of the columns. Call this concept m. We are ready to continue (with $Y(m)$ defined below):

$$\begin{aligned} \iota_G(f_4 f_3 f_2 f_1 f_0) = &\mathcal{D}(f_4)(\iota_G(f_3 f_2 f_1), \iota_G(f_0)) \\ = &\mathcal{D}(f_4)(\langle \texttt{hits Paul}, \text{VP}, «\{\langle t_0, w_0, a\rangle, \langle t_1, w_0, c\rangle\}»_{\mathscr{M}}\rangle, \\ &\quad \langle \texttt{John}, \text{NP}, \{a\}\rangle) \\ = &\langle \texttt{John}^\frown\square^\frown\texttt{hits Paul}^\frown\texttt{.}, \texttt{S}, \\ &\quad «\mathsf{C}_0.\mathsf{C}_1.\mathsf{C}_2.\mathsf{C}_3.\left(Y(m) \times Y(«\{a\}»_{\mathscr{M}}) \cap d^4_{23}\right)»_{\mathscr{M}}\rangle \\ = &\langle \texttt{John hits Paul.}, \text{S}, \{\varnothing\}\rangle \end{aligned} \tag{5.73}$$

The way to get there is as follows. The linking aspect orders the minimal members of the concept m. Assume that it does this on the basis of times < worlds < entities. (This does not follow, by the way, from our assumption on how it orders the minimal members of the concept of hitting!) Then

$$Y(m) = \{\langle t_0, w_0, a\rangle, \langle t_1, w_0, c\rangle\}. \tag{5.74}$$

It also orders the unique minimal member of the concept of John and gives us $\{a\}$. We take the product

$$Y(m) \times Y([\![\{a\}]\!]_{\mathscr{M}}) = \{\langle t_0, w_0, a, a\rangle, \langle t_1, w_0, c, a\rangle\}. \tag{5.75}$$

Next we intersect with d^4_{23}:

$$Y(m) \times Y(«\{a\}»_{\mathscr{M}}) \cap d^4_{23} = \{\langle t_0, w_0, a, a\rangle\}. \tag{5.76}$$

And then we eliminate the columns 0, 1, 2 and 3:

$$\mathsf{C}_0.\mathsf{C}_1.\mathsf{C}_2.\mathsf{C}_3.Y(m) \times Y(«\{a\}»_{\mathscr{M}}) \cap d^4_{23} = \{\langle\rangle\}. \tag{5.77}$$

The sentence is true in the model.

When we move to more complex cases, for example relations involving 3 entities (arising in the meaning of ditransitives, for example) we do not need to come up with an α such that, say,

$$\begin{aligned} (\!|\varphi(t, w, x, y, z)|\!)_{\mathscr{M}} &\subseteq (\!|\alpha(t, w, x)|\!)_{\mathscr{M}} \times M_{\mathrm{e}} \times M_{\mathrm{e}}, \\ \pi_{(23)}(\!|\varphi(t, w, x, y, z)|\!)_{\mathscr{M}} &\not\subseteq (\!|\alpha(t, w, y)|\!)_{\mathscr{M}} \times M_{\mathrm{e}} \times M_{\mathrm{e}}, \\ \pi_{(24)}(\!|\varphi(t, w, x, y, z)|\!)_{\mathscr{M}} &\not\subseteq (\!|\alpha(t, w, z)|\!)_{\mathscr{M}} \times M_{\mathrm{e}} \times M_{\mathrm{e}}. \end{aligned} \tag{5.78}$$

It is enough if we first find a concept that allows to separate two variables from a third and then continue as before.

The formulae above do not always exist. A case in point is the relation $<$. If taken as a relation on the natural numbers, we can use the formula $\alpha(y) := (y \neq 0)$. For there is no x such that $x < 0$, it is through this property that we can discriminate the positions. However, matters change when we look at it as a relation between integers. For the projection of $<$ onto both of its components is the set $\mathbb{Z}$ of integers. This means that for every x there is a number y that is bigger than x and for every y there is a number x that is smaller than y. Thus we have to use a different tool. One idea that actually always works is this.

Definition 5.2 A **sampler** is a function $\mathbb{S}$ from concepts to finite sets of tuples such that if $\mathfrak{c}$ is a concept, then there is exactly one minimal $R \in \mathfrak{c}$ with $R \supseteq \mathbb{S}(\mathfrak{c})$.

Samplers always exist. Let $\mathfrak{c}$ be a concept; fix a minimal member $\mathfrak{c}$ of R. Let Ξ be the set of permutations such that $\pi[R] \neq R$. (In fact, we can skip all permutations that are not sortally trivial. Here, a permutation π is sortally trivial if for the sequence $\vec{s}$ of sorts: $\pi(\vec{s}) = \vec{s}$.) For every $\pi \in \Xi$ pick a tuple $\vec{x}_\pi$ such that $\vec{x}_\pi \in R$ but $\vec{x}_\pi \notin \pi[R]$. By assumption for every $\pi \in \Xi$ such a tuple exists. Let

$$\mathbb{S}(\mathfrak{c}) := \{\vec{x}_\pi : \pi \in \Xi\}. \tag{5.79}$$

If we want to use a sampler to pick out a different minimal member U from $\mathfrak{c}$, then since that member is a permutation of the original set R, say $U = \rho[R]$, we can use in place of $\mathbb{S}(\mathfrak{c})$ the set $\rho(\mathbb{S}(\mathfrak{c}))$.

Example 5.4 In the example above, the following is a sampler for $«\mathsf{hit}'(t, w, x, y)»_{\mathscr{M}}$ picking out $R := (\!|\mathsf{hit}'(t, w, x, y)|\!)_{\mathscr{M}}$. It is $\{\langle t_0, w_0, a, c\rangle\}$. This is because the only permutations that are sortally trivial are the identity $\pi_{()}$ and $\pi_{(23)}$. Thus, $\Xi := \{\pi_{(23)}\}$ is enough. For the permutation $\pi_{(23)}$ we have $\pi_{(23)}(\langle t_0, w_0, a, c\rangle) = \langle t_0, w_0, c, a\rangle$, which is not in the relation. The set $\{\langle c, a, t_0, w_0\rangle\}$ instead picks out the member $\pi_{(0213)}[R]$, or if you will, the set $(\!|\mathsf{hit}'(y, x, t, w)|\!)_{\mathscr{M}}$. ⚽

Example 5.5 Assume one sort e and $M_e = \{a, b, c\}$. Let

$$R := \{\langle a, b, c\rangle, \langle a, c, b\rangle, \langle b, a, b\rangle, \langle b, b, a\rangle\}. \tag{5.80}$$

Then it turns out that $\Xi = \{\pi_{(01)}, \pi_{(02)}\}$, because the permutation (12) transforms R into itself. To fix $[\![R]\!]_{\mathscr{M}}$ to R, we use $\{\langle a, b, c\rangle\}$. ⚽

5.4 Concepts and LF

It seems that the introduction of concepts actually made matters worse. To derive meanings in a compositional way is not at all straightforward. When we compare this with other approaches (Montague Grammar, or DRT based approaches such as (Kamp and Reyle, 1993)) we ask ourselves whether it is really warranted to replace, say, DRSs by concepts. To see that one is virtually compelled to assume concepts, look at what the algorithm of Kamp and Reyle (1993) factually does. It translates the sentence (5.81) not directly but via a surface indexing.

$$\texttt{A big man sees a small cat.} \tag{5.81}$$

A surface indexing is an assignment of indices to the free variables of the corresponding DRS. Such indices were once assumed to be distributed by the parser in terms of annotations to the words of the surface string. Thus the input to the translation algorithm is (5.82) rather than (5.81). Note that the indices are also written using typewriter fonts. This highlights the fact that they are really there and they also have to be written using some characters of the alphabet. Making this absolutely clear is essential.

$$\texttt{A}_\texttt{1}\ \texttt{big}_\texttt{1}\ \texttt{man}_\texttt{1}\ \texttt{sees}_{(\texttt{1},\texttt{7})}\ \texttt{a}_\texttt{7}\ \texttt{small}_\texttt{7}\ \texttt{cat}_\texttt{7}\texttt{.} \tag{5.82}$$

Based on the input the translation is unique. The problem with this notion of syntax is that it uses material that is not in the actual surface string, namely indices. The indices in turn determine the translation into a DRS, or for that matter, into some predicate logical formula. It turns out that /$\texttt{man}_\texttt{0}$/ has a different translation than /$\texttt{man}_\texttt{1}$/. Therefore, in order for the proposed algorithm to work, we must assume that the grammar generates entries of the following form:

$$\langle \texttt{man}_\texttt{0}, \mathsf{man}'(x_0)\rangle, \langle \texttt{man}_\texttt{1}, \mathsf{man}'(x_1)\rangle, \langle \texttt{man}_\texttt{2}, \mathsf{man}'(x_2)\rangle, \cdots \tag{5.83}$$

It does not necessarily mean that the above entries are in the lexicon. For the indices may be taken to be, say, decimal strings; in this case we need a base entry

$$\langle \texttt{man}_\texttt{0}, \mathsf{man}'(x_0)\rangle \tag{5.84}$$

and ten unary functions (to append a digit to the index) to successfully generate all of these entries.

For a transitive verb we will have

$$\begin{array}{ll}\langle \texttt{sees}_{(0,0)}, \mathsf{see}'(x_0, x_0)\rangle, & \langle \texttt{sees}_{(1,0)}, \mathsf{see}'(x_1, x_0)\rangle, \\ & \langle \texttt{sees}_{(2,0)}, \mathsf{see}'(x_2, x_0)\rangle, \cdots \\ \langle \texttt{sees}_{(0,1)}, \mathsf{see}'(x_0, x_1)\rangle, & \langle \texttt{sees}_{(1,1)}, \mathsf{see}'(x_1, x_1)\rangle, \\ & \langle \texttt{sees}_{(2,1)}, \mathsf{see}'(x_2, x_1)\rangle, \cdots \\ \langle \texttt{sees}_{(0,2)}, \mathsf{see}'(x_0, x_2)\rangle, & \langle \texttt{sees}_{(1,2)}, \mathsf{see}'(x_1, x_2)\rangle, \\ & \langle \texttt{sees}_{(2,2)}, \mathsf{see}'(x_2, x_2)\rangle, \cdots \\ \cdots & \cdots \end{array} \tag{5.85}$$

This is where our principles come in. Recall that we have explicitly ruled out deletion. If there is no index on the surface, there has never been one in the beginning. So, at the deep phonological level we also have just /man/ and /sees/. Given that we apply compositionality at the deep phonological level and not the surface it might be deemed that we only need to propose a regular relation that deletes the indices. However, such an operation lacks any phonological motivation. In particular, since the symbols we use (smaller font size lowered numbers) do not appear in ordinary language, their use is ruled out by the fact that none of the symbols actually exists in the language itself. It is therefore excluded. Thus we rather have the following signs

$$\langle \texttt{man}, \mathsf{man}'(x_0)\rangle, \langle \texttt{man}, \mathsf{man}'(x_1)\rangle, \langle \texttt{man}, \mathsf{man}'(x_2)\rangle, \cdots \tag{5.86}$$

$$\begin{array}{lll}\langle \texttt{sees}, \mathsf{see}'(x_0, x_0)\rangle, & \langle \texttt{sees}, \mathsf{see}'(x_1, x_0)\rangle, & \langle \texttt{sees}, \mathsf{see}'(x_2, x_0)\rangle, \cdots \\ \langle \texttt{sees}, \mathsf{see}'(x_0, x_1)\rangle, & \langle \texttt{sees}, \mathsf{see}'(x_1, x_1)\rangle, & \langle \texttt{sees}, \mathsf{see}'(x_2, x_1)\rangle, \cdots \\ \langle \texttt{sees}, \mathsf{see}'(x_0, x_2)\rangle, & \langle \texttt{sees}, \mathsf{see}'(x_1, x_2)\rangle, & \langle \texttt{sees}, \mathsf{see}'(x_2, x_2)\rangle, \cdots \\ \cdots & \cdots & \cdots \end{array} \tag{5.87}$$

This means that the name of the actual variable has become immaterial beyond distinguishing positions. This is essentially what is meant by the Principle of Alphabetical Innocence.[1]

Principle 6 (Alphabetical Innocence) *Suppose a formula φ represents the meaning of a natural language string. Let s be a substitution that is injective on the variables of φ; and let $s(\varphi)$ be the result of replacing every occurrence of x_i by $s(x_i)$. Then $s(\varphi)$ is equivalent to φ.*

It is possible to derive this from our postulates on meaning. However, it is worth stating it on its own because it allows us to decide in a simple way whether a semantics is properly desyntactified. We shall apply the principle to the case at hand. It means that none of the predicate logical formulae properly capture the meaning of /man/ or /see/. For if the meaning of /man/ was expressed by, say, $\mathsf{man}'(x_0)$, then we should have

$$\mathsf{man}'(x_0) \leftrightarrow \mathsf{man}'(x_1). \tag{5.88}$$

[1] This name is due to Kit Fine, which he used during a lecture at UCLA.

But this is false in the standard semantics for predicate logic. Notice that even a formula such as $\bigvee_{i\in\mathbb{N}} \mathsf{man}'(x_i)$ is no good, since it is not invariant under the shift substitution $s : x_i \mapsto x_{i+1}$.

$$\nvDash \bigvee_{i\in\mathbb{N}} \mathsf{man}'(x_i) \leftrightarrow s\left(\bigvee_{i\in\mathbb{N}} \mathsf{man}'(x_i)\right) = \bigvee_{i\in\mathbb{N}-\{0\}} \mathsf{man}'(x_i) \tag{5.89}$$

We can now see why an approach of the sort advocated in Generative Grammar is no solution. Take, for example, the semantics of Heim and Kratzer (1998). For the purposes of presentation, I take a very simple example. The analysis of the sentence /`every man runs`/ proceeds as follows. The LF associated with this sentence is

$$\texttt{every man [8 [}t_8\ \texttt{runs]]} \tag{5.90}$$

This is interpreted bottom up. Notice that man' is the same as $\lambda x_0.\mathsf{man}'(x_0)$ and run' the same as $\lambda x_0.\mathsf{run}'(x_0)$:

$$\dfrac{\dfrac{\lambda P.\lambda Q.\forall x_0.P(x_0) \to Q(x_0)\ \ \mathsf{man}'}{\lambda Q.\mathsf{man}'(x_0) \to Q(x_0)} \quad \dfrac{\lambda P.\lambda x_8.P \quad \dfrac{x_8\ \ \mathsf{run}'}{\mathsf{run}'(x_8)}}{\lambda x_8.\mathsf{run}'(x_8)}}{\forall x_0.\mathsf{man}'(x_0) \to \mathsf{run}'(x_0)} \tag{5.91}$$

Essentially, the semantics does two things in sequence: first, the functions are applied to some variables, in this case x_8. The net effect of this is that the variable is *displayed*. In Generative Grammar this is done because variables are the interpretation of traces. This is the step of VP formation. The VP then has as its interpretation an open formula. Next, a step of function *abstraction* is performed. The element denoted by "8" does nothing but to abstract the variable x_8. Finally, the quantifier, being a function, takes the abstracted form as its argument.

The success of this proposal lies in the possibility to display and (re)abstract variables at each step of the derivation. This however demands synchronization of these two steps in semantics. For example, had we given the variable x_7 in place of x_8, the result would have been much different.

$$\begin{array}{c}\texttt{every} \qquad \texttt{man} \qquad \texttt{[8} \qquad \texttt{[}t_7\ \texttt{runs]]}\\[1em] \dfrac{\dfrac{\lambda P.\lambda Q.\forall x_0.P(x_0) \to Q(x_0)\ \ \mathsf{man}'}{\lambda Q.\mathsf{man}'(x_0) \to Q(x_0)} \quad \dfrac{\lambda P.\lambda x_8.P \quad \dfrac{x_7\ \ \mathsf{run}'}{\mathsf{run}'(x_7)}}{\lambda x_8.\mathsf{run}'(x_7)}}{\forall x_0.\mathsf{man}'(x_0) \to \mathsf{run}'(x_7)}\end{array} \tag{5.92}$$

For in the last step we have

$$
\begin{aligned}
&(\lambda Q.\forall x_0.\mathsf{man}'(x_0) \to Q(x_0))(\lambda x_8.\mathsf{run}'(x_7)) \\
&= \forall x_0.\mathsf{man}'(x_0) \to (\lambda x_8.\mathsf{run}'(x_7))(x_0) \\
&= \forall x_0.\mathsf{man}'(x_0) \to \mathsf{run}'(x_7)
\end{aligned}
$$

Thus only if the binder abstracts the same variable that the trace denotes do we get the correct quantification. The problems evidently get worse if we have more than one quantifier.

In light of Alphabetical Innocence we can now see why this project is bound to fail. For the meaning of [t_8 `run`] and [t_7 `run`] must be the same. Thus, movement has the side effect of displaying the variable. Now, quantifier movement was originally done to obtain alternate scopings (it was used to this effect by Montague, too, though not under this name). The idea was that different readings are the effect of a different structure beyond the level of VP.

`Every man loves some woman.` (5.93)

`every man` [8 [`some woman` [7 [t_8 t_7 `loves`]]]] (5.94)

`some woman` [7 [`every man` [8 [t_8 t_7 `loves`]]]] (5.95)

The underlying theme in Generative Grammar has been to make movement be the central device by which different readings are obtained. We can see however that this has nothing to do with movement, only with the order of quantification. For once we have displayed the variables Alphabetic Innocence strikes and we must be in a position to reabstract the correct variable. But how does the quantifier remember which variable it is supposed to bind?

The generativist will point to the indices in the syntactic structure to answer this question. However, we have also said that notational additions such as numbers cannot be part of the syntactic structure. Additionally, as we have just said, even if the indices are present in the syntax, they have no meaning in the semantics and therefore the idea of exposing and then abstracting a variable cannot work. If we therefore eliminate all numbers the material relevant for interpretation is only this:

[`every woman` [`some man` [t t `loves`]]] (5.96)

[`some man` [`every woman` [t t `loves`]]] (5.97)

(I hasten to add that even this contains information that the surface string does not show, for example, the number and places of occurrence of traces.) Now, suppose we were to interpret the LF directly. Then we would have to make sure we know (apart from the scopes of the quantifiers) that /`every man`/ is the subject and /`some woman`/ is the object. Unfortunately, we lose precisely this information once we decide to move the quantifier. We are lost.

The impasse has been created by thinking that the interpretation of the quantified NP can and must somehow be delayed. What is apparent, however, is that quite to the contrary the quantified NP must be interpreted immediately, upon inserting it into the structure. One way out of the dilemma (not the only one) is to allow the subject to combine first with the verb. Thus, one way to account for the difference in quantifier scope is to assume that the sentence has the following structures.

`some man [loves every woman]` (5.98)

`[some man loves] every woman` (5.99)

All that is required is to have two rules of quantification for a transitive verb. One where one binds the subject and the other where it binds the object.

This may be hard to digest but it has been observed that in certain constructions we actually do find the subject-verb constituent (see for example Steedman (1990)).

`Some man loves and the children adore every woman.` (5.100)

While Generative Grammar has insisted that the observed subject-verb constituent is just a constituent containing the object as well, we have rejected such analyses on two grounds. One is that syntax is not allowed to delete material. The other is that the empty material is of no actual help in establishing the correct semantics.

I should emphasize that in the literature on compositionality one rarely finds people taking offense at the use of free variables. The reason is that the issue of compositionality is often confused with offering just any sort of algorithm to compute the right meanings. The Tarskian truth conditions, formulated in terms of sets of assignments as values for propositions, are perfectly intelligible and rigorously formalized. It therefore looks like a perfect tool. But is it appropriate? Is the set of assignments sending x_8 (as opposed to x_7) to some man really the meaning of /man/? Indeed, one of the few advocates of bound variables, Pauline Jacobson, is actually more worried about how variables are properly administrated rather than whether the Tarskian semantics is a proper choice. Similarly, the literature in Categorial Grammar is full of proposals where free variables are used. If I am right, all these approaches are on the wrong track if they make use of variable names as opposed to linking aspects.

5.5 The Structure of Dutch

In this section we shall look at arguments in favour of a particular syntactic structure. The previous section already gave a glimpse of the idea that sentence structure can be motivated using purely semantic considerations. In the remainder of the chapter we shall develop this idea further. Traditionally in linguistics, arguments in favour of a particular syntactic structure were backed mostly by syntactic tests (substitution, movement and so on). These tests were surface tests. The tests themselves are based on certain background assumptions. Let us take the example of transformations.

`It is easy to please John.` (5.101)

`To please John is easy.` (5.102)

The correlation between (5.101) and (5.102) was taken to show that the sentence (5.101) contains a constituent /`to please John`/. The argument was that we can apply a movement transformation to (5.101) to get (5.102). As much as this sounds like a reasonable proposal, there is no reason to assume that (5.102) is derived from (5.101). Technically, we just have two different sentences. (Present day transformational grammar actually does *not* derive (5.102) from (5.101).) What makes this argument at all acceptable is the fact that there is not just a syntactic correlation; the transformation would not have been proposed to derive (5.102) from (5.101) if it had not been for the fact that they mean (approximately) the same thing. Indeed, the idea that gave rise to transformations in the first place was that they capture meaning correspondences on the basis of syntactic regularities. Even though Chomsky has changed the concept of transformation, the idea that they should not interfere with meaning has been an underlying theme all along. I give two examples that show how semantics is relevant.

There is a systematic syntactic correlation between a transitive sentence and one where subject and object are exchanged (ignoring subject verb agreement):

`John sees Mary.` (5.103)

`Mary sees John.` (5.104)

This does not work if one of them is a pronoun for reasons of case; and in other languages it might not work for case reasons. (Making the transformations suitably complex is a way to deal with that problem, however.) Yet in English this correlation is systematic. However, no one has proposed a transformation that derives one from the other. Similarly, the well known attachment paradoxes do not lead to the proposal of a transformation, to derive, say, (5.107) from (5.106):

`The police saw a man with a telescope.` (5.105)

`The police saw [a man with a telescope].` (5.106)

`The police [[saw a man] with a telescope].` (5.107)

The fact that the interpretation of passive sentences is different from their active counterparts has in fact in the 70ies been used to argue against deriving passive from active sentences[2]:

---

[2] It is a subtle matter to see in what ways such meaning facts can at all bear on the question whether one sentence is derived from another. This is because interpretation happens only once in a derivation. The argument would roughly be this. Suppose that meaning is established at the beginning of the derivation (at deep structure). Now suppose that S' is (more precisely: must be) derived from S through a transformation. Then the derivation that yields S' from its deep structure also derives S on the way. Same deep structure, same meaning. (A dual argument can be used if interpretation is established at LF.) Hence if the two sentences have different meaning they cannot stem from the same deep structure.

`Everyone in this class speaks two languages.` (5.108)

`Two languages are spoken by everyone in this class.` (5.109)

While in (5.109) the universal quantifier has a narrow scope (however only preferentially) (5.108) it has wide scope only.

It should be clear that the same remarks apply to the use of the substitution method to discover the tree structure of a sentence in a context free language. All these tests assume in one way or another a semantic correlation. It is interesting to note in this connection that the standard understanding of "strong generative capacity" was only the fact that a grammar could generate a language together with the right kind of structure without reference to any semantics. But how do we know that a language has that structure in the first place?

In my view, the answer lies in the fact that these languages are interpreted. The structure turns out to be necessary in order to derive the *interpreted* language not just its string part. We have met arguments of this sort before in Section 3.5. In this section I shall present cases from the literature, some of which have been the cause of intense debate. I shall show that the semantic theory developed in the previous chapter allows us to say something quite nontrivial about the syntactic structure of natural languages.

The first case is that of Dutch infinitives. Here is what they look like.

`Ik zeg dat de kinderen zwemmen.` (5.110)

I say that the children swim.

`Ik zeg dat Marie de kinderen leert zwemmen.` (5.111)

I say that Mary teaches the children to swim.

`Ik zeg dat Piet Marie de kinderen laat leren zwemmen.` (5.112)

I say that Piet lets Mary teach the children to swim.

`Ik zeg dat Jan Pier Marie de kinderen ziet laten leren zwemmen.` (5.113)

I say that Jan sees Piet let Mary teach the children to swim.

The order in which the elements appear in the Dutch sentences is quite different from English. All the NPs come first, followed by the verbs. Within the verbs we find first a finite verb and then infinitives. Second, the verbs line up in the same way as in English and not in reverse order. Thus we do not have

*`Ik zeg dat Marie de kinderen zwemmen leert.` (5.114)

*`Ik zeg dat Piet Marie de kinderen zwemmen leren laat.` (5.115)

*`Ik zeg dat Jan Pier Marie de kinderen zwemmen leren laten zag.` (5.116)

This word order is the order of German. But in Dutch this order is ungrammatical. However the reason it is ungrammatical is only that the finite verb is at the end and the nonraising verb at the beginning. Thus, to make any of the above grammatical, we just have to flip the verbs at either end of the sequence of verbs. If we did this, we would get grammatical sentences—but their meaning would be different from that of the German sentences in that same order. Thus we have to keep in mind that the difference between Dutch and German runs deeper than the surface order would make us believe. It will turn out that under our conception of strong generative capacity Dutch is not strongly context free, but German is. However, Dutch still is weakly context free. Let us see how we can establish this. First notice that the methods of Section 3.5 cannot be directly applied without inquiring into the nature of semantics. The reason is Theorem (3.4). It seems plausible that the fragment of Dutch is both unambiguous and monophone. Hence the reason for the impossibility cannot just be combinatorial. It must have to do with the way semantics works. We shall show below what that extra property is. Let us mention here that the claim that Dutch is not weakly context free is originally due to Huybregts (1984), which came at a time when Gazdar and Pullum were revisiting arguments by Chomsky and others concerning the non context freeness of languages. This culminated in the book (Gazdar et al., 1985), which presented an elaborate unification based context free grammar mechanism for natural language. This book provoked the idea that human languages are universally context free and this is why there was renewed interest in the question. Huybregts was aware of the semantic flavour of his argument and it took Shieber (1985) to get the point home that some languages are non context free after all. What Shieber showed was however that Swiss German (more exactly Züritüütsch, the dialect spoken in Zurich) was not even weakly context free. Thus, the argumentation remained strictly confined to form (be it syntax or morphology).

To be able to actually prove some facts about Dutch we are going to simplify and formalize matters somewhat. The simplification consists in ignoring tense, using only singulars and no finite forms. It is a trivial matter to extend the accounts below to the original case. I trust that the reader has knowledge of a few facts concerning CF languages (see Harrison (1978) or Kracht (2003)). These are that if $L \subseteq A^*$ is a CF string language and $R \subseteq A^*$ a regular string language, then $L \cap R$ also is CF. Another is that if $\varphi : A \to B^+$ is an arbitrary map and $L \subseteq A^*$ is CF then $\varphi[L]$ also is CF. (Notice that $\varphi(a)$ must be nonempty for all $a \in A$!) These techniques are used to infer that the fragment below "scales" up to the full language, that is to say, can be used to infer that Dutch as a whole and not just this selected fragment, is not CF. I shall not perform this argument since it essentially requires syntactic arguments (and more empirical facts about Dutch) and we are more interested in the issue of compositionality. But to make the sentences more realistic would be to obscure the problems that occur at a more fundamental level.

I shall in fact present various different formalizations, all leading basically to the same conclusion but different from each other in subtle but crucial respects.

I shall use predicate logic with constants for names and basic predicates. There are two sorts: individuals and events. The inclusion of events makes the formal semantics less trivial. It would similarly be possible to use time points or intervals, but events are actually easier to use. The arities of the verbs differ according to their meaning. The base verbs are unary and the raising verbs take two arguments of each sort. For example, $\mathsf{let}'(e_0, e_1, x_0, x_1)$ means "e_0 is an event of letting, whose subject is x_0, who is granting x_1 to perform e_1". Since x_1 is then also the subject of the embedded event e_1 (x_1 is said to "perform e_1") there is some nontrivial argument identification going on under merge. We shall also assume to have argument roles to further decompose the meanings of the verbs. Thus we actually regard $\mathsf{let}'(e_0, e_1, x_0, x_1)$ as an abbreviation.

$$\begin{aligned}&\mathsf{let}'(e_0,e_1,x_0,x_1) := \\ &\qquad \mathsf{let}'(e_0) \wedge \mathsf{thm}'(e_0,e_1) \wedge \mathsf{agt}'(e_0,x_0) \wedge \mathsf{ben}'(e_0,x_1) \wedge \mathsf{agt}'(e_1,x_1)\end{aligned} \tag{5.117}$$

The reason for this assumption will soon become apparent.

Thus, in addition to the standard vocabulary, the predicate logic will contain constants of type o ("object") for each name, constants of type e ("event") for each verb, constants of type $\langle e, o\rangle$ and $\langle e, e\rangle$ for argument roles and identity.

Example 5.6 We now present our first language. Our basic vocabulary is as follows:

$$\begin{array}{llll}\langle\mathtt{Piet}, & «x_0 = \mathsf{p}'»\rangle & \langle\mathtt{zwemmen}, & «\mathsf{swim}'(e_0, x_0)»\rangle \\ \langle\mathtt{Jan}, & «x_0 = \mathsf{j}'»\rangle & \langle\mathtt{let}, & «\mathsf{let}'(e_0, e_1, x_0, x_1)»\rangle \\ \langle\mathtt{Marie}, & «x_0 = \mathsf{m}'»\rangle & \langle\mathtt{leren}, & «\mathsf{teach}'(e_0, e_1, x_0, x_1)»\rangle \\ \langle\mathtt{het\ kind}, & «x_0 = \mathsf{c}'»\rangle & \langle\mathtt{zien}, & «\mathsf{see}'(e_0, e_1, x_0, x_1)»\rangle\end{array} \tag{5.118}$$

This is to say that the exponents are considered minimal units (if you will, letters of an alphabet) and their meanings are as given. For each of them there is a constant $f_{\vec{x}}$ with exponent $\vec{x}$ and it is interpreted as given above.

We assume that the only constituents are of the form, where $m = n$ or $m = n+1$.

$$\mathrm{NP}_0\text{␣}\mathrm{NP}_1\text{␣}\cdots\text{␣}\mathrm{NP}_{n-1}\text{␣}\mathrm{V}_0\text{␣}\mathrm{V}_1\text{␣}\cdots\text{␣}\mathrm{V}_{m-1} \tag{5.119}$$

The meaning of such an expression is the one that it ordinarily has in Dutch. If $n = m$ it is a concept of type $\langle e, o\rangle$, involving an event variable and an object variable. If $n = m + 1$ it is a concept of type $\langle e, o, o\rangle$.

First we present a grammar of Dutch that generates this language. Constituents are either strings or pairs of strings. NPs by themselves as well as Vs are strings. All other exponents are analysed as pairs $\langle\vec{x}, \vec{y}\rangle$ where $\vec{x}$ is a sequence of NPs and $\vec{y}$ a sequence of Vs. Thus they have the form (5.119). We shall use two functions: one integrates a verb and the second an NP.

We start with the base case. Let $\mathfrak{c} \circledcirc \mathfrak{d}$ be defined as follows. (a) It is partial and requires that $\mathfrak{c}$ is a 1-concept of type $\langle o\rangle$ and $\mathfrak{d}$ a 2-concept of type $\langle e, o\rangle$, that is, it is a relation between objects and events; (b) the result is obtained by identifying the object of $\mathfrak{c}$ with that of $\mathfrak{d}$. Since there is only one of each sort, we do not even need a linking aspect for this to be well-defined.

$$\mathcal{I}(c)(\langle\vec{x},\mathfrak{c}\rangle,\langle\vec{y},\mathfrak{d}\rangle) := \begin{cases} \langle\langle\vec{x},\vec{y}\rangle, \mathfrak{c} \oslash \mathfrak{d}\rangle & \text{if } \vec{x} \text{ is an NP and } \vec{y} \text{ a nonraising verb,} \\ \text{undefined} & \text{else.} \end{cases} \tag{5.120}$$

Now we deal with the recursion in the construction.

Say that a pair $\langle\vec{x},\vec{z}\rangle$ is of **Type A** if $\vec{x}$ is a sequence of n NPs and $\vec{z}$ a sequence of n Vs and $n > 0$.

$$\mathcal{I}(v)(\langle\langle\vec{x},\vec{z}\rangle,\mathfrak{c}\rangle,\langle\vec{y},\mathfrak{d}\rangle) \tag{5.121}$$
$$:= \begin{cases} \langle\langle\vec{x},\vec{y}{}^\frown\vec{z}\rangle, \mathfrak{c} \oslash' \mathfrak{d}\rangle & \text{if } \langle\vec{x},\vec{z}\rangle \text{ is of Type A and } \vec{y} \text{ a raising verb,} \\ \text{undefined} & \text{else.} \end{cases}$$

Here, $\mathfrak{c} \oslash' \mathfrak{d}$ is defined if and only if $\mathfrak{c}$ is of type $\langle e,o\rangle$ and $\mathfrak{d}$ of type $\langle e,e,o,o\rangle$. It identifies the event variable of $\mathfrak{c}$ with the second event variable of $\mathfrak{d}$ and the object variable of $\mathfrak{c}$ with the second object variable of $\mathfrak{d}$; then it quantifies the event variable away. To do this, we need to have a linking aspect that defines the notions "first" and "second" for concepts denoted by raising verbs in the appropriate way. This can be done by simply listing the critical sets for each of the raising verbs. The other strategy is semantic. We choose a linking aspect for thm' (since this is of type $\langle e,e\rangle$). This allows to distinguish the first and second event variable. For the object variables we actually take advantage of the thematic predicates agt' (giving us the first variable) and ben' (giving us the second).

Thus we get the following meaning of (English) "let Mary swim":

$$\text{«}\mathsf{let}'(e_0,e_1,x_0,x_1)\text{»} \oslash' \text{«}\mathsf{swim}'(e_0,x_0) \wedge x_0 = \mathsf{m}'\text{»} \tag{5.122}$$
$$= \text{«}\exists e_1.\mathsf{let}'(e_0,e_1,x_0,x_1) \wedge \mathsf{swim}'(e_1,x_1) \wedge x_1 = \mathsf{m}'\text{»}$$

The last function needed is the one that incorporates the NP. $\langle\vec{x},\vec{z}\rangle$ is of **Type B** if it is a sequence of n NPs followed by $n+1$ Vs. Define a function $\oslash''$ as follows. It is defined if and only if $\mathfrak{c}$ is of type $\langle e,o,o\rangle$ and $\mathfrak{d}$ of type $\langle o\rangle$. It identifies the object of $\mathfrak{d}$ with the second object of $\mathfrak{c}$ and then quantifies that away. Notice that we can define first and second object using the thematic predicate agt' (picking out the "first" argument). This will be the meaning of (English) "Piet let Mary swim":

$$\text{«}\exists e_1.\mathsf{let}'(e_0,e_1,x_0,x_1) \wedge \mathsf{swim}'(e_1,x_1) \wedge x_1 = \mathsf{m}'\text{»} \oslash'' \text{«}x_0 = \mathsf{p}'\text{»} \tag{5.123}$$
$$= \text{«}\exists x_1.\exists e_1.\mathsf{let}'(e_0,e_1,x_0,x_1) \wedge \mathsf{swim}'(e_1,x_1) \wedge x_0 = \mathsf{p}' \wedge x_1 = \mathsf{m}'\text{»}$$

With this definition we put

$$\mathcal{I}(n)(\langle\vec{y},\mathfrak{d}\rangle,\langle\langle\vec{x},\vec{z}\rangle,\mathfrak{c}\rangle) \tag{5.124}$$
$$:= \begin{cases} \langle\langle\vec{y}{}^\frown\vec{x},\vec{z}\rangle, \mathfrak{c} \oslash'' \mathfrak{d}\rangle & \text{if } \langle\vec{x},\vec{z}\rangle \text{ is of Type B and } \vec{y} \text{ an NP,} \\ \text{undefined} & \text{else.} \end{cases}$$

Let us now see why a context free grammar for this language cannot be given. Let us take a look at the sentence we just derived (cf. Fig. 5.2):

$$\texttt{Jan␣Marie␣Piet␣laten␣leren␣zwemmen} \tag{5.125}$$

In line with the assumptions that strings must contain the same number of NPs and Vs or at most one more V than NP, we can only propose the following parts (in addition to the words themselves):

$$\begin{aligned}
&\texttt{Jan␣Marie␣Piet␣laten␣leren␣zwemmen},\\
&\texttt{Marie␣Piet␣laten␣leren␣zwemmen},\\
&\texttt{Marie␣Piet␣laten␣leren},\\
&\texttt{Piet␣laten␣leren},\\
&\texttt{Piet␣laten}
\end{aligned} \tag{5.126}$$

In this case we are done: only the first two strings contain a raising verb. It is easy to see that this argument works in the general case, too. ⚽

This example worked because we have assumed the language has certain properties. Whether or not it actually does, is an empirical issue. Linguists have had serious difficulties assessing the nature of the constituents in the sentences above (from a

$$\begin{aligned}
&\iota(nf_{\text{Jan}}\,vnf_{\text{Marie}}\,vcf_{\text{Piet}}\,f_{\text{zemmen}}\,f_{\text{leren}}\,f_{\text{laten}})\\
&= \mathcal{I}(n)(\langle\texttt{Jan}, «x_0 = \mathsf{j}'»\rangle, \mathcal{I}(v)(\mathcal{I}(n)(\langle\texttt{Marie}, «x_0 = \mathsf{m}'»\rangle, \mathcal{I}(v)(\mathcal{I}(c)(\langle\texttt{Piet}, «x_0 = \mathsf{p}'»\rangle,\\
&\quad \langle\texttt{zwemmen}, «\mathsf{swim}'(e_0, x_0)»\rangle), \langle\texttt{leren}, «\mathsf{teach}'(e_0, e_1, x_0, x_1)»\rangle)))\\
&\quad \langle\texttt{laten}, «\mathsf{let}'(e_0, e_1, x_0, x_1)»\rangle))\\
&= \mathcal{I}(n)(\langle\texttt{Jan}, «x_0 = \mathsf{j}'»\rangle, \mathcal{I}(v)(\mathcal{I}(n)(\langle\texttt{Marie}, «x_0 = \mathsf{m}'»\rangle, \mathcal{I}(v)(\langle\langle\texttt{Piet}, \texttt{␣zwemmen}\rangle,\\
&\quad «\mathsf{swim}'(e_0, x_0) \wedge x_0 = \mathsf{p}'»\rangle, \langle\texttt{leren}, «\mathsf{teach}'(e_0, e_1, x_0, x_1)»\rangle)))\\
&\quad \langle\texttt{laten}, «\mathsf{let}'(e_0, e_1, x_0, x_1)»\rangle))\\
&= \mathcal{I}(n)(\langle\texttt{Jan}, «x_0 = \mathsf{j}'»\rangle, \mathcal{I}(v)(\mathcal{I}(n)(\langle\texttt{Marie}, «x_0 = \mathsf{m}'»\rangle, \langle\langle\texttt{Piet}, \texttt{␣leren␣zwemmen}\rangle,\\
&\quad «\exists e_1.\mathsf{swim}'(e_1, x_1) \wedge x_1 = \mathsf{p}' \wedge \mathsf{teach}'(e_1, e_0, x_0, x_1)»\rangle,\\
&\quad \langle\texttt{laten}, «\mathsf{let}'(e_0, e_1, x_0, x_1)»\rangle))))\\
&= \mathcal{I}(n)(\langle\texttt{Jan}, «x_0 = \mathsf{j}'»\rangle, \mathcal{I}(v)(\langle\langle\texttt{Marie␣Piet}, \texttt{␣leren␣zwemmen}\rangle,\\
&\quad «\exists x_1.\exists e_1.\mathsf{swim}'(e_1, x_1) \wedge \mathsf{teach}'(e_0, e_1, x_0, x_1) \wedge x_0 = \mathsf{m}' \wedge x_1 = \mathsf{p}'»\rangle,\\
&\quad \langle\texttt{laten}, «\mathsf{let}'(e_0, e_1, x_0, x_1)»\rangle)))\\
&= \mathcal{I}(n)(\langle\texttt{Jan}, «x_0 = \mathsf{j}'»\rangle, \mathcal{I}(v)(\langle\langle\texttt{Marie␣Piet}, \texttt{␣leren␣zwemmen}\rangle,\\
&\quad «\exists e_1.\mathsf{swim}'(e_1, \mathsf{p}') \wedge \mathsf{teach}'(e_0, e_1, x_0, \mathsf{p}') \wedge x_0 = \mathsf{m}'»\rangle,\\
&\quad \langle\texttt{laten}, «\mathsf{let}'(e_0, e_1, x_0, x_1)»\rangle)))\\
&= \mathcal{I}(n)(\langle\texttt{Jan}, «x_0 = \mathsf{j}'»\rangle, \langle\langle\texttt{Marie␣Piet}, \texttt{laten␣leren␣zwemmen}\rangle,\\
&\quad «\exists e_0.\exists e_1.\mathsf{swim}'(e_1, \mathsf{p}') \wedge \mathsf{teach}'(e_0, e_1, x_0, \mathsf{p}') \wedge x_0 = \mathsf{m}' \wedge \mathsf{let}'(e_2, e_0, x_2, x_0)»\rangle)\\
&= \langle\langle\texttt{Jan␣Marie␣Piet}, \texttt{laten␣leren␣zwemmen}\rangle,\\
&\quad «\exists x_0.\exists e_0.\exists e_1.\mathsf{swim}'(e_1, \mathsf{p}') \wedge \mathsf{teach}'(e_0, e_1, x_0, \mathsf{p}') \wedge x_0 = \mathsf{m}' \wedge \mathsf{let}'(e_2, e_0, x_2, x_0)\\
&\quad \wedge x_2 = \mathsf{j}'»\rangle\\
&= \langle\langle\texttt{Jan␣Marie␣Piet}, \texttt{laten␣leren␣zwemmen}\rangle,\\
&\quad «\exists e_0.\exists e_1.\mathsf{swim}'(e_1, \mathsf{p}') \wedge \mathsf{teach}'(e_0, e_1, \mathsf{m}', \mathsf{p}') \wedge \mathsf{let}'(e_2, e_0, x_2, \mathsf{m}') \wedge x_2 = \mathsf{j}'»\rangle
\end{aligned}$$

Fig. 5.2 A derivation

syntactic viewpoint). If we make the choice as above, there is not much chance for a CFG. Yet, one may complain that we have been biased: coordination facts indicate, for example, that the verb sequences can be constituents, too (see Groenink (1997)) and we have just excluded them. Therefore, we shall now ease the constituency of Dutch somewhat by admitting more subconstituents. There is another point where we might have made an arbitrary decision. The meaning of a sentence or complex expression is a function of the meanings of its parts. We have admitted this function to do only the following:

① identify some columns (= add an identity of the form $x_i = x_j$) and
② cylindrify (= apply an existential quantifier $\exists x_i$).

There does not seem to be much room for choices when to apply ①. After all, identifying two variables is to say something significant. On the other hand, applying ② seems to be negotiable from a meaning point of view. The difference between various choices seems to be rather of a technical nature. When a variable has been quantified away it is not available any more for identification. On the other hand, the more free variables we have the more difficult the job of identifying the right one gets.

Example 5.7 We shall extend the set of meaningful constituents to include all strings of NPs followed by Vs which are substrings of sentences. This means, effectively, that all sequences of names and verbs are licit that contain at most one nonraising V and where the NPs precede the Vs and the raising Vs precede the nonraising Vs. This, by the way, is a regular language. As interpretation we choose the one induced by these strings as parts of some sentence. In each combination of a V $\vec{x}$ and a V $\vec{y}$ following it, we shall identify the theme of $\vec{x}$ with the event nontheme of $\vec{y}$; we shall also identify the benefactor of $\vec{x}$ with the agent of $\vec{y}$. No existential quantification. This is a variant of $\textcircled{\wedge}''$ above. With respect to the NPs, matters are different. Consider the string /Jan␣Piet␣leren/. Is Jan the one who teaches? It depends. For the string could be embedded in the following different sentences:

$$\texttt{Jan Piet leren zwemmen} \tag{5.127}$$

$$\texttt{Marie Jan Piet leren laten zwemmen} \tag{5.128}$$

In (5.127), Jan is doing the teaching and Piet the swimming. In (5.128), Jan is not doing the teaching, it is Marie. However, if Jan is doing the teaching, Piet is the one who is being taught. (This is because they are adjacent and in Dutch the next NP is the beneficiary of the action carried out by the agent.) Thus, we assume that our language contains the following signs:

$$\langle \texttt{Jan␣Piet␣leren}, \text{«}\mathsf{teach}'(e_0, e_1, x_0, x_1) \wedge x_2 = \mathsf{j}' \wedge x_3 = \mathsf{p}'\text{»}\rangle \tag{5.129}$$

$$\langle \texttt{Jan␣Piet␣leren}, \text{«}\mathsf{teach}'(e_0, e_1, x_0, x_1) \wedge x_0 = \mathsf{j}' \wedge x_1 = \mathsf{p}'\text{»}\rangle \tag{5.130}$$

The more NPs we have in our string, the more signs we seem to get in this way. However, there are some more restrictions. The verb following the rightmost NP is certainly the highest. So in the following example we cannot make Piet the beneficiary of the teaching. Still, three signs remain:

$$\langle \texttt{Marie␣Jan␣Piet␣leren}, \quad (5.131)$$
$$«\mathsf{teach}'(e_0, e_1, x_0, x_1) \wedge x_2 = \mathsf{m}' \wedge x_3 = \mathsf{j}' \wedge x_4 = \mathsf{p}'»\rangle$$

$$\langle \texttt{Marie␣Jan␣Piet␣leren}, \quad (5.132)$$
$$«\mathsf{teach}'(e_0, e_1, x_0, x_1) \wedge x_0 = \mathsf{m}' \wedge x_1 = \mathsf{j}' \wedge x_2 = \mathsf{p}'»\rangle$$

$$\langle \texttt{Marie␣Jan␣Piet␣leren},$$
$$«\mathsf{teach}'(e_0, e_1, x_0, x_1) \wedge x_1 = \mathsf{m}' \wedge x_2 = \mathsf{j}' \wedge x_3 = \mathsf{p}'»\rangle$$

To show this, look at the following sentences containing them.

`Marie Jan Piet leren laten leren laten zwemmen` (5.133)
`Marie Jan Piet leren laten leren zwemmen` (5.134)
`Marie Jan Piet leren laten zwemmen` (5.135)

And so, with n NPs and one V we have n choices in general. Notice, however, that if the last V is nonraising, the number of different readings is just one. This is because the subject of the nonraising verb must be the last NP and the subject of the verb before it the second last NP and so on.

The only exception to this is when the string does not contain an NP. This case deserves some attention. In the case of raising verbs we need to take care of two event variables and two object variables. Each verb clearly identifies an order between its variables. Let the first verb introduce e_0 and e_1 and the second e_2 and e_3. Then we have to identify e_1 and e_2; after that we can quantify away e_1/e_2. The complex concept has only two free event variables. On the other hand, we do not really need to quantify away any variable. The concept establishes an order between the three variables (e_0, e_1 and e_3). For example, in /`leren laten`/ we have to combine «$\mathsf{let}'(e_0, e_1, x_0, x_1)$» with «$\mathsf{teach}'(e_0, e_1, x_0, x_1)$». Let us rename the variables in the second formula and return to ordinary predicates.

$$\mathsf{let}'(e_0, e_1, x_0, x_1) \wedge \mathsf{teach}'(e_2, e_3, x_2, x_3) \quad (5.136)$$

The result we want is (up to renaming)

$$\mathsf{let}'(e_0, e_1, x_0, x_1) \wedge \mathsf{teach}'(e_1, e_3, x_1, x_3). \quad (5.137)$$

Furthermore, given that we can identify a linear order on the event variables it is also possible to define a linear order on the object variables. This is because we can identify via the thematic roles which of the variables is actually the agent (beneficiary) of which event variable. In this way the newly formed concept can be effectively merged with any new concept. The effect is that the constituency in the verb cluster is completely free.

Let us see how we can derive the meanings of the sentences using these signs. In view of the last remark it appears that there is no other choice but to start by assembling the entire V cluster. For suppose we did not do that. Then we build signs with an NP-sequence followed by a V-sequence. These are multiply ambiguous, yet only one of the readings is the one needed in the sentence. It is just that as long as we do not have the last V, we do not know which one we should choose. Now, if we do not make a choice then we simply postpone the choice. However, if we do that we discard information about the relative order of the NPs (since this is not recorded in the semantics, only in the string). Thus the requirement we get is this: the NP cluster is right branching, while the V cluster has any structure we please. The easiest structure (but not the only one) is a right branching structure:

`[Jan [Piet [Marie [het kind [zien [laten [leren zwemmen]]]]]]]` (5.138)

Once again, however, Dutch is not context free. To see this one may appeal e. g. to Ogden's Lemma. I shall just point out that since the verb clusters each form a constituent, there must be infinitely many categories (one for each number of Vs). ⚽

I conclude this discussion with the following remarks. The structure is in basic agreement with CCG. It has indeed been proposed that the structure of Dutch involves a verbal cluster. Groenink (1997) has also argued from coordination data that the verbal cluster is more flexible in Dutch and German.

5.6 Arguing for Syntactic Structure

The previous section has shown that Dutch (or at least some "purified' version thereof) is indeed not weakly context free. The book (Gazdar et al., 1985) seems to have shown, however, that at least English is CF. Many syntactic theories seem to agree (see Rogers (1994) and Kracht (1995) for a demonstration that generative grammar of the 80ies essentially claimed the context freeness of English). In this section we shall look at some constructions of English that indicate that also English is not CF.

`John, Mary and Phil sang, danced and played drums, respectively.` (5.139)

This sentence effectively is the conjunction of "John sang", "Mary danced" and "Phil played the drums". Without the word /`respectively`/ it could be interpreted as saying that John, Mary and Phil *each* sang, danced *and* played drums.

`John, Mary and Phil sang, danced and played drums.` (5.140)

The interpretation of (5.140) requires only a basic sentential structure: we have a plural NP /John, Mary and Phil/ and a VP /sang, danced and played drums/. Each has a coordinated structure. However, (5.139) is much different. To make the argumentation self-contained we consider the following data.

Example 5.8 The language contains the following signs (compare the grammars P_1 to P_3 of Section 3.2). We choose a domain U of individuals. Intransitive verbs and nouns denote sets of individuals. There are n intransitive verbs v_i, $i < n$ and 2^n nouns. Verb forms are in the past, so that number distinctions do not exist. For every combination of v_i (or their negation) we assume that there is exactly one name n_j such that n_j satisfies that combination. The legitimate strings are defined by S (where V denotes any verb, N any name):

$$\begin{aligned} Y &:= (N \cdot \llcorner)^{+}\mathtt{and}_{\llcorner} \cdot N \\ Z &:= (V \cdot \llcorner)^{+}\mathtt{and}_{\llcorner} \cdot V \\ S &:= Y \cup Z \cup N \cup V \cup Y \cdot \llcorner \cdot Z \cdot (\mathtt{,}_{\llcorner}\mathtt{respectively})? \cdot \mathtt{.} \end{aligned} \tag{5.141}$$

Additionally we assume that if /respectively/ is present, the number of names and the number of verbs is the same. This defines a context free language (we leave the proof as an exercise). What we shall show here however is that no compositional CFG exists.

The meanings are as follows. (a) Strings from Y denote the sets of all denotations of the occurring names, (b) strings from Z denote the intersection of all the sets denoted by the individual members; (c) strings from $Y \cdot \llcorner \cdot Z$ denote the intersection of what Y denotes and what Z denotes; finally, (d) if $\vec{y}_i$, $i < n+1$, are some names and $\vec{z}_i$, $i < n+1$, some verbs, then the denotation of

$$\vec{y}_0{}_\llcorner \cdots \vec{y}_{n-1}{}_\llcorner\mathtt{and}_\llcorner\vec{y}_n{}_\llcorner\vec{z}_0{}_\llcorner \cdots \vec{z}_{n-1}{}_\llcorner\mathtt{and}_\llcorner\vec{z}_n\mathtt{,}_\llcorner\mathtt{respectively.} \tag{5.142}$$

is the intersection of the denotations of $/\vec{y}_i{}_\llcorner\vec{z}_i\mathtt{.}/$ for all $i < n+1$.

Let us see what happens if we attempt to interpret (5.139) using the same structure as for (5.140). In this case the following happens. The phrase /John, Mary and Phil/ is synonymous with /John, Phil and Mary/ and also /Mary, John and Phil/ and so on. However, this synonymy does not exist between (5.139) and (5.143) and (5.144).

John, Phil and Mary sang, danced and played drums, respectively. (5.143)

John, Mary and Phil sang, danced and played drums, respectively. (5.144)

It follows that /John, Mary and Phil/ is not a constituent in (5.139). Similarly we argue that neither /John, Mary/ nor /John, Phil/ nor /Mary and Phil/ can be constituents. And we can do the same with the verbs. The only constituents that we *can* form without running a risk of conflation are /John sang/, /Mary danced/ and /Phil played drums/.

It follows that in a construction involving /respectively/ we are forced to assume what is known as **crossover (crossing) dependencies**.

$$\mathrm{NP}_0\text{␣}\mathrm{NP}_1\text{␣}\cdots\text{␣and␣}\mathrm{NP}_{n-1}\text{␣}\mathrm{VP}_0\text{␣}\mathrm{NP}_1\cdots\text{␣and␣}\mathrm{VP}_{n-1},\text{␣}\mathtt{respectively.} \tag{5.145}$$

We can assume that we get these structures as follows. One method is to assume that exponents are pairs of strings $\langle\vec{x},\vec{u}\rangle$ such that $\vec{x}$ is an NP and $\vec{v}$ an agreeing VP. Let **Case A** be the following property.

$$\textbf{Case A} : \vec{v} \text{ does not end with } /\mathtt{respectively}/ \tag{5.146}$$

Furthermore, let $\circledS$ be the "obvious" conjunction of concepts. Assuming that NPs and VPs denote sets of individuals, $\circledS$ is the intersection of their minimal members, accompanied by existential closure (thus we get a 0-ary concept, also known as a truth value). For two 0-ary concepts, $\circledS$ is set intersection. (If that presents difficulties, you may replace concepts with standard relations.)

$$\begin{aligned} &r(\langle\langle\vec{x},\vec{u}\rangle,m\rangle,\langle\langle\vec{y},\vec{v}\rangle,n\rangle) \\ &\quad:= \begin{cases} \langle\langle\vec{x}^\frown\text{␣}^\frown\vec{y},\vec{u}^\frown\text{␣and␣}^\frown\vec{v}^\frown\mathtt{,␣respectively.}\rangle, m\circledS n\rangle & \text{in Case A,} \\ \langle\langle\vec{x}^\frown\text{␣}^\frown\vec{y},\vec{u}^\frown\text{␣}\vec{v}\rangle, m\circledS n\rangle & \text{else.} \end{cases} \end{aligned} \tag{5.147}$$

This creates a constituent $\langle\mathrm{NP}_i,\mathrm{VP}_i\rangle$ in (5.145), which we get with the following rule.

$$s(\langle\vec{x},m\rangle,\langle\vec{u},n\rangle) := \begin{cases} \langle\langle\vec{x},\vec{u}\rangle,\mathsf{C}_0.m\circledS n\rangle & \text{if } \vec{x} \text{ is an NP and } \vec{u} \text{ a VP,} \\ \text{undefined} & \text{else.} \end{cases} \tag{5.148}$$

Another option is to assume that the discontinuous NP-VP constituents are not even formed. In this case we use a modified version of r:

$$\begin{aligned} &r^*(\langle\vec{x},m_0\rangle,\langle\vec{u},m_1\rangle,\langle\vec{y},n_0\rangle,\langle\vec{v},n_1\rangle) \\ &\quad:= \begin{cases} \langle\vec{x}^\frown\text{␣}^\frown\vec{y},\vec{u}^\frown\text{␣and␣}^\frown\vec{v}^\frown\mathtt{,␣respectively.}\rangle, & \\ \qquad(\mathsf{C}_0.(m_0\circledS m_1))\circledS\mathsf{C}_0.(n_0\circledS n_0)\rangle & \text{in Case A,} \\ \text{undefined} & \text{else.} \end{cases} \end{aligned} \tag{5.149}$$

$$\begin{aligned} &r^{**}(\langle\vec{x},m_0\rangle,\langle\vec{u},m_1\rangle,\langle\langle\vec{y},\vec{v}\rangle,n_0\rangle) := \\ &\quad\begin{cases} \langle\langle\vec{x}^\frown\text{␣}^\frown\vec{y},\vec{u}^\frown\text{␣}^\frown\vec{v}\rangle,(\mathsf{C}_0.(m_0\circledS m_1))\circledS n_0\rangle & \text{not in Case A} \\ \text{undefined} & \text{else.} \end{cases} \end{aligned}$$

The first variant is more elegant. ⚽

Intermission 3 The grammar and interpretation of sequences of NPs is interesting in its own right.

$$\texttt{John, Paul and Mary} \quad (5.150)$$

$$\texttt{John, Paul or Mary} \quad (5.151)$$

Assume that coordination requires the presence of either /and/ or /or/. Assume further that meanings are concepts. Finally, the interpretation of a name is assumed to be a singleton set. There are then two choices for us. We can either interpret the coordinated NP as a relation between the named people, or as the set of all of them. In either option the basic laws of conjunction and disjunction (commutativity, associativity and idempotence) are satisfied. It is clear that the overall structure of a conjunction is not unique, even with all this being given. It is trivial to observe that we could in principle design ternary rules, for example. Or we may use wrapping. But we should not dismiss any of these options either, despite the fact that they are more complicated than the obvious right regular grammar.

In a compositional grammar this has noteworthy consequences. If one wishes to make /John and Mary/ a subconstituent of a sentence, then this can only be done if either /Mary and John/ cannot be substituted for it or else the resulting sentence has the same meaning. If you choose to have categories, one can of course discriminate a number of different coordinations, for example, by giving /John and Mary/ a different category than /Mary and John/. Apart from being rather unsatisfactory, the Principle of the Identity of Indiscernibles (see page 39) rules this out as well. (It does not under certain circumstances, however. One is agreement in languages where a conjunct controls the same agreement as its last member. Latin is such a case. In such circumstances, since /John and Mary/ controls feminine agreement and /Mary and John/ masculine agreement, they have different category.) ⚽

Notice that /respectively/ has more syntactic possibilities than given in this example. The preceding argument assumes that we are forming a compositional grammar. Alternatively and interestingly, even if one does not assume compositionality, the result follows. This has to do with the fact that we have restricted the available semantic functions.

English provides yet another construction that is quite problematic in phrase structure terms, namely *gapping*. This phenomenon is illustrated in the following sentence.

$$\texttt{John gave Mary a kiss and George Susan a flower.} \quad (5.152)$$

We understand this as the conjunction of two sentences:

$$\texttt{John gave Mary a kiss.} \quad (5.153)$$

$$\texttt{George gave Susan a flower.} \quad (5.154)$$

What is problematic about this construction is that it forces us to assume that we have a discontinuous constituent /John Mary a flower/. Let us see why this is so. Like the previous example, we assume that the meaning of sentences is a truth value. (This assumption can of course be modified, though the argument would not work as easily.) Suppose, we first fully compose the sentence (5.153). This will have as its meaning, say, a truth value. In this case it is impossible to interpolate the meaning of the verb so that it can be used to derive the meaning of (5.154). Notice that rather than having the full (5.154) we are actually missing the verb. It follows that (5.152) does not contain the constituent (5.153)!

Instead we are led to assume that (5.152) contains the constituents /`John Mary a kiss`/ and /`George Susan a flower`/. (This is essentially what Steedman (1990) claims. Though unlike him we do not use an ex post splitting of the first sentence, which makes no sense semantically. Instead, both sentences are formed in the same way from the parts.) More precisely, it contains the pairs ⟨`John`, `Mary a kiss`⟩ and ⟨`George`, `Susan a flower`⟩. The verb /`gave`/ is inserted into both of them. Since gapping is like conjunction in allowing any number of parts, we propose a solution similar to the one offered for "respectively".

Example 5.9 Here is a sketch of gapping. The constituents of the form /`George Susan a flower`/ are seen as pairs ⟨`George`, `Susan a flower`⟩. These pairs are coordinated via the mode c. After all of them are coordinated, the verb is linked with the conjunctive meaning and inserted between the first subject and the first object.

$$\begin{aligned}\mathcal{I}(c)(\langle\langle\vec{x},\vec{y}\rangle,m\rangle,\langle\langle\vec{u},\vec{v}\rangle,n\rangle) &:= \langle\langle\vec{x},\vec{y}^\frown\vec{u}^\frown\vec{v}\rangle,m\cup n\rangle\\ \mathcal{I}(i)(\langle\langle\vec{x},\vec{y}\rangle,m\rangle,\langle\vec{v},n\rangle) &:= \langle\vec{x}^\frown\vec{v}^\frown\vec{y},m\,\circledA^3\,n\rangle\end{aligned} \tag{5.155}$$

This accounts for this type of gapping. ⚽

It may seem to be disappointing that the syntactic structures are so irregular. Syntactic theories sometimes give the impression that syntactic structure (at least of English) is a matter of a few universal principles. This seems to be an artefact of the data that the theories wish to explain. No one theory succeeds in giving us a satisfactory account of all known phenomena and typically they tend to do well in a few areas and badly in others. I should also point out that in the literature there are no essentially different solutions to the problems shown above. Respectively-constructions have been used in (Kac et al., 1987) to show that English is not context free. Where the latter authors use the distribution of pronouns to show that the string language of English is not context free, here we have used the meanings to derive the same conclusion.

Exercise 5.9 Write a CFG to generate S from Example 5.8.

Chapter 6
Conclusion

In this book I have tried to build a theory that lets us ask (and sometimes even answer) questions concerning the structure of languages. Some of the results plainly validate some of our intuitions; others have been surprising (at least to me). The road has been fairly difficult not the least because exact results are difficult to obtain and because new techniques had to be found.

We are now at the end of our journey. Many questions have been answered and many new ones arose. I shall summarise this work with a few remarks.

- Some tangible results have been established. For example, it has been shown that it is not possible to reduce all ambiguous languages to unambiguous ones (at least if we want to keep the syntactic complexity). Or that concept based predicate logic with infinitely many variables does not have a compositional context free grammar. These results seem to be pretty robust. They cannot be made to disappear if minor changes are made to the languages.
- The study of interpreted languages really has just begun. We need to understand better in what ways the shift from string languages to interpreted languages changes our outlook on various issues. Mathematically, new combinatorial methods need to be developed. They might help us to understand better in what ways semantics determines syntactic structure.
- On the way I have tried to make progress also concerning the overall structure of language. For example, notions such as morphological transparency, realphabetization and abstraction were attempts at understanding why natural language apparently has more structure (in the sense of architecture in terms of levels or strata) than the present framework (and others) make believe.
- Negative results are typically hard to obtain. This contrasts with a lot of claims in the literature that suggest that certain phenomena force us to adopt or abandon a specific framework because of compositionality. Most of these results either follow because quite specific assumptions have been made at the outset or because the authors simply are not imaginative enough about counterstrategies. For example, I have not been able to show conclusively that there is no TAG for boolean logic if we allow the semantic functions to be partial, though it seems certain that this claim is true. Nor have I been able to find a countable language that is not independent.

M. Kracht, *Interpreted Languages and Compositionality*, Studies in Linguistics and Philosophy 89, DOI 10.1007/978-94-007-2108-1_6,

© Springer Science+Business Media B.V. 2011

- The results established here make use of some additional hypotheses about language, some of which are indispensable such as the hypothesis that rules do not destroy any structure. Others might be more controversial, for example that syntactic structures are sequences of strings and nothing else.
- The literature in formal semantics operates with high powered tools. Often however the justification in using them is only that they provide a functioning algorithm without clarifying whether or not that algorithm deserves the label "compositional". Our approach has been not to rely on particular mechanisms but rather to clarify identity criteria of meaning (such as alphabetic innocence) and see how much follows from them.

Appendix A
Useful Mathematical Concepts and Notation

For a set S we write $\operatorname{card} S$ for the cardinality of S. In other words, $\operatorname{card} S$ denotes the number of elements of S. The number n is the set of all numbers i (including 0) such that $i < n$. Thus, $3 = \{0, 1, 2\}$. (The interested reader may check that therefore $0 = \varnothing$, $1 = \{0\} = \{\varnothing\}$, $2 = \{\varnothing, \{\varnothing\}\}$ and $3 = \{\varnothing, \{\varnothing\}, \{\varnothing, \{\varnothing\}\}\}$.) Thus, $i < n$ and $i \in n$ are synonymous. Writing $f : k \to n$ means that f is a function defined on all numbers $< k$, with values $< n$.

We shall write $\langle x_0, x_1, \cdots, x_{n-1}\rangle$ for the tuple of length n consisting in x_0, x_1, etc., in that order. We make no commitment about the real nature of tuples; you may think of them as functions from the set n to the domain. (In that case they are the same as strings.) The length of $\vec{x} := \langle x_0, \cdots, x_{n-1}\rangle$ is denoted by $|\vec{x}|$. We write x_0 in place of $\langle x_0\rangle$ even though they are technically distinct. Tuple formation is not associative. So, $\langle x_0, \langle x_1, x_2\rangle\rangle$ is not the same as $\langle\langle x_0, x_1\rangle, x_2\rangle$. If $\vec{x} = \langle x_0, \cdots, x_{m-1}\rangle$ and $\vec{y} = \langle y_0, \cdots, y_{n-1}\rangle$ are tuples, the concatenation is denoted as follows.

$$\vec{x} \cdot \vec{y} := \langle x_0, \cdots, x_{m-1}, y_0, \cdots, y_{n-1}\rangle \tag{A.1}$$

Repetitions are not eliminated, so this is a sequence of length $m + n$.

Given two sets, A and B, $A \times B$ is the set of pairs $\langle a, b\rangle$ such that $a \in A$ and $b \in B$. Given an indexed family A_i, $i \in I$, of sets, $\mathsf{X}_{i\in I} A_i$ is the set of functions from I to the union of the A_i such that $f(i) \in A_i$ for all $i \in I$. (Thus, technically, $A_0 \times A_2$ is *not* the same as $\mathsf{X}_{i\in 2} A_i$, though the difference hardly matters.) Let A and B be sets. A **relation from** A **to** B is a subset of $A \times B$. We write $x\ R\ y$ in place of $\langle x, y\rangle \in R$. A **partial function from** A **to** B is a relation from A to B such that $x\ R\ y$ and $x\ R\ z$ implies $y = z$. A **function from** A **to** B is a partial function from A to B where for every $x \in A$ there is a $y \in B$ such that $x\ R\ y$. We write $f : A \to B$ to say that f is a function from A to B and $f : A \hookrightarrow B$ to say that f is a partial function from A to B. If $f : A \to B$ and $g : B \to C$ then $g \circ f : A \to C$ is defined by $(g \circ f)(x) := g(f(x))$. We write $\operatorname{dom}(f)$ for the set of all $a \in A$ such that f is defined on a. If $f : A^n \hookrightarrow B$ and $S \subseteq A$ then we write $f \restriction S$ for the following function

$$(f \restriction S)(\vec{x}) := \begin{cases} f(\vec{x}) & \text{if } \vec{x} \in S^n \text{ and } f(\vec{x}) \text{ is defined,} \\ \text{undefined} & \text{else.} \end{cases} \tag{A.2}$$

M. Kracht, *Interpreted Languages and Compositionality*, Studies in Linguistics and Philosophy 89, DOI 10.1007/978-94-007-2108-1,
© Springer Science+Business Media B.V. 2011

A somewhat simpler definition is

$$f \restriction S := f \cap (S^n \times A). \tag{A.3}$$

If $X \subseteq A$ is a set we write $f[X] := \{f(a) : a \in X, a \in \mathrm{dom}(f)\}$. This is the **direct image of** X **under** f. In particular, $\mathrm{rng}(f) := f[A]$ is the **range** of f. f is **surjective** or **onto** if $\mathrm{rng}(f) = B$. f is **injective** or **into** if for all x, y: if $f(x)$ and $f(y)$ are defined then either $x = y$ or $f(x) \neq f(y)$. A **permutation** is a surjective function $f : n \to n$. It is easily seen that if f is surjective it is also injective. There are $n! := n(n-1)(n-2)\cdots 2 \cdot 1$ permutations of an n element set ($n > 0$).

When $f : A \times B \to C$ is a function, we say that it is **independent** of its first argument if for all $x, x' \in A$ and $y \in B$, $f(x, y) = f(x', y)$. (If $A \neq B$ we also say that f is independent of A rather than of its first argument.) Pick $x \in A$ and define $\hat{f} : B \to C$ by $\hat{f}(y) := f(x, y)$. If f is independent of its first argument, $\hat{f}$ is independent of the choice of x. For partial functions there are some subtleties. We say that f is **weakly independent of** A if for all $x, x' \in A$ and $y \in B$, if $f(x, y)$ and $f(x', y)$ exist, they are equal. f is **strongly independent of** A if for all $x, x' \in A$ and $y \in B$, if $f(x, y)$ exists then so does $f(x', y)$ and they are equal. By default, for a partial function independence of A means weak independence. Independence of its second argument (or of B) is defined similarly. Similarly, if f has several arguments, it may be weakly of strongly independent of any of them.

If $f : A \to C$ and $g : A \to D$ are functions, then $f \times g : x \mapsto \langle f(x), g(y)\rangle$ is a function from A to $C \times D$. Every function from A to $C \times D$ can be decomposed into two functions, in the following way. Let $\pi_C : \langle x, y\rangle \mapsto x$ and $\pi_2 : \langle x, y\rangle \mapsto y$ be the projections from $C \times D$ to C and D, respectively. Then we have the general equation

$$f = (\pi_c \circ f) \times (\pi_D \circ f). \tag{A.4}$$

and so the functions $\pi_C \circ f$ and $\pi_D \circ f$ are the decomposition. This picture changes when we turn to partial functions. From a pair $f : A \hookrightarrow C$ and $g : A \hookrightarrow D$ we can form the partial function

$$(f \times g)(x) := \begin{cases} \langle f(x), g(x)\rangle & \text{if both } f(x) \text{ and } g(x) \text{ are defined,} \\ \text{undefined} & \text{else.} \end{cases} \tag{A.5}$$

Unfortunately, $f \times g$ does not allow to recover f and g uniquely. The problem is this: we have

$$\mathrm{dom}(f \times g) = \mathrm{dom}(f) \cap \mathrm{dom}(g). \tag{A.6}$$

However, from an intersection it is not easy to recover the individual sets. If $A = \{0\}$, $f = \{\langle 0, c\rangle\}$ and $g = \varnothing$ (the empty partial function) then $f \times g = \varnothing$. However, also $\varnothing \times \varnothing = \varnothing$.

Given a number n, a bijective function $f : n \to n$ is called a **permutation of** n. Π_n denotes the set of all permutations of n. Permutations are most conveniently described using the following notation. Pick a number $i < n$. The **cycle** of i is the largest sequence of the form $i, f(i), f(f(i)), \cdots$ in which no member is repeated. The set $\{i, f(i), f^2(i), \cdots\}$ is also called the **orbit** of i under f. We write this cycle in the form $(i f(i) f(f(i)) \cdots f^{k-1}(i))$. An example is (2567), which says that f maps 2 to 5, 5 to 6, 6 to 7 and 7 to 2. The **order of the cycle** is its length, k. So, the order is the smallest number k for which $f^k(i) = i$. For if $f^k(i) = f^m(i)$ for some $m < k$ then also $f^{k+1}(i) = f^{m+1}(i)$ (since f is a function), and $f^{k-1}(i) = f^{m-1}(i)$ (since f is bijective, so its inverse is a function, too). It follows that $f^{k-m}(i) = i$ and since $m < k$, we must have $m = 0$. (Else we have found a number $j > 0$ smaller than k such that $f^j(i) = i$.) Cycles can be cyclically rotated: for example, $(2567) = (5672)$. It is easy to see that any two distinct orbits are disjoint. A permutation thus partitions the set n into orbits, and defines a unique cycle on each of the orbits. In writing down permutations, cycles of length 1 are omitted. Cycles permute and can be cyclically rotated. Thus we write (2567)(3)(1)(04) and (2567)(04), (5672)(40)(3), (04)(2567) interchangeably. The permutation that changes nothing is also denoted by ().

A **group** is a structure $\mathscr{G} = \langle G, 1, ^{-1}, \cdot \rangle$, where $1 \in G$, $^{-1} : G \to G$ and $\cdot : G \times G \to G$ are such that for all $x, y, z \in G$:

1. $1 \cdot x = x \cdot 1 = x$.
2. $x^{-1} \cdot x = x \cdot x^{-1} = 1$.
3. $x \cdot (y \cdot z) = (x \cdot y) \cdot z$.

We say that x^{-1} is the **inverse** of x and that $x \cdot y$ (also written xy) is the **product** of x and y. The set Π_n forms a group. The product is defined by $(f \cdot g)(x) := f(g(x))$. The unit is the permutation (). The inverse is obtained as follows. The inverse of a cycle $(i_0 i_1 \cdots i_{k-1})$ is the cycle $(i_{k-1} i_{k-2} \cdots i_1 i_0)$. The inverse of a series of disjoint cycles is obtained by inverting every cycle individually. (Note that if c and d are disjoint cycles, then $c \cdot d = d \cdot c$.) A **subgroup** of $\mathscr{G}$ is a triple $\mathscr{H} = \langle H, 1^*, ^{-1^*}, \cdot^* \rangle$ where $H \subseteq G$, $1^* = 1$, $x^{-1*} = x^{-1}$ and $x \cdot^* y = x \cdot y$. It is stated without proof that if $\mathscr{H}$ is a subgroup of $\mathscr{G}$ then $|H|$ divides $|G|$.

A **signature** is a pair $\langle F, \Omega \rangle$ (often written simply Ω) where F is a set (the set of **function symbols**) and $\Omega : F \to \mathbb{N}$ a function, assigning each function symbol an arity. An **Ω-algebra** is a pair $\mathfrak{A} = \langle A, I \rangle$ such that for every $f \in F$, $I(f) : A^{\Omega(f)} \to A$. We also write $f^{\mathfrak{A}}$ for $I(f)$. A **partial Ω-algebra** is a pair $\mathfrak{A} = \langle A, I \rangle$ where for each $f \in F$, $I(f) : A^{\Omega(f)} \hookrightarrow A$. A **weak congruence** on $\mathfrak{A}$ is an equivalence relation $\Theta \subseteq A^2$ such that the following holds.

> If $a_i \,\Theta\, b_i$ for every $i < \Omega(f)$ and both $I(f)(a_0, \cdots, a_{\Omega(f)-1})$ and $I(f)(b_0, \cdots, b_{\Omega(f)-1})$ exist then they are equal.

Θ is **strong** if whenever $a_i \;\Theta\; b_i$ for all $i < \Omega(f)$ then $I(f)(a_0, \cdots, a_{\Omega(f)-1})$ exists iff $I(f)(b_0, \cdots, b_{\Omega(f)-1})$ exists as well. If Θ is a strong congruence we can construct the so-called **quotient algebra** $\mathfrak{A}/\Theta$.

$$\begin{aligned} a/\Theta &:= \{b : a\ \Theta\ b\} \\ A/\Theta &:= \{a/\Theta : a \in A\} \\ (I/\Theta)(f)(a_0/\Theta, \cdots, a_{\Omega(f)-1}/\Theta) &:= (f(a_0, \cdots, a_{\Omega(f)-1}))/\Theta \\ \mathfrak{A}/\Theta &:= \langle A/\Theta, I/\Theta\rangle \end{aligned} \tag{A.7}$$

It is to be observed that $(I/\Theta)(f)$ is well defined; the value of the function does not depend on the choice of representatives. Moreover, whether or not it is defined is also independent of the choice of representatives, since the congruence is strong.

A homomorphism between partial algebras $\mathfrak{A} = \langle A, I\rangle$ and $\mathfrak{B} = \langle B, J\rangle$ is a function $h : A \to B$ such that for all $f \in F$ and all $a_0, \cdots, a_{\Omega(f)-1} \in A$:

$$h(I(f)(a_0, \cdots, a_{\Omega(f)-1})) = J(f)(h(a_0), \cdots, h(a_{\Omega(f)-1})). \tag{A.8}$$

If $\mathfrak{A} = \langle A, I\rangle$ and $\mathfrak{C} = \langle C, J\rangle$ are partial algebras then the **product** of $\mathfrak{A}$ and $\mathfrak{C}$ is defined by

$$(I \times J)(f)(\langle a_0, c_0\rangle, \cdots, \langle a_{\Omega(f)-1}, c_{\Omega(f)-1}\rangle) := \langle I(f)(\vec{a}), J(f)(\vec{c})\rangle. \tag{A.9}$$

We write $\mathfrak{A} \times \mathfrak{C}$ for the product.

In the domain of algebra, the term functions and polynomial functions are very important. Their definition is notoriously difficult since one is often required to use variables where this creates problems due to choices of alphabetical variants. Instead, I offer the following definition, which only uses functions and compositions.

① All projections $p_i^n : A^n \to A$ defined by $p_i^n(a_0, \cdots, a_{n-1}) := a_i$ are term functions.

② If $g_i : A^{m_i} \to A$, $i < \Omega(f)$, are term functions and $p := \sum_{i<\Omega(f)} m_i$, then $f \circ \langle g_0, \cdots, g_{\Omega(f)-1}\rangle : A^p \to A$ is a term function where

$$f \circ \langle g_0, \cdots, g_{\Omega(f)-1}\rangle(\vec{c}_0, \cdots, \vec{c}_{\Omega(f)-1}) := f(g_0(\vec{c}_0), \cdots, g_{\Omega(f)-1}(\vec{c}_{\Omega(f)-1}))$$

is a term function.

③ If $g : A^n \to A$ is a term function and $i < j$ then $g \circ \Delta_{ij}^n : A^{n-1} \to A$ defined by $\left(g \circ \Delta_{ij}^n\right)(a_0, \cdots, a_{n-2}) := g(a_0, \cdots, a_{j-1}, a_i, a_j, a_{j+1}, \cdots, a_{n-1})$ also is a term function.

(For a partial algebra, replace "function" everywhere by "partial function".) Term functions are often described by means of terms such as $(x + y) \cdot z$ but this is inaccurate. A **polynomial** is defined to a term function over the expanded algebra $\mathfrak{A}^A$, where for each $a \in A$ we have added a constant $\underline{a}$ to the language, whose interpretation is fixed to A. (Alternatively, it is the closure under ①–③ of the set of functions containing $A^0 \to A : \varnothing \to a$ for each a.)

Symbols

References

Barker, Chris, and Pauline Jacobson, eds. 2007. *Direct Compositionality*. Oxford Studies in Theoretical Linguistics, vol. 14. Oxford: Oxford University Press.

Ben Shalom, Dorit. 1996. "Semantic Trees." PhD thesis, Department of Linguistics, UCLA.

Benaceraff, Paul. 1973. "Mathematical Truth." *Journal of Philosophy* 70:661–79.

Bittner, Maria. 2006. Online Update. "Temporal, Modal and de se Anaphora in Polysynthetic Languages." In *Direct Compositionality*, edited by Chris Barker and Pauline Jacobson, 363–404. Oxford: Oxford University Press.

Chomsky, Noam. 1986. *Barriers*. Cambridge, MA: MIT Press.

Chomsky, Noam. 1993. "A Minimalist Program for Linguistic Theory." In *The View from Building 20: Essays in Honour Sylvain Bromberger*, edited by K. Hale and S.J. Keyser, 1–52. Cambridge, MA: MIT Press.

Copestake, Ann, Dan Flickinger, Carl Pollard, and Ivan A. Sag. 2005. "Minimal Recursion Semantics: An Introduction." *Research on Language and Computation* 3:281–332.

Dixon, Robert M.W. 1994. *Ergativity*. Cambridge Studies in Linguistics, vol. 69. Cambridge: Cambridge University Press.

Dorr, Cian. 2004. "Non-Symmetric Relations." In *Studies in Metaphysics*, vol. 1, edited by Dean W. Zimmerman, 155–92. Oxford: Oxford University Press.

Erdélyi Szabó, Miklós, Lászó Kálmán, and Ági Kurucz. 2007. "Towards a Natural Language Semantics Without Functors and Operands." *Journal of Logic, Language and Information* 16:1–17.

Falk, Yehuda N. 2001. *Lexical-Functional Grammar: An Introduction to Parallel Constraint-Based Syntax*. Stanford, CA: CSLI.

Fiengo, Robert, and Robert May. 2006. *De Lingua Belief*. Cambridge, MA: MIT Press.

Fine, Kit. 2000. "Neutral Relations." *The Philosophical Review* 109:1–33.

Fine, Kit. 2003. "The Role of Variables." *Journal of Philosophy* 50:605–31.

Fine, Kit. 2007. *Semantic Relationism*. London: Blackwell.

Gärdenfors, Peter. 2004. *Conceptual Spaces*. Cambridge, MA: MIT Press.

Gazdar, Gerald, Ewan Klein, Geoffrey Pullum, and Ivan Sag. 1985. *Generalized Phrase Structure Grammar*. London: Blackwell.

Groenink, Annius. 1997. *Surface Without Structure. Word Order and Tractability Issues in Natural Language Analysis*. PhD thesis, University of Utrecht.

Harrison, Michael A. 1978. *Introduction to Formal Language Theory*. Reading, MA: Addison Wesley.

Heim, Irene, and Angelika Kratzer. 1998. *Semantics in Generative Grammar*. Oxford: Blackwell Publishers.

Hodges, Wilfrid. 2001. "Formal Features of Compositionality." *Journal of Logic, Language and Information* 10:7–28.

Huybregts, Riny. 1984. "Overlapping Dependencies in Dutch." *Utrecht Working Papers in Linguistics* 1:3–40.

IPA. 1999. *Handbook of the International Phonetic Association*. Cambridge: Cambridge University Press.

Jacobson, Pauline. 1999. "Towards a Variable Free Semantics." *Linguistics and Philosophy* 22:117–84.

Jacobson, Pauline. 2000. "Paycheck Pronouns, Bach-Peters Sentences, and Variable Free Semantics." *Natural Language Semantics* 8:77–155.

Jacobson, Pauline. 2002. "The (Dis)Organisation of the Grammar: 25 Years." *Linguistics and Philosophy* 25:601–26.

Janssen, Theo. 1997. "Compositionality." In *Handbook of Logic and Language*, edited by Johan van Benthem and Alice ter Meulen, 417–73. Amsterdam: Elsevier.

Kac, Michael B., Alexis Manaster-Ramer, and William C. Rounds. 1987. "Simultaneous-Distributive Co-ordination and Context-Freeness." *Computational Linguistics* 13:25–30.

Kamp, Hans. 1981. "A Theory of Truth and Semantic Representation." In *Formal Methods in the Study of Language*, edited by Jeroen Groenendijk. Amsterdam: Mathematisch Centrum.

Kamp, Hans, and Uwe Reyle. 1993. *From Discourse to Logic. Introduction to Modeltheoretic Semantics of Natural Language, Formal Language and Discourse Representation*. Dordrecht: Kluwer.

Keenan, Edward L., and Edward P. Stabler. 2001. *Bare Grammar. Lectures on Linguistics Invariants*. Stanford, CA: CSLI.

King, Jeffrey C. 2007. *The Nature and Structure of Content*. Oxford: Oxford University Press.

Kornai, András. 2007. *Mathematical Linguistics. Advanced Information and Knowledge Processing*. Berlin: Springer.

Korpela, Jukka. 2006. *Unicode Explained*. Sebastopol, CA: O'Reilly.

Kracht, Marcus. 1995. "Syntactic Codes and Grammar Refinement." *Journal of Logic, Language and Information* 4:41–60.

Kracht, Marcus. 2003. *Mathematics of Language*. Berlin: Mouton de Gruyter.

Kracht, Marcus. 2006. "Partial Algebras, Meaning Categories and Algebraization." *Theoretical Computer Science* 354:131–41.

Kracht, Marcus. 2008. "Is Adjunction Compositional?" *Research on Language and Computation* 6:53–77.

Lamb, Sydney M. 1966. *Outline of Stratificational Grammar*. Washington, DC: Georgetown University Press.

Landmann, Fred. 2004. *Indefinites and the Type of Sets*. Explorations in Semantics, vol. 3. Oxford: Blackwell.

Lasersohn, Peter. 2009. "Compositional Interpretation in Which the Meanings of Complex Expressions Are Not Computable from the Meanings of Their Parts." In *Theory and Evidence in Semantics*, edited by John Nerbonne and Erhard Hinrichs, 133–58. Stanford, CA: CSLI.

Leo, Joop. 2010. *The Logical Structure of Relations*. PhD thesis, Department of Philosophy, University of Utrecht.

Manaster-Ramer, Alexis. 1986. "Copying in Natural Languages, Context-Freeness and Queue Grammars." In *Proceedings of the 24th Annual Meeting of the Association for Computational Linguistics* 85–89. New York, NY: Stroudsburg, PA.

Manaster-Ramer, Alexis, and Peter Michalove. 2001. "Etymology vs. Phonology: The Treatment of */w/ After Sonorants in Armenian." *Münchener Studien zur Sprachwissenschaft* 61:149–62.

Manaster-Ramer, Alexis, M. AndrewMoshier, and R. Suzanne Zeitman. 1992. An Extension of Ogden's Lemma. Manuscript. Detroit, MI: Wayne State University.

Martín-Vide, Carlos, and Gheorghe Păun. 1998. "Structured Contextual Grammars." *Grammars* 1:33–55.

Matthews, Peter H. 1978. *Inflectional Morphology. An Introduction to the Theory of Word-Structure*. Cambridge Textbooks in Linguistics. Cambridge: Cambridge University Press.

Mel'čuk, Igor A. 1988. *Dependency Syntax: Theory and Practice*. SUNY Linguistics Series. Albany, NY: State University of New York Press.

Mel'čuk, Igor A. 1993–2000. *Cours de Morphologie Générale*, vols. 1–5. Montréal: Les Presses de l'Université de Montréal.

Miller, Philip H. 1999. *Strong Generative Capacity. The Semantics of Linguistic Formalisms*. Stanford, CA: CSLI.

Monk, Donald J. 1976. *Mathematical Logic*. Berlin, Heidelberg: Springer.

Onions, C.T. 1973. *The Shorter English Dictionary*. Oxford: Oxford University Press.

Pagin, Peter. 2003. Communication and Strong Compositionality. *Journal of Philosophical Logic* 32:287–322.

Parsons, Terence. 1994. *Events in the Semantics of English. A Study in Subatomic Semantics*. Current Studies in Linguistics, vol. 19. Cambridge, MA: MIT Press.

Pentus, Mati. 1997. "Product–Free Lambek–Calculus and Context–Free Grammars." *Journal of Symbolic Logic* 62:648–60.

Pollard, Carl, and Ivan Sag. 1994. *Head–Driven Phrase Structure Grammar*. Chicago, IL: The University of Chicago Press.

Pullurn, Geoffrey, and Kyle Rawlins. 2007. "Argument or No argument?" *Linguistics and Philosophy* 30:277–87.

Putnam, Hilary. 1975. "The Meaning of 'Meaning'." In *Mind, Language and Reality*, 215–71. Cambridge: Cambridge University Press.

Radzinski, Daniel. 1990. "Unbounded Syntactic Copying in Mandarin Chinese." *Linguistics and Philosophy* 13:113–27.

Rautenberg, Wolfgang. 2006. *A Concise Introduction to Mathematical Logic*. Berlin: Springer.

Rogers, James. 1994. *Studies in the Logic of Trees with Applications to Grammar Formalisms*. PhD thesis, University of Delaware, Department of Computer & Information Sciences.

Saussure, Ferdinand de. 2006. *Writings in General Linguistics*. Oxford: Oxford University Press.

Saussure, Ferdinand de. 2011. *Course in General Linguistics*. New York, NY: Columbia University Press.

Scollon, Ron, and Suzie Wong Scollon. 2003. *Discourses in Place. Language in the Material World*. London and New York: Routledge.

Shieber, Stuart. 1985. "Evidence Against the Context–Freeness of Natural Languages." *Linguistics and Philosophy* 8:333–43.

Staudacher, Peter. 1987. "Zur Semantik Indefiniter Nominalphrasen." In *Neuere Forschungen zur Wortbildung und Historiographie der Linguistik. Festgabe für Herbert E. Brekle*, edited by Brigitte Asbach-Schnithker and Johannes Roggenhofer, 239–58. Tübingen: Gunter Narr Verlag.

Steedman, Mark. 1990. "Gapping as Constituent Coordination." *Linguistics and Philosophy* 13:207–63.

Sternefeld, Wolfgang. 2006. *Syntax. Eine morphologisch motivierte generative Beschreibung des Deutschen*. 2 Vols. Tübingen: Stauffenberg Verlag.

Svenonius, Peter. 2007. "Paradigrn Generation and Northern Sámi Stems." In *The Basis of Inflectional Identity*, edited by Asaf Bachrach and Andrew Nevins. Oxford: Oxford University Press.

Szabó, Zoltán Gendler. 2000. "Compositionality as Supervenience." *Linguistics & Philosophy* 23:475–505.

Talmy, Leonard. 2000. *Toward a Cognitive Semantics*, vols. 1 & 2. Cambridge, MA: MIT Press.

Thue, Axel. 1914. Probleme über Veränderungen von Zeichenreihen nach gegebenen Regeln. (Problems Concerning Changing Strings According to Given Rules). *Skrifter utgit av Videnskapsselkapet i Kristiania, I. Mathematisk-naturvidenskabelig klasse*, 10.

Tomalin, Marcus. 2006. *Linguistics and the Formal Sciences. The Origins of Generative Grammar*. Cambridge Studies in Linguistics. Cambridge: Cambridge University Press.

Vermeulen, Kees F.M. 1995. "Merging Without Mystery or: Variables in Dynamic Semantics." *Journal of Philosophical Logic* 24:405–50.

Wechsler, Stephen. 1995. *The Semantic Basis of Argument Structure*. Dissertations in Linguistics. Stanford, CA: CSLI.

Werning, Markus, Wolfram Hinzen, and Edouard Machery, eds. 2012. *The Oxford Handbook of Compositionality*. Oxford: Oxford University Press.

Zadrozny, Wlodek. 1994. "From Compositional Semantics to Systematic Semantics." *Linguistics and Philosophy* 17:329–42.

Zeevat, Henk. 1989. "A Compositional Approach to Discourse Representation Theory." *Linguistics and Philosophy* 12:95–131.

Index

MIX
Papier aus verantwortungsvollen Quellen
Paper from responsible sources
FSC® C105338

If you have any concerns about our products,
you can contact us on
ProductSafety@springernature.com

In case Publisher is established outside the EU,
the EU authorized representative is:
Springer Nature Customer Service Center GmbH
Europaplatz 3, 69115 Heidelberg, Germany

Printed by Libri Plureos GmbH
in Hamburg, Germany